ENDANGERED AND THREATENED
ANIMALS OF FLORIDA AND T...

M000308777

NUMBER FIFTY-EIGHT
The Corrie Herring Hooks Series

Endangered and Threatened Animals of Florida and Their Habitats

CHRIS SCOTT

UNIVERSITY OF TEXAS PRESS, AUSTIN

Requests for permission to reproduce material from this work should be sent to
PERMISSIONS, UNIVERSITY OF TEXAS PRESS, P.O. BOX 7819, AUSTIN, TX 78713-7819.

∞ The paper used in this book meets the minimum requirements of ANSI/NISO
Z39.48-1992 (R1997) (Permanence of Paper).

Library of Congress Cataloging-in-Publication Data

Scott, Chris, 1961–
    Endangered and threatened animals of Florida and their habitats / Chris Scott.
      p.   cm.
    Includes bibliographical references and index (p.).
    ISBN 0-292-77774-4 (cl.: alk. paper) — ISBN 0-292-70529-8 (pbk.: alk. paper)
    1. Endangered species—Florida.   2. Habitat (Ecology)—Florida.   I. Title
QL84.22.F6S36   2004
333.95'42'09759—dc22   2003023540

Seminole Wind

JOHN ANDERSON

Ever since the days of old,
men would search for wealth untold.
They'd dig for silver and for gold,
and leave the empty holes.
And way down south in the Everglades,
where the black water rolls and the
    saw grass sways,
the eagles fly and the otters play,
in the land of the Seminole.

So blow, blow Seminole wind,
blow like you're never gonna blow
    again.
I'm calling to you like a long lost
    friend,
and I know who you are.
And blow, blow from the Okeechobee,
all the way up to Micanopy.
Blow across the home of the Seminole,
the alligator, and the gar.

Progress came and took its toll,
and in the name of flood control,
they made their plans and they drained
    the land,
now the glades are going dry.
And the last time I walked in the
    swamp,
I sat upon a cypress stump.
I listened close and I heard the ghost
    of Osceola cry.

So blow, blow Seminole wind,
blow like you're never gonna blow
    again.
I'm calling to you like a long lost
    friend,
and I know who you are. . . .

This book is dedicated to

my loving grandmother, the late

Gilberte "Gibbie" Langis,

a.k.a. Memére,
who, I believe,
should be a candidate
for sainthood;

and

to my dear friend

Dr. John "Doc" Schultz

(15 August 1949–10 July 1999),
a talented scientist and
undercover conservation officer,
who left us at a much too early age.

Contents

SPECIES ACCOUNTS

Preface

This book is intended to provide the reader with detailed, current, factual information on each of Florida's 67 animal species, subspecies, or populations designated as endangered or threatened by the Florida Fish and Wildlife Conservation Commission or the U.S. Fish and Wildlife Service. Descriptions of Florida's ecosystems (which these and every other native animal and plant depend on) and their current state are also included. Wherever possible, I have tried to accentuate the correlation between protection of habitats and protection of wildlife; it cannot be overemphasized.

Construction of the book entailed two distinct duties. The first was research and the actual writing of the text, which required hundreds of hours in front of the computer trying to avoid carpal tunnel syndrome while still trying to complete my self-imposed quota for the week. The second was photographing the fascinating assemblage of creatures discussed in the text, which often required trips of two or three days to some of the country's most unusual and beautiful locations. I much preferred the photography to the writing. The field trips were always exciting, whether or not the species sought was found, and provided a number of unusual and sometimes comical experiences. One such experience involved an attempt by myself and my son Matthew to photograph the threatened Atlantic salt marsh snake in the wild. Locating this species at any time other than low tide is extremely unlikely; however, after arriving at the site just after dark and discovering the tide to be just as high as it could possibly get, we decided to give it a shot. After several hours of wading and sinking chest-high in muddy water, or watery mud, we were still a quarter-mile and several hundred mosquito bites away from dry land, and then our flashlight died. If the *Guinness Book of World Records* had a category for the world's muddiest father and son, we would have won hands down. The beautiful photograph of the Atlantic salt marsh snake that appears in this book was taken by Barry Mansell, and it serves as testimony to the failure of our exhaustive search for the animal that October night.

Then there was the caterpillar incident. Over the years I have been bitten, stung, and envenomated by a variety of America's critters including rattlesnakes, scorpions, and even small alligators, and it has generally been my fault. While I was searching for scrub-jays and sand skinks in Ocala National Forest, again with my son, one cute, fuzzy little puss caterpillar somehow managed to fall down my shirt. Reacting to a sudden itching sensation on my chest, I rubbed the venomous quills of this unseen aggressor into my epidermis, which is exactly what you don't want to do. For the next several hours I felt as if someone had inflated the glands under my arm with about 200 psi of air.

The last incident I'll mention is one I

now consider humorous but a bit embarrassing. On one of my many trips to the Florida Keys to photograph species for this book, I happened on an amazingly tolerant peregrine falcon who permitted my very close approach. When I first spotted the bird—the fastest of all God's creatures, perched above a mangrove forest and keenly scanning its surroundings for an unsuspecting blue-winged teal or other feathered quarry, I quickly grabbed my camera and began my approach on foot. That euphoria stole over me, the feeling experienced by nature photographers when the rare opportunity for the perfect photograph of a prized animal presents itself in the wild. Stealthily approaching the falcon, I clicked off shots every few feet. The sun was at my back, increasing the probability of a once-in-a-lifetime peregrine shot. As this trusting, adult peregrine permitted me to approach within 20 feet with my 300-millimeter lens, I visualized, with certainty, the slides of the bird gracing the cover of

Audubon or *Wild Bird* magazines. After 30 frames or so, I was more than satisfied when the stately falcon took flight toward a flock of descending willets on an adjacent mudflat. Only then did I realize that I had no film in my camera.

If you are considering writing an article or book about the outdoors, and you're considering doing your own photography for the piece, I can offer the following advice: First, you'll probably save a lot of money and time by simply buying the needed photographs and rights from established nature photographers, and you'll have much more time to devote to your manuscript. Second, disregard the previous statement and get out there yourself, get muddy, beware of the savage puss caterpillar, and experience or reexperience the subject matter you are writing about firsthand. Your finished product will be enhanced as a result. Just remember to put film in your camera.

Acknowledgments

I owe a great deal of thanks to the many people who contributed their time and knowledge to this endeavor. The first group of people I wish to acknowledge merit special recognition for help that far exceeded any reasonable expectations. These individuals are Claudette Scott-Stude; Britton Jackson; James G. Duquesnel; Dr. Bobby Hattaway; and finally William Tanner, a good friend, for without his help, this book just may never have been completed.

The second and larger group of people also owed an enormous debt of gratitude include numerous field and laboratory biologists of various scientific disciplines, researchers, naturalists, land managers, volunteer editors, friends, and relatives who, among other things, reviewed portions of the manuscript, did their best to help me avoid errors, provided much needed photographs or illustrations, went out of their way to provide me with the latest data available, accompanied me (or allowed me to accompany them) on numerous field expeditions, and frequently provided me with a roof over my head and a cold beer during my many road trips. They are John Anderson, who allowed the use of the lyrics of his wonderful song "Seminole Wind"; Jimmy Buffett, for the constant inspirational support delivered via his many great tunes and my many excursions to that semi-imaginary nirvana Margaritaville; David L. Auth, Dr. Thomas C. Emmel, Dr. Richard Franz, Britt Keith, Joan L. Morrison, and Dr. Charles Woods of the University of Florida Museum of Natural History; Dr. Richard Barnowski of the University of Florida Agricultural Laboratory; R. D. "Dick" and Patty Bartlett; Robert E. Bennetts; Dr. Jim Bohnsack and Jeffrey Brown of the National Marine Fisheries Service; Ray Bullock of the Hibiscus Golf Club of Naples; staff of the Camera Shop of North Palm Beach; Clyde Caracara, David Leonard, Fred E. Lohrer, and Allison R. Mains of Archbold Biological Station; Jane Chabre, Elizabeth Forys, Phil Frank, Jeffrey A. Gore, Paul E. Moler (herpetologist extraordinaire), Timothy G. Roettiger, Ruth Stanbridge, and Don A. Wood of the Florida Game and Fresh Water Fish Commission; Joseph T. Collins and Suzanne L. Collins of the Center for North American Amphibians and Reptiles; Kendra Dean; Anne S. Deaton and James E. Weimer of the Florida Park Service; Mike DeCapita, Laura Jenkins, Lennie Jones, Boyd Kynard, Gloria Lee, Kim Livengood, Mary Moser, Jim Moyers, Dr. L. Karolee Owens, Frank Parauka, Lorna Patrick, Barry Stieglitz, Lloyd Stith, and Jane Tutton of the U.S. Fish and Wildlife Service; Patrick Elliott; Dan and Charla Fischer; Stephen Frink of Stephen Frink Photographic; Dr. Jerry Lee Gingerich; Kay Hale of the University of Miami; Dr. Bill Goodwin, Harold Hudson, Brenda S. Kittleson, Nancy Diersing, and Paige Gill of the Florida Keys National Marine

Sanctuary; Gregory C. Greer of International Expeditions; Roger Hammer of the Dade County Parks and Recreation Department; Bruce Hecker and Pamela Lyons of the National Aquarium, Baltimore; Geri Hylander and Dr. Peter Pritchard of the Florida Audubon Society; Paul and Lynn James; Stephanie Johnson; Dave Kenyon and Eve Rolandson of the Michigan Department of Natural Resources; Lynn Kirkland of the St. Augustine Alligator Farm; Pat Knox of the We Care Animal Center in Homestead; David A. Liebman; Larry Lipsky (deceased) and Debbie Lipsky; Dave Mack and Tammy Finks; David S. Maehr of Wilkinson and Associates, Inc.; Barry W. Mansell (if all of Florida's endangered species were to perish, at least Barry would, I believe, have a photograph of each and every last one); Paul and Kristen Markovich; Cyndi Marks of the Florida Bat Center; William Mertz of the La Paz Serpentarium, Baja California Sur, who contributed the exquisite drawing of the Squirrel Chimney cave shrimp; Mary Beth Mihalik of the Palm Beach County Solid Waste Authority; Arthur W. Mitchell of the Marine Resources Development Foundation, Key Largo; Donna M. Oddy and Michael Legare of NASA's Kennedy Space Center; Jeff Otteson; Bob Panko, Chuck Passek, William Reynolds, and Matt Stoffolano of Everglades National Park; Stuart L. Pimm of the Center for Environmental Research and Conservation; Rick Poley; Bill Pranty; Dave Prentiss and Katy NeSmith of the Florida Natural Areas Inventory; Jean Ribarich; Jeffrey Ritman; Bobby Roberts and Dick Sublette of *Florida Wildlife Magazine*; John V. Rossi, D.V.M., M.A.; Stephanie Rutan of the White Oak Plantation, Jacksonville; Dennis M. Sargent, chief of the Winter Park Fire Department; Konrad P. Schmidt of the Native Fish Conservancy; Jerry Schudda; Arnim Schuetz of Key West Naval Air Station; Matthew C. Scott, my son and favorite field companion; Karen M. Scott; Jeffrey Seminoff of the University of Arizona; Bob and Brenda Sinners; Bill and Jerry Tanner; Brian R. Toland of the Brevard County Natural Resources Management Office; Dr. Merlin D. Tuttle of Bat Conservation International; Doug Wechsler, Director of VIREO, Philadelphia Academy of Sciences; Angela Willhite; Debbie Wood and the staff of the Cornell Laboratory of Ornithology, Ithaca, New York; and Larry Wood and Wendy Cawley Maus of the Marinelife Center of Juno Beach.

I also wish to extend my deep appreciation to the entire staff of the University of Texas Press, especially Shannon Davies, Sheryl A. Englund, Leslie Tingle, Lorraine Atherton, and William Bishel.

Florida mastiff bat
(*Eumops glaucinus
floridanus*), Florida's
largest and rarest bat.
Photo by Pat Knox.

Gray bat (*Myotis grisescens*).
Photo by Merlin D. Tuttle.

Indiana bat (*Myotis sodalis*).
Photo by Merlin D. Tuttle.

Florida panther (*Puma concolor coryi*).
Photo by Jerry Lee Gingerich.

Florida black bear (*Ursus americanus floridanus*).
Photo by Barry Mansell.

Key deer (*Odocoileus virginianus clavium*) grazing on shoulder of heavily traveled road, No Name Key, Monroe County.

Big Cypress fox squirrel (*Sciurus niger avicennia*).

Lower Keys marsh rabbit (*Sylvilagus palustris hefneri*).
Photo by Elizabeth Forys.

Key Largo cotton mouse
(*Peromyscus gossypinus allapaticola*).

Key Largo wood rat
(*Neotoma floridana smalli*).
Photo by Phil Frank.

Perdido Key beach mouse (*Peromyscus polionotus trissyllepsis*). Photo courtesy U.S. Fish and Wildlife Service.

Choctawhatchee beach mouse (*Peromyscus polionotus allophrys*). Photo courtesy U.S. Fish and Wildlife Service.

Anastasia Island beach mouse (*Peromyscus polionotus phasma*).
Photo by Phil Frank.

Southeastern beach mouse (*Peromyscus polionotus niveiventris*).

Silver rice rat (*Oryzomys argentatus*).

Florida manatee (*Trichechus manatus latirostris*).

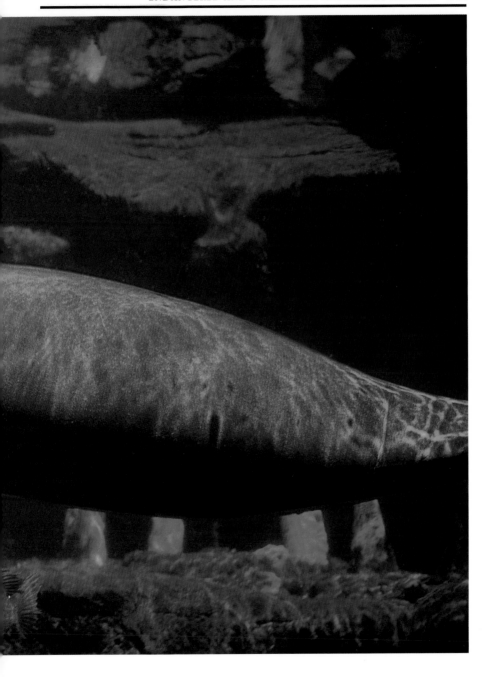

Clutch of Least tern eggs on a Florida beach. The well-camouflaged eggs and young of least terns are vulnerable to vehicular and pedestrian traffic, free-roaming dogs, and a number of natural predators. Photo by Gregory Greer.

Caribbean roseate terns (*Sterna dougallii dougallii*), Bush Key, Dry Tortugas. Photo by Dennis Mager, Florida Audubon Society.

Wood stork (*Mycteria americana*).

Whooping cranes (*Grus americana*), Osceola County.

Snowy plover (*Charadrius alexandrinus*). Photo by Glen Wood.

Florida sandhill crane (*Grus canadensis pratensis*).

Piping plover (*Charadrius melodus*) in winter plumage.

Male Everglades snail kite (*Rostrhamus sociabilis plumbeus*) with apple snail (*Polacea paludosa*). Photo by Robert Bennetts.

Adult southern bald eagle (*Haliaeetus leucocephalus leucocephalus*).

Audubon's crested caracara (*Caracara cheriway audubonii*).

Peregrine falcon (*Falco peregrinus*).

White-crowned pigeon (*Columba leucocephala*) on nest.
Photo by Rick Poley.

Male southeastern American kestral (*Flaco sparverius paulus*) with small bird. Photo courtesy Florida Fish and Wildlife Conservation Commission.

Painting of male ivory-billed woodpecker (*Campephilus principalis principalis*). Photo courtesy of Cornell Laboratory of Ornithology.

Florida scrub-jay (*Aphelocoma coerulescens*).

Red-cockaded woodpecker (*Picoides borealis*).

Bachman's warbler (*Vermivora bachmanii*), possibly extinct,
last recorded in 1988, last recorded in Florida in 1977.
Photo by J. H. Dick. Courtesy of V.I.R.E.O., Academy of
Natural Sciences of Philadelphia.

Cape Sable seaside sparrow (*Ammodramus maritimus mirabilis*). Photo by Stuart Pimm.

Kirtland's warbler (*Dendroica kirtlandii*). Photo by Bob Harrington, Michigan Department of Natural Resources.

Stuffed ivory-billed woodpeckers (*Campephilus principalis principalis*); female on left, male (with red crest) on right.
Photo courtesy Florida Fish and Wildlife Conservation Commission.

Male Florida grasshopper sparrow (*Ammodramus savannarum floridanus*) singing. Photo by Barry Mansell.

American crocodile (*Crocodylus acutus*).
Photo by Barry Mansell.

American alligator (*Alligator mississippiensis*).

Atlantic green turtle (*Chelonia mydas mydas*).

Atlantic green turtle neonate in sargasso grass.

Juvenile Atlantic loggerhead turtle (*Caretta caretta caretta*)
with wounds sustained from a shark bite.

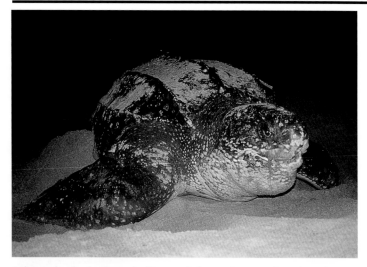

Atlantic leatherback turtle (*Dermochelys coriacea coriacea*) nesting
on beach in Palm Beach County. Photo by Larry Woods.

Atlantic hawksbill turtle (*Eretmochelys imbricata imbricata*).
Photo courtesy Sea World.

Atlantic ridley turtle (*Lepidochelys kempi*).
Photo by Peter Pritchard.

Bluetail mole skink (*Eumeces egregius lividus*) with rejuvenated tail.

Sand skink (*Neoseps reynoldsi*).

Atlantic salt marsh snake (*Nerodia clarki taeniata*). Photo by Barry Mansell.

Key ring-necked snake (*Diadophis punctatus acricus*), found by the author on No Name Key, Monroe County.

Eastern indigo snake (*Drymarchon corais couperi*).

Short-tailed snake (*Stilosoma extenuatum*) eating brown snake (*Storeria dekayi*).
Photo by Suzanne L. Collins and Joseph T. Collins.

Rimrock crowned snake (*Tantilla oolitica*). Photo by Jim Duquesnel.

Peninsula ribbon snake, Lower Keys population (*Thamnophis sauritus sackeni*). Photo by Barry Mansell.

Striped mud turtle, Lower Keys population (*Kinosternon bauri*).
Photo by Barry Mansell.

Shortnose sturgeon (*Acipenser brevirostrum*).

FOLLOWING PAGES: Key silverside
(*Menidia conchorum*).
Photo by Paige Gill.

Gulf sturgeon (*Acipenser oxyrinchus desotoi*). Photo by Noel Burkhead, U.S. Fish and Wildlife Service.

Okaloosa darter (*Etheostoma okaloosae*). Photo by Gray Bass.

Blackmouth shiner (*Notropis melanostomus*). Photo by Gray Bass.

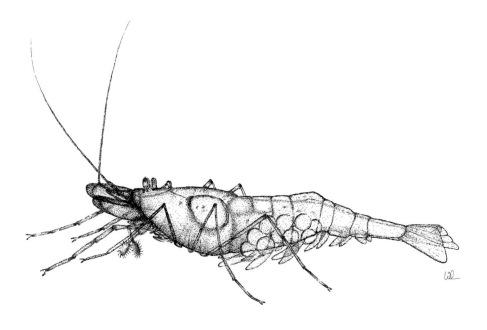

Squirrel Chimney cave shrimp (*Palaemonetes cummingi*)
possibly extinct. Illustration by William Mertz.

Schaus' swallowtail butterfly (*Papilio aristodemus ponceanus*).

Pillar coral (*Dendrogyra cylindrus*).
Photo courtesy Florida Keys National Marine Sanctuary.

Stock Island tree snail (*Orthalicus reses reses*).

Little blue heron (*Egretta caerulea*), designated a species of special concern by the state of Florida, Loxahatchee National Wildlife Refuge.

Rosy rat snake, or Lower Keys corn snake
(*Elaphe guttata guttata*), sold at the Orlando
International Reptile Expo (in violation of
federal law).

Alligator snapping turtle (*Macroclemys temmincki*), a species of special concern, inhabits some of Florida's larger Gulf drainages west of the Santa Fe and Suwannee rivers. North America's largest freshwater turtle has been exterminated throughout much of its range by trappers who harvest the turtle for its tasty flesh, which is sold.

ENDANGERED AND THREATENED
ANIMALS OF FLORIDA AND THEIR HABITATS

Listed Species

WHAT THEY ARE UP AGAINST

Visualize a hypothetical trip back in time, nearly 500 years. Imagine you are a scout accompanying the famous Spanish explorer Juan Ponce de Leon, whose ship in 1513 first landed on Florida's Atlantic coast, near present-day St. Augustine. You are assigned the year-long task of surveying this new subtropical paradise to describe its natural features, while, of course, keeping your eyes open for the fabled Fountain of Youth. At the end of a wondrous year, your journal contains detailed accounts of enormous expanses of wilderness. You have encountered continuous tracts of open pine woods, requiring several days to traverse, with stately trees, many over 2 feet in diameter; numerous tree islands composed of strange-looking tropical trees festooned with vibrant lush vegetation, a multitude of pale, delicate orchids, and clinging bromeliads. In your travels, you record a series of elevated ridges made of startlingly white sand in an arid, almost desert environment where dwarfed oaks flourish. You describe great expanses of freshwater marshes teeming with enormous alligators and countless wading birds. The many birds recorded in your travels include large flocks of bright green parakeets that nest in cypress swamps and forage on mulberries. There are large wild pigeons in flocks containing tens of millions of individuals; the flocks are so immense that they nearly darken the skies. While exploring an archipelago (now known as the Florida

Keys), you observe a slightly smaller, attractive dove. In the prairie region of the central peninsula you note a tremendous white and black vulture with orange, yellow, and purple on the neck, foraging on a deer carcass. Your journal describes colonies of small dark sparrows bearing a yellow patch above their eyes in the riverine salt marshes along the present-day St. Johns River and several hawk-size black and white woodpeckers, the males of which display brilliant red crests. (Today those birds are known as the Carolina parakeet, extinct 1937; the passenger pigeon, extinct 1914; and the Key West quail dove, extirpated, last recorded in Florida in 1966; the king vulture, extirpated, last recorded in Florida in 1766; the dusky seaside sparrow, extinct 1987; and the ivory-billed woodpecker, believed extinct, last recorded in Florida in 1969.)

The list of mammals observed would surely include large rookeries of seals basking on Atlantic beaches (West Indian monk seal, extinct, last confirmed report in 1952), where each summer several sea turtle species emerge from the ocean to lay their eggs. Among the rodents of various sizes and colors would be an abundant small, whitish mouse observed scampering through dune vegetation near an inlet (now known as Ponce de Leon Inlet); a larger, darker-pelaged mouse inhabiting wax myrtle thickets on a barrier island just east of St. Augustine; and another similar mouse, collected during a

Stuffed ivory-billed woodpeckers (Campephilus principalis principalis); *female on left, male (with red crest) on right. This species is now considered extinct by many authorities.* PHOTO COURTESY FLORIDA FISH AND WILDLIFE CONSERVATION COMMISSION.

laterned night stroll while camping in a maritime hammock on the southern Gulf Coast. (The mice are the pallid beach mouse, extinct, last recorded 1946; Anastasia Island cotton mouse, extirpated, last recorded 1901; Chadwick Beach cotton mouse, extinct, last recorded 1940s.) You encounter herds of ponderous buffaloes, weighing as much as a ton (eastern plains bison, extirpated, last recorded in Florida 1800s); and occasional pairs or trios of black-colored wolves, considerably smaller than the wolves of Spain (Florida's black race of red wolf, extinct, last reported in Florida 1922). You would not observe or record the water hyacinths that currently clog so many of Florida's waterways or the Australian pine, Brazilian pepper, or melaleuca, which cumulatively are now the most abundant of Florida's plants. You would not encounter starlings, English sparrows, brown anoles, marine toads, fire ants, black rats, or walking catfish.

Recently, while dining at a restaurant in the Florida Keys, I overheard a conversation much like this from a nearby table. "So what? We lose a rat here, a snail there. A minnow, a crayfish, a spider? Come on. Well, sure, I like manatees. They're kind of cute, and yes, I think we should do what we can to save the panther—it's a majestic animal. Clams and sport fish, yeah, save them, we can eat 'em. But when it comes to butterflies, bats, mice, and snakes, I mean, who cares? I hate snakes. I hear they are now protecting a beetle. What's next, a mosquito?" I have heard that sentiment expressed many times over the years, and often it is merely an affirmation of the beliefs the parties already share. When there are people present with an opposing view (you know, the environmentalists), they too are often ill equipped with factual, convincing arguments. I surmise, since you are reading this book, that you probably have some interest in the environment and may recognize that serious, possibly catastrophic environmental changes are on the calendar. I will do what I can to affirm the importance of and provide the reasons for restoring, protecting, and maintaining the environment, as nature designed it. Nature rarely makes mistakes; however, as illustrated by a 1993 Tom Toles cartoon regarding the fabled Noah's Ark, some people have a few questions about *Homo sapiens.* In this cartoon God tells Noah, "And bring two of every species so that they may all be preserved." Noah responds, "You mean except those that threaten jobs and economic development." God then rebuts, "No, I didn't make any mistakes. . . . Well, maybe one." In light of the above, I will also do what I can to arm the reader with current, factual information to dispel the myths regarding extinction and protection of the environment that remain in constant circulation.

One argument offered time and time again is that extinction is a natural process (this part is true), so we needn't be concerned about it (this part is not). Yes, it is true that extinction is a natural phenomenon; however, the rate of natural extinction is slow. Experts believe the natural frequency of extinction in all of North America to be only 3 species every century. Since the arrival of Europeans, this country alone has forever lost nearly 600 species, subspecies, or populations of native animals and plants. Of those, only one disappeared as a result of natural causes. Within the last several decades, the rate of extinction and endangerment of the world's species has accelerated to the point where it is difficult to track. Nearly half of Florida's vertebrate species are declining. In nearly all cases, the cause of the decline is directly related in one way or another to humans. According to Harvard University biologist E. O. Wilson, as many as 5 or 6 species become extinct worldwide with each passing hour, annually totaling some 45,000 to 50,000 species. Biologists consider the current rate of extinction to be as much as 10,000 to 25,000 times the natural rate, and the rate is increasing.

Within the contiguous United States, Florida is second only to California in terms of endangered and threatened animals and plants recognized by the U.S. Fish and Wildlife Service (105 species in Florida and 110 in California). An additional 277 Florida species are federally designated as proposed for endangered or threatened listing, candidate species, or species of management concern. The Florida Fish and Wildlife Conservation Commission, or FWC (until 1999 called the Florida Game and Fresh Water Fish Commission, or FG&FWFC), currently recognizes 118 animal species as endangered, threatened, or of special concern. The Florida Department of Agriculture and Consumer Services lists 496 plant species in the state as endangered, threatened, or commercially exploited. The location of Florida and California in the Sunbelt and the two states' close rankings as hotbeds of endangerment is no coincidence. Because both states offer a hospitable climate, they have rapidly become overpopulated and this in turn has resulted in widespread habitat destruction and degradation. Their location and climate also generally correlate with higher biodiversity, which means they have more species to lose, and both states have extensive seacoasts and numerous distinct ecosystems supporting multitudinous organisms.

Florida's environment and wildlife are jeopardized by a variety of threats. Our natural resources are subjected to many of the same environmental menaces as other states; however, Florida must contend with certain threats, such as invasive exotics, habitat loss and degradation, and biological accumulation of mercury, at a rate significantly higher than most states. Invasive exotic organisms have been especially troublesome to Florida's natural resources, and they are discussed in detail in the following chapter. Of all the threats to Florida's habitats and wildlife, none have taken more of a toll than the destruction, degradation, and fragmentation of habitats. Some human behaviors are more destructive than others, and some species are more vulnerable to the damage than others. Species with narrow ecological niches (habitat specialists) are more vulnerable to extinction than species with broad ecological niches (habitat generalists). So often we have altered our environment without a thought to the ramifications of our actions. This has at times resulted in cataclysmic changes affecting biodiversity for many years, sometimes permanently. Every organism in an ecosystem is intricately bound to others, and by altering one, we may alter many. To quote John Muir, "When we try to pick out anything by itself, we find it hitched to everything else in the universe." The loss of a single plant species may result in the extinction of as many as 30 other animals and plants, the so-called snowball effect.

Many humans place more value on a species or habitat if they recognize a direct benefit to the human race. For instance, people who enjoy fishing or hunting can appreciate the protection of a lake for its largemouth bass, or a track of flatwoods for the deer or wild turkeys it supports. The more that is learned about our environment, the more it appears

One of several signs posted on Tamiami Trail (US 41) in Collier County warning motorists of the presence of Florida panthers (Puma concolor coryi).

that all natural elements may provide a multitude of yet unknown benefits to humans. These may include cures for cancer, diabetes, AIDS, and other deadly or debilitating diseases. When it comes to the discovery of medically beneficial chemicals produced by plants and animals, we have just scratched the surface. Over half of all prescriptions filled contain chemicals originating from plants or animals, and less than 2 percent of the world's known plant species have been analyzed for medical uses thus far. A species of worm recently discovered in New England led to the discovery of a substance that may cure some types of cancer. A valuable new antibiotic was recently discovered in a frog's skin. Researchers in Arizona recently announced that properties found in the venom of Gila monsters (*Heloderma suspectum*) may eventually lead to a cure for diabetes. Beneficial chemicals are not restricted to tropical rain forests; they may occur in that parcel of Florida scrub you drove by today, the one with the sign announcing the construction of a new mall. Of the more than 3,000 plant species that could be used to feed humans, we rely on just 20 or so types (corn, rice, wheat, soybean, etc.) to obtain 90 percent of the world's food supply. Indigenous peoples of tropical Africa and South America, many of whom themselves are in danger of extinction, use a much more diverse array of native plants for food and medicinal purposes. Though humans have occupied Florida for at least 10,000 years, it wasn't until the arrival of Europeans, just a few hundred years ago, that our habitats and wildlife began to vanish at such an alarming rate.

Another notable threat to Florida's animals has increased steadily since the advent of personal mechanized transportation. The automobile is responsible for the death of tens of millions of the state's animals each year, and it represents the leading cause of death to several critically endangered species including Florida panthers and the Key deer. Automobile collisions killed 20 Florida panthers between 1980 and 1990; the entire population now consists of only 30 to 50 adults. During that same time period, at least 56 bald eagles, 234 black bears, and 400 Key deer were killed by automobiles on Florida's roadways. A stretch of SR46 north of Orlando between Sanford and

Sorrento has been the scene of numerous collisions between automobiles and black bears in the past two decades. The largest black bear ever recorded in Florida was a 630-pound male killed by a car near Naples in 1990; it was just one of 33 bears killed by autos that year alone. Other listed species killed by automobiles on Florida's roads include American crocodiles, alligators, indigo snakes, Lower Keys marsh rabbits, gopher tortoises, scrub-jays, kestrels, Key Largo wood rats, Everglades mink, and round-tailed muskrats, just to name a few. Biologists have been able to learn much about the animals inhabiting a particular area simply by examining the local road-kills. In one year, biologists at Payne's Prairie State Preserve near Gainesville recorded approximately 13,000 snakes killed by automobiles on less than three miles of U.S. Highway 441, the highway that bisects Payne's Prairie. Florida Park Service biologist Jim Weimer, who has been recording road mortality statistics at Payne's Prairie for many years, advised that during the 1970s (when traffic was much lighter than today), only 1 in 13 snakes reaching the roadway survived, and those that survived usually did so by retreating rather than crossing.

A look at a current, detailed road map of Florida will reveal virtually no large tracts of land remaining undivided by networks of roads and highways, which represent kill zones to our wildlife. Truth is, there are few places anywhere in Florida where one can be more than 10 miles from a paved road. In some areas, the placement of roads and associated road mortality have permanently isolated wildlife populations from other populations and have nearly eliminated certain

*American crocodile (*Crocodylus acutus*), roadkill on SR 905 (Card Sound Road).* CROCODILE LAKES NATIONAL WILDLIFE REFUGE, KEY LARGO, MONROE COUNTY.

*Red-shouldered hawk (*Buteo lineatus*) perched on speed-limit sign at Flamingo, Everglades National Park, Monroe County.*

wildlife populations from habitats adjacent to roadways. To make matters worse, the daily piles of bloodied fur, bones, feathers, or scales strewn about these kill zones attract vultures, caracaras, hawks, owls, and foxes, which are often killed while attempting to take advantage of an easy meal. There is probably not a motorist alive (myself included) who has not inadvertently hit some kind of animal, and sadly there are some individuals who feel it is their duty to run over snakes and other supposed vermin, sometimes going out of their way to do so.

Wildlife underpasses, erected in several locations where panthers and bears are known to cross roads, have proven very

successful. Mounted cameras have confirmed their use by those and many other species. Massachusetts has gone so far as to erect subterranean passageways to allow migrating spotted salamanders safe passage across roadways, which have also proven successful. Perhaps Florida should follow that proactive approach to protecting smaller, less publicly appealing, but ecologically important species such as snakes, salamanders, and muskrats by constructing subterranean tunnels in areas such as Payne's Prairie. In 1992 the Florida Legislature, recognizing the toll automobiles take on the state's wildlife, increased speeding ticket fines by 25 cents for every mile per hour above the

Bear "funnel tunnel" on SR 46, Seminole County. This type of tunnel has also proven effective in protecting Florida panthers and a number of other species.

speed limit. The proceeds go the state's Nongame Wildlife Program, helping to ease this division's increasing financial quandaries. It should be noted that in 1990 alone, automobile collisions with animals in Florida resulted in 380 human injuries and 4 fatalities.

Though steps have been taken to reduce the pollutants entering Florida's waters, substrates, and atmosphere (such as the outlawing of DDT), pollution remains a serious environmental threat. More pesticides and fungicides are used in Florida than in any other state. These chemicals, along with sewage from leaking septic tanks and other toxic substances, are carried into our lakes and rivers by stormwater runoff. Florida's groundwater quality ranks among the worst in the United States. Florida, which has more lakes than any other state, also has the nation's second most polluted lakes. The formerly pristine 50 square miles of Lake Apopka, once extremely popular with anglers who regularly landed trophy bass, is now much like a huge, foul-smelling bowl of antifreeze. In Miami, if police officers have to dive in the Miami River, they are required to wear specialized dive suits protecting their skin from bacteria, which often exceed safe levels by several thousand times. Florida's coastal and marine habitats are threatened by various forms of pollution. Nutrient-rich waters discharged from agricultural sites have caused repeated, concentrated algae blooms in Florida Bay and the Keys, obstructing water clarity and killing corals, sea grass beds, and other marine life. Thousands of colossal oil tankers travel Florida's offshore waters each year, increasing the chances of an environmental catastrophe along the lines of the *Exxon Valdez* spill.

Scientists now concede that global warming is one of the most serious environmental threats, but because it occurs slowly (by human standards) and cannot be seen, many people still refuse to believe it even exists. When more than 1,500 world-renowned scientists specializing in climatic conditions recently met to discuss global warming, they announced that they stand convinced that global warming does without a doubt exist. Fossil-fuel consumption, deforestation, agricultural production, and overpopulation are examples of human activities suspected of altering the earth's global heat balance. Increased atmospheric

Atlantic green turtle (Chelonia mydas mydas).

concentrations of carbon dioxide, methane, and other greenhouse gases are believed to be largely responsible for increases in mean global temperatures during the past century. (Greenhouse gases retain heat in the lower atmosphere, much the same way that glass walls hold the heat in a greenhouse.) Worldwide, 1999 was the warmest year on record. I don't believe a winter has passed for years now when, during a bitter cold spell, I haven't heard at least one person jokingly remark, "So this is global warming." Experts assert that atmospheric alterations may cause greater fluctuations in temperature extremes, both cold and hot. Long-term effects of ozone depletion are dangerous to humans as well as to the environment. The Environmental Protection Agency predicts an additional 200,000 skin cancer deaths in the United States during the next 50 years. As for the environment, scientists have made some somber predictions. Eventually, sea level rises of as much as 3 feet, attributed to melting glaciers, may engulf Florida's present coastline, consuming mangroves, salt marshes, beaches, and cities. Warmer oceans are likely to spawn more hurricanes, which are apt to be much more violent.

Another, more pressing threat to many of Florida's animals and plants, especially listed species, is exploitation. After the drug trade, wildlife exploitation is the world's largest illicit industry, at $20 billion a year. As John Muir put it, "Nothing dollarable is safe." In the name of making a buck, unscrupulous collectors ignore various state and federal laws to harvest species of reptiles, sea turtle eggs, tree snails, birds, butterflies, corals, orchids, sea shells, carnivorous plants, bromeliads, and other indigenous species for the pet trade or specialty markets. Bears are killed and sold, by the part, to overseas markets where gall bladders and other organs are worth their weight in gold. Before 1995, when box turtles were listed in Appendix 2 of CITES (the Convention on International Trade in Endangered Species of Wild Fauna and Flora), more than 200,000 box turtles were shipped to Europe annually, where they were sold as pets. Protected lands, including national and state parks, are often targeted by collectors because many sought-after species occur in higher densities in these areas. Having been a law enforcement officer for more than 15 years (5 of which involved the investigation and enforcement of conservation laws), I have firsthand knowledge of the magnitude of wildlife exploitation. While employed as an undercover federal agent investigating the poaching of reptiles and other animals and plants from national parks, I actually witnessed traffic jams and near fistfights between individuals feuding over who saw the snake first. In the spring of 1997, while working on a case in the western United States, I sat around a desert campfire with suspected poachers and was appalled as one of them boasted of illegally trapping dozens of raptors, including peregrine falcons, kestrels, Cooper's hawks, Harris' hawks, and red-tailed hawks. Everything, it seems, has a downside. Listing a species as endangered or threatened often causes its black market value to escalate. I am by no means suggesting, however, that these species should not be listed.

Without laws affording legal protection, many species would quickly perish.

As recently as the late 1960s and early 1970s, catalogs distributed by wildlife wholesalers offered just about any species of exotic animal imaginable. One 1960s price list offered for sale 81 species of birds (2,732 individuals), including several species of eagles, owls, kingfishers, purple gallinules, hornbills, thrushes, and flycatchers; 57 mammal species (1,180 individuals), including bears, clouded leopards, clawless otters, flying foxes (fruit bats), and a dozen or so primates; a total of 4,689 individual reptiles and

*U.S. Fish and Wildlife Service officer Lennie Jones with seized cooler containing loggerhead sea turtle (*Caretta caretta caretta*) parts, Collier County.*

amphibians representing 59 species, which consisted of several crocodile species, false gavials, king cobras, and Indian pythons; and 78 fish species (tens of thousands of individuals), including sharks, spiny eels, cichlids, and bat fish. That's from just one price list, mind you. The enactment of federal laws, such as the Endangered Species Act, Migratory Bird Conservation Act, and Lacey Act, along with similar state laws and international treaties such as CITES have now greatly reduced the trade in certain species, but a huge black market still exists. In recent years, nearly every kind of animal and plant has been assessed a monetary value by someone. For the year 2000, price lists from various animal dealers (Florida has more than any other state) offer for sale alligators, crocodiles, assorted deadly snakes, Galapagos tortoises, hedgehogs, sugar gliders, kangaroo rats, pocket gophers, centipedes, black widow spiders, even dung beetles. Unethical dealers readily take advantage of a number of loopholes in both state and federal laws. The various state and federal wildlife agencies are still kept busy with more traditional violations, such as deer poaching and illegal fish harvesting.

Many people have now heard about the mysterious worldwide decline of amphibians. Many amphibian species, having resiliently survived a profusion of natural threats since evolving from fish some 350 million years ago, have been decimated by this phenomenon. Its precise causes are yet unknown. Herpetologists theorize that acid rain, changes in ultraviolet radiation, and newly evolved viruses are among the more probable perpetrators. The southern dusky salamander, an abundant

*Rosy rat snake, or Lower Keys corn snake (*Elaphe guttata guttata*). Though protected by law, this specimen, admittedly collected in the Lower Keys, was sold by a South Florida reptile dealer at the Orlando International Reptile Expo, which draws 10,000 reptile enthusiasts annually.*

amphibian of the Silver Springs area in the Ocala National Forest until the 1970s, is all but gone now. Environmentalists fear the decline of this and other amphibians may be a sign that something is seriously wrong with our global environment.

Now, imagine taking another time voyage. This time, travel forward 100 years. Your great-grandchildren are now adults. Are there still panthers, indigo snakes, and wood storks? Do enormous Gulf sturgeon still make their yearly migration up the Suwannee River to spawn? Do Florida mastiff bats continue to emerge from unknown cavities somewhere south of Lake Okeechobee after the Florida sun has sunk into the Gulf of Mexico? Were enough tropical hardwood hammocks saved to assure the survival of Key Largo wood rats and cotton mice, rimrock crowned snakes, and Schaus' swallowtails? Was the Everglades saved, or were the valiant efforts and hopes of many tangled so tightly in the web of politics that they could not stop the coup-de-grace to Florida's heart and soul? Do sand skinks and bluetail mole skinks continue to swim through the sugar sand of the Lake Wales Ridge Florida scrub, or has this habitat itself become extinct? Do Floridians and tourists alike still gather in childlike excitement to take turtle walks on Florida's beaches each summer, or watch winter aggregations of gentle manatees in the transparent waters of Blue Springs, or is there no longer any reason to do so? Will enough components of Florida's ecosystems remain to sustain them? Will camping, hiking, and nature study with our children continue to enrich our lives, or will those activities be replaced by visits to the zoo or hours with a CD-Rom in the family computer? The answer to these questions is entirely up to us.

CHAPTER TWO

Biological Pollution

INVASIVE EXOTICS IN FLORIDA

The adverse effect of introduced invasive species of plants and animals on Florida's biodiversity certainly warrants a separate chapter in this book. Nearly 1,000 insect species, 36 herptile species, 35 fish species, 20 mammal species, and at least 22 species of birds have established breeding populations in Florida. Through day-to-day observations, the general public can often recognize the rapid destruction and fragmentation of various ecosystems and no doubt realizes this to be a factor in the decline of wildlife associated with these habitats. Most people, however, do not realize the magnitude of the harm associated with invasive, exotic species of flora and fauna. Biologists now believe that in many regions, including Florida, introduced plants and animals may constitute the most significant threat to entire ecosystems, as well as to several endangered and threatened species. At best, the damage to the delicate symmetry of our ecosystems caused by the proliferation of invasive exotics places a close second to the destruction, degradation, and fragmentation of habitat. What complicates the matter is that areas set aside for conservation purposes, such as national parks, are not safe from invasive exotics.

Some exotic species are ruinous to ecosystems where they do not occur naturally but pose no problems to the environment where they evolved, because nature generally provides a complex, nearly flawless system of checks and balances. Species naturally occurring within a particular area have developed specific habits and adaptations that improve their chances of survival. Within a healthy, functioning ecosystem, there are natural controls in place (e.g., predator-prey relationships) that hold populations of indigenous species in check. When species are removed from their natural range and introduced into regions where few or no natural controls exist, they may become problematic for native species. The lack of such controls may allow the introduced species to reproduce more successfully than the native species. In many cases, introduced species are larger and more aggressive than their native counterparts, which enables the newcomer to outcompete and occasionally eliminate the indigenous species.

Florida's balmy, subtropical climate (especially in southern Florida) has been conducive to the establishment of a multitude of alien organism populations, including various plants, insects, birds, reptiles, amphibians, fishes, and mammals. If one were to take a walk through any Dade County park and list the species of plants and animals observed, it is likely that the number of exotic, nonnative species would outnumber the native species. Though humans killed off Florida's only native parrot long ago, as many as 10 introduced parrot species can be seen in the greater Miami area. Visitors to southern and central Florida before the 1970s were likely to encounter numerous brilliantly colored native green anoles (*Anolis carolinensis*), commonly referred to as chameleons. Green anoles have occurred abundantly throughout Florida for at least 6 million years, and they are still quite common in more rural areas, especially in the northern third of the state. The brown anole (*Anolis sagrei* complex), an uninvited, more terrestrial cousin of the green anole, arrived in Florida from Cuba and the Bahamas just 30 or 40 years ago (probably as cargo on banana or cigar boats) and has now displaced the green anole in many urban and disturbed regions. Research by biologist Todd Campbell within Florida's Canaveral National Seashore has revealed that brown anoles are capable of rapidly displacing (extirpating) the native green anoles by outcompeting them and preying on their newborns. On one of Campbell's study plots, 125 green anoles and 18 brown anoles were counted in 1996. In 1997 only 12 green anoles were found, but the number of brown anoles skyrocketed to more than 300. Native green anoles have all but disappeared in many locales within peninsular Florida, while both the range and population of brown anoles continue to increase. The introduction of two subspecies of brown anoles into southern Florida, the Cuban brown (*Anolis s. sagrei*) and the Bahaman brown (*Anolis s. ordinatus*), and subsequent interbreeding between them has apparently resulted in a new race. These brown anoles rapidly became established in much of peninsular Florida and now differ significantly from the two originating subspecies; they will probably be endowed with their own subspecific designation at some point. Although Florida and other Sunbelt states are

*Brown anole (*Anolis sagrei*) complex, on fence, Palm Beach County. This aggressive, exotic anole species outnumbers the native green anole (*Anolis carolinensis*) throughout much of South Florida.*

more vulnerable to the establishment of exotic species, the problem of invasive, introduced species is now global.

Of the thousands of plant species that have become established in Florida, approximately one hundred are considered invasive enough to alter Florida's native ecosystems. Invasive exotic plants have become so serious a problem in many areas of the Sunshine State that in 1995 the state Legislature passed a bill to remove and control invasive exotics on public lands and appropriated up to 25 percent of existing CARL (Conservation and Recreation Lands) management funds to the task. The Florida Department of Environmental Protection (DEP) was designated the lead agency in the effort. It is now estimated that over 25 percent of the named plants in Florida are exotics. Among the most ecosystem-destructive plants are the Australian melaleuca tree (*Melaleuca quinquenervia*). Humans intentionally introduced this tree in Florida just after the turn of the century as a potential lumber tree and to dry up the Everglades, which at that time were considered useless wetlands that could and should be converted to agricultural land. Melaleuca has spread like wildfire in peninsular Florida, taking over a number of habitats including fresh and brackish water swamps and marshes, wet prairies, and pine flatwoods. It will grow virtually anywhere and endures both flood and drought. This domineering tree is invading the Everglades at a rate of 50 acres each day. Some experts now predict that melaleuca will become the dominant tree species in South Florida within the next decade. Melaleuca easily displaces native trees and rapidly alters many components of the ecosystem it takes over, including the hydrology. Invaded areas quickly become melaleuca monocultures, which support relatively few animal species. Its spread is enhanced by fire, which opens its seed capsules. Melaleuca, also called the paperbark tree, can be seen nearly anywhere in southern Florida; it is the tall, whitish tree with flaking bark that lines many canals and roadways. or information on organizing melaleuca eradication programs in your area, contact the Florida DEP at 407-275-4004.

The Australian pines *Casuarina equisetifolia, C. glauca,* and *C. cunninghamiana* are closely related immigrants from

*Melaleuca trees (*Melaleuca quinquenervia*) bordering canal in Palm Beach County, an Australian immigrant introduced into South Florida about a century ago to dry up the Everglades. In recent years this tree has been invading the Everglades at a rate of 50 acres per day.*

down under, introduced by humans as ornamentals. They have taken over tens of thousands of acres of southern and central Florida, particularly coastal areas, despite intensive efforts to eradicate them. Australian pines thrive on beaches where their shallow root configuration spreads out horizontally from the tree just below the surface. Nesting sea turtles have been observed struggling for hours on such beaches, becoming bloodied and exhausted in the attempt to excavate cavities in which to lay their eggs.

Two of Florida's most widespread and destructive invasive exotic plant species, Palm Beach County. Australian pines (Casuarina equisetifolia) *shade low-growing Brazilian pepper* (Schinus terebinthifolius).

The Brazilian pepper (*Schinus terebinthifolius*), referred to locally as Florida holly, is another widespread exotic that quickly populates disturbed areas within most any ecosystem. This highly invasive species was intentionally introduced as an ornamental in the late 1800s. Brazilian pepper is a dense bushy plant with red berries that often attains the height of a tree. A relative of poison ivy, it possesses a potent skin irritant that may cause a severe rash simply by brushing against it.

In northern Florida the kudzu vine (*Pueraria lobata*) is considered the most habitat-destructive exotic plant. This highly obtrusive immigrant from the Orient has been known to engulf entire buildings and large tracts of woodland.

Two species of introduced aquatic plants especially injurious to many of Florida's freshwater ponds, shallow lakes, swamps, and canals are the free-floating water hyacinth (*Eichornia crassipes*) and the immersed water hydrilla (*Hydrilla verticillata*). These plants have choked waterways and displaced native vegetation, significantly altering many of the state's aquatic habitats. Hydrilla reportedly takes over 1,500 more acres of aquatic habitat with each passing year. Hydrilla and hyacinth are both easily spread by boat propellers.

Exotic plants that are particularly deleterious to tropical hardwood hammocks and other ecosystems of southern Florida include latherleaf (*Colubrina asiatica*), sapodilla (*Manilkara zapota*), bowstring hemp (*Sansevieria hyacinthoides*), air potato (*Dioscorea bulbifera*), and downy myrtle (*Rhodomyrtus tomentosus*). Biologists fear that the invasion of nonnative cogon grass (*Imperata cylindrica*) into sandhill habitats would be ruinous to that vital Florida ecosystem. The list of introduced exotic pest plants established in Florida continues to grow, now including nearly 1,000 species. The Exotic Pest Plant Council is a nonprofit organization founded in Fort Lauderdale in 1984 to promote public awareness about the serious threat that invasive, exotic plants pose to our ecosystems.

The list of invasive exotic animals in Florida is also quite lengthy, second only to Hawaii's, and as with exotic plants, southern Florida harbors a much greater number than northern Florida. When it comes to exotic species, Dade, Broward, and Monroe counties can be considered the Ellis Island of Florida. At least 36 reptile and amphibian species, mostly lizards, have established breeding populations in Florida, with many more species recorded. Dade and Monroe counties are now home to more than 20 species of alien lizards, including geckos, anoles, iguanas, and curlytail lizards. The tiny Asian Brahminy blind snake (*Ramphotyphlops braminus*) is now well established in many South Florida and Florida Keys localities. This wee little snake (4.5–6.5 inches), which probably arrived in the roots of potted plants, readily establishes new populations by reproducing parthenogenetically (from unfertilized eggs).

Occasionally large boa constrictors and pythons capable of preying on dogs and cats are encountered, usually near urban areas. These are usually escaped pets. Biologists in Everglades National Park are now becoming concerned, however, that Burmese pythons (*Python molurus bivittatus*) may be reproducing in the wild. A number of these snakes, which can exceed 20 feet in length, have been encountered in mangrove habitats in and around the park. The gray-banded king snake (*Lampropeltis alterna*) is a harmless colubrid of the Chihuahuan Desert. One was found swimming across a brackish Key Largo canal. Florida has, so far, escaped the wrath of the brown tree snake (*Boiga irregularis*), which since being introduced to Guam in the 1940s has eliminated 9 of the country's 11 native bird species. Dave Roudebush

*A large, adult, exotic tokay gecko (*Gecko gecko*), found during the night by the author on the exterior of a residence in Key Largo, Monroe County.*

of the FG&FWFC encountered and shot three large Nile monitor lizards (*Varanus niloticus*) in February 1996, within the Crocodile Lakes National Wildlife Refuge in Key Largo. The refuge was established to protect a population of endangered American crocodiles (*Crocodylus acutus*). The aggressive monitors, which attain a length of 6 feet, regularly prey on crocodile eggs in their native Africa. The spectacled caiman (*Caiman crocodilus*), a grayish South American crocodilian 4 to 6 feet long, is clearly established and quite common in many Dade County canals. Though smaller than Florida's native alligator (*Alligator mississippiensis*), the more aggressive caiman competes with alligators for food in localities where both occur.

Several exotic amphibians are also well established in Florida, including marine toads (*Bufo marinus*). These enormous toads may reach 7 inches and weigh 3 pounds. A Neotropical native, the toad was intentionally released in Florida in an attempt to control insect pests on sugarcane. The extremely predaceous adults and tadpoles prey on native amphibians and compete with them for food. In some areas where marine toads occur, native species have all but disappeared. The immense parotoid glands of the species secrete a toxic substance that may be fatal to dogs and cats foolish enough to bite one. Cuban treefrogs (*Osteopilus septentrionalis*) are believed to have arrived in Key West during the early 1900s in vegetable shipments; they

*Gray-banded king snake (*Lampropeltis alterna*), a native of the Chihuahuan Desert, found swimming in a saltwater canal near John Pennekamp State Park in Key Largo, Monroe County.*

now occur at least as far north as Marion and Volusia counties. Also highly predaceous, this species is much larger than Florida's native treefrogs, which it readily consumes. Other factors that favor the establishment of these nonnative amphibians in South Florida include their ability to capitalize on major ecological disturbances, their high fecundity, and their plastic (adaptable) reproductive systems.

Florida's waterways are inhabited by more than 50 species of introduced fishes, more than any other state. Nearly half of them have established breeding populations. As with most exotics, nonnative fishes increase in both variety and abundance farther south, where warmer temperatures prevail. Many were released, intentionally or accidentally, by South Florida's numerous tropical fish dealers. Among the more habitat-disruptive species is the walking catfish (*Clarias batrachus*), an Old World inhabitant that now occurs in at least 22 Florida counties. Walking catfish were established soon after escaping from a Broward County fish farm in the 1960s. It threatens native fishes by consuming food supplies. The carnivorous oscar (*Astronotus ocellatus*), a South American native popular with aquarists, is now abundant in many South Florida waterways, where it competes with and preys on native fishes. During my many drives along Big Cypress National Preserve's Loop Road, I have found oscars and walking catfish to be among the most abundant and prolific fish present. The brown darter

Marine toad (Bufo marinus) in Palm Beach County, an enormous toad from South America, now common throughout much of South Florida. It preys on native amphibians and secretes a substance that may be fatal to household pets.

(*Etheostoma edwini*), introduced into a number of Panhandle drainages, has out-competed the endangered native Okaloosa darter (*E. okaloosae*) to near extinction. Other problematic introduced species include black acaras (*Cichlasoma bimaculatum*), pike killifish (*Belanesox belizansus*), Jack Dempsey (*Cichlasoma octofasciatum*), common carp (*Cyprinus carpio*), goldfish (*Carassius auratus*), and at least four species of *Tilapia*. Though the majority of exotics are freshwater or brackish species, saltwater species from foreign waters are occasionally encountered in Florida's coastal waters. In 1995 divers on Molasses Reef off Key Largo were astonished to find two Tierra batfish (*Platex tiere*), an Indian Ocean native.

The exotic mammals established in Florida, though much smaller in number than the nonnative herptiles or fishes, make up for their lack of diversity by the damage they cause to ecosystems. Three rodent species originating in Asia and arriving in the New World aboard European ships have played a significant role in the decline of many indigenous species of fauna and flora. The house mouse (*Mus musculus*) was probably the first to arrive in Florida, with records dating back to the early 1500s. Next to arrive (in the 1600s) was probably the black rat (*Rattus rattus*), a more aggressive species than most native rats. Black rats, also known as ship rats, quickly became established along the Atlantic, Gulf, and Pacific coasts and throughout much of the South. Although black rats became much less common in some areas after the arrival in the late 1700s of even larger and more aggressive Norway rats (*Rattus norvegicus*), they tend to remain more common than Norway rats in coastal areas. These

rodents, particularly the rats, are well known for carrying several virulent diseases, including bubonic plague, typhus, tularemia, and spotted fever. They also consume crops, mainly grains, worth millions of dollars each year.

The nutria (*Myocastor coypus*), a large, Neotropical, semiaquatic rodent, was intentionally released into Louisiana's marshes in the 1930s to multiply and later be harvested for their fur. Now well established on northwest Florida's Gulf Coast, these animals have damaged riparian habitats by depleting native vegetation and causing erosion.

Florida's most habitat-destructive introduced mammal is the wild boar (*Sus scrofa*), an enormous Old World swine. Wild boars, males of which may exceed 400 pounds, were imported into the United States during the late 1800s for hunting purposes. Their range now includes most of Florida, although Florida's wild boars are actually inter-grades between true European boars and feral hogs. With few natural predators, boars rummage through terrestrial and semiaquatic habitats, consuming large quantities of native vegetation and disturbing soils by rooting violently for food. Wild boars also prey on many animals, including the eggs and young of ground-nesting birds, rabbits, rodents, reptiles and their eggs, amphibians, and even young deer. On the up side, however, wild boars may have prevented the extinction of the Florida panther when South Florida's deer populations suffered extreme declines.

Then there are the rhesus macaque monkeys (*Macaca mulatta*) of Raccoon and Loggerhead keys (a.k.a. Key Lois). Bausch and Lomb and its subsidiary Charles River Laboratories have leased

*Wild boars (*Sus scrofa*), perhaps the most destructive introduced mammal in Florida, in terms of direct damage to habitat.* HIGHLANDS HAMMOCK STATE PARK, HIGHLANDS COUNTY.

these formerly pristine mangrove islands from the state of Florida since the 1970s. (Raccoon Key is within Great White Heron National Wildlife Refuge.) The islands are used by Bausch and Lomb for the sole purpose of breeding primates to produce offspring that are sold to medical and research laboratories. The free-roaming monkeys, which regularly escape to adjacent keys, have destroyed all of the islands' protected mangroves and other vegetation and have also degraded the water quality surrounding the islets. Biologists have for many years believed that the monkeys were adversely affecting nesting bird populations in the area, as well as destroying critical habitat of the federally endangered silver rice rat (*Oryzomys argentatus*). Despite

Bausch and Lomb's failure to comply with an agreement made with the FG&FWFC to correct these environmental issues, the state continues, year after year, to renew the company's $25 captive breeding permits. Two troops of rhesus monkeys have also become established in the Silver Springs area near Ocala National Forest and have at times become problematic in that area as well.

Other introduced mammal species established in Florida include Mexican red-bellied squirrels (*Sciurus aureogaster*), commonly seen on Elliott Key within Biscayne National Park, where they have caused significant damage to native thatch palms (*Thrinax* sp.). A population of sambar deer (*Cervus unicolor*), an Asian species that may exceed 600 pounds,

*Exotic rhesus macaque monkey (*Macaca mulatta*), Raccoon Key within Great White Heron National Wildlife Refuge, Monroe County. These free-roaming primates have destroyed much of what is supposed to be protected mangrove habitat on Raccoon and Loggerhead keys.* PHOTO BY JERRY LEE GINGERICH.

of millions of songbirds and small animals each year. A study in Michigan revealed that just one well-fed house cat killed more than 60 songbirds and 1,600 small mammals in 18 months. In Florida's Orange County alone, an average of 670 domestic cats are picked up by the Animal Control Department each month.

As exotic, invasive insects go, the fire ant (*Solenopsis invicta*) is often the first that comes to mind, especially if one has had the misfortune of inadvertently standing or sitting on a mound full of these tiny, painfully venomous ants with the temperament of a wolverine. The sting or bite of a fire ant is usually accompanied by a lingering stinging sensation, reddening of the skin, and inflammation. If humans are so affected by the fire ant's biocidal sting, you can imagine what happens to a small bird, rodent, or hatchling sea turtle when swarmed by an army of angry, biting fire ants. Despite considerable efforts to control imported fire ants in Florida, they now occur statewide and are apparently here to stay. Florida's only habitats not inhabited by fire ants are lakes, rivers, the submerged portions of swamps and marshes, and coral reefs. Fire ants threaten many of Florida's animal species, including ground-nesting birds, hatchling sea turtles, silver rice rats, amphibians, reptiles and their eggs, tree snails, and other invertebrates.

Judging from the portrayals of wild Florida in various television and magazine advertisements inviting vacationers to the Sunshine State, Florida's natural avifauna includes parrots, macaws, and flamingos. Birds such as parrots and parakeets, red-whiskered bulbuls (*Pycnonotus jocosus*), hill mynas (*Gracula religiosa*),

inhabits St. Vincent Island within St. Vincent National Wildlife Refuge, and black-tailed jackrabbits (*Lepus californicus*), native to the American Southwest, are commonly observed bounding across the grassy expanses of Miami's International Airport. In terms of predation, feral or free-roaming domestic cats (*Felis catus*) and dogs (*Canis familiaris*) are Florida's most destructive exotic mammals. Biologists studying the effects of free-roaming cats on native wildlife believe our lovable felines kill hundreds

*Domestic cat (*Felis catus*), Key Largo, Monroe County. Free-roaming domestic cats kill millions of native birds and mammals in the United States each year.*

red-crested cardinals (*Paroaria coronata*), muscovy ducks (*Cairina moschata*), scarlet ibis (*Eudocimus ruber*), spot-breasted orioles (*Icterus pectoralis*), ringed turtle doves (*Streptopelia risoria*), and Eurasian

collared doves (*Streptopelia decaocto*) may be common, even abundant, in portions of South Florida. None of these species is native, however, and they do not belong here. Florida's three most abundant and widespread exotic birds are also the most abundant and widespread exotic birds in each of the 48 contiguous states: European starlings (*Sturnus vulgaris*), house sparrows (*Passer domesticus*), and rock doves or domestic pigeons (*Columba livia*). These birds, fortunately, are largely restricted to urban areas and agricultural lands. The house sparrow and starling are aggressive species that compete with natives for nesting sites and food. As a cavity nester, the starling probably constitutes a more serious threat, as nesting cavities have become quite scarce in many regions.

Public education is crucial to curbing the further release of invasive nonnative species. Although we are just beginning to understand the complexity of our environment, we should now be smart enough to know that we cannot and should not attempt to forecast the effects of adding organisms to or removing them from the environment. It should be noted that Florida law (FG&FWFC 39-4.005 FAC) prohibits the intentional release of exotic species into the wild.

CHAPTER THREE

Saving Florida's Endangered Species

A RACE AGAINST THE CLOCK

Floridians, I believe, are a relatively environmentally conscious group; the problem is that there are just too many of them. A 1995 poll of 800 randomly selected Floridians revealed that 84.5 percent of them (86 percent of the Democrats, 83 percent of the Republicans in the sample) wanted to maintain or increase the amount of time and money spent protecting Florida's endangered species. A similar 1996 Florida State University poll of 879 Floridians demonstrated that "the public puts the protection of endangered species over property rights and job protection." When asked if property owners have the right to develop their property even if it harms public lands and waters, 84 percent responded no, and a whopping 94 percent believed that having laws to protect endangered species is important.

State and various local governments throughout the Sunshine State have initiated a number of innovative programs to benefit Florida's natural resources. Eco license plates, issued by the Florida Department of Motor Vehicles since 1990, have raised millions of dollars to help save two well-known listed species, the manatee and the panther. The manatee tags first became available in March 1990 and have been extremely popular. The additional fee a motorist pays for the tags is split between the Save the Manatee Trust Fund and Save Our State Environmental Education Trust Fund. As of 30 June 2002, Florida had issued 504,091 manatee tags, generating $28,600,882. Florida panther

specialty tags became available in October 1990 for an additional fee. By 30 June 2002, the 412,397 panther tags issued had generated $13,827,519. Revenue derived from panther tag sales is distributed between the Florida Panther Research and Management Trust Fund (45 percent), the Save Our State Environmental Education Trust Fund (40 percent), and the Florida Communities Trust Fund (15 percent). The handsome Indian River Lagoon tags, released in February 1995, generated more than $200,000 in their first year. All proceeds are used by the St. Johns River Water Management District to fund conservation projects involving the ecologically significant Indian River. Florida's specialty tags program really took off. By 2002, Floridians had 45 different specialty tags to choose from, more than any other state. Other new tags that generate revenue to benefit Florida's environment feature sea turtles, the Everglades, wild dolphins, Tampa Bay estuary, the state wildflower (*Coreopsis lanceolata*), and the message "Conserve Wildlife."

America's growing awareness and concern for endangered species is evident in the release of a special endangered-species series of postage stamps by the U.S. Postal Service in 1996. Several native Florida species are represented, including the Florida panther, American crocodile, manatee, piping plover, and Schaus' swallowtail butterfly.

Florida is also home to several conservation firsts, including the nation's first national wildlife refuge, Pelican Island, and the first national forest in the eastern United States, Ocala. Sadly, Florida is no longer home to the dusky seaside sparrow (*Ammodramus maritimus nigrescens*), which became extinct in 1987, making it the first animal to become extinct since the passage of the Endangered Species Act of 1973.

Floridians have proudly recognized particular natural elements as official state symbols. Included are the Florida panther (the state animal), Florida manatee (marine mammal), American alligator (reptile), largemouth bass (freshwater fish), Atlantic sailfish (saltwater fish), mockingbird (bird), zebra longwing (butterfly), horse conch (shell), sabal palm (tree), coreopsis (wildflower), agatized coral (stone), and Myakka fine sand (soil). It should be noted, however, with fewer than 50 panthers remaining and manatee populations declining each year, we soon may have to consider backup official animals.

Ecotourism has been increasingly recognized as a profitable industry in Florida and many other ecologically inviting locales. It has been the saving grace for biotically significant ecosystems worldwide that would have otherwise been lost to various types of degradation associated with the burgeoning human population. Ecotourism has provided convincing financial reasons for the people of many impoverished countries (and well-to-do countries) to preserve their remaining wild areas. By scanning the advertising sections of *Sierra, Wildbird, Audubon,* or any of the dozens of other outdoor and environmental publications, one can be overwhelmed by the number and price of ecotours offered. In addition to general

nature expeditions, various specialized but traditional outings are designed for birding, backpacking, whale watching, rock climbing, river running, scuba diving, and nature photography. A profusion of highly specialized excursions cater to butterfly or reptile enthusiasts; spelunkers; carnivorous plant fanciers; cactus, fern, wildflower, or mushroom lovers; survivalists; mountain bikers; fly-fishing devotees; and who knows what else.

Bird-watching or birding is America's most popular form of ecotourism and the form that generates the most revenue. In fact, Americans spend more money on birding than they do on baseball, our national pastime, and football combined. Sixty-five million Americans are involved in bird-watching or the feeding of birds. Of the estimated $18 billion that Americans spent annually on various wildlife-watching activities during the 1990s, as much as half went to birding activities. The industry of birding supports more than 200,000 jobs in this country alone. A combination of an unparalleled assemblage of temperate and subtropical habitats, diversity of birdlife, and numerous birding specialties that are unlikely to be encountered elsewhere accounts for the $500 million that birders spend annually in Florida. This revenue source could be in trouble, however. A review of the range maps at the rear of *A Field Guide to Birds* by Roger Tory Peterson will reveal numerous captions noting shrinking bird populations, such as "now absent from many sections," "decline in recent decades," "diminishing," "an overall decline," "has disappeared from," "formerly more widespread," and "nearly gone from." Many species of birds, particularly songbirds, have been declining at an annual rate of 2–4 percent for some time now. For more than 25 years, Clemson University scientists have been monitoring songbird migrations over the Gulf of Mexico; their radar data show sharp and progressive declines. The comparison of radar images from Louisiana and Texas reveals that the number of northbound spring migrants may have declined as much as 50 percent since the 1960s. An overall decline of Neotropical migrants is attributed to the loss of habitat in both breeding and wintering grounds. University of Florida biologists are investigating the nexus between mercury (bioaccumulation) and the dramatic decline of wading birds in the Everglades over the last several decades.

Though the concept of ecotourism is a good one, we as nature lovers must be careful not to love to death the creatures and places we travel long distances and pay a premium price to experience. Humans, regardless of title or intention, stress any environment they invade. Overzealous birders, attempting to lure a rare bird into view by repeatedly blaring tape-recorded bird calls, may disrupt nesting birds to the point of abandoning their nest. Microenvironments such as decaying logs, rock piles, loose tree bark, and detritus accumulations provide vital cover, moisture, food reserves, hibernacula, and incubation chambers for countless herptiles, mammals, and invertebrates. Reptile enthusiasts using snake sticks often cause irreparable damage to these sites in their quest for specimens. Egg-bearing sea turtles are no doubt highly stressed when mobbed by loud, enthusiastic crowds of human tourists as soon as

they emerge from the surf onto tropical beaches. Likewise, boats and rafts carrying camera-toting whale watchers to calving grounds, with hopes of photographing or better yet petting whales, have been known to separate mother whales from their calves. The ever-increasing number of ecotourists visiting Mexico's Sierra Madre to witness the enormous congregations of wintering monarch butterflies has prompted developers to deforest portions of the butterflies' habitat to build additional visitor accommodations. Some of Africa's national parks are receiving so many visitors that cheetahs and other timid creatures are abandoning the protected areas for locales where they are more exposed to poachers. In Costa Rica, where ecotourism is now the largest industry, so much rain forest has been altered to house the thousands of tourists that the wildlife that attracts the visitors has suffered as a result. In Florida, divers and swimmers frequently trespass into posted manatee areas to interact with the gentle giants, ignoring the numerous signs warning them not to do so. Interacting with manatees may seem innocuous to well-intentioned visitors, but many cases of mother-calf separation as a result of encounters with divers have been documented.

The benefits associated with ecotourism, however, clearly outweigh the negative aspects. Environmental conditions in Costa Rica, Florida, and elsewhere would be worse without ecotourism. Governments hoping to reap the full financial benefits of ecotourism must make concerted efforts to protect sizable tracts of wilderness and wildlife populations. It is the responsibility of visitors to acquaint themselves with the do's and don'ts of the area visited and to exercise proper ecological etiquette at all times.

HISTORY

The history of protection of Florida's natural resources is one of contrasts and changes, changes in both the environment and the public's attitude about the environment. There are eerie tales of extreme environmental abuse, politics, and accounts of early Audubon Society conservation wardens who lost their lives protecting wildlife. Florida's natural resources, considered by early frontiersmen to be inexhaustible, were not, and many species suffered drastic declines by the late 1800s.

Millions of wading birds were killed for the fashionable plume industry centered in New York. Rookeries of herons, egrets, ibises, and spoonbills were easily reached by gun- and club-toting poachers on johnboats. By the turn of the century, most of Florida's wading birds had been killed. Only one known pair of reddish egrets remained, and roseate spoonbills teetered on the brink of extinction. In 1891 the Florida Legislature outlawed the taking of and commerce in wading birds, which had virtually no effect in the lawless Everglades, where poachers continued the slaughter. In response to the ongoing and illegal annihilation of wading birds, the Florida Audubon Society was established in 1901 to protect the remaining birds. Being an Audubon warden was a dangerous job. The first Audubon warden, Guy Bradley, was murdered in 1905, and Warden Columbus McLeod was murdered in 1908. For the next 20 years, conservationists waged a

relentless war against the illicit plume industry, which was finally brought to its knees in 1930. The populations of reddish egrets, roseate spoonbills, and other Florida wading birds have now rebounded after state and federal laws prohibited the killing of these birds.

During that same era, the once ubiquitous Carolina parakeets were being exterminated wherever they could be found, often just for sport. When one of these gregarious parakeets was shot and fell to the ground, its panicked mate and other flock mates were often picked off, one by one, as they fluttered above the dead or dying birds. Florida remained the parakeets' last stronghold, but efforts to save them came too late; the last Carolina parakeet died in captivity in 1918.

Nonetheless, Florida's early years of wildlife conservation were not without victories. The state certainly had its share of colorful characters, many of whom helped shape efforts of future conservationists globally. Among them were J. N. "Ding" Darling, appointed by President Franklin Roosevelt to head the Bureau of Fisheries and Wildlife in the 1930s, and Marjory Stoneman Douglas, author of *The Everglades: River of Grass.*

Florida's history of wildlife conservation begins in the nineteenth century. In 1830 fewer than 35,000 people inhabited Florida, which works out to about 1,000 acres of land per resident. In 1845 Florida became the twenty-seventh state; its total population was approximately 70,000. In 1875 nonresident hunting licenses were required by law, and in 1877 Florida's first conservation laws were enacted, creating hunting seasons. During the 1880s the state paid a $5 bounty for each bear, panther, and wolf killed. In contrast, the

*Great egret (*Casmerodius albus*), one of many species of Florida wading birds nearly hunted to extinction during the late 1800s.*

1890s brought the first laws protecting manatees and wading birds, though the laws concerning birds were largely ignored.

By 1900 the population of Florida had exceeded half a million, reducing the acres per human to about 66. Notable events of the early 1900s included the establishment of the Florida Audubon Society and the U.S. Forest Service. The responsibility of managing Florida's game and fish species was traded back and forth between the state and counties. In 1903 President Theodore Roosevelt designated Pelican Island as the nation's first national wildlife refuge. The United States and Canada signed the Migratory Bird Convention in 1916 to protect avifauna that migrated between the two countries. A similar treaty signed by Mexico in

1936 strengthened the protection of migratory birds. Florida's real estate craze began in the 1920s with a flood of new settlers. In 1927 political chicanery allowed Lake Okeechobee, Florida's largest freshwater lake, to be classified as saltwater so that commercial fishing could continue there unregulated. In 1936 the National Wildlife Federation was established. The Pittman-Robertson Act was passed by the U.S. Congress in 1937, authorizing states to utilize excise taxes from the sale of firearms and hunting gear for conservation purposes. State laws protecting the American alligator were passed in 1939, but despite the laws, rampant harvesting continued.

By 1940 the state's population had reached 1,897,414, with about 18.3 acres per Floridian. Declines of many wildlife species were evident, though concern was primarily directed at game species and alligators, which produced valuable hides. In 1946 the first biologists were hired by the FG&FWFC; soon, more than 160 conservation officers were employed throughout the state. In 1949 the conservation officers were renamed wildlife officers, and in 1950 new officers were required to attend a law enforcement academy in an attempt to modernize the commission. That year also brought some protection for panthers and black bears; they were listed as game animals, which provided closed seasons. The panther was afforded full protection under Florida law in 1958. The war on the introduced, lake-clogging water hyacinth was waged in earnest in 1952 by the FG&FWFC.

By 1960 Florida was the tenth most populous state, with 4,951,560 residents, leaving only about 7 acres for every resident. In the 1960s a new awareness of the sensitivity of our environment became widespread. If you were around during that decade, you will surely remember slogans such as "Give a Hoot, Don't Pollute" and "Only You Can Prevent Forest Fires," and the TV commercial featuring the tearful native American canoeing along a polluted, littered waterway. The 1962 book *Silent Spring*, by Rachel Carson, alerted the public to the harmful effects of pesticides such as DDT on birds and other wildlife. The harvest of alligators was totally banned in 1962, and in 1966 the species was declared endangered under the Endangered Species Preservation Act. The FG&FWFC, at that time a division of the Department of Natural Resources, was delegated the authority to administer game and freshwater fish laws in 1969.

The 1970s were pivotal years for Florida's environment and for those protecting it. By 1970 Florida's population had reached 6,789,443, which left barely 5 acres for each Floridian. Several notable events occurred in 1970, including the first Earth Day and the formation of the Environmental Protection Agency, which was responsible for establishing standards of environmental quality, including the Clean Air Act. Wildlife officers were empowered to enforce all state laws, not just conservation laws. In 1971 the enormous construction project known as the Cross Florida Barge Canal, which began in the 1960s, was successfully halted by conservationists, who were able to establish that damage to the environment would far outweigh the need for such a conduit. Greenpeace, an international organization known for its proactive efforts to protect the environment, was established in the same year. In 1972 FG&FWFC published the first official state list of endangered species (followed up in 1977 with an endangered species program), and state environmental laws were passed protecting groundwater and wetlands, creating five water management districts. The federal Endangered Species Act passed in 1973, without a doubt the most significant year in the country's history in terms of protecting listed species and their habitat. The U.S. Department of the Interior distributed $26.5 million to various states for acquisition of conservation lands. By 1977 the American alligator, which had been critically endangered in recent years, had responded so favorably to state and federal protection that it was downlisted from endangered to threatened. In 1979 the FG&FWFC established a 24-hour toll-free hotline for the Wildlife Alert Reward Program (1-800-432-2046), which encouraged the public to report wildlife violations. Also in 1979 the wonderful program called CARL (Conservation and Recreation Lands) was born. (It received a needed economic boost in 1990 when the Preservation 2000 Act was passed.)

By 1980 there were approximately 9.7 million Floridians, making Florida the fourth most populous state and dropping the acreage per person to 3.6. The state Nongame Act was established in 1980, and in 1984 the FG&FWFC set itself apart from many other state conservation agencies by demonstrating an interest in protecting all native species, not just animals that gobbled or those with antlers. The Nongame Wildlife Program, later renamed the Bureau of Nongame Wildlife, was established to study and conserve wildlife species defined by what they are not, which includes the great majority of Florida's wildlife. Another significant 1981 event was the establishment of the Florida Natural Areas Inventory, a joint effort of the Department of Environmental Protection and the Nature Conservancy. The inventory is staffed by highly qualified scientists who compile and maintain a comprehensive database of Florida's biodiversity.

The early 1980s were a trying time for environmentalists and the environment. Secretary of the Interior James Watt repeatedly sided with environmental exploiters. Conservationists rejoiced in 1983 when Watt resigned and again in 1995 when he was convicted of several criminal violations. In 1982 a combination of tragic factors (predominantly human-caused) resulted in the slow and agonizing death of about 1,200 deer in the Everglades. In 1988 western cougars were transplanted to Florida as part of an experimental program to impede the genetic erosion of the remaining small population of Florida panthers.

By 1990 the state's population had exploded to 13,365,000, and nearly 1,000 new Floridians were arriving each day (not to mention a record-breaking 41 million visitors from around the world). The acreage per resident had now dwindled to 2.7. Florida's ecosystems and wildlife and the agencies responsible for protecting them were faced with a steadily increasing number of threats. In 1991 the Florida Legislature passed the Marine Turtle Protection Act, enhancing existing laws. In 1993 the Florida Department of Natural Resources and Department of Environmental Regulation merged to create the new Department of Environmental Protection. In 1995 history repeated itself, as flooding killed nearly 90 percent of the Everglades deer herd.

Florida's population had soared to 15,982,378 by the year 2000, and by 2002 it was up to 16,396,515, leaving just a little over two acres for every Floridian. Experts with the University of South Florida Bureau of Economic and Business Research predict that by 2024 Florida will surpass New York as the third most populous state and that by 2030 the Sunshine State will be crammed with nearly 25 million people. Crammed, indeed: there would be only 1.3 acres for every Florida resident. South Florida alone would be home to an expected 7.5 million people. Collier County on the southwest coast, Osceola County in Central Florida, and Flagler County in northeastern Florida expect population increases of 100 percent or more by 2030. The state is growing faster than India, Haiti, and Mexico. Florida's burgeoning human population will certainly create problems for those responsible for protecting the state's endangered and threatened animals and their habitats.

GOVERNMENT AS ENVIRONMENTAL STEWARDS

The role of the Florida Fish and Wildlife Conservation Commission (FWC) has evolved from the state's gamekeeper, when it paid out cash bounties for killing panthers and rattlesnakes, to informed caretaker of all, not just some, of Florida's biodiversity. Making up for lost time, dedicated biologists with the Bureau of Nongame Wildlife have conducted numerous, science-based investigations, the results of which have saved many native species and habitats from annihilation. As with all governmental agencies, politics have played a role in the commission since its inception in 1913. It is now one of the most distinguished state conservation agencies and was honored as one of the nation's five most effective fish and wildlife agencies. A review of the FWC publication *Florida Wildlife* (and its several predecessors, going back to *Florida Woods and Waters,* first published in 1929) provides a fascinating chronology of the changes in Floridian perspectives on natural resources.

Mention Richard Milhous Nixon and most Americans will immediately think of Watergate and a betrayal of the public trust. A few of us, however, remember Nixon as the president who put into action the first environmental law that had a real bite, the Endangered Species Act of 1973 (ESA). Signing the act into law on 28 December 1973, President Nixon proclaimed, "Nothing is more priceless and more worthy of preservation than the rich array of animal life with which our country has been blessed."

The ESA of 1973 was written as an equal-opportunity law (in theory at least) affording protection to all species great and small, giving no preference to popular celebrated species or so-called higher life-forms. Under the law, the Secretary of the Interior, who oversees the U.S. Fish and Wildlife Service, and the Secretary of Commerce, who oversees the U.S. Marine Fisheries Service, share the responsibility of enforcing the act as it pertains to fauna. Fish and Wildlife is generally responsible for terrestrial and freshwater species, and Marine Fisheries is responsible for marine and anadromous species.

Without the ESA and other federal and state conservation laws, the species listed below as well as many others probably would exist only in photographs and memories. Fortunately, the ESA will preserve the opportunity for us and future generations to experience true wilderness and behold these splendid creatures in their element.

Bald Eagle (*Haliaeetus leucocephalus*)

A victim primarily of DDT, the national bird also suffers from habitat destruction and shooting. By 1963 only about 400 breeding pairs remained in the lower 48 states. Conservation efforts (including banning the domestic use of DDT and protecting nesting habitat) have increased the number of breeding pairs to more than 4,000 and climbing. Recovery efforts have proven so successful that the species was downlisted from endangered to threatened in 1995.

American Alligator
(*Alligator mississippiensis*)
The recovery of the American alligator, largest of North American reptiles, is one of the ESA's greatest success stories. This crocodilian, revered for its hide and meat, was hunted to the brink of extinction by 1972, when biologists estimated that as much as 99 percent of Florida's gator population had been hunted out. Protection offered by the ESA and state regulatory laws allowed the alligator to make a tremendous and rapid recovery. In 1977 it was downlisted to threatened, and by 1988 alligators had become so abundant that limited harvests were permitted in Florida. Currently, it remains listed solely because of its similarity to the endangered American crocodile (*Crocodylus acutus*).

Eastern Brown Pelican
(*Pelecanus occidentalis carolinensis*)
Once in serious trouble as a result of the biological accumulation of DDT, this bird experienced a remarkable recovery on the Atlantic Coast, especially in Florida, and in Alabama, where it was delisted in 1985. In recent years, the brown pelican is easily observed on any given day in nearly every coastal area of Florida.

Peregrine Falcon (*Falco peregrinus*)
Just 25 years ago, fewer than 40 pairs of these magnificent, streamlined speedsters nested in the lower United States, with none nesting in the East. Another victim of DDT, the peregrine may have joined the ranks of the now extinct passenger pigeon and Carolina parakeet, if not for the ESA. The peregrine was delisted in 1995, thanks to successful ESA recovery actions including outlawing DDT, captive propagation, and reintroduction programs.

*American alligator (*Alligator mississippiensis*) basking with Florida Cooters (*Pseudemys floridana*), Wakulla Springs State Park, Wakulla County. Alligators are once again a common sight throughout much of Florida as a direct result of the Endangered Species Act of 1973.*

More than 1,000 pairs of peregrines now nest in the United States, including many that nest on ledges of skyscrapers in New York and other large cities.

Whooping Crane (*Grus americana*)

Only 16 whoopers remained on Earth in 1941. The ESA furnished various recovery actions, including much-needed protection along the cranes' migration route of more than 2,000 miles. Captive propagation programs and the establishment of experimental populations, including Florida's reintroduced nonmigratory population, have kept this bird alive as a species.

Kirtland's Warbler (*Dendroica kirtlandii*)

In 1974, when the annual count of singing male Kirtland's warblers on the Michigan breeding grounds totaled only 167, biologists became seriously concerned for the species' survival. Intensive and expensive recovery efforts (including habitat restoration, prescribed burns, and cowbird eradication) established under ESA guidelines proved successful. By 1995 the population had rebounded to more than 1,500 individuals.

California Gray Whale (*Rhachianectes glaucus*)

By the 1940s the whaling industry had reduced the world population of these gentle giants to only 4,000 to 6,000. Protection afforded by the ESA and the Marine Mammal Protection Act was instrumental in restoring populations to a level (more than 20,000) where the species could be delisted in 1995. Unfortunately, the ESA arrived too late for the Atlantic gray whale, which was whaled into extinction years before it was enacted.

California Condor (*Gymnogyps californianus*)

After soaring above southern California's mountains for tens of thousands of years, the immense California condor rapidly became one of the earth's rarest creatures. The once safe montane home of the condor became overpeopled and unsuitable. By the 1980s the species appeared doomed. When only a handful of wild condors remained, the last birds were removed from the wild in a last-ditch effort to save them. Those efforts paid off. As part of an ESA captive breeding and reintroduction program, the first group of six condors was released into the wilds of Arizona's Vermillion Cliffs in 1996. Condors were extirpated from Arizona in the 1920s. During 2001 and 2002, it was almost common for visitors to Grand Canyon National Park to observe condors riding the thermals above the canyon.

Black-footed Ferret (*Mustela nigripes*)

Feared extinct for years, a population of ferrets was discovered near Meeteetse, Wyoming, in 1981. This population was decimated by a canine distemper epidemic later that decade. By funding a captive propagation program using 18 surviving ferrets, the ESA salvaged the species from extinction. Several hundred offspring have been reared, and some have been reintroduced back into the wild at various locations within their historic range.

In recent years the U.S. Fish and Wildlife Service (USF&WS) and many state conservation agencies have been developing recovery plans for listed species with a multispecies or ecosystem approach. In

Clearcut sand pine scrub (Panhandle coastal scrub),
FRANKLIN COUNTY.

its 1992 *Report to Congress: Endangered and Threatened Species Recovery Program,* the USF&WS asserts, "More and more the Service is recognizing that concentration on conserving individual species from extinction is inadequate when other interdependent species that are members of the same ecosystem continue to decline. The Service is directing increased attention to producing multi-species or ecosystem recovery plans that address the needs of other species that are not primary targets of the plan." This approach just makes sense. It should prove more cost-effective and may prevent species that would have eventually become listed from reaching that point; like crime prevention, it can prevent a potential problem from becoming a real problem. Examples of such recovery plans currently in effect in Florida include the Pine-Rockland Ecosystem Plan, the Florida Scrub Plants Plan, and the Sand Skink/Blue-tailed Mole Skink Plan. The rationale of ecosystem plans, after all, is the primary reason for writing this book: to demonstrate just how critical the protection of ecosystems is to the protection of individual species.

CHAPTER FOUR

Florida's Habitats

Mother Nature has blessed Florida with an astounding diversity of animals and plants, in terms of the number of species represented and the number of endemics (species whose range is confined to Florida). Florida's opulent biodiversity includes more than 3,800 plant species. Florida specimens of 95 different tree species are of record size, and native trees contain the world's heaviest and lightest woods. Animal diversity is equally impressive, with more than 100 mammal species (including 28 dolphins, porpoises, and whales), 460 birds, 128 reptiles, 62 amphibians, and 130 fishes. Florida's 50,000 invertebrate species include 3,000 species of butterflies and moths, 700 spiders, 83 freshwater snails, 121 terrestrial mollusks, 52 freshwater mussels, and numerous other insects, arachnids, diplopods, bivalves, crustaceans, corals, and sea fans.

In addition to diversity, Florida boasts a high rate of endemism, of both natural communities and organisms. Among the state's thousands of vascular plant taxa, 275 species, subspecies, or distinct populations are considered endemic. Among the fauna, 61 mammal species or subspecies, 26 birds, 10 amphibians, 43 reptiles, 11 freshwater fishes, and 410 terrestrial and freshwater invertebrates (including 67 mollusks, 193 beetles, 36 arachnids, 42 grasshoppers, 23 decapods, and 17 butterflies and moths) are considered endemic to Florida. Regions of the state that contain particularly high numbers of endemics are the Central Ridge (Highlands, Polk, Orange, Lake, and Marion counties), the Florida Keys and extreme southern Florida (Dade, Monroe, and Collier counties), and the Apalachicola River basin (Franklin, Liberty, Gulf, and Bay counties).

Florida's rich faunal diversity is supported by a diverse assemblage of habitat types, several of which are unique to the state. This section discusses more than 25 primary habitat types in Florida, with information on the many habitat subtypes or variants as well. The Florida Natural Areas Inventory describes no fewer than 82 distinct natural communities occurring in Florida, 13 of which are endemic.

Habitats such as pine flatwoods, mixed-hardwood forests, and freshwater swamps are widespread in the southeastern United States; others such as Florida scrub, tropical hardwood hammocks, and living coral reefs are indeed unique to Florida. Without leaving the state, one can experience the steep, wooded ravines and bluffs that border portions of the Apalachicola River, which resemble Appalachian forests, and the following day dive among brilliantly colored tropical fish and coral formations in the Keys, which are, as biologist and author Skip Lazell put it, "the only West Indies one can drive to." Florida's array of flora and fauna is interesting because it contains a blend of temperate and tropical as well as eastern and western components.

Numerous temperate species reach the southernmost limit of their range in Florida (seal salamander, eastern chipmunk), and many West Indian or other tropical species find their northernmost limits here as well (white-crowned pigeon, manatee). Scrub and dry prairie ecosystems are geographically isolated islands of habitat that were historically more widespread and contiguous with similar arid habitats now largely restricted to western North America. Stranded in Florida with these remnant habitats are disjunct populations of western taxa, including scrub-jays, burrowing owls, and caracaras, whose main populations occur no farther east than Texas. When attempting to characterize a particular habitat that does not clearly fit a habitat description or that has characteristics of several different habitats, one must remember that habitats commonly grade into adjacent habitats, making identification troublesome. Also, anthropogenic alterations often make characterization difficult (e.g., tropical pineland where fire has been suppressed for five or more years may strongly resemble tropical hammock).

Nearly 1,200 miles of coastline outlines Florida's 58,664 square miles on three sides, providing various estuarine and marine communities inhabited by countless life-forms. Inland are thousands of freshwater wetlands (lakes, ponds, rivers, marshes, swamps, bogs), which harbor myriad aquatic organisms. Florida's various terrestrial and subterranean ecosystems are also occupied by a profusion of animal life. Unlike many states, especially western states, where life zones are defined by altitudinal differences measured in thousand-foot increments,

Florida's habitats and dominant fauna and flora may change dramatically with variances of just several inches. Typically, the tip of a peninsula (such as southern Florida) will have fewer species than the base (northern Florida). The subtropical climate of southern Florida and the Keys, however, coupled with the many stenothermal tropicopolitan species restricted to extreme southern Florida, considerably offsets the peninsula effect, particularly for plants. The diversity of South Florida's native animal life is generally lower than in northern Florida (especially for herpetofauna, avifauna, and mammals), but there are also a number of tropical animal species restricted in range to South Florida.

Biologists now recognize the importance of ecosystem preservation in the effort to protect individual species. In recent years, state and federal conservation and land management agencies have been employing multispecies or ecosystem approaches to recovery actions. The more we know about interrelationships between the many organisms forming an ecosystem and the niches each organism occupies, the better we can protect individual elements.

In writing this book, it occurred to me that the text contains a preponderance of rather disturbing information concerning the natural state of our natural state, so I was pleased to report some good information for a change. At a time when the federal government and many states are reducing monies directed toward environmental causes in the name of balancing budgets, Florida is demonstrating its candor in protecting the environment by spending more money on land acquisition than any other state. In 1990 the Florida

Legislature made a conscious commitment to acquire and protect its remaining ecologically significant lands from development. The venture, appropriately named the Florida Preservation 2000 Act, or Preservation 2000 for short, included a proposed $300 million annual land acquisition budget through the year 2000. Major recipients of this funding are the Conservation and Recreation Lands (CARL) and the Save Our Rivers programs. To quote state representative Peter Wallace, "Floridians buy and protect more environmentally endangered lands each year than any other state. In fact, we buy more land for conservation than the federal government does throughout the whole country." There is some bad news, however. In-depth scientific studies conducted by state biologists have concluded that protecting Florida's biodiversity through habitat acquisition would require approximately twice the $3 billion authorized under Preservation 2000.

THE CARETAKERS OF FLORIDA'S HABITATS

A number of state and federal land management agencies are responsible for administering Florida's public lands, which include some of the most unique, beautiful, and ecologically significant lands in North America.

The Florida Park Service, a division of the Florida Department of Environmental Protection, manages more than 140 sites throughout the state. The state park service pursues the same basic conservation goals as the federal park service: to protect natural and cultural resources, and to maintain and restore environments to conditions that existed prior to the arrival of Europeans. State park lands protect examples of virtually every ecosystem type found in Florida. Lands managed by the Florida Park Service include parks, preserves, recreation areas, geological sites, archeology sites, botanical sites, and reserves.

The Florida Fish and Wildlife Conservation Commission manages a number of wildlife management areas statewide, including Cecil M. Webb in southwest Florida; Three Lakes, Bull Creek, and Triple N Ranch in central Florida; Gulf Hammock in the Gulf Hammock region; Andrews, Guana River, and Big Bend in northern Florida; and Gaskins in the Panhandle.

State Forest Service lands include central Florida's Lake Wales Ridge and Withlacoochee state forests, Goethe State Forest in north-central Florida, and the Panhandle's Blackwater River State Forest.

The National Park Service is responsible for managing several Florida units, the largest and most familiar being the 1.5 million acres of Everglades National Park. Other national park lands in Florida include Dry Tortugas National Park, Biscayne National Park, Big Cypress National Preserve, Cape Canaveral and Gulf Islands national seashores, and several small national monuments.

The U.S. Fish and Wildlife Service (usf&ws) oversees several large and small national wildlife refuges throughout Florida, including the country's first, Indian River County's Pelican Island; Merritt Island in Brevard County; St. Marks in Wakulla County; Loxahatchee in Palm Beach County; Florida Panther and Ten Thousand Islands in Collier and Monroe counties; J. N. "Ding" Darling on Sanibel Island in Lee County; Lake Wales Ridge in Polk and Highlands counties;

Crocodile Lakes, Key Deer, Great White Heron, and Key West, all in the Keys.

The National Oceanic and Atmospheric Administration oversees the Florida Keys National Marine Sanctuary and several smaller marine sanctuaries in the Florida Keys.

Florida has three large national forests (totaling more than a million acres) managed by the U.S. Forest Service: Ocala in north-central Florida, Osceola in northern Florida, and the largest, Apalachicola, in Florida's Big Bend region.

Several of Florida's military bases have made considerable efforts to protect and maintain their ecosystems, which harbor numerous listed species. The Nature Conservancy has worked with some posts to further conservation efforts. The country's 400 military bases occupy more than 25 million acres, ranking third in landholdings among federal agencies. Florida bases containing substantial tracts of ecologically significant lands include Key West Naval Air Station on Boca Chica Key, Avon Park Air Force Base in central Florida, and the Panhandle's half-million-acre Eglin Air Force Base. Lands owned and managed by the Miccosukee and the Seminole Indian tribes also contain pristine tracts of rare and endangered habitats and wildlife.

Nongovernmental conservation agencies owning notable landholdings within Florida include The Nature Conservancy, the nation's largest private, science-based conservation organization, which acquires environmentally threatened lands through heritage programs. The Nature Conservancy owns or manages several of Florida's ecologically unique and most scenic tracts, including several Lake Wales Ridge preserves, Ordway

Preserve near Gainesville, and the Panhandle's Apalachicola River Bluffs and Ravines Preserve. The Florida Audubon Society is Florida's oldest and largest (32,000 members) conservation organization. Since its inception in 1900, the society has maintained a persistent presence in Tallahassee, lobbying for environmentally beneficial legislation, opposing harmful legislation, and participating in important projects such as Everglades restoration activities. It manages approximately 50 sanctuaries statewide and its Center for Birds of Prey in Maitland, which has treated thousands of raptors, including nearly 100 bald eagles. The Florida Audubon Society is not affiliated with the National Audubon Society, which owns and manages southwest Florida's famous Corkscrew Swamp Sanctuary. A few large private landholdings are maintained largely to benefit wildlife, including Archbold Biological Station near Lake Placid.

Ten representative land acquisitions procured via the Preservation 2000 Act, CARL, or related programs are described below. These sites, managed by several different land management agencies, support many listed species.

Lake Wales Ridge Ecosystems: Superb examples of ancient Florida scrub. In Highlands and Polk counties; lead managers FWC and USF&WS.

Archie Carr Sea Turtle Refuge: Site of the world's second largest loggerhead sea turtle rookery. In Brevard and Indian River counties; lead managers USF&WS and Florida Park Service.

Tate's Hell/Carrabelle Tract: Protects water quality of Apalachicola Bay (North America's most productive estuary) as well as critical habitat for several listed species, including red-cockaded woodpeckers and black bears. In Franklin County; lead manager U.S. Forest Service.

Hammocks of the Lower Keys: Preserves many of the last Lower Keys tropical hardwood hammocks and the assortment of listed species they harbor. In Monroe County; lead manager USF&WS.

Topsail Hill: Perhaps the most outstanding assemblage of the Panhandle's coastal habitats, which include 30-foot dunes, Panhandle coastal scrub, and two freshwater lakes. Home to critically endangered Choctawhatchee beach mice, red-cockaded woodpeckers, and Godfrey's golden asters. In Walton County; lead manager Florida Park Service.

Green Swamp: Florida's second largest wetlands system, after the Everglades. Includes headwaters for five major rivers. In Lake and Polk counties; lead managers FWC and Florida Park Service.

Southeastern Bat Maternity Caves: Safeguards bat maternity and roosting sites as well as habitat of Georgia blind salamanders and other listed species. In Alachua, Citrus, Jackson, Marion, and Sumter counties; lead manager FWC.

Fakahatchee Strand: The country's finest example of strand swamp, the greatest diversity of native orchids in the United States, and several remaining Florida panthers. In Collier County; lead manager Florida Park Service.

East Everglades/Frog Pond: An enormous water storage area that is critical to the various Everglades ecosystems. In Dade County; lead managers National Park Service and South Florida Water Management District.

Florida's First Magnitude Springs: Scattered sites acquired to protect some of the world's premier first-magnitude springs and their unique, often endemic inhabitants. In Hernando, Jackson, Leon, and Wakulla counties; lead managers U.S. Forest Service, Jackson County, Florida Park Service, and FWC.

FLORIDA SCRUB ECOSYSTEMS

With all but a diminutive tract occurring in coastal Alabama, this unique, ancient ecosystem is generally endemic to the Sunshine State. This habitat is known by several other names, including "sand pine scrub," "rosemary scrub," "oak scrub," and, in portions of Polk and Highlands counties, "slash pine scrub." Most scrub communities are generally dominated by shrubs rather than trees. Scrub is a xeric, almost desert habitat occurring on the well-drained, sandy soils of inland ridges, ancient shorelines, or coastal uplands. The substrate is characterized as a brilliant white, infertile, quartz-derived sugar sand, though the presence of clay in some regions gives the sand a yellow or gray color. The sugar sand of scrub occurring on the Lake Wales Ridge (a pre-Pleistocene dune system) is often 100 to 200 feet deep. Dominant scrub vegetation often includes sand pine (*Pinus clausa*) and several evergreen, sclerophyllous, shrubby oaks: myrtle oak (*Quercus myrtifolia*), Chapman's oak (*Q. chapmanii*), Archbold oak (*Q. inopina*), and sand live oak (*Q. geminata*). Other characteristic scrub plants include rosemary (*Ceratiola ericoides*), rusty lyonia (*Lyonia ferruginea*), scrub hickory (*Carya carya floridana*), and various ground lichens. The plants of scrub ecosystems, particularly those on the Lake Wales Ridge, have a high rate of endemism, with at least 40 percent occurring nowhere else on Earth. Several species are known from only one or two sites. Endemic or listed scrub plants include scrub blazing star (*Liatris ohlingerae*), scrub mint (*Dicerandra frutescens*), pygmy fringe tree (*Chionanthus pygmaeus*), scrub plum (*Prunus geniculata*), and the Florida ziziphus (*Ziziphus celata*).

Scrub communities are pyrogenic, perpetuated by infrequent high-intensity fires that occur every 10 to 70 years.

Apparently never a dominant ecosystem in Florida, however, scattered pockets of scrub did occur throughout much of the peninsula where dunes and sandbars were abandoned by receding ancient seas. Currently, this critically endangered ecosystem is restricted to a few increasingly smaller, isolated tracts, many of which are slated for development. The distinctiveness of the scrub biota was not widely recognized until just recently, thus conservation efforts came late. Unfortunately, the most commonly heard sound in scrub habitats is the noise of construction equipment.

Florida scrub has one of the highest concentrations of endangered and threatened species of any ecosystem in the

*Florida scrub habitat near Sebring, Highlands County, on Central Florida's Lake Wales Ridge. Note sugar-white sand, sand pine (*Pinus clausa*), Florida rosemary (*Ceratiola ericoides*), and scrubby oaks (*Quercus sp.*). One of Florida's most endangered and species-rich habitats.*

country, and as for plants, the list of endemic scrub fauna is long. Listed or endemic animals inhabiting scrub communities include Florida scrub-jays (*Aphelocoma coerulescens*), Florida mice (*Podomys floridanus*), sand skinks (*Neoseps reynoldsi*), bluetail mole skinks (*Eumeces egregius lividus*), eastern indigo snakes (*Drymarchon corais couperi*), short-tailed snakes (*Stilosoma extenuatum*), pine snakes (*Pituophis melanoleucus mugitus*), gopher tortoises (*Gopherus polyphemus*), gopher frogs (*Rana capito*), Florida scrub lizards (*Sceloporus woodi*), Lake Placid funnel wolf spiders (*Sosippus placidus*), and several scarab beetles, to name a few.

Typical birds of Florida scrub habitats include eastern towhees (*Pipilo erythrophthalmus*), mockingbirds (*Mimus polyglottos*), common ground-doves (*Columbina passerina*), bobwhites (*Colinus virginianus*), and white-eyed vireos (*Vireo griseus*). Characteristic scrub mammals include oldfield mice (*Peromyscus polionotus*), raccoons (*Procyon lotor*), southeastern pocket gophers (*Geomys pinetis*), and bobcats (*Lynx rufus*). The herpetofauna includes racers (*Coluber constrictor*), eastern coachwhip snakes (*Masticophis flagellum flagellum*), hog-nosed snakes (*Heterodon*), six-lined racerunners (*Cnemidophorus sexlineatus*), and oak toads (*Bufo quercicus*). An enormous variety of insects and arachnids occur, including red widow spiders (*Latrodectus bishopi*), nocturnal scrub velvet ants (*Photomorphus archboldi*), Lake Wales Ridge velvet ants (*Dasymutilla archboldi*), and many others. Florida scrub ecosystems quite possibly contain plant, insect, arachnid, or perhaps even small fossorial reptile species that have

yet to be discovered. Because many scrub species are so isolated and localized, extinction may precede discovery.

Scrubby Flatwoods
This hybrid between true scrub and pine flatwoods occurs at elevations slightly higher than flatwoods and slightly lower than scrub. Because of this they are generally drier and better drained than flatwoods but damper than scrub. The flora and fauna are influenced by both communities, but several species, including Archbold oak and scrub palmetto (*Sabal etonia*), are often most common in scrubby flatwoods. Many animals found in true scrub but not flatwoods occur in this habitat, including Florida scrub lizards, bluetail mole skinks, sand skinks, scrub-jays, and Florida mice. Some flatwoods species also occur in scrubby flatwoods, including pine woods treefrogs (*Hyla femoralis*).

Inland Peninsular Scrub
Florida scrub is restricted to three fairly distinct geographical regions within the state. Inland peninsular scrub is the oldest, most distinctive, and most endangered of the three. It occupies a narrow, broken, north-to-south chain of isolated ridgetop fragments from southern Clay County to Highlands County, known collectively as the Central Florida Ridge. It includes the Lake Wales Ridge. Currently, the largest intact parcel of scrub occurs within Ocala National Forest. The areas now comprising inland peninsular scrub were once islands protruding from a shallow sea. This ecosystem was forged in the late Pleistocene, when Florida's climate was cooler and drier than it is today. As the weather became warmer

and moister, 5,000 to 7,000 years ago, scrub habitat receded substantially.

Early settlers to the Lake Wales Ridge found scrub to be useless and unproductive for their needs. Not until citrus growers learned to graft citrus bud wood onto lemon rootstock were they able to grow citrus on well-drained scrub sands. By the end of World War II, citrus growers had converted most of the Lake Wales Ridge scrub habitat to orange groves. Northern areas were lost first, but devastating freezes during the late 1970s and 1980s forced growers southward along the ridge. Other threats soon appeared, including residential and commercial development, which collectively destroyed over 80 percent of the original inland scrub.

Considerably more endemics inhabit inland peninsular scrub than coastal scrub. Areas where pristine or nearly pristine inland scrub can be found include Ocala National Forest, Avon Park Air Force Bombing Range, Archbold Biological Station, Saddleblanket Lakes Preserve, Lake Apthorpe Preserve, Catfish Creek Preserve, Arbuckle Lake State Preserve, and the following state park lands: Gold Head Branch, Blue Springs, Wekiwa Springs, Rock Springs Run, Lake Kissimmee, Lake Louisa, and Highlands Hammock. The new 10,000-acre Lake Wales Ridge National Wildlife Refuge will occupy numerous scattered sites in Polk and Highlands counties.

The story behind Archbold Biological Station, a private, nonprofit ecological research station near Lake Placid in Highlands County, is an interesting one. Established in 1941 by Richard Archbold, an explorer and heir to the early Standard Oil Company fortune, the station contains 5,000 acres of pristine scrub habitat and manages an adjacent 3,000 acres for the FWC (Lake Placid Scrub Preserve). These lands contain globally significant habitats, including more than 100 chaste rosemary balds, a Florida scrub variant. Archbold died in 1976, leaving his estate to Archbold Expeditions, the foundation that provides core funding for the station. It accommodates a staff of resident scientists and a continual flow of visiting biologists who come to study the unique plants and animals of Central Florida ridge habitats. Much of what is now known about Florida scrub-jays, sand skinks, Florida mice, and many endemic scrub plants is based on research conducted at Archbold. The biodiversity recorded on the grounds of Archbold Biological Station is astounding. Recorded to date are 40 mammal species, 64 herptiles, 25 fishes, 208 birds, 535 vascular plants, and more than 4,500 insects and arachnids, including the greatest diversity of ant species in North America, 105. Fred Lohrer, Archbold's information manager, reported in 1996 that the station's entomologist, Mark Deyrup, was continuing to discover new insect species, including sand-burrowing ants, beetles, and pygmy mole crickets.

The general public is welcome to visit Archbold (certain areas only) and enjoy the self-guided nature trail, butterfly garden, and an informative 18-minute video on Florida scrub. Contact Archbold Biological Station at 941-465-2571 for more information.

Peninsular Coastal Scrub

Peninsular coastal scrub occurs in narrow strips along Florida's Atlantic and Gulf coasts, occupying dunes of the ancient Pamlico and Silver Bluff coastlines. Scrub habitats are rare on the Gulf Coast, occurring in disjunct meager parcels from the area of Cedar Key, Levy County, south to Marco Island, Collier County (formerly). Scrub occurs along Florida's Atlantic Coast in a similarly fragmented pattern from St. Johns County south to northern Broward County. No sizable tracts of scrub remain in Broward County, however. In December 1995 Palm Beach County purchased the 212-acre Yamato Scrub site in Boca Raton, which now constitutes the southernmost tract of Florida scrub. Coastal scrub hosts a fairly large number of listed species, though less than inland scrub. Locations supporting peninsular coastal scrub include Cedar Keys Scrub State Preserve, Rookery Bay National Estuarine Research Reserve, Savannas State Reserve, Jonathan Dickinson State Park, Hobe Sound National Wildlife Refuge, and Merritt Island National Wildlife Refuge.

Panhandle Coastal Scrub

The panhandle coastal scrubs are limited in distribution to Gulf coastal areas and barrier islands from the area of Gulf State Park in Baldwin County, Alabama, east to eastern Franklin County of Florida's Panhandle. Locations where panhandle coastal scrub is protected include St. George Island and St. Joseph Peninsula state parks, Henderson Beach and St. Andrew's state recreation areas; St. Vincent National Wildlife Refuge; and Apalachicola National Estuarine Research Reserve.

State and Federally Listed or Endemic Animal Species of Florida Scrub Ecosystems

S, State

F, Federal

E, Endangered

T, Threatened

SSC, Species of Special Concern, a state classification

SMC, Species of Management Concern, a federal classification

CAND, Candidate, a federal classification

INLAND, Inland peninsular scrub

PENINSULAR, Peninsular coastal scrub

PANHANDLE, Panhandle coastal scrub

BIRDS

Florida scrub-jay (*Aphelocoma coerulescens*), S & F-T; INLAND, PENINSULAR (endemic)

Southeastern American kestrel (*Falco sparverius paulus*), S-T, F-SMC; INLAND, PENINSULAR, PANHANDLE

Loggerhead shrike (*Lanius ludovicianus*), F-SMC; INLAND, PENINSULAR, PANHANDLE

MAMMALS

Florida mouse (*Podomys floridanus*), S-SSC, F-SMC; INLAND, PENINSULAR

Florida black bear (*Ursus americanus floridanus*), S-T, F-SMC; INLAND, PENINSULAR, PANHANDLE

Southeastern beach mouse (*Peromyscus polionotus niveiventris*), S & F-T; PENINSULAR

REPTILES AND AMPHIBIANS

Gopher tortoise (*Gopherus polyphemus*), S-SSC, F-SMC; INLAND, PENINSULAR, PANHANDLE

Sand skink (*Neoseps reynoldsi*), S & F-T; INLAND (endemic)

Bluetail mole skink (*Eumeces egregius lividus*), S & F-T; INLAND (endemic)

Florida scrub lizard (*Sceloporus woodi*), F-SMC; INLAND, PENINSULAR (endemic)

Island glass lizard (*Ophisaurus compressus*), F-SMC; INLAND, PENINSULAR, PANHANDLE

Short-tailed snake (*Stilosoma extenuatum*),

S-T, F-SMC; INLAND, PENINSULAR
Eastern indigo snake (*Drymarchon corais
couperi*), S & F-T; INLAND, PENINSULAR,
PANHANDLE
Florida pine snake (*Pituophis melanoleucus
mugitus*), S-SSC, F-SMC; INLAND,
PENINSULAR, PANHANDLE
Southern hog-nosed snake (*Heterodon
simus*), F-SMC; INLAND, PENINSULAR,
PANHANDLE
Dusky gopher frog (*Rana capito sevosa*),
S-SSC, F-CAND; PANHANDLE.
Florida gopher frog (*Rana c. aesopus*),
S-SSC, F-SMC; INLAND, PENINSULAR,
PANHANDLE

ARACHNIDS

Lake Placid funnel wolf spider (*Sosippus
placidus*), F-SMC; INLAND (endemic)
Red widow spider (*Latrodectus bishopi*),
not listed; INLAND (habitat endemic)

INSECTS

Archbold anomala scarab beetle (*Anomala
eximia*), F-SMC; INLAND (endemic)
Aphodius tortoise commensal scarab beetle
(*Aphodius troglodytes*), F-SMC; INLAND
Copris tortoise commensial scarab beetle
(*Copris gopheri*), F-SMC; INLAND
Scrub Island burrowing scarab beetle
(*Mycotrupes pedester*), F-SMC;
PENINSULAR (endemic)
Tortoise commensal scarab beetle
(*Onthophagus polyphemus*), F-SMC;
INLAND
Scrub palmetto flower scarab beetle
(*Trigonopelastes floridana*), F-SMC;
most common in scrubby flatwoods
Frost's spring serican scarab beetle (*Serica
frosti*), F-SMC; INLAND (endemic)
Florida asaphomyian tabanid fly
(*Asaphomyia floridensis*), F-SMC;
INLAND (endemic)

Elizoria june beetle (*Phyllophaga elizoria*),
not listed; INLAND, PENINSULAR (endemic)
Florida scrub millipede (*Floridobolus pen-
neri*), not listed; INLAND only (endemic)
East coast scrub grasshopper (*Melanoplus
indicifer*), not listed; PENINSULAR Atlantic
coast only (endemic)
Ocala claw-cercus grasshopper (*Melanoplus
sp.*), not listed; INLAND only (endemic)
Trail Ridge scrub grasshopper (*Melanoplus
sp.*), not listed; INLAND only (endemic)
Broad cercus scrub grasshopper (*Melanoplus
forcipatus*), not listed; INLAND only
(endemic)
Highlands tiger beetle (*Cicindela highlandensis*), F-SMC; INLAND only (endemic)

HIGH PINE COMMUNITIES

Some authorities separate the high pine
communities into two habitats, sandhill
and clayhill, because of different soil
characteristics. Most, however, group
sandhill with clayhill because of their
many similarities. Both habitat types
occur on hilly terrain and possess deep,
well-drained sandy soils that are relatively sterile. Clayhill sands contain various
amounts of Miocene clays that retain
some moisture and allow plants typically
associated with lower, more mesic habitats to flourish. By comparison, the yellowish or white sandhill soils are generally more xeric and porous. Sandhill and
clayhill are both fire climax communities requiring frequent ground fires (every
2–5 years for sandhill and 3–5 years for
clayhill) to facilitate pine and wiregrass
reproduction and inhibit hardwood
encroachment.

Sandhill is more widespread in Florida
than clayhill, occuring throughout much
of central and northern Florida (as far

Southern ridge, sandhill community, Archbold Biological Station, Highlands County, with active burrow of gopher tortoise, a keystone species.

*Gopher tortoise (*Gopherus polyphemus*), a keystone species within sandhill habitats, where its burrows provide refuge to more than 350 animal species.*
ARCHBOLD BIOLOGICAL STATION, HIGHLANDS COUNTY.

south as Martin, Highlands, and Lee counties) and the Panhandle. Clayhills are primarily restricted to inland portions of the Panhandle and Big Bend region barely extending into northwestern peninsular Florida. In the Panhandle and Big Bend regions, sandhill generally occurs south of clayhill communities; however, fingers of sandhill do reach northward to the Alabama line in several areas. Where sandhill and clayhill merge, differentiating the two is difficult.

Historically, the vegetative makeup of many high pine communities consisted of longleaf pine (*Pinus palustris*) and

wiregrass (*Aristida stricta*) associations. Along the southern Lake Wales Ridge where a sandhill subtype known as Southern Ridge sandhill occurs, South Florida slash pine (*Pinus elliottii* var. *densa*) replaces longleaf pine as the dominant conifer. Nearly all of Florida's virgin longleaf pine forests were logged by the end of the Great Depression. Forestry practices also eradicated wiregrass from many sites. Only a few isolated tracts of Florida's old-growth longleaf pine forest remain today (fewer than 3,000 acres), and wiregrass is not known to reoccupy sites naturally once it has been eliminated.

Foresters typically replaced logged longleaf pine with slash pine (*Pinus elliottii*), sand pine, or loblolly pine (*P. taeda*), altering the biodiversity of those areas. Shortleaf pine (*Pinus echinata*) replaced longleaf pine in many clayhill communities.

High pine communities are maintained by frequent, low-intensity fires, as opposed to scrub, which requires infrequent, high-intensity fires. Longleaf pine is Florida's most fire-adapted pine species, remaining in a grass stage for several years. This relatively slow-growing and long-lived (up to 500 years) pine also provides a denser, more rot-resistant and valuable timber than other Florida pines. Because its growth is much slower than other pines, the longleaf pine was usually replaced with other species.

Several species of deciduous oaks are commonly associated with high pine communities. Turkey oak (*Quercus laevis*) is the most characteristic oak of sandhill communities; longleaf pine and turkey oak associations are among the most prevalent sandhill subtypes. Oaks become the dominant species in sandhill communities now devoid of pines because of timbering or fire suppression. Other sandhill oak species include sand post oak (*Quercus margaretta*) and bluejack oak (*Q. incana*). Oaks associated with clayhill communities include running oak (*Quercus pumila*), southern red oak (*Q. falcata*), blackjack oak (*Q. marilandica*), bluejack oak, and post oak (*Q. stellata*). Plant species commonly occurring in both high pine communities include persimmon (*Diospyros virginiana*), bracken fern (*Pteridium aquilinum*), winged sumac (*Rhus copallina*), goat's rue (*Tephrosia virginiana*), golden aster (*Chrysopsis* spp.), partridge pea (*Cassia fasciculata*), and Indian grass (*Sorghastrum* spp.). Plants restricted to or occurring more frequently in sandhill communities include gopher apple (*Licania michauxii*) and sparkleberry (*Vaccinium arboreum*). Plants restricted to or occurring more frequently in clayhill communities include mockernut hickory (*Carya tomentosa*), black cherry (*Prunus serotina*), black gum (*Nyssa sylvatica* var. *biflora*), and sweet gum (*Liquidambar styraciflua*).

Wiregrass is the most important groundcover species. It provides a dense groundcover, which in itself retards succession by hardwoods and provides fuel for the periodic fires needed to maintain these habitats. Other groundcover species occurring in one or both high pine communities include piney woods dropseed (*Sporobolus junceus*), goldenrod (*Solidago* spp.), hair grass (*Muhlenbergia capillaris*), and low-bush blueberry (*Vaccinium myrsinites*). Various herbaceous species may occur, including blazing star (*Liatris pauciflora*), splitbeard bluestem (*Andropogon ternarius*), green eyes (*Berlandiera subacaulis*), and dog tongue (*Eriogonum tomentosum*). Several listed plants occur in high pine communities, including clasping warea (*Warea amplexifolia*), Panhandle golden aster (*Pityopsis flexuosa*), and sandhill pigeon-wing (*Clitoria fragrans*).

High pine communities are among Florida's most important ecosystems in terms of biodiversity. A plenitude of animals inhabit sandhill and clayhill ecosystems. Of all the high pine denizens, the gopher tortoise is arguably the most important keystone animal species and generally the species that first comes to mind when sandhills are mentioned. A species of special concern in Florida, gopher tortoises are threatened or endangered in other southeastern states within its range. Gopher tortoises excavate burrows as long as 40 feet and about 10 feet deep that are an extremely important component of high pine ecosystems. More than 350 animal species are known to use gopher tortoise burrows as shelter from adverse weather conditions and as refuge from predators and fire. Several arthropod species are actually tortoise burrow endemics, which are directly dependent on tortoise burrows for survival. Included in this group are gopher tortoise robber flies (*Machimus polyphemus*), which may never leave the burrow. Other animals (some of which are listed) closely associated with tortoise burrows include tortoise burrow anthomyiid flies (*Eutrichota gopheri*), tortoise burrow dance flies (*Drapetis* sp.), gopher tortoise hister beetles (*Chelyoxenus xerobatis*), two tortoise commensal noctuid moths (*Idia gopheri* and *Schinia rufipinna*), tortoise commensal scarab beetles (*Onthophagus polyphemus*), copris tortoise commensal scarab beetles (*Copris gopheri*), gopher tortoise aphodius beetles (*Aphodius troglodytes*), and dusky and Florida gopher frogs. Other species that regularly use gopher tortoise burrows include eastern indigo snakes, Florida mice, burrowing owls (*Speotyto cunicularia*), eastern diamondback rattlesnakes (*Crotalus adamanteus*), rabbits, skunks, opossums, lizards, and toads. Gopher tortoise populations have decreased significantly rangewide mainly because of habitat loss, harvesting for food (now illegal), gassing of burrows by rattlesnake collectors (now illegal), road mortality, illegal collection, and recent increases in upper respiratory tract disease, or URTD. URTD is a chronic bacterial infection that causes a slow,

agonizing death for tortoises. The spread of this contagious disease by infected tortoises released into wild populations represents a continuing threat. Declines of tortoise populations would certainly result in declines of the obligate commensals and other associated species.

High pine communities support a number of other listed species, including red-cockaded woodpeckers (*Picoides borealis*), southeastern American kestrels, short-tailed snakes, Sherman's fox squirrels (*Sciurus niger shermani*), and Florida pine snakes. High pine birdlife includes brown-headed nuthatches (*Sitta pusilla*), red-headed woodpeckers (*Melanerpes erythrocephalus*), hairy woodpeckers (*Picoides villosus*), eastern bluebirds (*Sialia sialis*), and pine warblers (*Dendroica pinus*). The southeastern pocket gopher is a characteristic high pine mammal, which like the gopher tortoise excavates burrows that harbor endemic invertebrates. The herpetofauna also includes six-lined racerunners (*Cnemidophorus sexlineatus*), southeastern five-lined skinks (*Eumeces inexpectatus*), southern fence lizards (*Sceloporus undulatus*), scarlet snakes (*Cemophora coccinea*), hog-nosed snakes (*Heterodon* spp.), coachwhip snakes, crowned snakes (*Tantilla relicta*), and southern toads (*Bufo terrestris*).

In the years to come, mature longleaf pine forests may not occur outside protected public lands. Centuries of fire suppression, coupled with widespread clear-cutting, commercial and recreational development, and current forestry practices of harvesting young trees (red-cockaded woodpeckers require pines 60 to 90 years old), may prohibit future generations from experiencing the grandeur of old-growth longleaf ecosystems. Until recently, the failure to propagate wiregrass has hindered efforts to restore natural longleaf and wiregrass communities. The Apalachicola Bluffs and Ravines Preserve, a 6,300-acre Nature Conservancy site acquired in 1985, accommodated an extensive longleaf pine–wiregrass ecosystem until the 1950s. At this site Nature Conservancy biologists learned techniques to regenerate wiregrass and longleaf pine, offering a new ray of hope.

Examples of high pine communities can be found at Ocala National Forest's Riverside Island (nearly chaste sandhill), Blackwater River State Forest (clayhill), The Nature Conservancy's Ordway Preserve in Putnam County and Janet Butterfield Brooks Preserve in Hernando County, Archbold Biological Station in Highlands County (Southern Ridge sandhill), and the following Florida state park and preserve lands: Gold Head Branch, Wekiwa Springs, Ichetucknee Springs, Manatee Springs, San Felasco Hammock, O'Leno, Suwannee River, and Torreya.

State and Federally Listed Animal Species of High Pine Ecosystems

S, State
F, Federal
E, Endangered
T, Threatened
SSC, Species of Special Concern, a state classification
SMC, Species of Management Concern, a federal classification
CAND, Candidate, a federal classification

*Gregory Seaman of The Nature Conservancy's Apalachicola Bluffs and Ravines Preserve holding wiregrass (*Aristida stricta*) seedling.*

BIRDS

Bachman's sparrow (*Aimophila aestivalis*), F-SMC

Henslow's sparrow (*Ammodramus henslowii*), F-SMC (wintering species)

Stoddard's yellow-throated warbler (*Dendroica dominica stoddardi*), F-SMC

Kirtland's warbler (*Dendroica kirtlandii*), S & F-E (possibly in migration)

Southeastern American kestrel (*Falco sparverius paulus*), S-T, F-SMC

Red-cockaded woodpecker (*Picoides borealis*), S-T, F-E

Burrowing owl (*Speotyto cunicularia*), S-SSC (ecotones)

MAMMALS

Florida panther (*Puma concolor coryi*), S & F-E (historically)

Florida mouse (*Podomys floridanus*), S-SSC, F-SMC

Eastern chipmunk (*Tamias striatus*), S-SSC (clayhill)

Florida black bear (*Ursus americanus floridanus*), S-T, F-SMC; usually transient in high pine habitats, prefers flatwoods

Sherman's fox squirrel (*Sciurus niger shermani*), S-SSC, F-SMC

REPTILES AND AMPHIBIANS

Gopher tortoise (*Gopherus polyphemus*), S-SSC, F-SMC

Eastern indigo snake (*Drymarchon corais couperi*), S & F-T

Sand skink (*Neoseps reynoldsi*), S & F-T (turkey oak barrens)

Short-tailed snake (*Stilosoma extenuatum*), S-T, F-SMC

Florida pine snake (*Pituophis melanoleucus mugitus*), S-SSC, F-SMC

Southern hog-nosed snake (*Heterodon simus*), F-SMC

Dusky gopher frog (*Rana capito sevosa*), S-SSC, F-CAND

Florida gopher frog (*Rana c. aesopus*), S-SSC, F-SMC

Florida bog frog (*Rana okaloosae*), S-SSC, F-SMC (ecotones)

INSECTS

Aphodius tortoise commensal scarab beetle (*Aphodius troglodytes*), F-SMC

Eastern beard grass skipper (*Atrytone arogos*), F-SMC

Copris tortoise commensal scarab beetle (*Copris gopheri*), F-SMC

Spiny Florida sandhill scarab beetle (*Gronocarus multispinosus*), F-SMC (endemic)

Tortoise commensal scarab beetle (*Onthophagus polyphemus*), F-SMC

Ocala burrowing scarab beetle (*Peltotrupes youngi*), F-SMC

Tortoise commensal noctuid moth (*Idia gopheri*), F-SMC

Tortoise commensal noctuid moth (*Schinia rufipinna*), F-SMC

PINE FLATWOODS AND DRY PRAIRIE HABITATS

Pine flatwoods and dry prairies are quite flat. They occur at lower elevations and are moister than sandhill and Florida scrub communities. The acidic, fine, sandy soils of these habitats are poorly drained and therefore commonly remain wet during the rainy months. As with other upland ecosystems in Florida, fire is essential in the maintenance of these habitats; it reduces competition from or succession to hardwood habitats.

Four species of pines represent the keystone tree species of these ecosystems:

Pine flatwoods, Avon Park Bombing Range, Polk County.

the longleaf pine, most common on higher sites in the Panhandle and northern and central peninsular Florida; slash pine, which has much the same range in Florida and often occurs together with longleaf pine; the south Florida slash pine, which occurs in central and southern Florida; and the pond pine (*Pinus serotina*), which is most common in the lowest, wettest flatwoods of the Panhandle and northern Florida but occurs as far south as Wekiwa Springs State Park in Orange County. Mature pine flatwoods are often quite open but can be fairly dense in some areas. The interior of flatwoods is usually well lit and has an understory of various plants that can vary with geographical location and type of dominant pine species. Longleaf pine flatwoods often have an abundance of wiregrass, but saw palmetto (*Serenoa repens*) and gallberry (*Ilex glabra*) are

usually dominant in slash pine flatwoods. Florida's pine flatwood communities contain many endemic and listed plants, including cutthroat grass (*Panicum abscissum*), big yellow milkwort (*Polygala rugelii*), coastal plain wild indigo (*Baptisia simplicifolia*), Florida beargrass (*Nolina atopocarpa*), mock pennyroyal (*Hedeoma graveolens*), yellow squirrel-banana (*Deeringothamnus rugelii*), Edison's St. John's-wort (*Hypericum edisonianum*), and wiregrass gentian (*Gentiana pennelliana*).

Pine flatwoods and dry prairies may border titi swamps, cypress domes, freshwater or salt marshes, or high pine and scrub communities. Ecotonal areas often contain elements of both abutting communities.

Pine flatwoods are found throughout the southeastern coastal plain, and in Florida they occur commonly as far

Dry prairie habitat, Highlands County.

south as Palm Beach and parts of Collier County. Dry prairies occur as far north as Wakulla County but are most concentrated to the north and west of Lake Okeechobee in Okeechobee, Highlands, Polk, De Soto, and Glades counties. Data obtained from a landsat satellite show that dry prairie currently covers approximately 2,000 square miles (about 4 percent) of Florida. Unfortunately, less than 17 percent of Florida's dry prairie occurs on protected lands.

Dry prairies are generally treeless, and dominant plant species include grasses such as wiregrass, broomsedge (*Andropogon virginicus*), arrowfeather (*Aristida purpurascens*), bottlebrush three-awn (*Aristida spiciformis*), and saw palmetto. Cabbage palms (*Sabal palmetto*) do occur, sometimes in dense stands, in some dry prairies. (Refer to the section on temperate hardwood communities

for additional information on prairie hammocks.) Florida's dry prairies resemble the grasslands of western North America; however, dry prairies in Florida receive nearly twice the rainfall of their western counterparts. Without Florida's recurrent lightning fires and the current use of prescribed burning, dry prairies would quickly be succeeded by trees. Central Florida's prairie ecosystems harbor disjunct relict populations of several western grassland species far from their principal, contiguous range.

The most significant difference between pine flatwoods and dry prairies is the latter's lack of trees. This distinction allows dry prairies to support listed wildlife such as Florida sandhill cranes (*Grus canadensis pratensis*), Audubon's crested caracaras (*Caracara cheriway audubonii*), burrowing owls, and endangered Florida grasshopper sparrows

(*Ammodramus savannarum floridanus*), which do not typically inhabit pine flatwoods. Other dry prairie species rarely encountered in flatwoods include eastern meadowlarks (*Sturnella magna*) and field sparrows (*Spizella pusilla*). Critically endangered whooping cranes, another prairie-land species, have recently been reintroduced into Osceola County's Kissimmee Prairie region by the USF&WS, with hopes that a stable, nonmigratory population can be established. This phase of the Whooping Crane Recovery Plan began in 1992 with a long-term goal of producing 25 breeding pairs in the Sunshine State. The caracara trox (*Trox howelli*), a unique beetle species, is known from only two specimens, one from Florida's dry prairie region (found in a caracara's nest) and one from Texas.

Species likely to be found in pine flatwoods but not dry prairies include red-cockaded woodpeckers, Bachman's sparrow, brown-headed nuthatches, fox squirrels (*Sciurus niger*), pine woods treefrogs, flatwoods salamanders (*Ambystoma cingulatum*), southern fence lizards, and pine woods snakes (*Rhadinaea flavilata*). Insect species largely or wholly restricted to pine flatwood communities include yellow-banded typocerus (*Typocerus flavocinctus*), least Florida skippers (*Amblyscirtes alternata*), and southern dusted skippers (*Atrytonopsis hianna loammi*). The Panama City crayfish (*Procambarus econfinae*), a state-listed crustacean, is known only from a wet flatwoods area near Panama City, where human encroachment now threatens its existence.

Mammals that may occur in both habitats include white-tailed deer (*Odocoileus virginianus*), black bears, Florida panthers, bobcats, gray fox (*Urocyon cinereoargenteus*), least shrews (*Cryptotis parva*), cotton rats (*Sigmodon hispidus*), and cotton mice (*Peromyscus gossypinus*). The herpetofauna often includes box turtles (*Terrapene carolina* ssp.), eastern diamondback rattlesnakes, racers, eastern coachwhip snakes, southern ring-necked snakes (*Diadophis punctatus punctatus*), eastern tiger salamanders (*Ambystoma tigrinum tigrinum*), and oak toads (*Bufo quercicus*). Birds utilizing both communities include great horned owls (*Bubo virginianus*), southeastern American kestrels, and both turkey and black vultures. Insects include cabbage palm longhorn beetles (*Osmopleura chamaeropis*).

In the recent past, pine flatwoods covered much of Florida's low-lying, level terrain. Dry prairies, on the other hand, have been restricted to portions of the peninsula for some time. It is estimated that pine flatwoods still cover nearly 50 percent of Florida's land area; however, many experts believe—now that most of the favored well-drained upland sites (high pine and scrub) have been lost to development—flatwood and dry prairie habitats will soon be heavily exploited. Although development has only recently become a significant threat to Florida's flatwood and dry prairie ecosystems, humans have exploited them in other ways for some time.

Forestry practices, including lumbering, pulpwood extraction, naval stores industries, and range practices including cattle ranching have had detrimental effects. The practice of harvesting mature, old-growth pine forests has dramatically reduced or extirpated populations of red-cockaded woodpeckers, which require sizable tracts of large, mature trees. Additionally, clear-cutting flatwoods adversely affects Florida's 25 cavity-nesting bird species. The U.S. Forest Service has now begun to leave several large snags (some containing cavities) when logging tracts of forest. This practice benefits cavity-nesting species and such perch-hunting species as southeastern American kestrels and loggerhead shrikes. Humans have been extracting gum for the production of rosins and turpentine from Florida's longleaf and slash pines for several centuries. These practices and the equipment, herbicides, and insecticides used can be harmful to ecosystems. Humans have also altered pine flatwoods and dry prairie habitats, both of which are pyrogenic communities, by suppressing fires. Cattle overgrazing has deleteriously affected flatwoods and dry prairie habitats by depleting natural vegetation and cover used by wildlife. Invasive exotic vegetation, particularly melaleuca and Brazilian pepper, have been troublesome to South Florida's slash pine flatwoods. The rooting propensities of two abundant exotic animals, feral hogs and nine-banded armadillos, have extensively damaged many flatwood and prairie communities. Other threats include severe weather events. The direct strike of a hurricane can be very damaging to flatwoods. Hurricane Opal, a category 3 storm that struck Florida's Panhandle in October 1995, downed tens of thousands of longleaf and slash pine trees, including trees utilized by endangered red-cockaded woodpecker colonies.

Healthy examples of pine flatwoods can be found at Florida's three national forests (Apalachicola, Osceola, and Ocala); state forests (Blackwater River and Withlacoochee); many state park units, including Payne's Prairie, Ochlockonee River, Myakka River, Honeymoon Island, Rock Springs, Tosohatchee, Blackwater River, Faver-Dykes, and Jonathan Dickinson; and Eglin Air Force Base and the Avon Park Air Force Bombing Range. Dry prairie habitats can be seen along Route 721 in and near the Brighton Seminole Indian Reservation, at the Avon Park Bombing Range, Prairie Lakes State Preserve, Three Lakes Wildlife Management Area, Myakka River State Park, and the Audubon Society's Kissimmee Prairie Preserve.

State and Federally Listed Animal Species of Pine Flatwoods and Dry Prairie Ecosystems

S, State
F, Federal
E, Endangered
T, Threatened
SSC, Species of Special Concern, a state classification
SMC, Species of Management Concern, a federal classification
CAND, Candidate, a federal classification
PINE, Pine flatwoods
DRY, Dry prairie

BIRDS
Bachman's sparrow (*Aimophila aestivalis*), F-SMC; PINE, DRY, particularly ecotones
Henslow's sparrow (*Ammodramus henslowii*), F-SMC; DRY, PINE
Florida grasshopper sparrow (*Ammodramus savannarum floridanus*), S & F-E; DRY

Stoddard's yellow-throated warbler
(*Dendroica dominica stoddardi*),
F-SMC; PINE
Kirtland's warbler (*Dendroica kirtlandii*),
S & F-E, PINE (migratory transient)
Southeastern American kestrel (*Falco spar-
verius paulus*), S-T, F-SMC; DRY, PINE
Whooping crane (*Grus americana*), S-SSC,
F-T (experimental population); DRY
Florida sandhill crane (*Grus canadensis
pratensis*), S-T; DRY
Loggerhead shrike (*Lanius ludovicianus*),
F-SMC; DRY
Red-cockaded woodpecker (*Picoides
borealis*), S-T, F-E; PINE
Audubon's crested caracara (*Caracara
cheriway audubonii*), S & F-T, DRY
Burrowing owl (*Speotyto cunicularia*), S-SSC,
DRY

MAMMALS
Florida panther (*Puma concolor coryi*), S &
F-E; PINE, DRY
Florida black bear (*Ursus americanus
floridanus*), S-T, F-SMC; PINE, DRY
Insular hispid cotton rat (*Sigmodon
hispidus insulicola*), F-SMC, PINE
Florida mastiff bat (*Eumops glaucinus
floridanus*), S-E, F-CAND; PINE
Big Cypress fox squirrel (*Sciurus niger
avicennia*), S-T, F-SMC; PINE
Sherman's short-tailed shrew (*Blarina caro-
linensis shermani*), S-SSC, F-SMC; PINE

REPTILES AND AMPHIBIANS
Eastern indigo snake (*Drymarchon corais
couperi*), S & F-T; DRY, PINE
Southern hog-nosed snake (*Heterodon
simus*), F-SMC; DRY, PINE
Florida pine snake (*Pituophis melanoleucus
mugitus*), S-SSC, F-SMC; PINE, DRY
Island glass lizard (*Ophisaurus compressus*),
F-SMC; PINE

Flatwoods salamander (*Ambystoma cingu-
latum*), F-SMC; PINE
Florida gopher frog (*Rana capito aesopus*),
S-SSC, F-SMC; PINE (occasional)
Dusky gopher frog (*Rana c. sevosa*), S-SSC,
F-CAND; PINE (occasional)

CRUSTACEANS
Panama City crayfish (*Procambarus
econfinae*), S-SSC; PINE

INSECTS
Caracara trox (*Trox howelli*), F-SMC; DRY
Eastern beard grass skipper (*Atrytone
arogos*), F-SMC; PINE

TEMPERATE HARDWOOD COMMUNITIES

Hardwood forests, of which there are
several distinct types, occupy more
acreage in northern Florida, particularly
in the Panhandle, but extend southward
in the peninsula through portions of central and southern Florida. These natural
communities, unlike high pine communities, are generally nonpyrogenic. The
term "hardwood" itself, like "evergreen,"
is somewhat ambiguous. "Hardwood" is
most often used to describe broad-leaved
trees, and "softwood" is used when describing conifers. In some cases, however,
those terms are not descriptive; some
conifers, such as slash pine, have very
hard wood, and the wood of some broad-
leaved trees, such as willows (*Salix*), is
quite soft. The diversity of flora and fauna
occurring in these ecosystems varies
considerably from north to south (and
with elevation and topographic relief),
reaching the greatest variance along the
Panhandle's Apalachicola River corridor,
which includes bottomland forest, floodplain forest, bluffs, slope forest, upland

hardwood forest, and upland mixed hardwood forest. There are more species of trees and shrubs occurring in this region than in any other region in the continental United States or Canada. These mixed mesophytic forests contain numerous trees and other plant species that occur in the Appalachians and reach their southernmost distributional limit here.

Slope Forest

Slope forest, also known as ravine forest, is unique to Florida and, biologically, one of the richest habitats in the state. The exceptional number of plant and animal species results from a distributional crossroads of subtropical and temperate biotas. Several plant species (e.g., maidenhair fern, *Adiantum* sp.) and animal species (e.g., Little Mountain jumping spider, *Habrocestum parvulum*) inhabiting slope forest are more typical of piedmont forests or even southern Appalachian forests. Though these forests are floristically related to the Appalachian forests, they are ecologically quite akin to the temperate cloud forests of Mexico, which occur at approximately 6,000 feet elevation. The ravines caused by seeping steepheads, a geomorphic feature, are unique to this area of northern Florida and a tiny portion of adjacent southwestern Georgia. Slope forests occurring in Florida are mesic, climax communities, with closed canopies and generally cooler microclimates than high pine communities, which they often merge with above the slopes. Forests at the base of slopes often merge with moister bottomland forest. Seepage streams often occur in ravine forests, producing hydric conditions locally.

Several endangered endemic trees inhabit slope forest, including Florida

Floodplain hardwood forest, Florida Caverns State Park, Jackson County.

torreya (*Torreya taxifolia*) and Florida yew (*Taxus floridana*). These species as well as the oakleaf hydrangea (*Hydrangea quercifolia*) are adapted to growing on steep slopes. The critically imperiled torreya is now vulnerable to extinction. This conifer was heavily logged during the mid-1800s. After clear-cutting the forests, foresters often replaced original tree species with slash pines. Then, in the 1950s, a series of mysterious fungal attacks, possibly spurred by environmental changes, decimated remaining torreya populations at a rate of 10 percent every four years. Other trees associated with slope forests include mockernut hickory, black walnut (*Juglans nigra*), southern magnolia (*Magnolia grandiflora*), American holly (*Ilex opaca*), mountain laurel

(*Kalmia latifolia*), white oak (*Quercus alba*), and American beech (*Fagus grandifolia*). Other plants include strawberry bush (*Euonymus americanus*), rattlesnake plantain (*Goodyera pubescens*), Sebastianbush (*Sebastiania fruticosa*), and sarsaparilla vine (*Smilax pumila*). There are often considerable differences in the flora occurring at the cooler, moister, lower elevations of slope forests and that at the more xeric, higher elevations. More temperate species tend to colonize north-facing slopes, which receive less winter sunlight than south-facing slopes.

Many slope forest animals and plants also inhabit upland hardwood and mixed hardwood forests. Among the more unusual animals inhabiting slope forest are Torreya trap-door spiders (*Cyclocosmia torreya*) and southern copperheads (*Agkistrodon contortrix contortrix*); the snake's occurrence represents a southern extension of its range. This area of Florida harbors the third highest concentration of reptile and amphibian species in the United States.

Of Florida's several varieties of temperate, predominantly hardwood communities, slope forests are the most vulnerable to human disturbance. Activities such as timbering often open the forest canopy, thus upsetting the delicate, shaded microclimate of the forest. Uncontrolled collecting of rare plant and animal species and illegal dumping within slope forest ravines also rank among the more serious threats.

Upland Hardwood Forest and Mixed Hardwood Forest

Although the hardwood forests of northern Florida, particularly the Panhandle, often contain many of the plant species found in slope forests, the mixed hardwood forests of central and southern Florida are quite different. Both upland and mixed forest types are generally mesic, closed canopy, climax communities. Unlike hardwood forests in the Appalachians, the canopy of Florida's hardwood forests frequently contains broadleaf evergreens. Climate, more than any other factor, is responsible for the slight differences that distinguish upland hardwood forest from mixed hardwood forest. Mixed hardwood forests commonly occur in most of peninsular Florida (especially central and southern portions); the northern Panhandle's closest counterpart is called upland hardwood forest. The warmer, subtropical climate of most of peninsular Florida does not support some of the more northern tree species common in Panhandle forests. These include American beech, white oak, and shortleaf pine. Tree diversity decreases as one travels south through Florida's peninsula and increases again in extreme southern Florida and the Keys, where tropical hardwood hammocks occur.

Typical mammals of Florida's various hardwood communities include white-tailed deer, skunks, raccoons, opossum, golden mice (*Ochrotomys nuttalli*), eastern wood rats (*Neotoma floridana*), gray squirrels (*Sciurus carolinensis*), eastern chipmunks, and Florida black bears. Habitat-destructive introduced feral hogs are quite common in many areas.

Birdlife includes such species as red-eyed vireos (*Vireo olivaceus*), Acadian flycatchers (*Empidonax virescens*), wood thrush (*Hylocichla mustelina*), hooded warbler (*Wilsonia citrina*), pileated woodpeckers (*Dryocopus pileatus*), red-shouldered and broad-winged hawks

(*Buteo* spp.), and Cooper's hawks *Accipiter cooperii*). Many species of birds utilize hardwood forests during migration.

Characteristic reptiles include gray, yellow, red, and Gulf hammock rat snakes (*Elaphe* spp.); southern ring-necked snakes; five-lined, broadhead, and southern coal skinks (*Eumeces* spp.); and green anoles. Typical amphibians occurring in Florida's hardwood communities include southeastern slimy salamanders (*Plethodon grobmani*); seal salamanders (*Desmognathus monticola*), which occur in associated riparian microhabitats in the extreme western Panhandle; Apalachicola dusky salamanders (*Desmognathus apalachicolae*); and gray, green, and squirrel treefrogs (*Hyla* spp.).

Listed insect species inhabiting Florida's hardwood and mixed hardwood habitats include sugarfoot moth flies (*Nemopalpus nearcticus*) and Say's spiketail dragonfly (*Cordulegaster sayi*). Other insects generally unique to hardwood habitats include Horn's, long, and profound june beetles (*Phyllophaga* spp.); coral hairstreaks (*Harkenclenus titus mopsus*); King's hairstreaks (*Satyrium kingi*); comma anglewings (*Polygonia comma*); and pitted myrmica ants (*Myrmica punctiventris*).

**Bottomland Hardwood Forest
and Floodplain Hardwood Forest**
The terms "bottomland hardwood forest" and "floodplain hardwood forest" are often used synonymously; there are, however, several distinctions between the two. Both bottomland forest and floodplain forest are fairly widespread in the coastal plain of the southeastern United States, but their geographical distribution within Florida is restricted. Bottomland forests

occur in portions of peninsular Florida as well as the Panhandle, and true floodplain forest is limited to the alluvial floodplains of several Panhandle rivers. Both types are mesic to hydric communities harboring many of the same dominant tree species, though bottomland forest, unlike floodplain forest, is inundated with water only irregularly. Bottomland forests generally become deluged with water after very heavy downpours or severe floods; floodplain forests have a regular hydroperiod and are regularly inundated during the rainy season. Except during the winter where deciduous trees dominate, the canopy is generally dense and closed in both habitats. Both forests are stable communities that often take a century or more to mature. Fires are rare in both forest types; their understories are variable, ranging from open to nearly impenetrable.

Both forest types consist of mixed mesophytic hardwoods, and they share many of the same species. Dominant trees occurring in bottomland forest include live oak (*Quercus virginiana*) and water oak (*Q. nigra*), white cedar (*Chamaecyparis thyoides*), loblolly pine and spruce pine (*Pinus glabra*), red maple (*Acer rubrum*), American hornbeam (*Carpinus caroliniana*), and sweet gum. Characteristic trees of floodplain forest include some of those same species in addition to diamondleaf oak, overcup oak, swamp chestnut oak, water hickory (*Carya aquatica*), and others. The plant life of floodplain forest is often richer because of alluvial deposits transported from the piedmont and mountainous regions of Georgia or Alabama. Though more hydric than bottomland forest, floodplain forest is not as hydric as true floodplain swamp, with which it often merges.

Bottomland and floodplain forests (particularly the latter) contain an assemblage of semiaquatic animals that rarely occur in other terrestrial hardwood communities. They include the American alligator, water snakes (*Nerodia*), swamp snakes (*Seminatrix*), mud snakes and rainbow snakes (*Farancia*), cottonmouths (*Agkistrodon*), amphiuma salamanders (*Amphiuma*), sirens (*Siren*), several frog species, beavers (*Castor canadensis*), Homosassa shrews (*Sorex longirostris eionis*), wood ducks (*Aix sponsa*), and several species of wading birds. The four-toed salamander (*Hemidactylium scutatum*) is restricted in distribution (within Florida) to several apparently isolated tracts of bottomland hardwood forest. These populations are separated by nearly 200 miles from their main population in the southern Appalachians.

Both of these forest types are threatened by certain human activities. Although the moist, often wet floors of these forests have saved them from most residential or commercial development, many have been heavily timbered in the past and the healing process is exceptionally slow. Both forest types, but particularly floodplain hardwood forests, like floodplain swamps, are vulnerable to changes in water quality and impoundments that alter a site's hydroperiod.

Xeric Hammock, Maritime Hammock, and Prairie Hammock

Xeric hammock is, as its title suggests, quite dry, considerably drier than slope, upland hardwood, and mixed hardwood forests and much drier than bottomland and floodplain forests. This natural community occurs in rather small, isolated parcels and is nowhere contiguous. Xeric hammock, also known as oak hammock, is an advanced successional tier of sandhill communities and, less frequently, scrub habitats and is considered to be the climax community of both habitats.

Plants occurring in xeric hammocks generally do not differ from the originating habitat. Xeric hammocks range from dual-leveled forests (canopy and forest) to multistoried, more mature forests. Oaks of several species usually dominate these hammock communities. The most common oaks include live oak, blackjack oak, sand live oak, and laurel oak. Other trees occupying xeric hammocks include pignut hickory (*Carya glabra*), southern magnolia, and red bay (*Persea borbonia*). Other characteristic plants include saw palmetto (the most common understory species), black cherry, and beautyberry (*Callicarpa americana*). Many of the animal species found in xeric hammocks occur in other hardwood habitats, and several species typically associated with sandhill or scrub habitats, such as Florida pine snakes, inhabit xeric hammocks.

Fires are among the two most ominous threats to xeric hammocks and are capable of causing consequential and permanent changes resulting in succession to other plant communities. Areas supporting this habitat have generally been free of fire for at least three decades. The other serious threat to hammocks is development, particularly residential. The high, dry land and picturesque large oaks of the hammocks unfortunately invite homesite development.

Maritime hammock, or coastal hammock, occurs or occurred in many of the state's coastal regions and for the purposes of this book is included in the coastal strand category, along with a variety of distinct coastal habitats. It too, as a rule, is drier than most of Florida's hardwood communities, though it is not necessarily a dry habitat. In fact, the interior of maritime hammock may be quite mesic, which helps to retard fire. Dominant trees include live oak, cabbage palm, and red bay. Maritime hammock ranks among the most threatened hardwood and mixed hardwood communities. Coastal development has taken a serious toll on Florida's maritime hammocks and eliminated them from many areas. They have also been invaded by exotic species, particularly plants. The listed Stoddard's yellow-throated warbler (*Dendroica dominica stoddardi*) is an inhabitant of Panhandle maritime hammocks.

Prairie hammocks are relatively small, rounded patches of live oaks and cabbage palms, occurring sporadically throughout portions of peninsular Florida. These two trees are so constant in these hammocks that they are often referred to as palm-oak hammocks. These hammocks generally occur on slightly elevated rises within wet prairie, dry prairie, mesic flatwoods, or marl prairie communities and are the terminal successional stage of those habitats. Prairie hammocks are often mesic, but lower sites may become inundated with water for several days. Fire is rare except on drier sites.

Sites where slope forest can be visited include Torreya State Park and The Nature Conservancy's Apalachicola Bluffs and Ravines Preserve, both in the eastern Panhandle. Other types of Florida's hardwood and mixed hardwood communities can be found in the following areas in Alachua County: San Felasco Hammock

State Preserve, Devil's Millhopper State Geological Site, Cross Creek hammock, Alachua sink, and Newman's sink. Clay County has the Goldhead branch hammock, Leon County has the Woodyard hammock, Highlands County has Highlands Hammock State Park, Wakulla County has Wakulla Springs State Park, and Jackson County has Three Rivers State Recreation Area and Florida Caverns State Park. Additional hardwood communities can be found in the floodplains of the Apalachicola, Ochlockonee, Suwannee, Yellow, Choctawhatchee, Escambia, and other large river corridors.

State and Federally Listed Animal Species of Florida's Temperate Hardwood Communities

S, State

F, Federal

E, Endangered

T, Threatened

SSC, Species of Special Concern, a state classification

SMC, Species of Management Concern, a federal classification

CAND, Candidate, a federal classification

BIRDS

Ivory-billed woodpecker (*Campephilus principalis*), S & F-E (now believed to be extinct)

Stoddard's yellow-throated warbler (*Dendroica dominica stoddardi*), F-SMC

Bachman's warbler (*Vermivora bachmanii*), S & F-E (formerly?)

Limpkin (*Aramus guarauna*), S-SSC (seasonal visitor, floodplain forest)

Little blue heron (*Egretta caerulea*), S-SSC (seasonal visitor, floodplain forest)

Snowy egret (*Egretta thula*), S-SSC (seasonal visitor, floodplain forest)

Tricolored heron (*Egretta tricolor*), S-SSC
(seasonal visitor, floodplain forest)
White ibis (*Eudocimus albus*), S-SSC
(seasonal visitor, floodplain forest)
Wood stork (*Mycteria americana*), S & F-E
(seasonal visitor, bottomland forest)

MAMMALS
Sherman's short-tailed shrew (*Blarina
carolinensis shermani*), S-SSC, F-SMC
Florida panther (*Puma concolor coryi*),
S & F-E
Big Cypress fox squirrel (*Sciurus niger avicen-
nia*), S-T, F-SMC (maritime hammock)
Homosassa shrew (*Sorex longirostris eionis*),
S-SSC (floodplain forest)
Eastern chipmunk (*Tamias striatus*), S-SSC
Florida black bear (*Ursus americanus
floridanus*), S-T, F-SMC

REPTILES AND AMPHIBIANS
Eastern indigo snake (*Drymarchon corais
couperi*), S & F-T (particularly ecotones)
Pine barrens treefrog (*Hyla andersoni*),
S-SSC (ecotones, Panhandle)
Florida pine snake (*Pituophis melanoleucus
mugitus*), S-SSC, F-SMC (xeric hammock)
Florida gopher frog (*Rana capito aesopus*),
S-SSC, F-SMC (xeric hammock only)
Florida bog frog (*Rana okaloosae*), S-SSC,
F-SMC (ecotones, Panhandle)
Short-tailed snake (*Stilosoma extenuatum*),
S-T, F-SMC (xeric hammocks only)

ARACHNIDS
Torreya trap-door spider (*Cyclocosmia
torreya*), F-SMC

INSECTS
Say's spiketail dragonfly (*Cordulegaster
sayi*), F-SMC (at spring seepages)
Sugarfoot moth fly (*Nemopalpus
nearcticus*), F-SMC

SOUTH FLORIDA ROCKLAND HABITATS

Tropical hammock and tropical pine-land are often described in separate sections, but both communities are geographically restricted to extreme southern Florida, where they occur on slightly elevated outcrops of exposed limestone containing tropical vegetation. The two communities often intergrade in locations where fire has been suppressed. Florida's rockland communities are among the most endangered habitats in North America. They harbor an astounding biodiversity, which includes many endemic and listed animals and plants.

Rockland habitats developed during the mid-Pleistocene and Miocene periods. They occur on three different geological formations: Key Largo limestone, Miami limestone, and Tamiami limestone. While exploring these habitats, particularly those occurring on Miami and Key Largo limestone, you will likely encounter exposed limestone protruding from the ground. Key Largo limestone occurs from Soldier Key south to northern and eastern portions of Big Pine Key. Miami limestone occupies the largest area, from southern Palm Beach County south and west to the Long Pine Key region of Everglades National Park on the mainland and also in the Lower Keys, including portions of Big Pine Key. Tamiami limestone, the oldest formation by far, occurs primarily in the Big Cypress Swamp region of southwest Florida. So little remains of undisturbed rockland ecosystems that they appear on a map of South Florida as tiny dots surrounded by urban encroachment.

Tropical Hammock

Soon after venturing into the dark, mysterious interior of a tropical hardwood hammock, you will be sure you are in a very special place, divergent from any other habitat in the contiguous United States. These junglelike stands of unusual, mostly tropical trees look like scattered islands on upland sites of the extreme southern Florida mainland and the Keys. Hammock soils, though generally fertile and organic, are often thinly distributed over the ubiquitous limestone substrate. Water-filled limestone depressions, combined with a layer of decaying leaves and organic material and the hammock's dense canopy, maintain a moist, shaded microclimate that protects these rock-rooted plant communities from fire. Tropical hammocks of the mainland and Lower Keys tend to be small, and those on Key Largo are larger and less fragmented. The largest hammock that occurred on the Miami limestone ridge, Brickell Hammock, occupied the area that is now downtown Miami. Tropical hammocks were heavily logged by early settlers for valuable timber, especially mahogany. The two greatest contemporary threats are habitat loss and invasive exotics. Florida Keys hammocks are in greater danger than mainland hammocks because many remaining Keys hammocks occur on private property and are not protected. Exotic animals and plants when introduced into South Florida ecosystems (lacking the natural controls present in their native range) are often more aggressive, larger, or more prolific than native species, often displacing natives as a result. The beautiful and formerly ubiquitous green anole is now seldom seen in many areas, having been displaced by larger, nonnative brown anoles. In several north Key Largo hammocks, introduced European black rats now outnumber the critically endangered Key Largo wood rats. Endangered tree snails are attacked by exotic fire ants as they descend to the ground to lay eggs. Invasive exotic organisms represent the greatest threat to Florida's protected lands such as parks and refuges and their native species.

Tropical hammocks represent the advanced successional stage of tropical pineland. Vegetation is composed predominantly of tropicopolitan, evergreen, broad-leaved trees and shrubs, common to the Greater Antilles or Bahamas. More than 200 species of Caribbean trees and shrubs have been found here, and many of them occur nowhere else in the United States. Characteristic trees include gumbo-limbo (*Bursera simaruba*), mahogany (*Swietenia mahogani*), strangler fig (*Ficus aurea*), wild tamarind (*Lysiloma latisiliqua*), pigeon plum (*Coccoloba diversifolia*), poisonwood (*Metopium toxiferum*), black ironwood (*Krugiodendron ferreum*), and soldierwood (*Colubrina elliptica*). Tree species endemic to Lower Keys hammocks include pisonia (*Pisonia rotundata*), cupania (*Cupania glabra*), yellowheart satinwood (*Zanthoxylum flavum*), and false boxwood (*Gyminda latifolia*). Florida's tropical hammocks are festooned with myriad tropical epiphytic bromeliads, ferns, and beautiful orchids, and they support a variety of vines, grasses, forbs, and herbs. Overcollection has caused serious declines in many species, especially orchids and bromeliads, and the apparent extinction of several species. Among the most pernicious exotic plants to invade Florida's hammocks are Brazilian pepper, sapodilla, bowstring hemp, latherleaf, and African ground orchids (*Oeceoclades maculata*).

Extracts from the beneficial, endangered lignum-vitae (*Guaiacum sanctum*, or the tree of life) have been used successfully to treat rheumatism and tuberculosis. Two critically endangered hammock cacti, Key tree cactus [*Pilosocereus* (synonym *Cereus*) *robinii* var. *deeringii*] and Big Pine tree cactus (*P. r.* var. *robinii*), were both overcollected for many years. The Key variety is now known from only five localities, the Big Pine from only two. South Florida's tropical hardwood hammocks are home to numerous other plant species listed as threatened or endangered.

Florida's tropical hardwood hammocks support a rich diversity of mammals, birds, herpetofauna, insects, and mollusks, with a high degree of endemism. These rare biotic communities are also inhabited by many listed species, some critically endangered. In recent years, Schaus' swallowtail butterflies (*Papilio aristodemus ponceanus*) and Stock Island tree snails (*Orthalicus reses reses*) teetered on the verge of extinction. Survival of Schaus' swallowtail depends largely on two plant species that occur only in tropical hammocks, torchwood (*Amyris elemifera*) and wild lime (*Zanthoxylum fagara*). Southern Florida's tropical hardwood hammocks harbor a number of insect species that occur nowhere else and also many tropical insect species at the northernmost periphery of their

Tree snails of South Florida's tropical hardwood hammocks have been overcollected for decades, so much so that a number of subspecies are now extinct in the wild. UNDISCLOSED LOCATION, MONROE COUNTY.

range. This category includes Miami blue butterflies (*Hemiargus thomasi bethune-bakeri*), dingy purplewing and Florida purplewing butterflies (*Eunica*), Bahama swallowtails (*Papilio andraemon bonhotei*), Florida whites (*Appias drusilla neumoegenii*), Bush and Jamaican sulfur butterflies (*Eurema*), Chevrolat's stenodontes beetles (*Stenodontes chevrolati*), Strohecker's eburias (*Eburia stroheckeri*), white-spotted longhorn beetles (*Linsleyonides albomaculatus*), and Jamaican fungus ant (*Trachymyrmex jamaicensis*). Pesticides and snail collectors have decimated the wild populations of Stock Island tree snails. Snail collectors are also to blame for the extinction of several color phases of Florida tree snails (*Liguus fasciatus*) that formerly inhabited South

Florida's tropical hammocks. The threatened white-crowned pigeon (*Columba leucocephala*) is a keystone species of Florida's rockland communities. These frugivorous pigeons nest colonially on mangrove islets but forage almost exclusively on fruit-bearing hammock trees on the mainland, continually dispersing seeds along their commutes. The mangrove cuckoo (*Coccyzus minor*) is one of several endemic birds that nest in tropical hammocks. Tropical hammocks are important to numerous migrating and wintering songbirds. The herpetofauna of South Florida's rockland habitats is diverse and interesting, with many distinct races or local variants of wide-ranging species, most of which are listed. They include Lower Keys populations

Tropical hardwood hammock community, Key Largo Hammocks Botanical State Park, North Key Largo, Monroe County.

or subspecies of brown snakes (*Storeria*), ribbon snakes (*Thamnophis*), the corn snake known as the rosy rat snake (*Elaphe guttata guttata*), and the Key ring-necked snake (*Diadophis punctatus acricus*). Distinct Upper Keys and adjacent mainland races include Deckert's phase rat snakes (*Elaphe obsoleta deckerti*), Barbour's phase coral snakes (*Micrurus fulvius barbouri*), and rimrock crowned snakes (*Tantilla oolitica*).

Significant tropical hammock sites still exist within Everglades and Biscayne national parks; Crocodile Lakes and Key Deer national wildlife refuges; the Florida Park Service sites of Key Largo Hammocks, Collier-Seminole, Bahia Honda, Hugh Taylor Birch, Lignum-Vitae Key, MacArthur, John Pennekamp, and Long Key; and the Dade County parks of Matheson, Snapper, Fuchs, Castellow, and Addison.

Tropical Pineland

Like tropical hammocks, rockland pine forests occupy slightly elevated rimrock areas with numerous oolitic limestone protrusions. That is where the similarities end, however. Soils of Florida's limestone pinelands (and most pinelands) are generally well drained; however, unlike sandhill and scrub pinelands, rockland soils are exceedingly shallow accumulations of sand or marl. South Florida slash pine is the dominant tree species, with Key thatch palms (*Thrinax morrisii*) and silver palms (*Coccothrinax argentata*) often present. Plant species occurring in rockland pinewoods of the mainland but not in Lower Keys sites include varnish leaf (*Dodonaea viscosa*) and beautyberry (*Callicarpa americana*). The flora restricted to Lower Keys pinewoods

includes dune lily thorn (*Catesbaea parviflora*) and a species of poinciana, *Caesalpinia pauciflora*. Tropical pinelands support a diverse herbaceous flora, especially at mainland sites (more than 250 species), with few epiphytic components. Mainland tropical pinelands typically have sparse understories, but the understory of Lower Keys pinewoods is often dense. Few significant tracts of tropical pinelands remain. Several remain in the Lower Keys (Big Pine, No Name, Little Pine, Cudjoe, and Sugarloaf keys) and locally within the Miami and the Big Cypress limestone regions of the mainland. Tropical pineland plants display various adaptations to the fires that periodically sweep through this community. Conditions typical of this community (meager fuel accumulations) rarely allow crown fires to develop.

Florida's tropical pinelands support a diverse assemblage of wildlife. Mammals include raccoons, white-tailed deer (mainland), and Key deer (Lower Keys). Mainland sites may harbor Florida black bears, Big Cypress fox squirrels, and the occasional Florida panther. The avifauna is similar to that of central Florida pine flatwoods. Several species, however, were recently extirpated as breeding birds from South Florida's pinelands, including the red-cockaded woodpecker, southeastern American kestrel, eastern bluebird, brown-headed nuthatch, and summer tanager (*Piranga rubra*). The herpetofauna of tropical pineland includes squirrel treefrogs (*Hyla squirella*), reef geckos (*Sphaerodactylus notatus notatus*), and several species discussed in the tropical hammocks section. Myriad insect species occur, and several are habitat endemics, including Florida duskywing butterflies

Tropical rockland pineland community, National Key Deer Refuge, Big Pine Key, Monroe County.

(*Ephyriades brunnea floridensis*), Rockland grass skippers (*Hesperis meskei*), and Bartram's hairstreaks (*Strymon acis bartrami*).

By 1920, nearly all of the rockland pine forests on the mainland had been logged. Pinelands were also cleared to plant pineapples, coconut palms, grapefruit, mangos, and avocados. Land clearing was laborious and time consuming until the advent of the rock plow in 1950. With the new device, nearly all the remaining tropical pinelands were quickly converted to agricultural fields. Remnant parcels were, and are, seriously jeopardized by development. By the year 2000, only 2 percent of Florida's tropical pinelands remained intact outside protected lands. Invasive exotic plants threaten remaining sites, both on and off protected lands. Among the most detrimental species are melaleuca and Brazilian pepper.

Rockland pine forests can be visited in the Long Pine Key area of Everglades National Park, Key Deer National Wildlife Refuge, Big Cypress National Preserve, the area around the old Richmond Air Field in Dade County, and two Dade County properties, Deering Estate at Cutler and Navy Wells Pineland Preserve.

Readers are encouraged to ask government officials to seek appropriations for acquisition of rockland habitats, help conservation organizations acquire threatened lands, and assist the state CARL Program with lobbying or letter-writing campaigns for state land purchases.

State and Federally Listed or Endemic Animal Species of South Florida Rockland Habitats

S, State
F, Federal
E, Endangered
T, Threatened
SSC, Species of Special Concern, a state classification
SMC, Species of Management Concern, a federal classification
CAND, Candidate, a federal classification
HAMMOCK, Tropical hammocks
PINELAND, Tropical pinelands

BIRDS

White-crowned pigeon (*Columba leuco-cephala*), S-T, F-SMC; HAMMOCK, PINELAND (endemic)

Antillean nighthawk (*Chordeiles gund-lachii*), not listed; PINELAND (U.S. range limited to the Lower Keys)

Southeastern American kestrel (*Falco sparverius paulus*), S-T, F-SMC; PINELAND

Bachman's warbler (*Vermivora bachmanii*), S & F-E; HAMMOCK, PINELAND (possibly extinct)

Loggerhead shrike (*Lanius ludovicianus*), F-SMC; PINELAND

MAMMALS

Florida mastiff bat (*Eumops glaucinus floridanus*), S-E, F-CAND; HAMMOCK, PINELAND

Florida panther (*Puma concolor coryi*), S & F-E; HAMMOCK, PINELAND (mainland only)

Key Largo wood rat (*Neotoma floridana smalli*), S & F-E; HAMMOCK (Upper Keys endemic)

Key Largo cotton mouse (*Peromyscus gossypinus allapaticola*), S & F-E; HAMMOCK (Upper Keys endemic)

Key deer (*Odocoileus virginianus clavium*), S & F-E; PINELAND, HAMMOCK (Lower Keys endemic)

Key Vaca raccoon (*Procyon lotor auspicatus*), F-SMC; HAMMOCK, PINELAND (Keys endemic)

Key West raccoon (*Procyon lotor incautus*), F-SMC; HAMMOCK, PINELAND (Lower Keys endemic)

Big Cypress fox squirrel (*Sciurus niger avicennia*), S-T, F-SMC; PINELAND, HAMMOCK (South Florida endemic)

Sherman's fox squirrel (*Sciurus niger shermani*), S-SSC, F-SMC; PINELAND (peripheral species)

Insular hispid cotton rat (*Sigmodon hispidus insulicola*), F-SMC; PINELAND

Florida black bear (*Ursus americanus floridanus*), S-T, F-SMC; PINELAND, HAMMOCK (mainland only)

REPTILES AND AMPHIBIANS

Key ring-necked snake (*Diadophis puncta-tus acricus*), S-T, F-SMC; PINELAND, HAMMOCK (Lower Keys endemic)

Eastern indigo snake (*Drymarchon corais couperi*), S & F-T, HAMMOCK, PINELAND

Rosy rat snake (*Elaphe guttata guttata*), S-SSC, HAMMOCK, PINELAND (Lower Keys endemic)

Deckert's phase yellow rat snake (*Elaphe obsoleta deckerti*), not listed; HAMMOCK, PINELAND (endemic)

Barbour's phase eastern coral snake (*Micrurus fulvius barbouri*), not listed; HAMMOCK (endemic)

Florida Keys mole skink (*Eumeces egregius egregius*), S-SSC, F-SMC; HAMMOCK, PINELAND (Keys endemic)

Lower Keys striped mud turtle (*Kinosternon bauri*), S-E; HAMMOCK, PINELAND, riparian habitats (Lower Keys endemic)

Lower Keys Florida brown snake (*Storeria*

dekayi victa), S-T; HAMMOCK, PINELAND
(Lower Keys endemic)
Rimrock crowned snake (*Tantilla oolitica*),
S-T, F-SMC; HAMMOCK, PINELAND
(endemic)
Lower Keys peninsula ribbon snake (*Thamnophis sauritus sackeni*), S-T; PINELAND,
riparian habitats (Lower Keys endemic)

ARACHNIDS

Key gnaphosid spider (*Cesonia irvingi*),
F-SMC; HAMMOCK (endemic)

INSECTS

Schaus' swallowtail butterfly (*Papilio aristodemus ponceanus*), S & F-E;
HAMMOCK (endemic)
Florida leafwing butterfly (*Anaea troglodyta floridalis*), F-SMC; PINELAND (endemic)
Florida atala butterfly (*Eumaeus atala florida*), F-SMC; HAMMOCK, PINELAND
(endemic)
Bartram's hairstreak butterfly (*Strymon acis bartrami*), F-SMC; PINELAND (endemic)
Big Pine Key ataenius dung beetle (*Ataenius superficialis*), F-SMC; PINELAND (Lower
Keys endemic)
Big Pine Key conehead katydid
(*Belocephalus micanopy*), F-SMC;
PINELAND (Lower Keys endemic)
Keys short-winged conehead katydid
(*Belocephalus sleighti*), F-SMC; mainly
PINELAND, edges of HAMMOCK (endemic)
Keys scaly cricket (*Cycloptilum irregularis*),
F-SMC; HAMMOCK (endemic)
Handsome flower scarab (*Rutela formosa*),
not listed; HAMMOCK (endemic)
Klot's skipper (*Euphyes pilatka klotsi*), not
listed; PINELAND (Lower Keys endemic)

MOLLUSKS

Stock Island tree snail (*Orthalicus r. reses*),
S-E, F-T; HAMMOCK (Lower Keys endemic)

Florida tree snail (*Liguus fasciatus*), S-SSC;
HAMMOCK (endemic)

COASTAL STRAND HABITATS

Florida's coastal strand ecosystems are actually an assemblage of various microhabitats that change considerably along the state's nearly 1,200 miles of coastline. They include communities described in other sections, such as Florida scrub, pine flatwoods, and hardwood forests. In this treatment, "coastal strand" refers to Atlantic or Gulf shoreline vegetation zones including beach, foredunes, grassland, scrub, flatwoods, maritime hammock, and tropical forest. In typical usage, coastal strand does not include wetland communities such as mangrove swamps and coastal marshes. Coastal strand ecosystems are among the most threatened in the state. Human activities have heavily damaged beaches and adjacent habitats throughout much of Florida. Counties where beachfront habitats have been severely altered include Volusia, Palm Beach, Broward, Dade, Monroe, and Pinellas.

Foredunes, formed by sand banking where stable plant growth occurs, are imperative to maintaining beaches. Most of the sand of Florida's beautiful beaches originated from granite high in the Appalachian Mountains. Over the course of millions of years it has eroded and made its way to the Atlantic and Gulf coasts, dispersing farther southward by ocean currents. Several peninsula Gulf beaches have sand composed primarily of finely ground shell and coral particles. Scores of high-rise hotels, apartment buildings, and condominiums were built directly on the fragile foredunes of many

*Coastal strand community, Honeymoon Island State Park, Pinellas County. Note flock of whimbrels (*Numenius phaeopus*) on dune.*

of Florida's beaches. Seawalls often con-structed to shield the costly structures from storms cause powerful waves to erode frontage beaches. Once that occurs, the continuing and costly practice of beach restoration begins. This involves dredging sand from offshore deposits and redepositing it back on the beach. Beach renourishment efforts cost Florida tax-payers as much as $46 million a year in the 1990s. Jetties, built on the majority of Florida's inlets, also cause the adjacent beaches to erode, often leading to the same expensive maintenance efforts. Those and other human alterations cause much of Florida's beach sand simply to be carried away. State and federal laws now prevent many construction activi-ties on foredunes; however, Florida's laws

pertaining to seawall construction lag behind regulations in other coastal states. North Carolina and South Carolina now prohibit construction of all new artificial sea barriers.

Global warming constitutes an almost certain threat to coastal habitats, though how soon and how severe the changes will be is not certain. Global warming is unfortunately a reality. Worldwide, the rate of rise in the sea level has increased substantially during the last half-century. Hurricanes, although natural, are another serious threat to coastal ecosystems and can be very destructive to foredunes. A direct strike from a severe hurricane to the last stronghold of an endangered species, such as the Perdido Key beach mouse, could potentially result in its extinction. Such an extinction would not be natural, despite our classification of hurricanes as acts of God. Human-related activities (for instance, habitat destruction and predation by domestic cats) cause the unnatural circumstances (in this case, isolated populations) that may render species more vulnerable to extinction from natural events. Another example is artificial lights erected along Florida's coastline, which represent a threat specific to sea turtles. Lights sometimes interfere with the ability of hatchling sea turtles to find their way to the safety of the ocean.

Sea oats (*Uniola paniculata*), which occur on the foredunes of nearly all Florida beaches, stabilize dunes by growing both upward and horizontally. Horizontal growth is achieved by rhizomes (rootlike stems) that penetrate the sand. Other vegetation may vary significantly with latitude, especially vegetation beyond the foredunes. On Florida's northeast coast, typical foredune vegetation includes railroad vines (*Ipomoea stolonifera* and *I. pes-caprae*), bitter panicum (*Panicum amarum*), beach dropseed (*Sporobolus virginicus*), and prostrate beach spurge (*Chamaesyce bombensis*). Grassland and herbaceous flats contain muhly grass (*Muhlenbergia capillaris*), beach cordgrass (*Spartina patens*), prickly pear (*Opuntia stricta*), capeweed (*Phyla nodiflora*), and beach pennywort (*Hydrocotyle bonariensis*). A scrub zone is often present in this region where species such as wax myrtle (*Myrica cerifera*), yaupon (*Ilex vomitoria*), saw palmetto, southern red cedar, cabbage palm, and myrtle oak can be found. Maritime hammocks in northeastern Florida often contain live oak, laurel oak, southern magnolia, black cherry, and rusty lyonia (*Lyonia ferruginea*). Farther south on Florida's coasts, a number of more tropical plant species appear, including sea grape (*Coccoloba uvifera*), blackbead (*Pithecellobium keyense*), West Indian bluestem (*Andropogon semiberbis*), Spanish stopper (*Eugenia foetida*), and marlberry (*Ardisia escallonoides*). The coastal forests of extreme southern Florida and the Keys become full-fledged tropical hardwood hammocks. The more pristine coastal strand communities of the Panhandle typically have an abundance of rosemary shrubs in backdune areas, where woody goldenrod (*Chrysoma pauciflosculosa*) and sand live oak also occur. In Franklin County, sand pine scrub meets the Gulf of Mexico in an ecotone of white, sandy beach.

There are now many invasive exotic plants well established in Florida's coastal strand habitats, especially in South Florida. Two exotics that are considered particularly deleterious to natural communities are Australian pine and Brazilian pepper. Both rapidly take over ecosystems, displacing native vegetation.

Coastal strand habitats, particularly beach and dune areas, are home to several critically endangered animals. Among them are five beach mouse (*Peromyscus polionotus*) subspecies: the endangered Choctawhatchee, St. Andrew, Anastasia Island, and Perdido Key beach mice and the threatened southeastern beach mouse. A sixth subspecies, the Santa Rosa beach mouse, is a federal species of concern. A seventh subspecies, the pallid beach mouse (*Peromyscus polionotus decoloratus*) once found in dune areas of Volusia and Flagler counties, is now extinct. The Chadwick Beach cotton mouse (*Peromyscus gossypinus restrictus*), another endemic coastal strand mammal that just recently became extinct, formerly inhabited the Englewood Beach area of Charlotte County. The Anastasia Island cotton mouse (*Peromyscus gossypinus anastasae*), now extirpated in Florida, still occurs on Cumberland Island, Georgia. Beaches and dune areas provide important, natural nesting sites for several listed birds, including least terns (*Sterna antillarum*), Caribbean roseate terns (*Sterna dougallii*), southeastern snowy plovers (*Charadrius alexandrinus tenuirostris*), black skimmers (*Rynchops niger*), and American oystercatchers (*Haematopus palliatus*). Scores of peregrine falcons (*Falco peregrinus*) migrate and hunt along Florida's coasts each year, with many also wintering in the state. Brown pelicans, an abundant coastal species in Florida, are rare in many other parts of its range. Numerous other gulls, terns, and shorebirds depend on Florida's coastal strand ecosystems for nesting, feeding, and wintering grounds.

The herpetofauna of Florida's coastal strand habitats is fairly rich. The reptiles most dependent on the beaches and dunes of the coastal strand are undoubtedly sea turtles. The beaches of the state's east-central coast are among the most important nesting sites in the world for Atlantic loggerhead turtles (*Caretta caretta caretta*), and many Atlantic green turtles (*Chelonia mydas mydas*) nest there as well. Three other sea turtles, the leatherback (*Dermochelys coriacea*), Atlantic ridley (*Lepidochelys kempi*), and Atlantic hawksbill (*Eretmochelys imbricata imbricata*), occasionally nest

on Florida's shores. Other listed reptiles of coastal strand habitats are gopher tortoises and eastern indigo snakes. Common herptiles include the six-lined racerunner (*Cnemidophorus sexlineatus sexlineatus*), racers, the eastern coachwhip snake, and the coastal dunes crowned snake (*Tantilla relicta pamlica*), an endemic restricted to coastal strand habitats of Florida's south-central Atlantic Coast. Several listed or endemic insects occur in coastal strand habitats, including Woodruff's ataenius beetles (*Ataenius woodruffi*), Panhandle beach scarab beetles (*Polylamina pubescens*), Panhandle beach anomala beetles (*Anomala flavipennis okaloosensis*), Florida coast scarabs (*Ataenius rudellus*), and Florida forestiera borers (*Nesostizocera floridana*).

Intact coastal strand ecosystems can be found in the Gulf Island and Cape Canaveral national seashores; Merritt Island, St. Vincent, and Egmont Key national wildlife refuges; Eglin Air Force Base; The Nature Conservancy's Blowing Rocks Preserve; and the state parks or recreation areas of Amelia Island, Little Talbot Island, Anastasia, Flagler Beach, Sebastian Inlet, Fort Pierce Inlet, St. Lucie Inlet, J. D. MacArthur, John U. Lloyd, Delnor-Wiggins Pass, Cayo Costa, Caladesi Island, Honeymoon Island, Anclote Key, St. George Island, St. Joseph Peninsula, St. Andrews, Henderson Beach, Grayton Beach, and Perdido Key.

State and Federally Listed Animal Species of Coastal Strand Ecosystems

S, State

F, Federal

E, Endangered

T, Threatened

SSC, Species of Special Concern, a state
classification
SMC, Species of Management Concern,
a federal classification
CAND, Candidate, a federal classification

BIRDS

Southeastern snowy plover (*Charadrius
alexandrinus tenuirostris*), S-T, F-SMC
Piping plover (*Charadrius melodus*), S &
F-T
Stoddard's yellow-throated warbler
(*Dendroica dominica stoddardi*),
F-SMC
Peregrine falcon (*Falco peregrinus*), S-E, F-T
Southeastern American kestrel (*Falco
sparverius paulus*), S-T, F-SMC
American oystercatcher (*Haematopus
palliatus*), S-SSC
Southern bald eagle (*Haliaeetus leuco-
cephalus leucocephalus*), S & F-T
Osprey (*Pandion haliaetus*), S-SSC in
Monroe County only
Brown pelican (*Pelecanus occidentalis*),
S-SSC
Black skimmer (*Rynchops niger*), S-SSC
Least tern (*Sterna antillarum*), S-T
Caribbean roseate tern (*Sterna dougallii*),
S & F-T

MAMMALS

Choctawhatchee beach mouse (*Peromyscus
polionotus allophrys*), S & F-E
Santa Rosa beach mouse (*Peromyscus
polionotus leucocephalus*), F-SMC
Southeastern beach mouse (*Peromyscus
polionotus niveiventris*), S & F-T
St. Andrew beach mouse (*Peromyscus
polionotus peninsularis*), S-E, F-CAND
Anastasia Island beach mouse (*Peromyscus
polionotus phasma*), S & F-E
Perdido Key beach mouse (*Peromyscus
polionotus trissyllepsis*), S & F-E

REPTILES AND AMPHIBIANS

Atlantic loggerhead turtle (*Caretta caretta
caretta*), S & F-T
Atlantic green turtle (*Chelonia mydas
mydas*), S & F-E
Atlantic leatherback turtle (*Dermochelys
coriacea coriacea*), S & F-E
Atlantic hawksbill turtle (*Eretmochelys
imbricata imbricata*), S & F-E
Atlantic ridley turtle (*Lepidochelys kempi*),
S & F-E
Gopher tortoise (*Gopherus polyphemus*),
S-SSC, F-SMC
Island glass lizard (*Ophisaurus compressus*),
F-SMC
Florida Keys mole skink (*Eumeces egregius
egregius*), S-SSC, F-SMC
Cedar Key mole skink (*Eumeces egregius
insularis*), F-SMC
Eastern indigo snake (*Drymarchon corais
couperi*), S & F-T
Southern hog-nosed snake (*Heterodon
simus*), F-SMC
Florida pine snake (*Pituophis melanoleucus
mugitus*), S-SSC, F-SMC

INSECTS

Panhandle beach scarab beetle (*Polylamina
pubescens*), F-SMC
Woodruff's ataenius (*Ataenius woodruffi*),
F-SMC

SUBTERRANEAN HABITATS

Many Floridians and tourists alike are
aware of the state's numerous freshwater
springs, many of which are popular public recreation areas. Unknown to many
Floridians, however, is the vast network
of caves, sinks, and deep wells existing
below ground statewide in the limestone
aquifer. Even more unfamiliar are the
peculiar, ghostly creatures that never

venture from the dark, lonely recesses of their subterranean natural communities. By definition, terrestrial caves include caves devoid of standing water or areas within aquatic caves above water, such as ceilings and unsubmerged fissures. Aquatic caves, on the other hand, are permanently or periodically submerged. In this treatment, both cave communities are grouped together, as many Florida caves contain portions falling under both definitions. Subterranean ecosystems differ from other Florida habitats in that they support relatively few plant species, and those present, mostly algae, mosses, and liverworts, are generally restricted to areas that admit some light, called the twilight zone.

Cave fauna, however, is more diversified, incorporating mammals, fishes, amphibians, insects, arachnids, and crustaceans, with an exceptionally high proportion of endemics. At least 7 of Florida's 17 recognized bat species use caves for roosting, maternity, or hibernation. Two of Florida's three endangered bats, the gray bat (*Myotis grisescens*) and the Indiana bat (*Myotis sodalis*), are highly dependent on subterranean habitats. Other Florida bats with a strong nexus to caves include southeastern brown bats (*Myotis austroriparius*), little brown bats (*Myotis lucifugus*), Keen's bats (*Myotis keenii*), and big brown bats (*Eptesicus fuscus osceola*). Gray rat snakes (*Elaphe obsoleta spiloides*) have been observed positioned at cave entrances at dusk striking at emerging bats.

Unlike bats and other troglodytes (cave dwellers) that spend time above

Cave, Florida Caverns State Park, Jackson County.

ground, animals known as troglobites spend most or all of their lives in the dark zone just beyond the twilight zone and in the deep zone (the farthest zone from the entrance), where air is inert. Troglobites have developed evolutionary, morphological adaptations for cave life, including loss of pigmentation and working eyes, neither of which is needed in total darkness. Troglobites of Florida's aquatic caves include Georgia blind salamanders (*Haideotriton wallacei*), which would be more appropriately named Florida blind salamanders since most populations are known from Florida. The type locality, however, is a well in Dougherty County, Georgia, hence the name. Other aquatic Florida troglobites include several gastropods, cave isopods, and cave shrimp. Typical terrestrial troglobites include several cave springtails, cave mites, and cave spiders. A number of troglodytic crayfish species (*Procambarus* spp.) are Florida endemics, each known from only one site: Santa Fe cave crayfish (*P. erythrops*), Putnam County cave crayfish (*P. morrisi*), Silver Glen Springs cave crayfish (*P. attiguus*), and big-cheeked cave crayfish (*P. delicatus*). Others occur at just a few localized sites, such as the Orange-Seminole cave crayfish (*P. acherontis*), Miami cave crayfish (*P. milleri*), Orange Lake cave crayfish (*P. franzi*), Withlacoochee light-fleeing crayfish (*P. lucifugus lucifugus*), and Alachua light-fleeing crayfish (*P. lucifugus alachua*). Other notable troglodytic crustaceans include the Squirrel Chimney cave shrimp (*Palaemonetes cummingi*, federally listed as threatened), swimming little Florida cave isopods (*Remasellus parvus*), Florida cave amphipods (*Crangonyx grandimanus*), and Hobbs

cave amphipods (*Crangonyx hobbsi*). Many of Florida's troglobitic invertebrates are listed species. All depend on organic detritus from outside sources or nitrogen-rich bat guano for their nutritional requirements.

Another group of animals found in Florida's subterranean communities is the troglophiles. Troglophiles may occupy subterranean environments and moist areas outside caves. Native troglophiles include three-lined salamanders (*Eurycea longicauda guttolineata*) in the Panhandle, several fishes, crickets, and cave orb spiders. Fish species sometimes encountered in aquatic caves or subterranean streams are gambusia (*Gambusia affinis*), yellow bullhead (*Ictalurus natalis*), American eel (*Anguilla rostrata*), and redeye chub (*Notropis harperi*). Florida naturalist Barry Mansell has reported observations of ghostly white catfish with vestigial eyes in aquatic caves of Jackson County. Mansell believes this fish, yet to be officially described or recognized by science, is of the genus *Ictalurus.*

Sinkholes, or sinks, are another limestone, groundwater habitat accommodating life-forms (crayfish, isopods, and amphipods) similar to those of caves and, to a lesser extent, springs. Sinkholes are depressions in limestone, often deep and usually having permanent, though fluctuating, levels of clear, alkaline waters, with a high mineral content. Aquatic vegetation such as cattail (*Typha domingensis*), smartweed (*Polygonum* spp.), duckweed (*Lemna* spp.), and bog moss (*Mayaca fluviatilis*) may be present. Florida, referred to as the sinkhole capital of the United States, has an abundance of sinks. Sinks are important

Georgia blind salamander (Haideotriton wallacei), *a Species of Special Concern, one of many albinistic, troglobitic creatures inhabiting subterranean habitats of Florida's Panhandle.*

to many animals, including several listed or endemic species, such as Squirrel Chimney cave shrimp, Hobbs cave amphipods, Santa Fe cave crayfish, Orange-Seminole cave crayfish, Putnam County cave crayfish, and striped newts (*Notophthalmus perstriatus*). Larger sinkholes with expansive surface water, known as sinkhole lakes, also attract animals associated with lakes, such as wading birds, fishes, amphibians, and turtles.

Subterranean ecosystems, aquatic and terrestrial, are extremely delicate environments with stable, constant temperatures, humidity, air circulation patterns, chemical characteristics, and detrital inputs. Even minor perturbative events can result in large kills of cave fauna.

Threats include agricultural, industrial, and residential pollutants, especially pesticides and herbicides (which may simply leach through soils); erosion and siltation caused by destruction of vegetation at sink perimeters; changes in detrital input; pumping of water; collection of fauna; invasive exotic species; and disturbance of fauna or nutrient reserves by spelunkers and divers. Humans have slaughtered entire bat colonies in some caves and caused partial or total abandonment of others, depleting the guano that supplies important nourishment for many cave invertebrates. Degradation of surface habitats may also threaten cave fauna. Santa Fe cave crayfish, a former resident of Suwannee County's Hildreth

Cave, has not been encountered there
since the site became a garbage dump
in the 1970s. The Oklawaha sponge
(*Dorsilia palmeri*), North America's only
freshwater sink-inhabiting sponge, formerly inhabited a Levy County sink but
is now feared extinct. The introduced
flathead catfish (*Pylodictis olivaris*), an
enormous, midwestern crayfish-eating
species, now occurs in several Panhandle
aquatic caves and springs. It is now a
criminal offense to vandalize or pollute
caves, damage or disturb natural features,
or to remove, harm, or kill any animal
indigenous to Florida's caves (Title 39,
810.13 F.S.).

Florida's largest assemblage of terrestrial caves is found in the Panhandle,
especially Jackson County and surrounding areas. The majority of aquatic spring
caves and sinks occur in the karst
districts of central and northern Florida.
Unfortunately, numerous sites are on
private lands, many of which are gravely
endangered. Subterranean habitats on
public lands include the state park units
at Florida Caverns, Falling Waters,
Torreya, and Devil's Millhopper and
several locations within the Apalachicola
and the Ocala national forests.

State and Federally Listed Animal Species of Florida's Subterranean Habitats

S, State
F, Federal
E, Endangered
T, Threatened
SSC, Species of Special Concern, a state
   classification
SMC, Species of Management Concern,
   a federal classification
CAND, Candidate, a federal classification

MAMMALS
Gray bat (*Myotis grisescens*), S & F-E
Indiana bat (*Myotis sodalis*), S & F-E

REPTILES AND AMPHIBIANS
Georgia blind salamander (*Haideotriton wallacei*), S-SSC, F-SMC

SPONGES
Oklawaha sponge (*Dorsilia palmeri*),
   F-SMC (endemic, possibly extinct)

CRUSTACEANS
Florida cave amphipod (*Crangonyx grandimanus*), F-SMC
Hobbs cave amphipod (*Crangonyx hobbsi*),
   F-SMC
Squirrel Chimney cave shrimp
   (*Palaemonetes cummingi*), F-T
Orange-Seminole cave crayfish
   (*Procambarus acherontis*), F-SMC
Santa Fe cave crayfish (*Procambarus erythrops*), S-SSC

FRESHWATER SWAMPS AND RELATED COMMUNITIES

The *Random House College Dictionary*
defines swamps as "tracts of wet, spongy
land, often having a growth of certain
types of trees and other vegetation, but
unfit for cultivation." Well, luckily for
Florida's swamp inhabitants, large tracts
of nearly pristine swampland were, at
first, left undisturbed, mainly because
they were considered useless for cultivation, while much of the surrounding
upland habitat was easily converted
to agricultural fields. In spite of that,
approximately half of Florida's original
wetlands, including many swamps, are
now gone. Although large and very wild
swamps still remain in Florida, the large

stands of virgin old-growth bald cypress (*Taxodium distichum*) were felled long ago. Demands for timber, particularly cypress, beginning in the late 1800s led to intensive logging of swamps statewide. When swamps were timbered, old-growth forest was often succeeded by gum, ash, bay, or other trees, altering the swamp's physical makeup and biodiversity. Hydroperiods, water quality, fire frequency, and accumulations of organic matter in swamps have been altered by human activities. Mining of peat and other organic substrates from swamps is among the most destructive practices. Detritus deposits, an important component of the swamp, take many years, often hundreds of years, to accumulate after they are depleted by mining. Though

swamps are not as endangered as other Florida ecosystems, many continue to be threatened by development, phosphate mining, pollution, and other human activities.

Many people ask how a swamp differs from a marsh. Basically, a swamp is forested, a marsh is not. A variety of swamp types occur in Florida: river swamps (including whitewater and blackwater floodplain swamps), cypress swamps and strands, dome swamps, freshwater tidal swamps, basin or gum swamps, and bogs and seepage wetlands (including baygalls and seepage slopes).

Bogs (also known as bog swamps) and seepage wetlands are among the most distinctive of Florida's swamps. Bogs are basin wetlands that occupy small sites

Cypress swamp, Fish-eating Creek, Glades County.

in scattered locations, most frequently in northern Florida. Bogs obtain moisture through a capillary action and generally have a deep peat substrate. Typical trees and plants of Florida bogs include titi (*Cyrilla racemiflora*), red bay, sweet bay (*Magnolia virginiana*), dahoon holly (*Ilex cassine*), sphagnum moss (*Sphagnum* spp.), and several carnivorous plants. Seepage slopes and baygalls are closely related. Unlike bogs, both communities receive moisture through a downslope seepage; however, like bogs, they have acidic soils, and baygalls often have sphagnum mats. Of the two, baygalls are more swamplike, often having dense forest canopies of evergreen hardwoods and a rather open understory. Baygalls occupy peat-filled seepage depressions, sometimes at the base of seepage slopes. Water percolating downslope through loamy or sandy soils maintains the moisture levels of seepage slope communities. Florida's seepage habitats contain numerous endemic and highly specialized plants and animals, including insectivorous plants, orchids, and a diverse array of amphibians. Among the amphibians are Florida bog frogs, pickerel frogs (*Rana palustris*), carpenter frogs (*Rana virgatipes*), four-toed salamanders, seal salamanders, and Gulf hammock dwarf sirens (*Pseudobranchus striatus lustricolus*). The pine barrens treefrog, a species of special concern, occurs in three widely separated populations from New Jersey to Florida's Panhandle, where it is generally restricted to seepage communities. Several species of small freshwater snails (*Aphaostracon* and *Cincinnatia*) inhabit spring run and seepage microhabitats. Of the 45 or so carnivorous plant species known in North America, over

50 percent occur in Gulf Coast bogs and seepage communities. More than 12 species may occur within a single site.

The marl prairies or dwarf cypress (*Taxodium ascendens*) savannas of southern Florida are often more marshlike than swamplike. These and other swamp and swamplike habitats support an incredible biodiversity, including many listed species. Different swamp types have different vegetative components, and changes become dramatic as one travels from the temperate north to the subtropical south. Dominant tree species include cypresses, sweet gum (*Liquidambar styraciflua*), water hickory, water tupelo (*Nyssa aquatica*), swamp black gum (*Nyssa sylvatica* var. *biflora*), sweet bay, ogeechee lime (*Nyssa ogeche*), water ash (*Fraxinus caroliniana*), and southern red maple. Regrettably, exotic melaleuca has invaded many South Florida swamps, rapidly displacing native trees. Common shrubs and vines of Florida swamps include titi, black titi (*Cliftonia monophylla*), fetterbush (*Lyonia lucida*), dahoon holly, poison ivy (*Toxicodendron radicans*), bamboo vine (*Smilax laurifolia*), pepper vine (*Ampelopsis arborea*), and, in extreme southern Florida, strangler fig. Epiphytes and insectivorous plants are also well represented, with Spanish moss (*Tillandsia usneoides*), numerous bromeliads and orchids, pitcher plants (*Sarracenia* spp.), sundews (*Drosera* spp.), bladderworts (*Utricularia* spp.), and butterworts (*Pinguicula* spp.). Unfortunately, orchids, bromeliads, ferns, and carnivorous plants have been severely overcollected in some areas.

A swamp's lush vegetation and abundant water attract a wide variety of resident and transient wildlife. Larger mammals such as Florida panthers, Florida black bears, river otters (*Lutra canadensis*) and bobcats commonly utilize swamp habitats. Beavers, once extirpated by trappers, have made a comeback in some North Florida swamps. Other swamp-inhabiting mammals include Everglades minks (*Mustela vison evergladensis*), Big Cypress fox squirrels, raccoons, southeastern shrews, and golden mice. River swamps have fairly diverse fish populations, including darters (*Etheostoma*) and minnow (*Hybognathus*) species. Invertebrates are well represented by myriad insects, arachnids, crustaceans, and leeches. Butterflies associated with Florida swamps include textor skippers (*Amblyscirtes aesculapius*), Duke's skippers (*Euphyes dukesi*), southern swamp skippers (*Poanes yehl*), Hessel's hairstreaks (*Mitoura hesseli*), and Appalachian eyed browns (*Satyrodes appalachia appalachia*). Not surprisingly, nearly 20 mosquito species occur here.

It is also not surprising that Florida's swamps contain a rich variety of herpeto-fauna, beginning with the well-known American alligator and venomous cottonmouth and including 19 semiaquatic snake species or subspecies, three-foot amphiuma salamanders (*Amphiuma means*), dwarf sirens (*Pseudobranchus striatus*), and several species of treefrogs (*Hyla*) and true frogs (*Rana*). Even more varied is the birdlife of Florida's swamps. Birds of prey that nest in swamps include swallow-tailed kites (*Elanoides forficatus*), Mississippi kites (*Ictinia mississippiensis*), and barred owls (*Strix varia*). Characteristic swampland birds

are wood storks; wood ducks; more than a dozen ibis, egret, and heron species; limpkins (*Aramus guarauna*); and Swainson's, Bachman's (historically), and prothonotary wood warblers. Two recently extinct species, the Carolina parakeet (*Conuropsis carolinensis*) and the ivory-billed woodpecker (*Campephilus principalis*), were former inhabitants of northern Florida swamps.

Living examples of several different swamp types can be visited in the flood-plains of the Blackwater, Apalachicola, Chipola, Suwannee, and Oklawaha rivers; Okefenokee and nearby Pinhook swamps in northern Florida; Ocala National Forest; Lake Panasoffkee; Green Swamp near Lakeland (Florida's second largest wetland ecosystem); Upper St. Johns River basin in central Florida; Six-mile Cypress Swamp; Corkscrew Swamp Sanctuary; Big Cypress National Preserve in southern Florida; and state park lands of Fakahat-chee Strand, San Felasco Hammock, Tosahatchee, Wakulla Springs, Highlands Hammock, and Myakka River.

State and Federally Listed Animal Species of Florida's Freshwater Swamps

S, State

F, Federal

E, Endangered

T, Threatened

SSC, Species of Special Concern, a state classification

SMC, Species of Management Concern, a federal classification

CAND, Candidate, a federal classification

FISH

Blackmouth shiner (*Notropis melanosto-*

mus), S-E, F-SMC (in oxbows of the
Blackwater River at ecotones of river
swamp and floodplain)
Tessellated darter (Etheostoma olmstedi
maculaticeps), S-SSC (in blackwater
streams)
Suwannee bass (Micropterus notius notius),
S-SSC
Bluenose shiner (Pteronotropis welaka),
S-SSC

BIRDS

Roseate spoonbill (Ajaia ajaja), S-SSC (in
South Florida's dwarf cypress savannas)
Limpkin (Aramus guarauna), S-SSC
Little blue heron (Egretta caerulea), S-SSC
Reddish egret (Egretta rufescens), S-SSC,
F-SMC
Snowy egret (Egretta thula), S-SSC
Tricolored heron (Egretta tricolor), S-SSC
White ibis (Eudocimus albus), S-SSC
Southern bald eagle (Haliaeetus leuco-
cephalus leucocephalus), S-T, F-T
Wood stork (Mycteria americana), S & F-E
Bachman's warbler (Vermivora bachmanii),
S & F-E

MAMMALS

Florida panther (Puma concolor coryi), S &
F-E
Everglades mink (Mustela vison evergladen-
sis), S-T
Sherman's short-tailed shrew (Blarina
carolinensis shermani), S-SSC, F-SMC
Southeastern brown bat (Myotis austrori-
parius), F-SMC
Gray bat (Myotis grisescens), S & F-E
Indiana bat (Myotis sodalis), S & F-E
Big Cypress fox squirrel (Sciurus niger
avicennia), S-T, F-SMC
Sherman's fox squirrel (Sciurus niger
shermani), S-SSC (dome swamp and
baygall communities)

Homosassa shrew (Sorex longirostris
eionis), S-SSC
Florida black bear (Ursus americanus
floridanus), S-T, F-SMC

REPTILES AND AMPHIBIANS

American alligator (Alligator mississippien-
sis), F-T(S/A), S-SSC
Eastern indigo snake (Drymarchon corais
couperi), S & F-T (frequents environs of
swamps where it feeds on water snakes
and rodents)
Barbour's map turtle (Graptemys barbouri),
S-SSC, F-SMC (riverine ecotones)
Alligator snapping turtle (Macroclemys
temmincki), S-SSC, F-SMC
Suwannee cooter (Pseudemys concinna
suwanniensis), S-SSC (riverine ecotones)
Gulf hammock dwarf siren
(Pseudobranchus striatus lustricolus),
F-SMC
Flatwoods salamander (Ambystoma cingu-
latum), F-SMC
Pine barrens treefrog (Hyla andersoni),
S-SSC
Florida bog frog (Rana okaloosae), S-SSC,
F-SMC
Short-tailed snake (Stilosoma extenuatum),
S-T, F-SMC (an upland species that has
been found hibernating in sphagnum
bogs within sandhill communities)

MOLLUSKS

Florida arc mussel (Alasmidonta wright-
iana), F-SMC (possibly extinct)
Southern kidneyshell mussel
(Ptychobranchus jonesi), F-SMC

LAKES, RIVERS, STREAMS, SPRINGS, AND RELATED ECOSYSTEMS

Florida is a very aquatic state, with thousands of lakes and hundreds of rivers,

streams, and springs. In descriptions of these aquatic ecosystems, lakes or lacustrine habitats are often separated from riverine ecosystems, which include rivers, streams, and spring runs; however, they attract many, but not all, of the same faunal species. It is primarily for that reason that lacustrine and riverine ecosystems have been combined in this treatment. Both lacustrine ecosystems and riverine ecosystems could be further divided into a series of subtypes, based on differences in origin, topography, hydrology, substrate composition, and other factors. Lacustrine subdivisions would include clastic upland lakes, coastal dune lakes, coastal rockland lakes, flatwood or prairie lakes, river floodplain lakes and swamp lakes, sandhill upland lakes, and sinkhole lakes. Riverine communities could be divided into alluvial rivers, blackwater rivers, seepage streams, and spring-run streams. Springs or spring-run streams differ from other riverine systems in that they derive most, if not all, of their water from artesian openings in underground aquifers. Springs have been described in more detail than the others because they support a large number of listed and endemic species. For more detailed accounts of each subdivision, I recommend *Guide to the Natural Communities of Florida*, prepared by the Florida Natural Areas Inventory and Florida Department of Environmental Protection. The fauna chiefly associated with these aquatic ecosystems includes fishes, crustaceans, and mollusks; however, a multitude of birds, mammals, insects, and reptile and amphibian species are closely associated with Florida's aquatic habitats as well. Species occurring in ecotonal areas are influenced by adjacent terrestrial ecosystems.

Florida has more lakes than any other state. Though the state boasts many unpolluted, nearly pristine lakes, Florida's lakes, as a whole, rank as the second most polluted lakes in the nation. Natural lakes and ponds occur statewide but are most abundant on the Central Florida Ridge. Lake Okeechobee is by far Florida's largest lake, followed by Lake George, Lake Kissimmee, Lake Apopka, and Lake Istokpoga. Rivers are the source for many of Florida's lakes. The Kissimmee River is the source of a series of small lakes before spilling into Lake Okeechobee, and the St. Johns River is

Florida's Apalachicola River, view from The Nature Conservancy's Apalachicola Bluffs and Ravines Preserve, Liberty County. The mighty Apalach separates the eastern and central time zones.

the source for Lake George, Lake Woodruff, Lake Monroe, Lake Jessup, Lake Harney, and numerous smaller lakes. Rivers occur throughout Florida, with the most in the Panhandle, north central Florida, and along the Gulf Coast. Florida's five largest rivers (in descending order) are the Apalachicola, the Suwannee, the St. Johns (occurring entirely within the state), the Choctawhatchee, and the Escambia.

Florida's freshwater lake and riverine ecosystems support a rich ichthyofauna of more than 125 species. Recreationally important fishes include Florida largemouth bass (*Micropterus salmoides floridanus*), crappie (*Pomoxis nigromaculatus*), bluegill and sunfish, and catfish (*Ictalurus* spp.). Native endangered or threatened fishes include anadromous shortnose and Gulf sturgeons (*Acipenser*), Okaloosa darters, blackmouth shiners, and crystal darters (*Crystallaria asprella*). The lake-dwelling Kissimmee sponge (*Ephydatia subtilis*), known only from its type locality, Lake Kissimmee, has not been found in many years and may be extinct. The listed herpetofauna associated with these aquatic ecosystems or adjacent riparian habitats includes American alligators, alligator snapping turtles, Barbour's map turtles, and Suwannee cooters. Gopher frogs and Florida bog frogs use ponds or streams for breeding sites. Florida manatees (*Trichechus manatus latirostris*) use rivers as corridors when migrating from Atlantic or Gulf waters to inland springs. Bald eagles and ospreys nest on towering trees that border the lakes and rivers that supply fish to feed their young. Other characteristic birds include herons, egrets, ibis, and endangered wood storks. Florida's rivers, streams, lakes, and spring-run ecosystems are home to a panoply of crustaceans, mollusks, and insect species. Some insects use swift-flowing waters of streams and rivers for their larval stage; others require still waters of lakes, slow rivers, or oxbows of swift rivers for reproduction.

The Apalachicola River separates the eastern and central time zones and carries by far the largest volume of water of any Florida river. The Apalachicola River system travels through Georgia, Alabama, and Florida on its journey to the Gulf of Mexico. This system includes the Flint and Chattahoochee rivers and, in part, the Chipola River. Quantities of silt transported from the piedmont plateau are deposited throughout this alluvial river's floodplain. The system is ecologically significant, supporting more than 115 species of fishes (3 are endemic), more than 20 snail species (5 are endemic), and 40 clam species (3 are endemic). This grand river passes through some of the country's rarest habitats, including slope forest and bluffs.

Springs are abundant in Florida's northern peninsula and Big Bend regions, where the water-filled, permeable limestone of the Floridian Aquifer is just below the earth's surface. Florida has more large springs (which include river rises and karst windows) than any other state, or any country for that matter. About 30 of Florida's largest springs are classified as first-magnitude springs, which discharge an average of more than 100 cubic feet of water per second. Among them are Marion County's Silver, Silver Glen, and Rainbow springs; Columbia County's Ichetucknee Springs;

Wakulla County's Wakulla, Spring Creek, Kini, and River Sink springs; and three separate Blue Springs, one each in Volusia County, Madison County, and Jackson County. Smaller springs and springlike habitats occur throughout much of Florida, including South Florida's unusual warm-water pseudosprings, which are technically artesian wells.

Florida's many clear, continuously flowing springs are extremely popular with locals and tourists alike. They are also important to wildlife, including numerous listed species. Nearly a dozen endemic snail species, federally listed as species of management concern, inhabit Florida springs. Other listed species inhabiting springs or riverine habitats associated with springs include Suwannee cooters and Florida manatees, indisputably the most popular denizen. Each winter, several hundred manatees seek refuge in the tepid waters of several Florida spring runs, with large congregations gathering at Volusia County's Blue Springs. Spring runs are jeopardized by pollution and other similar threats affecting riverine and lake ecosystems, but they also face several of the same overuse and misuse threats endangering caves. In Florida, springs are commonly closely associated with aquatic caves and sinkholes and sometimes share the same animal species, especially invertebrates.

Florida's springs can be visited at Ponce de Leon Springs State Recreation Area, Wakulla Springs State Park, Gold Head Branch State Park, Ichetucknee Springs State Park, Manatee Springs State Park, Peacock Springs State Recreation Area, Silver River State Park, Rainbow Springs State Park, Blue Spring State Park, Rock Springs Run State Recreation

Snorkeler at Silver Glen Springs, Ocala National Forest, Marion County. This is one of over 30 first-magnitude springs (those springs which discharge over 100 cubic feet of water per second) found in Florida.

Area, Wekiwa Springs State Park, and Homosassa Springs State Wildlife Park, and several locations within Ocala National Forest, including Alexander, Silver Glenn, and Juniper springs.

A number of human activities are known to damage these aquatic ecosystems. Damming of rivers and streams drastically alters habitats downstream and upstream from the dam, and channelization is detrimental to several ecosystems. The long-term effects of the channelization of the Kissimmee River on a freshwater marsh downstream known as the Everglades is a classic example. The straightening of the Kissimmee River eliminated as much as 95 percent (35,000 acres) of its riparian habitat, particularly marshland. Other Florida rivers that have endured extensive channelization include the Apalachicola and Caloosahatchee rivers. Pollutants are another constant threat to aquatic ecosystems. Orange County's Lake Apopka is Florida's fourth largest lake, and its most polluted. Runoff from area muck farms and pollutants, including raw sewage and citrus wastage, seriously degraded water quality and induced plankton blooms in the lake. The lake's bottom has a four-foot layer of muck. Water hyacinth appeared and spread, quickly choking the lake and displacing native pondweed and eelgrass. Bass and other gamefish diminished and nearly disappeared. The St. Johns River Water Management District has now begun an extensive $19 million project to restore Lake Apopka.

Invasive exotic plants and animals have become especially troublesome to some of Florida's river, lake, and spring ecosystems. Water hydrilla and water hyacinth, introduced and established years ago, have become a menace by choking waterways and obstructing their navigability. Herbicides have proved fairly successful in eradicating the free-floating hyacinth and the rooted hydrilla. Native manatees and introduced Asian grass carp (*Ctenopharyngodon idella*), both hardy herbivores, have also been effective in reducing the rapidly growing aquatic plants. More than 50 species of nonnative fishes have been recorded in Florida's waterways and many have established breeding populations. More alien fishes inhabit rivers than lakes, and most occur in southern Florida. They include oscars, black and Midas cichlids (*Cichla-soma*), several species of tilapia, and walking catfish. Exotic fishes often outcompete and displace native fishes. The Asiatic clam (*Corbicula fluminea*), an aggressive exotic bivalve that arrived in Florida in 1960, now occurs in virtually all of its rivers. It is the suspected culprit in the decline of several native mussel species.

State and Federally Listed Animal Species of Florida Lake, Riverine, Stream, and Spring Ecosystems

S, State
F, Federal
E, Endangered
T, Threatened
SSC, Species of Special Concern, a state classification
SMC, Species of Management Concern, a federal classification
CAND, Candidate, a federal classification
LAKE, Lakes
RIVER, Rivers or streams
SPRING, Springs and related habitats

FISHES
Shortnose sturgeon (*Acipenser brevirostrum*), S & F-E; RIVER
Atlantic sturgeon (*Acipenser oxyrinchus oxyrinchus*), S-SSC; RIVER
Gulf sturgeon (*Acipenser oxyrinchus desotoi*), S-SSC, F-T; RIVER
Crystal darter (*Crystallaria asprella*), S-T, F-SMC; RIVER
Bluestripe shiner (*Cyprinella callitaenia*), F-SMC; RIVER
Lake Eustis pupfish (*Cyprinodon variegatus hubbsi*), S-SSC; LAKE (endemic)
Harlequin darter (*Etheostoma histrio*), S-SSC; RIVER

Okaloosa darter (*Etheostoma okaloosae*),
S & F-E; RIVER

Southern tessellated darter (*Etheostoma
olmstedi maculaticeps)*, S-SSC; RIVER

Key silverside (*Menidia conchorum*), S-T;
LAKE (coastal rockland lakes in the Keys)

Suwannee bass (*Micropterus notius notius*),
S-SSC; RIVER, SPRING

Chipola bass (*Micropterus notius coosae*),
S-SSC; RIVER

Blackmouth shiner (*Notropis melanostomus*), S-E, F-SMC; RIVER

Bluenose shiner (*Pteronotropis welaka*),
S-SSC; RIVER, SPRING

BIRDS

Limpkin (*Aramus guarauna*), S-SSC; RIVER,
SPRING

Little blue heron (*Egretta caerulea*), S-SSC;
LAKE, RIVER, SPRING

Snowy egret (*Egretta thula*), S-SSC; LAKE,
RIVER, SPRING

Tricolored heron (*Egretta tricolor*), S-SSC;
LAKE, RIVER, SPRING

White ibis (*Eudocimus albus*), S-SSC; LAKE,
RIVER, SPRING

Southern bald eagle (*Haliaeetus leucocephalus leucocephalus*), S & F-T; LAKE,
RIVER

Black rail (*Laterallus jamaicensis*), F-SMC;
LAKE (marshy lake borders)

Wood stork (*Mycteria americana*), S & F-E;
LAKE, RIVER

Osprey (*Pandion haliaetus*), S-SSC in
Monroe County only; LAKE, RIVER

Everglades snail kite (*Rostrhamus sociabilis
plumbeus*), S & F-E, LAKE, RIVER

Least tern (*Sterna antillarum antillarum*),
S-T; RIVER

MAMMALS

Everglades mink (*Mustela vison
evergladensis*), S-T; RIVER

Southeastern brown bat (*Myotis austroriparius*), F-SMC; RIVER, LAKE

Gray bat (*Myotis grisescens*), S & F-E;
RIVER, LAKE

Indiana bat (*Myotis sodalis*), S & F-E;
RIVER, LAKE

Florida manatee (*Trichechus manatus
latirostris*), S & F-E; RIVER, SPRING (also
Lake Okeechobee)

REPTILES AND AMPHIBIANS

Gulf hammock dwarf siren (*Pseudobranchus striatus lustricolus*), F-SMC; LAKE
(endemic, also drainage ditches)

Pine barrens treefrog (*Hyla andersoni*),
S-SSC; RIVER (seepage streams)

Dusky gopher frog (*Rana capito sevosa*),
S-SSC, F-CAND; LAKE (breeding)

Florida gopher frog (*Rana capito aesopus*),
S-SSC, F-SMC; LAKE (breeding)

Florida bog frog (*Rana okaloosae*), S-SSC,
F-SMC; RIVER (seepage streams, endemic)

American alligator (*Alligator mississippiensis*), S-SSC, F-T (similar appearance to the
American crocodile); LAKE, RIVER, SPRING

Barbour's map turtle (*Graptemys barbouri*),
S-SSC, F-SMC; RIVER, SPRING

Striped mud turtle, Lower Keys population
(*Kinosternon bauri*), S-E; LAKE (coastal
rockland lake)

Alligator snapping turtle (*Macroclemys
temmincki*), S-SSC, F-SMC; RIVER, LAKE,
SPRING

Suwannee cooter (*Pseudemys concinna
suwanniensis*), S-SSC; RIVER, SPRING
(endemic)

SPONGES

Kissimmee sponge (*Ephydatia subtilis*),
F-SMC; LAKE (endemic, may be extinct)

CRUSTACEANS

Florida cave amphipod (*Crangonyx grandi-*

manus), F-SMC; SPRING (associated with aquatic caves)

Orange-Seminole cave crayfish (*Procambarus acherontis*), F-SMC; SPRING (endemic)

Black Creek crayfish (*Procambarus pictus*), S-SSC, F-SMC; RIVER (endemic)

INSECTS

Zigzag blackwater caddisfly (*Agarodes ziczac*), F-SMC; RIVER, SPRING (endemic)

Say's spiketail dragonfly (*Cordulegaster sayi*), F-SMC, RIVER, SPRING (seepage streams)

American sand-burrowing mayfly (*Dolania americana*), F-SMC; RIVER

Bronze clubtail dragonfly (*Gomphus townesi*), F-SMC; RIVER

Westfall's clubtail dragonfly (*Gomphus westfalli*), F-SMC; RIVER

Blackwater sand-filtering mayfly (*Homoeoneuria dolani*), F-SMC; RIVER

Apalachicola twilight skimmer dragonfly (*Neurocordulia clara*), F-SMC; RIVER

Provost's ochrotrichian microcaddisfly (*Ochrotrichia provosti*), F-SMC; RIVER, SPRING (endemic)

Little oecetis longhorn caddisfly (*Oecetis parva*), F-SMC; LAKE (endemic, may be extinct)

Florida oxyethiran microcaddisfly (*Oxyethira florida*), F-SMC; LAKE, RIVER

Variegated clubtail dragonfly (*Progomphus bellei*), F-SMC; LAKE, RIVER,, SPRING

Three-tooth long-horned triaenodes caddisfly (*Triaenodes tridonta*), F-SMC (precise microhabitat unknown, but surely riparian)

MOLLUSKS

Florida arc mussel (*Alasmidonta wrightiana*), F-SMC; RIVER (endemic, possibly extinct)

Fat three-ridge mussel (*Amblema neislerii*), F-SMC; RIVER

Blue Spring hydrobe snail (*Aphaostracon asthenes*), F-SMC; SPRING (endemic)

Wekiwa Springs hydrobe snail (*Aphaostracon monas*), F-SMC; SPRING (endemic)

Dense hydrobe snail (*Aphaostracon pycnus*), F-SMC; SPRING (endemic)

Fenny Spring hydrobe snail (*Aphaostracon xynoelictus*), F-SMC; SPRING (endemic)

Helicoid spring snail (*Cincinnatia helicogyra*), F-SMC; SPRING (endemic)

Enterprise silt snail (*Cincinnatia monroensis*), F-SMC; SPRING (spring seepage run, endemic)

Ichetucknee silt snail (*Cincinnatia mica*), F-SMC; SPRING (endemic)

Pygmy silt snail (*Cincinnatia parva*), F-SMC; SPRING (endemic)

Ponderous silt snail (*Cincinnatia ponderosa*), F-SMC; SPRING (endemic)

Seminole silt snail (*Cincinnatia vanhyningi*), F-SMC; SPRING (endemic)

Wekiwa silt snail (*Cincinnatia wekiwae*), F-SMC; SPRING (endemic)

Purple bankclimber mussel (*Elliptoideus sloatianus*), F-SMC, RIVER

Narrow pigtoe mussel (*Fusconaia escambia*), F-SMC; RIVER

Albany snail (*Goniobasis albanyensis*), F-SMC; RIVER

Southern sandshell mussel (*Lampsilis australis*), F-SMC; RIVER

Shiny-rayed pocketbook mussel (*Lampsilis subangulata*), F-SMC; RIVER

Oval pigtoe mussel (*Pleuroblema pyriforme*), F-SMC; RIVER

Southern kidneyshell mussel (*Ptychobranchus jonesi*), F-SMC; RIVER

Choctaw pearly mussel (*Villosa choctawensis*), F-SMC; RIVER

FRESHWATER AND SALTWATER MARSH COMMUNITIES

Marshes, both freshwater and saltwater, are prairielike, treeless, or nearly treeless wetlands where herbaceous plants are the dominant floral species. The water depth fluctuates regularly but remains shallow.

Freshwater Marshes, Including the Everglades

A number of fairly distinct types of freshwater marshes occur in Florida, including wet prairie, submerged marsh, cattail marsh, water lily marsh, flag marsh, and saw grass marsh. Dominant plant species vary considerably with latitude and physiological makeup. They include such species as pondweed (*Potamogeton* spp.), saw grass (*Cladium jamaicensis*, which is actually a sedge), cordgrass (*Spartina bakeri*), St. John's wort (*Hypericum fasciculatum*), white water lily (*Nymphaea odorata*), fire flag (*Thalia geniculata*), bulrush (*Scirpus*), spike rush (*Eleocharis elongata*), pickerelweed (*Pontederia cordata*), and cattail (*Typha domingensis*). Marshes have a rich plant diversity (more than 300 taxa have been recorded in some marsh ecosystems), and wet prairies generally have the highest plant diversity. Fire frequency and hydroperiods also vary considerably among freshwater marsh types. Submerged and water lily marshes generally have the longest hydroperiods and lowest fire frequencies; wet prairies typically have the shortest hydroperiods and highest fire frequencies. Saw grass, cattail, and flag marshes usually fall somewhere in between.

Florida's freshwater marshes also support a large number of animal species. Characteristic invertebrates

Storm over freshwater marsh, Loxahatchee National Wildlife Refuge, Palm Beach County.

include various insects (mosquitoes, dragonflies, mayflies, and others); mollusks, including apple snails (*Pomacea paludosa*) and Seminole ramshorn (*Planorbella duryi*); and crayfish (*Procambarus alleni* and *P. fallax*). Typical fishes include mosquito fish, Florida gar (*Lepisosteus platyrhincus*), largemouth bass, and several species of bluegill. Reptiles and amphibians are well represented. The American alligator is *the* characteristic marsh reptile. Although occurring in many aquatic habitats, these formidable crocodilians reach their greatest abundance in marshes. Several semiaquatic snakes inhabit freshwater marshes, including crayfish snakes (*Regina*), black swamp snakes (*Seminatrix*), peninsula ribbon snakes, three species of water snakes (*Nerodia*), and venomous cottonmouths. Common turtles include mud turtles (*Kinosternon*),

Florida softshell turtles (*Apalone ferox*), and cooters and redbelly turtles (*Pseudemys*). Florida's freshwater marshes also teem with amphibians, including several species of sirens, a large aquatic salamander, several species of treefrogs, cricket frogs (*Acris*), and several species of true frogs (Rana).

Florida's freshwater marshes attract many of the same bird species found in salt marshes. Typical species include herons, egrets, ibises, bitterns, rails, common yellowthroat (*Geothlypis trichas*), boat-tailed grackle (*Quiscalus major*), and red-winged blackbirds (*Agelaius phoeniceus*). The endangered wood stork is an indicator species of healthy marshes. The Everglades nesting population of wood storks has dropped from approximately 6,000 birds in the 1960s to about 500 in recent years. Representative mammals include

Wet prairie, Ocala National Forest, Marion County.

raccoons, marsh rabbits (*Sylvilagus palustris*), and river otters. Listed animal species associated with Florida's freshwater marshes include the Cape Sable seaside sparrow, snail kite, Florida sandhill crane, Everglades mink, Florida panther (southern Florida only), and round-tailed muskrat.

Easily the most renowned of Florida's freshwater marshes is South Florida's 40-by-100-mile sheet-flow ecosystem known as the Everglades. Saw grass marsh comprises a significant portion of the Everglades landscape, but the system also includes other habitats, such as tropical hardwood hammocks, rockland pine forests, cypress swamps, dwarf cypress forests, sloughs, alligator holes, mangrove swamps, and other estuarine habitats bordering Florida Bay. Alligator holes, which are pondlike depressions dug and maintained by adult alligators, are an important component of the Everglades landscape, providing refuge to many aquatic and semiaquatic species during the winter dry season.

Not only is the Everglades Florida's most famous ecosystem, but it is also its most exploited and impaired. Historically, the Everglades watershed covered a vast area originating just south of present-day Orlando. It was and is strongly influenced by the Kissimmee River and Lake Okeechobee. When the first Europeans arrived in South Florida, it was a harsh and nearly impenetrable wilderness. Within a relatively short time, during the late 1800s and early 1900s, humans drastically altered and exploited the famous river of grass.

In the late 1800s the multimillion-dollar plume industry, centered in New York City, motivated South Florida

settlers, American Indians, and hunters from near and far to slaughter unmercifully millions of wading birds, harvesting their pretty feathers as decorations for ladies' hats. Entire rookeries were shot by marksmen armed with .22-caliber rifles. After nearly a quarter-century of carnage, some species, including reddish egrets and roseate spoonbills, were reduced to a dozen or fewer pairs. The Florida Audubon Society, incorporated in 1901, was instrumental in pressing for legislation that protected wading birds, undoubtedly saving some species from extinction. Plume harvesting was just one of many threats to come.

The most serious threat to the entire Everglades landscape has been the replumbing of the glades that began in the early 1900s. Early settlers attempted to tame this wilderness by draining the Everglades and converting wetlands to agricultural fields, not an easy task, but one tried in earnest. That was coupled with attempts to redirect large quantities of fresh water from its natural flow to Florida Bay toward several quickly growing Atlantic Coast cities. This was accomplished by excavating a network of enormous canals, totaling about 1,400 miles. The natural sheet flow was also precluded by the construction of huge levees and dikes and by the extensive straightening of the Kissimmee River by the Army Corps of Engineers. Today the amount of water, with the exception of rainfall, that enters Everglades National Park is for the most part controlled by the South Florida Water Management District. Currently the megalopolis of southeastern Florida uses more water each year than Everglades National Park receives. Scientists also blame the diversion of Everglades water for the slow death of Florida Bay. A momentous and unnatural increase of salinity in Florida Bay has precipitated the death of massive sea grass beds. Large and persistent algae blooms began forming in Florida Bay in the fall of 1991. The formerly healthy body of water, which supported large populations of fish, crustaceans, mollusks, sponges, and wading birds, is now ill. Nature's sheet-flow design, which evolved some 5,000 years ago, has not functioned properly for nearly a century now.

In 1995 catastrophic flooding caused the highest water levels in more than 30 years (after two years of unusually heavy precipitation) and took a serious toll on the Everglades flora and fauna. The severe flooding would probably not have occurred if the Everglades had been functioning as designed by Mother Nature. An estimated 90 percent of the Everglades deer herd was lost as a result of the flooding. An entire population of endangered Cape Sable seaside sparrows inhabiting Everglades National Park is believed to have perished. Biologists fear the persistent high water of 1995 may cause a number of lasting, possibly permanent changes to the environment. Large tracts of drowned maples, bays, strangler figs, live oaks, and other trees may die, losing their leaves and their ability to provide shade to the understory and floor of numerous tree islands within the Everglades ecosystem. As these trees take decades to mature, the microclimate of the hammocks may be altered for many years. Though flooding has been pernicious for many species, a few species may have benefited from extreme water levels. A number of aquatic plants

and fishes occurring in formerly droughty localities are now abundant.

Nearly 500,000 acres of former Everglades wetlands is now the Everglades Agricultural Area. Massive sugarcane plantations were established to the east and southeast of Lake Okeechobee. The federal government has subsidized Everglades sugarcane growers and furnished free water for irrigation and cheap drainage since 1934. Sugarcane plantation owners are often at odds with environmentalists, who assert that the pollutants and nutrient-rich runoff from the plantations are deleterious to the delicate ecosystems to their south. Attempts to divert that runoff water away from the Everglades have altered other habitats by producing an unnatural abundance of cattails. The conflicts between the Everglades and the sugar barons have prompted government officials to seek serious remedies to the problems at hand.

Monumental plans are now being put into action to restore the Everglades. More than 25 federal, state, and local governmental agencies will be involved in some aspect of the grand scheme. The restoration is projected to cost what some people consider an excessive sum. Others, however, consider the alterations absolutely essential and a small price to pay. Proposals include the remeandering of the Kissimmee River, which may exceed $400 million and is the largest project undertaken by the Army Corps of Engineers since the Panama Canal. It may be necessary to alter Lake Okeechobee's water level at a cost of several hundred million dollars more. Converting sugarcane plantations into water-holding areas or stormwater treatment areas to filter polluted waters may cost nearly a billion. The estimated expense of widening and deepening certain canals to supply the Everglades with more water is $300 million. The strategic removal of particular levees to promote the natural sheet flow will cost at least $230 million. The eradication of invasive, introduced, exotic plants will run into the tens of millions of dollars. Other projects deemed necessary would restore the natural flow of water between the Everglades and Big Cypress Swamp, restore the flow of water to southeastern Dade County, and, last but definitely not least, restore the natural balance of fresh and salt water to Florida Bay. Those final three tasks are expected to cost hundreds of millions of dollars.

Mercury (specifically methylmercury, a toxic, organically bound form of mercury) is another serious threat to the Everglades. Toxic levels of mercury have been found in many faunal species and apparently are responsible for several Florida panther deaths within Everglades National Park; the local largemouth bass have also been rendered unsuitable for consumption by mercury levels. Official notices were posted warning the public not to eat certain fishes caught in Florida Bay more than once a month. So where did this toxic substance suddenly come from? A number of theories exist. Some authorities contend that methylmercury occurs naturally in the Everglades, in deep subterranean peat accumulations, and that drainage of the wetlands has exposed the mercury and allowed it to accumulate in the food chain. Others believe that airborne introduction from burning sugarcane fields, paint and medical wastes, and fossil-fuel power plants

is to blame. Increased mercury levels in water and the atmosphere are not restricted to the Everglades or Florida, for that matter. More research is needed to determine the causes and solutions to this environmental hazard.

The threats seem to be proliferating. South Florida's wading birds are threatened by a parasitic disease known as eustrongylidosis. The larvae of a roundworm (*Eustrongylides ignotus*), which thrives in nutrient-rich runoff waters, are readily eaten by fish, which are consumed by wading birds, which when infected may weaken and die. Numerous threats to the Everglades and other freshwater marshes stem from the introduction of exotic plants and animals. Exotics are more prevalent in southern Florida, with more than 200 exotic plant species recorded in the Everglades alone. Among the most detrimental are melaleuca, Brazilian pepper, Australian pine, and downy myrtle, which have upset the natural balance of many ecosystems. Florida's marsh communities have also been invaded by a multitude of problematic exotic animals. One example is the blue tilapia (*Tilapia aurea*), a species that devours quantities of native marsh vegetation. Off-road vehicles such as four-wheel-drive trucks, all-terrain three and four wheelers, swamp buggies, and half- and full-tracks damage marshlands by forming deep ruts that may cause an unnatural channeling of water. A single pass of a vehicle may cut ruts that remain for years. Off-road vehicles and airboats also disturb wildlife, particularly nesting birds.

Marjory Stoneman Douglas (whose name is synonymous with conservation and the Everglades) said in regard to saving the Everglades, "It isn't a question of being optimistic or pessimistic. It's got to be done. The Everglades is a test. If we pass it, we get to keep the planet."

Excellent examples of Florida's freshwater marsh ecosystems can be visited at Everglades National Park, at Loxahatchee National Wildlife Refuge, along the Kissimmee and St. Johns river corridors, and at Payne's Prairie in Alachua County.

Salt Marshes

Salt marshes differ from freshwater marshes in several ways, but the most obvious differences involve water salinities and hydroperiods. Salt marsh hydroperiods are directly linked to tides. Florida's salt marshes occupy coastal intertidal zones where wave energy is low. Their estuarine environments are much the same as those occupied by mangrove swamps, except that salt marshes generally predominate north of the freeze line and mangrove swamps generally predominate south of the line. Salt marshes, like mangrove swamps, are among the earth's most biologically productive ecosystems, and they are quite prolific in many coastal areas of northern Florida and the Panhandle, with wide expanses occurring at the mouths of larger rivers. Florida's salt marshes are filled with various salt-tolerant grasses, sedges, and rushes, and usually have a network of drainage creeks. Their characteristic flora includes extensive dense growths of black needlerush (*Juncus roemerianus*) and smooth cordgrass (*Spartina alterniflora*). At slightly higher elevations, shoreside of the black needlerush low marsh, and on berms and ridges within the marsh, there are often annual and perennial glassworts (*Salicornia* spp.),

leather ferns (*Acrostichum aureum*), saltworts (*Batis maritima*), beach dropseed, salt meadow cordgrass (*Spartina patens*), salt marsh asters (*Aster tenuifolius*), sea oxeye (*Borrichia* spp.), saltgrass (*Distichlis spicata*), and other salt marsh vegetation. Vegetation occupying higher adjacent areas often includes saltbush (*Baccharis halimifolia*), Christmas berry (*Lycium carolinianum*), and sea blite (*Suaeda linearis*). Mangroves often occur sparingly in more southern salt marshes.

The diversity of animal life occurring in salt marshes exceeds that of freshwater marshes, primarily because of the additional marine affinities. Salt marsh animals have evolved various adaptations enabling them to endure harsh, saline

Brackish salt marsh, Lower Suwannee National Wildlife Refuge, Levy County.

environments. Some animals, especially mammals, survive by moving back and forth between salt marshes and adjacent terrestrial habitats. Animals that take advantage of that strategy, known as transient species, include raccoons, marsh rabbits (*Sylvilagus palustris*), cotton rats (*Sigmodon hispidus*), and cotton mice. Rice rats and round-tailed muskrats, a species of special concern, have adapted well to salt marsh life, as have endangered Florida salt marsh voles, which exist nowhere but salt marshes. Manatees are periodic visitors to the deeper waters on the outer periphery of salt marshes.

Mollusks and crustaceans are well represented in salt marsh communities. Typical species include commercially valuable oysters (*Crassostrea virginica*), blue crabs (*Callinectes sapidus*), and shrimp, along with marsh snails (Littorinidae and Ellobiidae), periwinkle snails (*Littorina irrorata*), mud snails (Nassariidae), ribbed mussels (*Geukensia demissa*), coffee bean snails (*Melampus coffeus*), marsh crabs (*Sesarma* spp.), and fiddler crabs (*Uca* spp.). The hundreds of benthic microalgae and phytoplankton taxa inhabiting salt marshes are an important food source for crustaceans, mollusks, and other organisms. The extensive burrows of fiddler crabs are believed to stimulate the growth of smooth cordgrass, a keystone salt marsh species.

Typical salt marsh insects and arachnids include juice-feeding planthopper grasshoppers (*Prokelesia marginata*), tissue-eating tettigoniid grasshoppers (*Orchelimum concinnum*), wasps, and spiders. Characteristic birds of Florida's salt marshes include Worthington's and Marian's marsh wrens (*Cistothorus palustris griseus* and *C. p. marianae*);

Cape Sable, Scott's, and Wakulla seaside sparrows (*Ammodramus maritimus* ssp.), all listed taxa; rails; ospreys; fish crows (*Corvus ossifragus*); and numerous wading birds. The recently extinct dusky seaside sparrow was restricted to the salt marshes of Volusia and Brevard counties. As one would expect, the herpetofauna of salt marshes is relatively depauperate. The few species generally restricted to salt marsh environments include Atlantic, Gulf, and mangrove salt marsh snakes (*Nerodia clarki*) and diamondback terrapins (*Malaclemys terrapin*). The American alligator, though generally thought of as a freshwater inhabitant, is actually quite common in some salt marsh communities.

An immense number of fishes, including many commercially and recreationally important species, spend all or part of their lives in salt marshes. They include common snook (*Centropomus undecimalis*), tarpon (*Megalops atlanticus*), spot (*Leiostomus xanthurus*), red drum (*Sciaenops ocellatus*), and mullet (*Mugil* spp.). Smaller fishes such as minnows, killifishes, gambusia, and pinfish favor shallow waters, and larger sharks and rays are often present in deeper waters.

In addition to providing food, refuge, and nursery grounds to myriad lifeforms, salt marshes also act as buffers, protecting Florida's coastline from violent storms. They also reduce, to some degree, the harmful effects of pollution by functioning as a filter. Since 1900 human activities have degraded the health of many of Florida's salt marshes. To accommodate the exploding urbanization along Florida's coastline, many salt marshes were filled. Approximately half of Tampa Bay's salt marshes have been filled and converted to commercial or residential sites. Thousands of dikes and marsh impoundments were constructed to control bothersome mosquitoes, a common salt marsh denizen. Marsh impoundments have altered natural water fluctuations, causing population declines and extirpations of plant and animal species, and induced the invasion of exotic species. Impoundment of Brevard County's salt marshes is largely to blame for the demise of the dusky seaside sparrow. Recently, in an effort to restore marshes to their natural condition, a number of impoundments have been removed. After years of spraying DDT over America's salt marshes to repress mosquitoes, the practice was finally recognized as another ominous environmental threat with dire, long-lasting consequences. Salt marshes are also threatened by the dumping of industrial and domestic wastes in or near them. Until recently, it was a fairly common practice for smaller towns to discharge sewage directly into salt marshes. Future sea level rises associated with global warming are expected to constitute a serious threat to all coastal ecosystems.

Nearly pristine salt marshes can be visited at Merritt Island, Cedar Keys, and St. Marks national wildlife refuges; Everglades National Park and Canaveral and Gulf Islands national seashores; and the state park lands of Fort Clinch, Amelia Island, Little Talbot Island, Big Talbot Island, Guana River, Anastasia, Waccasassa Bay, Cedar Key Scrub, St. George Island, St. Joseph Peninsula, Ecofina River, and Big Lagoon.

Floridians can help preserve the marshes associated with Indian River by purchasing the Indian River Lagoon license plate, which displays a common snook, when renewing their automobile registration.

State and Federally Listed Animals of Florida's Marsh Ecosystems

S, State
F, Federal
E, Endangered
T, Threatened
SSC, Species of Special Concern, a state classification
SMC, Species of Management Concern, a federal classification
CAND, Candidate, a federal classification
FRESH, Freshwater marsh
SALT, Salt marsh and brackish marsh

FISHES

Shortnose sturgeon (*Acipenser brevirostrum*), S & F-E; SALT
Gulf sturgeon (*Acipenser oxyrinchus desotoi*), S-SSC, F-T; SALT
Atlantic sturgeon (*Acipenser oxyrinchus oxyrinchus*), S-SSC; SALT
Common snook (*Centropomus undecimalis*), S-SSC; SALT
Salt marsh topminnow (*Fundulus jenkinsi*), S-SSC; SALT
Mangrove rivulus (*Rivulus marmoratus*), S-SSC; SALT

BIRDS

Wakulla seaside sparrow (*Ammodramus maritimus juncicolus*), S-SSC, F-SMC; SALT
Cape Sable seaside sparrow (*Ammodramus maritimus mirabilis*), S & F-E; FRESH, SALT
Scott's seaside sparrow (*Ammodramus maritimus peninsulae*), S-SSC; SALT
Florida grasshopper sparrow (*Ammodramus savannarum floridanus*), S & F-E; FRESH
Limpkin (*Aramus guarauna*), S-SSC; FRESH

Worthington's marsh wren (*Cistothorus palustris griseus*), S-SSC; SALT

Marian's marsh wren (*Cistothorus palustris marianae*), S-SSC; SALT

Little blue heron (*Egretta caerulea*), S-SSC; FRESH, SALT

Reddish egret (*Egretta rufescens*), S-SSC, F-SMC; SALT

Snowy egret (*Egretta thula*), S-SSC; FRESH, SALT

Tricolored heron (*Egretta tricolor*), S-SSC; FRESH, SALT

White ibis (*Eudocimus albus*), S-SSC; FRESH, SALT

Florida sandhill crane (*Grus canadensis pratensis*), S-T; FRESH (wet prairies)

Whooping crane (*Grus americana*), S-SSC, F-T (experimental population); FRESH (wet prairies)

Southern bald eagle (*Haliaeetus leucocephalus leucocephalus*), S & F-T; FRESH, SALT

Black rail (*Laterallus jamaicensis*), F-SMC; SALT, FRESH

Wood stork (*Mycteria americana*), S & F-E; FRESH, SALT

Osprey (*Pandion haliaetus*), S-SSC in Monroe County only; SALT, FRESH

Everglades snail kite (*Rostrhamus sociabilis plumbeus*), S & F-E; FRESH

MAMMALS

Sherman's short-tailed shrew (*Blarina carolinensis shermani*), S-SSC, F-SMC; FRESH (wet prairies)

Florida panther (*Puma concolor coryi*), S & F-E; FRESH, occasionally SALT

Florida salt marsh vole (*Microtus pennsylvanicus dukecampbelli*), S & F-E; SALT (endemic)

Everglades mink (*Mustela vison evergladensis*), S-T; primarily FRESH, occasionally SALT (endemic)

Round-tailed muskrat (*Neofiber alleni*), F-SMC; FRESH, SALT

Silver rice rat (*Oryzomys argentatus*), S & F-E; SALT, FRESH (endemic)

Sanibel Island rice rat (*Oryzomys palustris sanibeli*), S-SSC; FRESH, SALT (endemic)

Key deer (*Odocoileus virginianus clavium*), S & F-E; SALT (endemic)

Key Vaca raccoon (*Procyon lotor auspicatus*), F-SMC; SALT (endemic)

Key West raccoon (*Procyon lotor incautus*), F-SMC; SALT (endemic)

Insular hispid cotton rat (*Sigmodon hispidus insulicola*), F-SMC; FRESH, SALT

Lower Keys marsh rabbit (*Sylvilagus palustris hefneri*), S & F-E; SALT (endemic)

Florida manatee (*Trichechus manatus latirostris*), S & F-E; SALT, FRESH (waterways within)

REPTILES AND AMPHIBIANS

American alligator (*Alligator mississippiensis*), S-SSC, F-T (similar appearance to the American crocodile); FRESH, SALT

American crocodile (*Crocodylus acutus*), S & F-E; occasional in SALT, prefers mangrove swamps and saline lakes

Eastern indigo snake (*Drymarchon corais couperi*), S & F-T; FRESH, SALT (ecotones)

Atlantic salt marsh snake (*Nerodia clarki taeniata*), S & F-T; SALT (endemic)

Gulf salt marsh snake (*Nerodia c. clarki*), F-SMC; SALT

Peninsula ribbon snake, Lower Keys population (*Thamnophis sauritus sackeni*), S-T; SALT, FRESH (endemic)

MANGROVE COMMUNITIES

Mangrove communities in Florida are often composed of three mangrove species, closely related buttonwood trees (*Conocarpus erectus*), and a number of other salt-tolerant plant species. The web of life is probably more apparent in these mangrove ecosystems than in any other type of ecosystem in Florida. The leaves, twigs, and other organic particles or detritus that accumulate in mangrove swamps are broken down by simple organisms, the bacteria and fungi at one end of the food chain. These small particles are consumed by larger organisms such as shrimp and small fish, which are consumed by larger fish, which in turn are preyed on by bald eagles, ospreys, crocodiles, and other organisms representing the other end of the food chain. That process is imperative to maintaining the biodiversity of the ecosystem as well as surrounding habitats. Mangrove communities are also crucial to the survival of many marine species because the provide nursery grounds and shallow-water refuges in the mangrove's intricate root systems. Among them are many species important to commercial and recreational fishing industries, such as snook, tarpon, mangrove snapper (*Lutjanus apodus*), spiny lobster (*Panulirus argus*), oysters, and pink shrimp (*Penaeus duorarum*). This ecosystem also supports larger animals, including endangered Florida manatees and threatened Florida black bears. In fact, research has revealed that bears in southwest Florida use mangrove forests extensively. Mangroves also serve as land stabilizers by trapping sediments washed in by the sea and out from the mainland, thus maintaining and protecting coastal areas. The canopy towering above the shallow, nutrient-rich water and prop roots provides nesting and roosting sites to many birds. One such listed species, the white-crowned pigeon,

feeds on native fruits of nearby tropical hammocks. Florida prairie warblers (*Dendroica discolor paludicola*) and Cuban yellow warblers (*Dendroica petechia gundlachi*) nest almost exclusively in mangroves. Numerous wading birds, shorebirds, pelicans, magnificent frigatebirds (*Fregata magnificens*), mangrove cuckoos, kingfishers, cormorants, songbirds, and raptors use mangroves for nesting, roosting, or foraging activities. Invertebrate species commonly associated with mangroves include mangrove crabs (*Aratus pisonii* and *Goniopsis cruentata*). Insect species largely restricted to mangrove communities include the mangrove skipper (*Phocides pigmalion okeechobee*), mangrove buckeye (*Junonia evarette*), and the Cape Sable longhorn beetle (*Heterachthes sablensis*). Mangrove communities also serve as filters, lessening the effect of pollution on coral reefs, sea grass beds, and other sensitive ecosystems on their seaward side.

Mangroves are essentially tropical or subtropical species that are restricted to coastal regions of Florida's peninsula. Mangroves increase in number and size as one travels south. They reach their greatest abundance in the Ten Thousand Islands wilderness of Collier County and in the Florida Keys. Black mangrove (*Avicennia germinans*), the most cold-tolerant and widely distributed species, has been recorded as far north as Shell Island, Bay County, on the Gulf Coast and sporadically to St. Johns County on the Atlantic Coast. Northern stragglers are usually scrawny, waist-high shrubs. The white mangrove (*Laguncularia racemosa*) has been recorded as far north as the Cedar Keys of Levy County on the Gulf Coast and Volusia County

Mangrove community, John Pennekamp Coral Reef State Park, Key Largo, Monroe County.

on Florida's Atlantic Coast. The red mangrove (*Rhizophora mangle*) occurs on Florida's Gulf Coast as far north as Hernando County (rarely) and to Brevard County on the east coast. Since the early 1900s, mangroves have been slowly migrating northward along Florida's coasts. Though the species are absent from the coastal regions of other southeastern states, mangrove swamps thrive on Bermuda, which lies in the Gulf Stream 570 miles east of North Carolina's Outer Banks. The buttonwood tree, a close ally of the white mangrove, has virtually the same distributional limits as red mangroves.

Each mangrove species occupies its own niche within the ecosystem. Not being as salt-tolerant as other mangroves,

buttonwood trees typically occupy the innermost perimeter of the mangrove forest. White mangrove aggregations are generally closest to shore, with black mangroves growing slightly farther from shore and red mangroves at the outermost perimeter. Each mangrove species has evolved specialized processes to survive in harsh saltwater environments. Buttonwood, white mangrove, and black mangrove are salt-excreting species; they excrete excess salt through salt glands on their leaves. Red mangrove is a salt-exclusion species; it separates fresh water from sea water through a reverse-osmosis process. Red mangroves are known for their characteristic prop roots that spread out from the tree's base. Black mangroves use an extensive system of cable roots and pneumatophores (upright projections of the root system) that encircle the tree's base, sometimes appearing some distance from the base. White mangroves only rarely develop pneumatophores. True mangrove species reproduce by dropping partially developed propagules into the water, which are carried off by currents, sometimes far off, to mudflats or beaches. Seedling development of white and black mangroves is neither as obvious nor as specialized as it is for red mangroves. Mangrove coastal environments are similar to those of salt marshes farther north. Though mangroves can prosper in fresh water, they are outcompeted by hardier freshwater vascular plants. Conversely, other trees, even the domineering exotic melaleuca, have difficulty invading mangrove communities. Other plant species associated with mangrove habitats are glasswort (*Salicornia virginica*), saltwort, sea lavender (*Limonium carolinianum*), Christmas berry (*Lycium carolinianum*), and sea purslane (*Sesuvium portulacastrum*).

Before mangrove species were afforded legal protection, thousands upon thousands of acres were lost to commercial and residential development. Large parcels of mangroves were destroyed in Broward and Dade counties, Marco Island (Collier County), and the Tampa Bay area. Fortunately, significant tracts of Florida's mangrove habitat were saved, with nearly 500,000 acres existing today (90 percent of those are in Dade, Monroe, Collier, and Lee counties). The state of Florida has taken steps to restore mangrove habitat in many localities where it had been destroyed by human activities. Threats to mangrove communities

include dredge and fill operations, impounding or diking mangrove habitats (which alters natural water levels), and oil spills and other forms of pollution.

Extensive healthy stands of mangrove forest can be seen at Everglades and Biscayne national parks; Collier Seminole, John Pennekamp, Long Key, Bahia Honda, John D. MacArthur, and Cayo Costa state park lands; and J. N. "Ding" Darling, Ten Thousand Islands, Key Deer, Key West, and Great White Heron national wildlife refuges.

State and Federally Listed Animal Species of Mangrove Communities

S, State
F, Federal
E, Endangered
T, Threatened
SSC, Species of Special Concern, a state classification
SMC, Species of Management Concern, a federal classification
CAND, Candidate, a federal classification

FISH

Gulf sturgeon (*Acipenser oxyrinchus desotoi*), S-SSC, F-T (occasional)
Common snook (*Centropomus undecimalis*), S-SSC
Mangrove rivulus (*Rivulus marmoratus*), S-SSC
Key silverside (*Menidia conchorum*), S-T

BIRDS

Roseate spoonbill (*Ajaia ajaja*), S-SSC
White-crowned pigeon (*Columba leucocephala*), S-T, F-SMC
Little blue heron (*Egretta caerulea*), S-SSC
Reddish egret (*Egretta rufescens*), S-SSC, F-SMC

Snowy egret (*Egretta thula*), S-SSC

Tricolored heron (*Egretta tricolor*), S-SSC

White ibis (*Eudocimus albus*), S-SSC

Peregrine falcon (*Falco peregrinus*), S-E, F-T

Southeastern American kestrel (*Falco sparverius paulus*), S-T, F-SMC

American oystercatcher (*Haematopus palliatus*), S-SSC

Bald eagle (*Haliaeetus leucocephalus*), S & F-T

Wood stork (*Mycteria americana*), S & F-E

Osprey (*Pandion haliaetus*), S-SSC, Monroe County only

Brown pelican (*Pelecanus occidentalis*), S-SSC

Mangrove clapper rail (*Rallus longirostris insularum*), F-SMC

Black skimmer (*Rynchops niger*), S-SSC

MAMMALS

Everglades mink (*Mustela vison evergladensis*), S-T

Key deer (*Odocoileus virginianus clavium*), S & F-E

Florida panther (*Puma concolor coryi*), S & F-E (rarely)

Southeastern brown bat (*Myotis austroriparius*), F-SMC (has wintered in mangroves)

Silver rice rat (*Oryzomys argentatus*), S & F-E

Key Vaca raccoon (*Procyon lotor auspicatus*), F-SMC

Key West raccoon (*Procyon lotor incautus*), F-SMC

Big Cypress fox squirrel (*Sciurus niger avicennia*), S-T, F-SMC

Lower Keys marsh rabbit (*Sylvilagus palustris hefneri*), S & F-E (ecotones)

Florida manatee (*Trichechus manatus latirostris*), S & F-E

Florida black bear (*Ursus americanus floridanus*), S-T,F-SMC

REPTILES AND AMPHIBIANS

American crocodile (*Crocodylus acutus*), S & F-E

American alligator (*Alligator mississippiensis*), S-SSC, F-T (similar appearance to the American crocodile)

Rosy rat snake, or Lower Keys corn snake (*Elaphe guttata guttata*), S-SSC

Peninsula ribbon snake, Lower Keys population (*Thamnophis sauritus sackeni*), S-T

Atlantic green sea turtle (*Chelonia mydas mydas*), S & F-E

Atlantic hawksbill turtle (*Eretmochelys imbricata imbricata*), S & F-E

Atlantic loggerhead sea turtle (*Caretta caretta caretta*), S & F-T

Atlantic ridley turtle (*Lepidochelys kempi*), S & F-E

Striped mud turtle, Lower Keys population (*Kinosternon bauri*), S-E

Atlantic salt marsh snake (*Nerodia clarki taeniata*), S & F-T

Eastern indigo snake (*Drymarchon corais couperi*), S & F-T (ecotones)

CORAL REEFS AND RELATED MARINE ECOSYSTEMS

This category encompasses, besides living tropical coral reefs, vermetid reefs, worm reefs, oculina banks, and deep coral banks, plus artificial reefs and live-bottom and sea grass communities.

Living Tropical Coral Reefs

The coral reefs found in Florida's waters constitute yet another distinctive ecosystem unique to the Sunshine State. Florida's tropical coral reefs have been and continue to be immensely important to the state's economy. Commercial and recreational fishing and other reef-related activities (diving, snorkeling, ecotourism) have become a multibillion-dollar industry. The Florida Keys coral reef is the only living reef in the continental United States and the third largest on the planet. This particular reef system parallels the Florida Keys, several miles offshore between the Keys and the Straits of Florida, from the area of Key Biscayne south and west to the Dry Tortugas. Similar reef structures occur as far north as Palm Beach County; however, living corals are no longer constructing these reef formations.

Coral reefs are an assemblage of minuscule, columnar bodied, tentacled coral animals called polyps. These polyps affix themselves to limestone skeletons that, over time, create reefs. The most common and largest of the Florida Keys reef structures are bank reefs. The largest reef formations form on the Atlantic side of the larger keys, thus the largest bank reefs occur in the waters adjacent to the upper and lower Florida Keys, which occupy more longitudinal landmass. Coral species are most diverse on these outer bank reefs. The shallow waters between the bank reefs and the Keys archipelago accommodate the smaller, roundish patch reefs and sea grasses. The coralliferous structures of the reef, though they appear stable, are quite delicate and vulnerable to human incursions. Simply dropping an anchor onto a reef or

Living coral reef, Florida Keys National Marine Sanctuary, Monroe County. Though only about one tenth the size of Australia's Great Barrier Reef, coral reefs of the Florida Keys receive about 10 times the number of divers.
PHOTO COURTESY THE FLORIDA KEYS NATIONAL MARINE SANCTUARY.

brushing against coral formations when snorkeling or diving can destroy or seriously injure corals that took decades, possibly centuries, to construct. Many of the Keys reefs have sustained severe damage from vessel collisions and groundings. Coral reefs form and survive only in tepid, transparent, nutrient-free waters. The deeper sunlight can penetrate reef waters, the deeper the coral species can flourish. Events that diminish water quality in reef areas (such as introduction of nutrients from sewage, stormwater runoff, or fertilizers) adversely affect the health of living coral reefs by reducing water clarity and increasing algae blooms and coral diseases. Until 1990 the City of Key West continued to pump untreated sewage less than a mile offshore, and despite being outlawed for decades, several thousand cesspools still remain in the Keys. Scientists are increasingly concerned about the flow of nutrient-rich water into reef sites. Significant increases in deadly algae blooms on living coral at John Pennekamp State Park have been documented. A primary source is believed to be the nearby community of Ocean Reef, with its four fertilized golf courses and a thousand luxury yachts. For years, reef-toxic, nutrient-rich nitrogen fertilizer and raw sewage from boats have been washed out to neighboring coral reefs via a corridor called Dispatch Creek. Nutrient-rich runoff, even from hundreds of miles away, can have disastrous effects on reef systems. Runoff from the deforested rain forest of Venezuela's Orinoco River has produced detrimental effects on coral reefs of the Grenadine Islands, hundreds of miles away.

Natural events such as hurricanes and extended cold fronts may also damage reefs. Historically, the Florida Keys and the coastal area of extreme southeastern Florida have had the highest probability of direct hurricane strikes of any other area in Florida. Another malady for Florida's precious living coral reefs is known as white-line disease, which is capable of spreading at an extremely rapid rate. This affliction destroys primarily the beautiful star corals (*Montastrea* spp.), but it also kills or damages at least 17 other coral species. It was first reported in Florida in the summer of 1996 and is now widespread in the Keys. White-line disease has killed nearly 50 percent of the star coral in some areas, turning the formerly colorful coral into bleached skeletons.

The Florida Keys living coral reefs harbor a spectacular diversity of animal species. Hundreds of fish species, soft and stony corals, sponges, octopuses, shelled mollusks, crustaceans, algae, marine worms, birds, sea turtles, and marine mammals occur there, either as residents or visitors. Representatives of two classes of corals (Hydrozoa and Anthozoa) are found in this system. The most prevalent hydrozoan coral on shallow reefs is fire coral, or *Millepora,* with two species present, crenulated fire coral (*Millepora alcicornis*) and bladed fire coral (*Millepora complanata*). Fire corals are notorious for the painful sting they inflict when touched. The anthozoans are more diverse and include, at last count, 42 species of octocorals, 63 stony corals, and numerous forms of false corals, anemones, and zoanthids. Octocorals are represented by sea whips, sea fans, other gorgonians, sea plumes, and soft corals. Stony corals, or Scleractinia, secrete limestone skeletons and are critical to reef building processes.

Commercial harvesting and personal collecting of coral are serious threats to many coral species. Two species of black coral (*Antipathes pennacea* and *A. dichotoma*), formerly occurring in the Florida Keys, have been extirpated by commercial and personal collecting. Pillar coral (*Dendrogyra cylindrus*), an endangered species, has been heavily collected, as have flower corals (*Mussa angulosa* and *Eusmilia fastigiata*) and several brain corals. Strict state and federal laws now prohibit collection of most corals. Unlike stony corals, however, not all of Florida's soft corals are protected from collection. At least 20,000 pieces of soft coral, worth $15 million–20 million, are harvested from Florida's waters annually. Approximately 600,000 pounds of live rock are also removed annually from the state's waters for use in saltwater aquariums. The extraction of coral rock from marine habitats reduces the natural refuges used by countless sea creatures.

Many listed species frequent reef ecosystems, including sea turtles, especially the Atlantic green turtle and Atlantic hawksbill turtle. Florida manatees and several whale species are occasional visitors. The Caribbean monk seal, formally a native of the Keys, is now extinct. Approximately 450 species of fishes have been identified in the Keys coral reef ecosystems. They are of various shapes, sizes, and colors, including queen angelfish (*Holacanthus ciliaris*), rock beauty (*Holacanthus tricolor*), butterflyfish (*Chaetodon* spp.), parrotfish

(*Scarus* spp.), green and spotted moray eels (*Gymnothorax* spp.), and larger species such as manta rays (*Manta birostris*) and nurse sharks (*Ginglymostoma cirratum*). Occasionally whale sharks (*Rhincodon typus*), the largest of all fish, attaining a length of 60 feet, are seen here. The Key blenny is known from only one locality near Looe Key and one locality off Honduras. Fishes prized by anglers in reef habitats include grouper, snapper, hogfish, yellowtail, and barracuda. The harvest of another reef resident, the spiny lobster, is also important to the economy of the Florida Keys, with revenue now exceeding $15 million annually.

Well-known reef sites in the Upper Keys include Pacific Reef, French Reef, Molasses Reef, and Alligator Reef. In the Lower Keys, well-known sites include Looe Key, Maryland Shoal, Sambo Reefs, Marquesas Key, and the Dry Tortugas. Noteworthy examples of living coral reef formations can be seen at Biscayne National Park; Florida Keys, Key Largo, and Looe Key national marine sanctuaries; John Pennekamp Coral Reef State Park, and Fort Jefferson National Monument.

Because so many fishermen, boaters, divers, and snorkelers love our extraordinary living coral reefs, many are now in poor health and all are in jeopardy of being loved to death. For hundreds of years humans have exploited them, harvesting lobster, fish, sea turtles, shellfish, and beautiful corals. Visitation to Florida's coral reefs has increased so dramatically in the past two decades that experts now fear these reef ecosystems will not be able to sustain the ever-increasing use. About a dozen state and federal agencies share the responsibility of environmental management of the Keys coral reefs. The division of responsibilities among so many governmental agencies can, at times, complicate rather than simplify problematic issues. Options under consideration include closing the most heavily visited reefs, limiting numbers of divers and snorklelers on certain reefs, and creating artificial reefs to provide alternative dive sites. The Florida Marine Patrol, National Park Service, and Florida Department of Environmental Protection enforce laws enacted to preserve coral reefs and their inhabitants; however, that usually means that a violation is investigated after the damage has been done. Education, therefore, is the most important tool available to protect these sensitive ecosystems for future generations.

The Florida Keys Marine Sanctuary became a reality on 16 November 1990, when an act of Congress afforded protection to the extraordinary marine landscape of the Florida Keys Reef Tract. At 2,800 square nautical miles, it is the country's second largest marine sanctuary, running the entire length of the Keys from Biscayne Bay to the Dry Tortugas. It will soon encompass the previously established Key Largo National Marine Sanctuary and the Looe Key National Marine Sanctuary. Marine sanctuaries are managed by the National Oceanic and Atmospheric Administration. Managed much the same way as Australia's Great Barrier Reef Marine Park, the sanctuary is structured for multiple uses. Permitted activities include sport and commercial fishing with hook and line, limited take of lobster and stone crabs, diving, and boating, as long as they do not undermine the fundamental health and integrity of the area. Prohibited activities include dredging and filling, removing or damaging natural features, anchoring in a manner damaging to coral, discharging pollutants into water, and spearfishing. Some areas will remain closed for all but scientific research activities.

Sanctuary Guidelines for Boaters and Fishermen

NEVER drop an anchor onto or drag an anchor across a reef. Anchor buoy systems are in use at Looe Key NMS and several areas offshore from Key Largo.

BE extremely careful not to ground your boat. Groundings damage reefs and sea grass beds.

NEVER discharge bilge water at reefs.

NEVER dump trash or monofilament line at sea; it is illegal and harmful to wildlife.

MAINTAIN a considerable distance from mangroves when birds are nesting or roosting.

MAINTAIN safe distances from other boats and divers.

OBEY regulations pertaining to size and catch limits of fish.

Sanctuary Guidelines for Divers and Snorkelers

NEVER collect coral from reefs without permits; it is illegal.

NEVER touch coral. It may look firm, but even brushing against formations can seriously damage polyps.

WEAR float-coats so gear adjustments can be made without standing on coral.

DON'T feed fish or other fauna.

Report the illegal collecting of coral or conch shells, polluting of waters, or damaging of reefs to the Florida Marine Patrol at 1-800-DIAL-FMP. The livelihoods of many Florida Keys residents are directly dependent on the continuous flow of tourists to this archipelago to participate in one of many reef-related activities. The Florida Keys receive ten times as many divers annually as Australia's Great Barrier Reef, which is ten times larger. Florida's living coral reefs comprise the most popular diving destination on the planet.

Vermetid Reefs

These reefs occur in the shallow Gulf waters in the area of Marco Island and the Ten Thousand Islands in extreme southwestern Florida. The reef formations were produced by *Petaloconchus,* a wormlike mollusk species that is no longer constructing reefs, although it is still found in this region. Vermetid reefs provide shelter to stone crabs (*Menippe mercenaria*) and other marine fauna.

Worm Reefs

Worm reefs occur off Florida's Atlantic coast from Merritt Island to Key Biscayne. The best examples are found offshore from St. Lucie and Martin counties. They are constructed in fairly shallow waters by colonies of marine worms (*Phragmatopoma lapidosa*). The fragile tube formations, constructed of sand grains glued together, provide refuge and nursery grounds for spiny lobsters and many fishes.

Oculina Banks

These unusual, little known, and biologically important reefs are named after the ivory tree coral (*Oculina varicosa*) that builds them. Oculina banks generally occur in deeper waters (to 160 feet) well offshore from the Atlantic coastline, from Nassau County to St. Lucie County. Dense formations of ivory tree corals sometimes occur at the edge of the continental shelf. Oculina banks support a great diversity of marine life, including gastropod mollusks, bivalves, anemones, crabs, shrimp, black sea bass (*Centropristis striata*), and groupers. Because *Oculina* is a branching coral, it is vulnerable to damage from nets, dredges, anchors, and fishing tackle. Slow-growing oculina banks are also threatened by oil and gas exploration, red tides, and severe weather events.

Deep Coral Banks

Even less understood than vermetid and oculina reefs are the deep coral reefs at depths of 145–290 feet off the Gulf and Atlantic coasts of Florida. These banks resemble oculina banks but are formed by several species of branching corals, including *Enallopsammia profunda* and *Lophelia prolifera.* Commercially sought-after deep-sea crabs (*Geryon* spp.) inhabit deep coral banks with various other crustaceans and fish.

Artificial Reefs

Artificial reefs include many kinds of submerged man-made structures and vessels that have become permanent underwater fixtures, providing living quarters for a multitude of marine life. These structures include wrecked ships and aircraft, piers, bridge pilings, and oil platforms. Probably Florida's most unusual artificial reef is a surplus NASA rocket submerged in May 1996. Species utilizing artificial reefs often include many of the same species found in nearby bank reef or live-bottom communities. Many sunken vessels, such as the 1733 San Pedro Spanish fleet in about 18 feet of water off Indian Key and the *Blackthorn* shipwreck off Pinellas County, are well known to divers.

Live-bottom and Sea Grass Communities
These two ecologically important habitats are linked in many ways to coral reef ecosystems. Live-bottom communities occupy sea floors, artificial reefs, seawalls, and other submerged surfaces with a solid substratum, even boat bottoms. Live-bottom, also known as hardbottom, occurs where there is less than an inch of sediment on the limestone substrata. This biotic community is found in the shallow Atlantic and Gulf waters adjacent to the Keys, in Florida Bay, and several other offshore locations. Soft corals outnumber stony corals and include sea whips (*Pterogogia*), sea feathers, and sea plumes (*Pseudopterogorgia*), corky sea fingers (*Briareum asbestinum*), and sea fans (*Gorgonia ventalina*). The stony corals that do occur include rose coral (*Manicina areolata*), smooth starlet coral (*Siderastrea* spp.), and golfball coral (*Favia* spp.). Live-bottoms often harbor a variety of sponges, including vase, cake, sheepswool, loggerhead, stinker, grass, and bleeding sponges. Sponges are the chief dietary staple of the endangered hawksbill turtle. Solution holes, formed during the last ice age, are numerous in live-bottom communities. These craters provide refuges for spiny lobsters and myriad other creatures. Other characteristic sea life of live-bottom communities consists of queen conchs (*Strombus gigas*), basket starfish (*Astrophyton muricatum*), crabs (stone, arrow, and coral species),

and various annelid worms. Common fishes include oyster toadfish (*Opsanus tau*), damselfish (*Pomacentrus planifrons*), black margate (*Anisotremus surinamensis*), angelfish, and parrotfish.

Sea grasses cover approximately 3,300 square miles of southwest Florida's Gulf estuaries and bays, shallow open waters of Florida Bay, and much of the area adjacent to the living coral reefs of the Keys. In terms of biological importance, this ecosystem is among the most productive on the planet, serving as nursery and feeding grounds to multitudinous forms of marine life. Of the six species of sea grasses found in Florida, turtle grass (*Thalsassia testudinum*), manatee grass (*Syringodium filiforme*), and shoal grass (*Halodule wrightii*) are the most widespread and important. Sea grasses are the only flowering plants that live their entire lives exclusively in sea water. Vast numbers of algal species and invertebrates occur in sea grass biotas; among them are sea urchins, anemones, sponges, clams, spiny lobsters, and gastropods, including queen conchs and Florida fighting conchs (*Strombus alatus*). Larger, commercially important fishes, including sea bass, snappers (Lutjanidae), and drums (Sciaenidae), use sea grass beds as nursery grounds, as do many smaller species. Turtle grass in particular provides important food and shelter to sea turtles, hence the name. Green sea turtles are well known for congregating in sea grass beds. Bottlenose dolphins (*Turisiops truncatus*) and Florida manatees also frequent sea grass communities. Dredge-and-fill operations threaten sea grass beds by altering water clarity, thus reducing the penetration of light and interfering with photosynthesis by the keystone plant species.

State and Federally Listed Animal Species of Coral Reefs and Related Marine Ecosystems

S, State

F, Federal

E, Endangered

T, Threatened

SSC, Species of Special Concern, a state classification

SMC, Species of Management Concern, a federal classification

CAND, Candidate, a federal classification

FISHES

Common snook (*Centropomus undecimalis*), S-SSC

Key blenny (*Starksia starcki*), S-SSC

BIRDS

Osprey (*Pandion haliaetus*), S-SSC (Monroe County only)

Southern bald eagle (*Haliaeetus leucocephalus leucocephalus*), S & F-T

Brown pelican (*Pelecanus occidentalis*), S-SSC

Black skimmer (*Rynchops niger*), S-SSC

Least tern (*Sterna antillarum*), S-T

Caribbean roseate tern (*Sterna dougallii*), S & F-T

MAMMALS

Florida manatee (*Trichechus manatus latirostris*), S & F-E

Right whale (*Eubalaena glacialis*), S & F-E

Sei whale (*Balaenoptera borealis*), S & F-E (rare visitor)

Finback whale (*Balaenoptera physalus*), S & F-E

Humpback whale (*Megaptera novaeangliae*), S & F-E

Sperm whale (*Physeter macrocephalus*), S & F-E (rare visitor to shallow waters)

REPTILES

Atlantic green sea turtle (*Chelonia mydas mydas*), S & F-E

Atlantic hawksbill turtle (*Eretmochelys imbricata imbricata*), S & F-E

Atlantic loggerhead sea turtle (*Caretta caretta carretta*), S & F-T

Atlantic leatherback sea turtle (*Dermochelys coriacea coriacea*), S & F-E

Atlantic ridley turtle (*Lepidochelys kempi*), S & F-E

CORALS

Pillar coral (*Dendrogyra cylindrus*), S-E

SPECIES ACCOUNTS

The following accounts describe in detail Florida's 67 animal species, subspecies, and populations (excluding whales) designated as endangered or threatened by the federal or state government.

The U.S. Fish and Wildlife Service (USF&WS) defines "endangered species" as any species in danger of extinction throughout all or a significant portion of its range. The Florida Fish and Wildlife Conservation Commission (FWC) defines the term as any species, subspecies, or isolated population so few or depleted in number or so restricted in range or habitat (because of either manmade or natural factors) that it is in imminent danger of extinction or extirpation from the state or may attain such status within the immediate future.

"Threatened species" is defined by the USF&WS as any species likely to become an endangered species within the foreseeable future throughout all or a significant portion of its range. The FWC applies the term to any species, subspecies, or isolated population that is acutely vulnerable to environmental alteration, that is declining in number at a rapid rate, or whose range or habitat is declining in an area at a rapid rate, and as a consequence is destined or very likely to become an endangered species within the foreseeable future.

Those definitions, however, are deceptively simple. Determining which animals will be placed on the official lists of endangered or threatened species and receive protection is far from easy.

THE LISTING PROCESS: SO MANY SPECIES, SO LITTLE TIME

The listing process, at both the state and federal levels, is lengthy, involving many factors, not the least of which are politics and money. The majority of Floridians would certainly promote efforts to protect and preserve populations of Florida manatees, sea turtles, and Florida panthers, even if it meant paying a few extra tax dollars each year. On the other hand, the general public may be much less willing to protect species such as the Lake Placid funnel wolf spider. The Endangered Species Act was supposed to treat all species the same (think of it as an Equal Opportunity law applied to animals instead of job seekers), but here in the real world, it does not.

The state classification "species of special concern" and the federal designations "candidate" and "species of management concern" are used to classify animal species, subspecies, or populations that FWC or USF&WS biologists believe may be declining or are vulnerable to certain threats that may eventually result in listing them as threatened or endangered. In reviewing these lists, one may notice several apparent inconsistencies. Species such as the Florida mastiff bat and St. Andrew beach mouse, although considered endangered under Florida law, are ranked as mere candidate species by the USF&WS. Conversely, the endemic Squirrel Chimney cave shrimp, listed by the USF&WS as threatened, is not listed at all by the state of Florida. The Florida arc mussel, a species not recognized in any fashion by the FWC and listed as a mere species of management concern federally, has perhaps the most limited distribution of any North American mussel; it has not been seen since the 1930's and may very well be extinct. Many native invertebrates, such as the round-necked romulus beetle (*Romulus globosus*), are not listed by either agency despite being one of the rarest of Florida's insects, with just a handful of specimens ever recorded. As with most complex contemporary issues, these contradictions involve, among other things, legitimate professional disagreements, budgetary constraints and politics, and common sense. Money is the primary reason that all species do not receive equal protection. In many instances, one agency may allow the other agency to take the lead role in the listing and recovery efforts of a particular species so that it may devote more time and dollars to other species. Still, there is not enough money, nor are there enough biologists, to study and protect all of the species already listed from Florida or to add to the lists all the species that meet the criteria. Generally the largest and more publicly appealing species receive the most funding and thus the most protection. Invertebrates typically receive the lowest priority, with exceptionally rare species such as the round-necked romulus beetle not being listed by either agency.

STATE SPECIES OF SPECIAL CONCERN, FEDERAL CANDIDATE SPECIES, AND FEDERAL SPECIES OF MANAGEMENT CONCERN

The 51 Florida animals officially recognized as species of special concern by the FWC are afforded some degree of legal protection. Under Florida law, no person shall take, possess, transport, or sell any species of special concern or parts thereof or their nests or eggs except as authorized by commission regulations or by permit. Each of these species

1. has a significant vulnerability to habitat modification, environmental alteration, human disturbance, or human exploitation that may, in the foreseeable future, result in its becoming a threatened species, unless appropriate protective or management techniques are initiated or maintained, or

2. may already meet certain criteria for designation as a threatened species but conclusive data are limited or lacking, or

3. may occupy such an unusually vital or essential ecological niche that should it decline significantly in numbers or distribution, other species would be adversely affected to a significant degree, or

4. has not sufficiently recovered from past population depletion.

Species designated by the USF&WS as candidate species or species of management concern are not afforded legal protection under the Endangered Species Act; however, "the Service encourages their consideration in environmental planning, such as in environmental impact analysis under the National Environmental Policy Act of 1969." A total of 133 Florida animals are so designated. In 1996 the USF&WS revised and simplified the list of species formerly classified as candidates, which encompassed nearly 4,000 species in three separate categories: C-1, C-2, and C-3. Under the current system, only the 182 animals formerly deemed C-1 species retain the candidate classification; the USF&WS believes it has enough scientific information to warrant proposing them for listing as endangered or threatened under the Endangered Species Act. The remaining majority are now called species of management concern. The report issued by the USF&WS, dated 28 February 1996, states that other species "may be found to be in greater danger of extinction than some present candidate taxa."

HOW TO USE THE SPECIES ACCOUNTS

Each species account gives the following information about the animal being described:

Name: Includes common and scientific names.

Listed Status: Provides the current official state (FWC) and federal (USF&WS) designations and date of listing. For this treatment, "listed" includes endangered, threatened, species of special concern, and species of management concern. (See the appendix at the end of the Species Accounts for a list of species of special concern, candidate species, and species of management concern.) If applicable, the international designation under the Convention on International Trade in Endangered Species (CITES) is also noted.

Description: Describes identifying characteristics of the species in question, which may include size, shape, weight, coloration, scalation, plumage, voice, seasonal variations, and other distinctive physical characteristics. Characteristics that differentiate the species from closely related races or species similar in appearance are noted.

Distribution: Includes the current as well as historic geographic range of the species, subspecies, or population. In the case of listed subspecies or populations, the range of the species is also given.

Biology: Identifies the habitats utilized by the species, detailing (when known) habitat specialization or preference, seasonal variations of habitat use, and specific uses (such as nesting or foraging) of certain habitats, with an emphasis on elements of habitat that a species may depend on for survival. Species can generally be characterized as either habitat specialists (species that tend to be restricted to and adapted to a specific habitat or microhabitat) or habitat generalists (species that may utilize a variety of habitats and are not restricted to a particular environmental niche). Information on the animal's life history, activity patterns, reproductive biology, diet, predators, longevity, and other items of general interest are included in this section.

Cause of Decline, Threats: Describes contemporary and historic threats to the species, subspecies, or population in question.

Current Trend: Classifies the population of the species as:

Increasing—known to be increasing in numbers, or the threats to its continued existence in the wild are lessening.

Stable—known to have stable numbers in the recent past, and threats have remained relatively constant or diminished in the wild.

Declining—known to be decreasing in numbers, or threats to its existence are increasing in the wild.

Unknown—requires additional survey work to determine current status.

Extirpated—believed to be extinct in the wild statewide.

Extinct—believed to be extinct in the wild rangewide.

Florida Mastiff Bat
Eumops glaucinus floridanus
FAMILY MOLOSSIDAE; Order Chiroptera
LISTED STATUS
FWC: Endangered, listed 1993
USF&WS: Candidate
Description: The Florida mastiff bat, also known as Wagner's mastiff bat, is Florida's largest bat. The dimensions and weight of a male found in a residence in Coral Gables, Dade County, on 5 June 1995 were: total length 5.6 inches (143.2 mm), forearm length 2.5 inches (64.60 mm), wing 7.4 inches (188 mm), weight 1.27 ounces (36 g). The leathery ears are large (0.8–1.2 inches, 19.9–31 mm) and the way they join together between the eyes distinguishes this species from other bats. Weight averages 1–1.75 ounces (30.2–46.2 g). Florida mastiff bats are slightly larger than Caribbean and South American races. This species, like other molossids, or free-tailed bats, has a tail that extends beyond the tail membrane. The short, glossy pelage may be sable brown, grayish, or black. The grayish underparts are lighter.
Distribution: The Florida mastiff bat is Florida's only endemic bat. The range of this subspecies, one of the state's rarest animals, is limited to extreme southern Florida; in recent history it has not been reported outside Dade, Broward, and Charlotte counties. Pleistocene fossil records from Brevard and Dade counties indicate this species is not a recent immigrant to Florida.

Many recent locality records are from the vicinity of Coral Cables (Dade County), where it was apparently fairly common in the 1950's and early 1960's. At that time, specimens collected were often associated with residential structures and were found roosting in Spanish tile roofs, which are popular in the area. During the mid-1960's there was an apparent sharp population decline, and since 1967 this species has been recorded only three times in Florida. In 1979 eight mastiff bats were discovered roosting in an abandoned red-cockaded woodpecker cavity in a longleaf pine tree near Punta Gorda in Charlotte County. The site was destroyed, however, as part of a highway construction project. For six weeks in 1980, biologists intensively searched for mastiff bats in the Miami area and along the Gulf Coast, with negative results. In 1988 a gravid female flew into a balcony of a seventh-floor office in a Coral Gables high-rise. From June through September 1989, another intensive search for this species was conducted in Florida's nine southernmost counties. A number of evening bats (*Lycticeius humeralis*), Brazilian free-tailed bats (*Tadarida brasiliensis*), and northern yellow bats (*Lasiurus intermedius*) were recorded, but again no evidence of Florida mastiff bat populations was found. Then, on 5 June 1995, an adult male flew down a chimney of a Coral Gables residence and landed on a couch, startling the bat-fearing residents of the house. The bat was evicted by tossing it out the front door with a pair of hot-dog tongs. The bat, which sustained internal injuries and was severely traumatized, was rescued by Pat Knox of the We Care Animal Center in Homestead. After five months of recovery, the bat was fitted with a radiocollar and released by biologists who hoped to use this opportunity to discover more about the species' habits and the mysterious location of a mastiff bat colony. As luck would have it, the collar malfunctioned as soon as the bat flew out of sight and no tracking signal was ever received.

There are more Florida mastiff bats out there, and they appear to be breeding, but where they are and how many there are remains a mystery.

Biology: Little is known of the habitat, habits, and life history of this very rare animal. It is known that this subspecies roosts in cavities and utilizes human-made sites such as chimneys, Spanish tile roofs, and abandoned buildings. The tendency to associate the Florida mastiff bat with artificial sites may be attributed to the increasing scarcity of natural cavities in South Florida. Several cavity-nesting birds, including the southeastern American kestrel and eastern bluebird, are now extirpated as breeding species in Dade County. Before 1964, Florida mastiff bats were often found roosting in tile roofs and cavities of royal palm trees (*Roystonea regia*) in the Coral Gables area. Studies in Cuba of the closely related Cuban mastiff bat (*Eumops glaucinus glaucinus*) revealed that of 33 roosting sites, 10 were in buildings and 9 were in tree cavities.

Because presettlement Coral Gables comprised tropical hardwood hammock and rockland pine forest, there is reason to believe that those two ecosystems constitute the primary natural habitats of this subspecies. The eight specimens discovered in Charlotte County in 1979 were in a pine flatwoods habitat.

Mastiffs generally hunt for their insect quarry at heights above 35 feet (10.6 m). They have been observed leaving roosts well after dark and are known to fly at higher elevations than most bats, which may preclude their detection during field investigations. These bats are known to emit loud, high-pitched, shrilling calls that can be heard and identified at considerable distances. Males have a scent gland on the chest that produces a musky odor, possibly used to mark females at communal roosting sites. Mastiff bats have a low reproductive rate, with females birthing no more than one pup each year. Although they possess fairly good eyesight, these bats rely heavily on echolocation to navigate and to find insect prey. Flying bats emit high-frequency sound waves at a rate of up to 200 per second; they are able to hear the echoes reflected back to them and use the echos to locate prey and avoid objects in their flight path in the dark. Swift-flying mastiff bats are capable of detecting prey at up to 16.5 feet (5 m) in open skies. An examination of a fecal sample from the Charlotte County roosting site revealed the proportions of these insect families in the bats' diet: 55 percent Coleoptera, 15 percent Diptera, and 10 percent Hemiptera. Bats, the only major predators of night-flying insects, including mosquitoes, should be regarded as extremely beneficial organisms.

CAUSE OF DECLINE, THREATS

Habitat Destruction: Loss of suitable habitat, particularly roosting and nesting sites, is believed to be a primary cause of decline for this subspecies. So much of the forested area of Broward and Dade counties has been destroyed that a number of species that depend on wooded habitats have now disappeared from the region. Trees containing cavities are not common, and competition for sites is extremely high. Dead trees and snags are usually felled by property owners. Hurricane Andrew, which swept unmercifully through Dade County on 24 August 1992, downed many of the remaining trees throughout a 30-mile-wide strip from the Atlantic to the Gulf in Dade, Monroe, and Collier counties.

Pesticides: Some biologists consider the repeated spraying of pesticides to control mosquitoes in South Florida primarily responsible for the decline of this and other bat species in recent decades. All six bat species that regularly inhabit southern Florida have also decreased. Decreased populations of flying insects in areas where pesticides are heavily used reduces the prey base of bats and insectivorous birds.

Other Threats: Bats, like snakes, are among the most persecuted animals on Earth, and when humans encounter bats, the bat is never triumphant. Mendacious beliefs that bats become entangled in human hair and regularly spread rabies and other diseases to humans have unfortunately prompted many uninformed people to kill bats on sight.

CURRENT TREND: *Declining.*

Endangered Bats of the Panhandle
Gray Bat
Myotis grisescens
Indiana Bat
Myotis sodalis
FAMILY VESPERTILIONIDAE; Order Chiroptera

LISTED STATUS
Gray Bat
FWC: Endangered, listed 1975
USF&WS: Endangered, listed 1976
Indiana Bat
FWC: Endangered, listed 1974
USF&WS: Endangered, listed 1967

Description
Gray Bat: The pelage, or fur, of this species is uniformly gray after molting or brownish between molts. All other southeastern *Myotis* species are bicolored or tricolored. Also, unlike other *Myotis* species, the wing membrane connects to the ankle rather than the base of the toe. The calcar, located behind the ankle, is not keeled. Adults weigh an average of 0.28–0.35 ounces (8–10 g) and measure 3.1–3.8 inches (80–96 mm) in total length. Forearm length measures 1.6–1.8 inches (40–46 mm).

Indiana Bat: This medium-sized *Myotis* species, sometimes called the social bat, is about the same size as the gray bat. It closely resembles the little brown bat but has smaller, more delicate hind feet and the hairs on the hind feet are very short. Unlike the little brown bat, this species' calcar is noticeably keeled and the braincase is typically smaller, lower, and more narrow. Total length of adults ranges from 2.9 to 3.9 inches (73–100 mm), averaging 3.5 inches (88 mm). Forearm measures 1.4–1.6 inches (35–41 mm), averaging 1.5 inches (38 mm). Adults weigh 0.1–0.35 ounces (3–10 g), averaging 0.2 ounces (6.2 g). Females attain a slightly larger size and weight than males. The pelage is two-toned or three-toned, with a dull brownish gray dorsally and a lighter buffy or whitish color ventrally. The shoulder regions are often darker. The fur is lighter at the tips than at the base.

Distribution: The ranges of both species are closely associated with major cave systems.

Gray Bat: Populations of gray bats occur sporadically over portions of 12 states in the south-central United States but are primarily concentrated in the karst regions of Kentucky, Tennessee, Alabama, Arkansas, and Missouri. The range of the gray bat is widespread; however, only 5 percent or less of the caves within its range are suitable for occupation. In Florida the species is largely restricted to several caves in Jackson County, although small aggregations may occur in suitable karst habitat in surrounding counties. This species is migratory. Populations that winter in Florida caves are believed to summer in Tennessee and northern Alabama. An estimated 95 percent of gray bats hibernate in only eight cave systems, three in Missouri, two in Tennessee, and one each in Arkansas, Kentucky, and Alabama. Population estimates, based primarily on the presence of guano deposits on the floors of caves and stains on the cave ceilings, indicate declines of approximately 89 percent in Kentucky, 72–81 percent in Missouri, 61 percent in Arkansas, and 76 percent in Alabama and Tennessee.

Indiana Bat: Though considerably more widespread than the gray bat, within Florida this species is much more rare,

with but a single specimen known. The Indiana bat inhabits cave regions from portions of southern New England and extreme southern Ontario through portions of the Midwest, south to portions of Alabama, Georgia, and extreme northwestern Florida. Over 85 percent of all Indiana bats are believed to hibernate in seven cave systems or mines: three in Missouri, two each in Kentucky and Indiana. The species has also experienced significant population declines. The sole Florida record was found in October 1955 in Old Indian Cave, Jackson County (Florida Caverns State Park).

Biology: It would be difficult to discuss these two species without delving into the subject of bats as a whole. Although other mammals, such as flying squirrels, may achieve a semiflight by volplaning from a higher to lower altitude, only bats can accomplish true flight. "Chiroptera," the name of the order that bats belong to, means "handwing." The bone structure of a bat's arm is identical to that of a human, but its elongated fingers are connected by a double membrane to form the wing. Likewise, bats are the only mammals known to use echolocation to detect prey, predators, or obstructions in darkness. They emit high-frequency, low-intensity sounds and then analyze the returning echoes to locate objects, much like sonar. Some large frugivorous bats, including flying foxes, lack the ability to echolocate.

In contrast to other, more batty parts of the world, Florida can fairly be described as depauperate in terms of bat fauna. The recent discovery of two Caribbean species in the Florida Keys (a generally batless region) raised the total number of bat species recorded in Florida to 18. Bats occur in temperate and tropical regions worldwide but reach their greatest diversity in the tropics. With nearly 1,000 species, bats represent approximately one quarter of all known mammal species. They range in size from Thailand's tiny bumblebee bat (*Craseonycteris thronglongyai*), weighing no more than a penny, to the enormous flying foxes (genera *Pteropus* and *Aproteles*) of Indonesia, which possess 6-foot wingspans and weigh approximately 2 pounds. Nearly 70 percent of bat species feed chiefly on flying insects, with about 29 percent considered frugivorous (fruit-eating) and approximately 1 percent being prey specialists. Pallid bats (*Antrozous pallidus*) prey on flightless arthropods, including venomous scorpions. The echolocation of fishing bats (*Noctilio leporinus*) is so refined that they can detect the fin of a minnow as it grazes the water's surface and effectively forage by gaffing small fish with their feet.

To declare bats simply beneficial is an understatement; they are extremely beneficial and an integral part of entire ecosystems. The endangered lesser Sanborn's long-nosed bat (*Leptonyctteris sanborni*) is the primary pollinator of such Sonoran Desert keystone plants as the tree-size saguaro cactus (*Cereus giganteus*) and the tequila-producing mescal pardo (*Agave sobria*); it also pollinates another 100 other plant species. Bats also pollinate important food crops such as bananas, mangos, peaches, figs, and dates and are important seed dispersers for a multitude of plant species. Statistics provided by Merlin D. Tuttle, of Bat Conservation

International, Inc. (BCI), of Austin, Texas, suggest that a colony of big brown bats numbering only 150 individuals can potentially save local farmers tens of thousands of dollars by devouring millions of crop-destructive cucumber beetles. On a typical summer night, the 40 million–50 million Brazilian free-tailed bats that emerge from three nursery caves near San Antonio, Texas, consume about 1 million pounds of insects; statewide in Texas, this species eats an estimated 18,000 metric tons of mosquitoes and other insects yearly. The loss of large numbers of bats greatly increases farmers' need for chemical pesticides, which in turn, jeopardizes myriad plant and animal species. Even bat droppings, or guano, serves a useful purpose. Guano reserves in caves sustain unique ecosystems, including bacteria, and have long been used by humans in the production of antibiotics, gasohol, detergents, and waste detoxification processes. The extent of medical applications is yet unknown.

According to BCI, more than 50 percent of American bat species are in "severe decline." Because large numbers roost or hibernate together, certain species are vulnerable to extirpation as a result of a single catastrophic event, including severe floods or indiscriminate slaughter by humans. Another factor rendering bats prone to extinction is their relatively slow reproductive rate, among the slowest of all mammals.

Bats, like snakes and spiders, are feared by many humans who consider them worthless vermin, but the first thing needed to convert bat haters to bat lovers is factual information. Contrary to popular folklore, bats are no more predisposed to rabies than other mammals, they are generally not aggressive, they are not blind (most have excellent vision), they are not mice with wings, and they do not get tangled in the hair of humans. Bats constantly groom themselves and rank among the world's cleanest animals. They are also remarkably resistant to disease.

Most bats, including the gray and Indiana bats, drink by scooping water from rivers, ponds, lakes, and occasionally swimming pools. Most are capable swimmers. The foraging habitat of both the gray bat and the Indiana bat is quite similar. These species typically forage for flying insects above riparian habitats, especially streams but also rivers, ponds, and lakes. The bodies of water most frequently used are bordered by mature forest with dense vegetative growth at the water's edge. Indiana bats are more likely than gray bats to forage within the forest itself. Moths (Lepidoptera), represent the primary food item for Indiana bats; mayflies (Ephemeroptera) constitute the gray bat's chief insect quarry. Gray bats have been observed defending foraging territories, and it is likely the Indiana bat does so as well. Biologists believe the two species compete for prey in some areas. Forests, especially floodplain forests, are very important to both species. It is believed that they routinely use forested corridors when traveling between caves and foraging habitats, which usually occur within one or two miles of one another. Gravid females of both species use relatively warm caves during the summer for nursery or maternity purposes. Males and subadult females also form colonies in warm caves, often referred to as bachelor

colonies. The temperature of typical gray bat maternity caves ranges between 58 and 77 degrees F (14–25 degrees C). Unlike gray bats, which seldom roost outside caves or cavelike environments, Indiana bats often roost and bear young under the loose bark of dead trees in streamside habitats.

Gray bats and Indiana bats typically mate before hibernating, the gray in September or October and the Indiana from late August to early October, but occasionally during the winter and the early spring. Females of both species typically hibernate after mating and emerge from hibernation before males; males may not hibernate for two or three weeks after mating, emerging long after females. Females generally retain sperm over the winter and become pregnant after emerging from their hibernacula. Both species bear a single young, sometime between late May and early June. Young are typically capable of flight within 20–25 days. Gray bats from warmer climes tend to develop more rapidly. Gray bats, and presumably Indiana bats, are sexually mature after two years.

These migratory species may travel more than 300 miles between summer and winter habitats. In late summer most of Florida's gray bat population migrates to the colder hibernation caves of Tennessee and northern Alabama, which maintain temperatures of 43–52 degrees F (6–11 degrees C). The hibernation caves used by Indiana bats are often cooler, with temperatures of 39–46 degrees F (4–8 degrees C). During hibernation, bats of both species form dense congregations in their respective hibernation caves to conserve body heat. Gray bat hibernacula may have as many as 170 gray bats per square foot. Indiana bats pack into their hibernation caves with 300–480 of them per square foot. A few hundred (mostly males) of the esti-mated 10,000 gray bats that summer in Florida have been known to winter in Florida caves, most in Jackson County's Old Indian Cave, one of the few Florida caves cold enough to sustain hibernating gray bats or Indiana bats. Historically, thousands of gray bats hibernated in this cave, but human disturbance caused most bats to abandon the site by the mid-1970's. Both gray and Indiana bats hibernate for approximately six months.

Known or suspected predators of these bats include several species of owls, certain hawks and falcons, snakes, especially rat snakes (*Elaphe* spp.), raccoons, skunks, and domestic cats. Newborn bats that fall to ground may fall prey to cockroaches and other small predators. The average longevity of both species is about 5 years, with long-lived individuals surviving 18 years, possibly as long as 30 years. Females often outlive males.

CAUSE OF DECLINE, THREATS

The threats and causes of decline are identical, or nearly so, for both species. **Habitat Destruction, Human Disturbance, and Related Threats:** The loss of suitable hibernation, maternity, and roosting sites constitutes the most prominent contemporary threat. Numerous cave systems formerly used by these and other bats have been destroyed by residential and commercial development. Others have been rendered unsuitable by the intentional blocking of cave entrances by humans. Many bats have died or were forced to abandon

caves when the creation of additional openings changed their microclimate or the installation of poorly designed gates blocked the natural air flow. The destruction and degradation of woodland habitats and stream channelization within summer ranges are also among the more serious threats to both species. Populations have also been extirpated by repeated disturbance by spelunkers, vandals, even well-meaning but careless biologists, and the commercialization of caves as tourist attractions, which often includes electrical lighting and guided tours. Disturbance to bat colonies that would have previously seemed inconse-quential may well prove harmful to bats. Human intrusion into occupied maternity caves often incites mother bats to take wing and flurry for several minutes. The mother's absence during this critical time may cause the body temperature of the young to drop precar-iously low. Disturbing a hibernating colony is often even more perilous. Hibernating bats flushed into flight must use energy reserves that they will be unable to replenish until the spring, substantially weakening them and less-ening their chance of surviving the win-ter. A single arousal from hibernation may cost a bat more energy than it would burn in a month or more of undisturbed hibernation.

Cave Flooding: Damming of streams or rivers to create lakes and reservoirs has permanently flooded a number of caves used by gray bats or Indiana bats. Also, floods spurred by severe weather events have decimated bat colonies. A single severe flood of the bat cave at Kentucky's Mammoth Cave National Park drowned 300,000 Indiana bats.

Human Persecution: In decades past, human crusades were regularly organized to exterminate bat colonies when discovered. Because these bats form large hibernating and maternity congregations, they are extremely vulnerable to intentional annihilation. In 1973 approximately 250,000 gray bats occupying Alabama's Hambrick Cave were suffocated after fires were set at the cave's entrance. Many similar incidents have been documented. Legal protection and increased awareness of bat conservation issues have helped, but the intentional killing of bats continues.

Other Threats: *Pesticides and other contaminants.* Pesticides and pollutants may threaten bats in two ways. Dangerously high levels of PCBs, DDEs, DDT, heptudilor expoxide, and lead have been found in the tissues of gray bats; these substances may pose a direct threat to bats. The use of pesticides also depletes the bat's prey base of insects.

Freezing of hibernacula. Large kills have occurred when traditional hibernacula sites have been destroyed by urban sprawl, forcing bats to utilize unsuitable sites where temperatures drop below levels that they can endure.

Mining of bat guano (historic threat). During the Civil War, large quantities of bat guano were removed from caves to make gunpowder. Experts suspect this activity took a heavy toll on gray bats at that time.

CURRENT TREND

Gray Bat: *Stable* to *increasing* in some regions, *declining* in others. Total population estimated at more than 1.5 million.

Indiana Bat: *Stable* overall, but *declining* locally. Total population numbers approximately 400,000.

Florida Panther

Puma concolor coryi

FAMILY FELIDAE; Order Carnivora

LISTED STATUS

FWC: Endangered, listed 1958

USF&WS: Endangered, listed 1967

CITES: Appendix 1

Description: The scientific or Latin name of an animal often reveals quite a bit about the species or subspecies. In the case of the Florida panther, the genus and species names (*Puma concolor*) mean "cat of one color," and *coryi* refers to the naturalist Charles B. Cory, who first described this subspecies of cougar in 1896. Florida's official state animal is a large, well-muscled, tawny cat with a long, thick tail. The larger males average 7 feet 2 inches (220 cm) in length (including tail) and weigh 110–154 pounds (50–70 kg); females average 6 feet 2 inches (188 cm) in length and weigh 71–99 pounds (32–45 kg). The heaviest panther recorded in Florida was a male captured in Hendry County in 1989 that weighed 154 pounds (70 kg). In contrast, other subspecies of cougars may weigh 265 pounds (120 kg) or more. Adult panthers are unspotted and uniformly tawny above with whitish chin, lips, throat, and underparts. The head is fairly small. The tail is approximately half the length of the cat's body and head and is lighter below than above. Kittens have bold spots, a banded tail, and bright blue eyes, but all those markings diminish rapidly after six months. Many people, including life-long Floridians, associate the term "panther" with the black panther, the melanistic Old World leopards (*Panthera pardus*) or New World jaguars (*Panthera onca*), and therefore mistakenly believe

Florida panthers to be black. There are no records of melanistic panthers ever occurring in Florida.

The Florida panther generally has longer legs, smaller feet, a slimmer tail, smaller overall dimensions, and darker color than western cougars. The Florida subspecies differs from other subspecies by the characteristic cowlick on the ridge of the back; white flecking about the head, shoulders, and neck; and a right-angle crook at the end of the tail. The cowlick and crooked tail are more prevalent in the Big Cypress Swamp population than in the Everglades National Park population.

Panther tracks typically display four toes (with no claw marks) surrounding a wide pad with three pronounced lobes along the rear border. Front pads of adult panthers are 1.6–2.3 inches (4–6 cm) wide, slightly larger than rear pads. The tracks of panthers, even kittens six months or older, are considerably larger than the tracks of bobcats, and domestic dog tracks usually have visible claw marks. Typical of felines, panthers have pivotal forelimbs and retractable claws. Their teeth include large canines to kill and grip prey and sharp-edged molars that are used to shear flesh.

Distribution: The current range of the Florida panther is but a tiny remnant of its former distribution. Breeding populations are now largely restricted to southern Florida, particularly Collier and Hendry counties, but also portions of Dade, Monroe, Lee, and Glades counties. Two primary reproducing populations exist. One occupies large tracts of protected lands within Big Cypress National Preserve, Big Cypress Seminole Indian Reservation, Florida Panther National Wildlife Refuge, and Fakahatchee Strand State Preserve and large parcels of private land north of I75 in Collier, Hendry, and Glades counties. The other includes Everglades National Park and adjacent areas. Recent sightings have also been confirmed in Broward, Palm Beach, Martin, Highlands, Alachua, Osceola, Volusia, and St. Johns counties, but those animals are believed to be stragglers or, in northern counties, possibly escaped captives.

Historically, this subspecies ranged throughout much of the southeastern United States and southern Mississippi Valley but was eliminated from every state but Florida by human encroachment. Each year, sightings of panthers are reported from a number of formerly inhabited states; however, Florida remains the only state where populations have been verified. As many as 30 subspecies of *Puma concolor* range from Canada to the southernmost tip of South America, making it one of the most widely distributed New World mammals.

Biology: The species as a whole (commonly called cougar, mountain lion, or puma) is an excellent example of a habitat generalist; it successfully exploits many habitats, ranging from snow-covered alpine habitats to blistering, arid, treeless deserts to steamy, tropical rain forests. Florida cats utilize hardwood hammocks, cabbage palm forests, pine flatwoods, cypress swamps and prairies, mixed swamp forests, freshwater marshes, and even dense thickets of introduced Brazilian pepper; uplands however, are favored over wetlands. These cryptic felines have the uncanny ability to evade visual detection when approached by humans, often by remaining perfectly still. Few people who have spent their entire lives in the midst of cougar country have ever caught a glimpse of one. The author has been fortunate enough to observe *Puma concolor* in the wild on three occasions, twice in Arizona, once in Florida. The use of radiotelemetry, which began in the 1980's, has provided biologists with a wealth of information on the behavior and habitat use of these elusive felines. Panthers typically use upland habitats for denning and diurnal resting sites but will hunt in upland and wetland habitats.

The adult male's home range is immense, often 200 square miles or more, and may overlap the range of several females. Males are polygamous, breeding with several females whose home ranges occur within his home range. The female's home range, though smaller, is expansive, at more than 70 square miles, and usually includes localities supporting an abundance of prey, which benefits a mother rearing kittens.

Panthers are chiefly nocturnal and crepuscular but may be partially diurnal, especially during the winter months. The diet of adult panthers (in recent decades) consists mainly of four mammal species: white-tailed deer, raccoons, feral hogs, and nine-banded armadillos, the last two being introduced or relatively new immigrants. Historically, white-tailed deer were the principal large prey item, probably regularly supplemented by raccoons and other smaller vertebrates. A healthy panther will take a deer or hog every 7–10 days. The species has possibly the highest power-to-weight ratio of any feline. These cats are capable of bringing down prey much larger than themselves and have slain deer and

hogs by biting through the skull. The remains of a black bear have been found in panther scat. Prey is stalked in the typical cat manner, approaching closely by slow, careful movements and attacking with a high-speed charge. After the kill, large prey is typically dragged to an area of dense brush. There the cat will devour large meaty portions as well as the liver, heart, and lungs. Cats often gorge themselves, consuming more than 30 pounds at a sitting. After feeding, the panther often covers the remainder of the prey with vegetative matter and then returns to feed several times. Most smaller prey are eaten completely; an exception is the armadillo, whose shell and tail are left behind. Unlike some western races, Florida panthers rarely prey on domestic livestock, and there is only one record of a panther attacking a human. Adult panthers have virtually no natural predators, other than other panthers.

Mating may take place year round, but the season peaks between November and March. Panthers are generally solitary animals; however, males and females often spend a week together copulating repeatedly. Mature females tend to become gravid on a two-year cycle. The gestation period is 90–96 days. Litters vary from one to four kittens, averaging two. Dens are often located in dense saw palmetto thickets. Typical dens are merely shallow depressions scraped out of the soil. Kittens weigh approximately 1.1 pounds (500 g) at birth and are blind and defenseless. Their eyes open after three weeks, and they grow rapidly for several months. They remain at the den for 2 months and stay with the mother for 12–18 months. After 10–12 months, the kittens often accompany the mother on hunting expeditions. After 18 months or so, the kittens are able to provide for themselves and establish territories of their own. Once the kittens have dispersed, the mother is ready to mate again. Offspring become sexually mature after 18–30 months.

CAUSE OF DECLINE, THREATS

Habitat Destruction and Fragmentation, Human Encroachment: The Florida panther is a cat of the wilderness, something that Florida has less and less of with every passing day. These cats have demonstrated some tolerance of human encroachment, but the ever-increasing human population of South Florida is pushing the extinction envelope. The reduction and fragmentation of Florida's wilderness brings with it a number of other spin-off threats, including inbreeding and increased vulnerability to disease and hurricanes, all of which, singularly or collectively, could cause the extinction of our state animal.

Automobile Collisions: Automobile collisions are the leading cause of panther deaths each year. Twenty panthers were killed by automobiles between 1980 and 1990, with 8 panther deaths in 1990 alone.

Poaching: Although it is widely known that Florida panthers are an endangered species, critically imperiled with extinction, poaching remains the second leading cause of mortality.

Mercury Poisoning: Mercury poisoning has caused the death of one panther and is suspected in the death of at least two others. The presence of toxic levels of mercury in panthers, which occupy the top of the food chain, is evidence that

this extremely harmful liquid metal has contaminated much of the Everglades food chain.

Inbreeding: A century ago, genetic material was exchanged throughout the species' range. Florida populations are now isolated, and genetic exchange no longer occurs. Some of the race's distinctive characteristics, including the kinked tail and cowlick on the spine, are believed to be the result of long-term inbreeding. Inbreeding is also believed to be the cause of several serious physiologic mutations. Many males now suffer from a malady in which one testicle does not descend into the scrotum, and 93 percent of such a cat's sperm is abnormal. Heart abnormalities have also been found.

Disease and Parasites: Several potentially fatal infectious diseases, including feline panleukopenia, parvovirus, and feline calicivirus, have been detected in many of the remaining panthers. Many panthers are also infected with hookworms (*Ancylostoma pluridentatum*), which can be problematic with old and very young cats. Rabies caused the death of a radiocollared cat in 1989.

Intraspecific Aggression: Currently, 37 percent of panther mortality results from panthers killing other panthers. Aggression between these large cats is not abnormal, but it becomes a detrimental factor when the entire population consists of only 30–80 animals. The majority of panthers killed are young males who enter the territories of larger, more aggressive males. Fortunately, the loss of younger males affects the population less than the loss of breeding females or older males.

CURRENT TREND: *Stable.* With only 30–80 panthers (30–50 adults) remaining in the wild, however, this species remains in grave danger of extinction. The number of panthers occurring in Florida before the arrival of Europeans has been estimated at 1,400.

Florida Black Bear

Ursus americanus floridanus
FAMILY URSIDAE; Order Carnivora
LISTED STATUS
FWC: Threatened (except in Apalachicola National Forest and Baker and Columbia counties, where it is considered a game species), listed 1978
USF&WS: Species of management concern
CITES: Appendix 3

Description: The black bear, although the smallest of North America's three bear species, is now Florida's largest terrestrial mammal (the larger Plains bison was extirpated in the 1800's). Adults average 4–6 feet (130–180 cm) in length (head and body) and 2.5–3.5 feet (80–105 cm) in height at the shoulder. Adult males, which average 299 pounds (136 kg), attain a greater size than females, which average 198 pounds (90 kg). The largest black bear recorded in Florida was a 630 pound (286 kg) behemoth killed by a car in Collier County in 1990. An adult male's rear foot averages nearly 3 inches (7.5 cm) wide and is 5.5–8.6 inches (14–22 cm) long; an adult female's foot is 2.6–3.7 inches (6.5–9.5 cm) wide and 5.3–7.1 inches (13.5–18 cm) long. The front feet of an adult male can be 3.5–5.5 inches (9–14 cm) wide and 3.3–5.9 inches (8.5–15 cm) long; the female's can be 3 inches (7.5 cm) wide by 3–4.3 inches (7.5–11 cm) long. The

footprint of the black bear is distinctive. Bears are formidable predators with powerful jaws and large sharp teeth and claws. The head is elongated, and the snout is light brown or tan. The skull has 42 teeth. The tail is small and rarely measures over 5 inches (12.7 cm) long; it is often not visible. Typical pelage color of Florida black bears is uniformly black, with a white or light-colored chest patch present on some animals. Some bears in the southern part of the state appear somewhat brownish, but the color of these bears is not as light as the cinnamon phase of black bears frequently encountered in western states. Individual animals of other subspecies of black bear may be tan, gold, gold and white, orange, pinto with patches of black and white, silvery-blue, and even pure white.

Black bear scat often resembles dog scat, except that it is usually larger and often contains berries, seeds, mammal hair, and insects. Trees scarred by a bear's teeth and claw marks are telltale signs of occupied territory.

Distribution: Eighteen subspecies of black bear are distributed from Alaska and northern Canada south through much of the United States into the highlands of Mexico. Though still widespread, the area now occupied by black bears is but a small fraction of the area inhabited before Europeans arrived in North America.

The historic range of the Florida subspecies covered most of the Panhandle and peninsular Florida, excluding the Keys. Bears also inhabited forested barrier islands. The range of the subspecies outside Florida is limited to portions of southern Georgia and Alabama. The range of the black bear in Florida was widespread and contiguous before the arrival of Europeans; now, although bears regularly occur or have been recently recorded in 50 of Florida's 67 counties, the range has been severely fragmented and continues to shrink as humans encroach on the last large tracts of forest. The current range of the black bear in Florida consists of five large populations and a number of smaller populations, distributed sporadically from portions of the Panhandle and northern peninsular Florida south to the tip of the mainland. South Florida is the only location east of the Mississippi River where black bears and panthers inhabit the same area. The five largest populations occur in Big Cypress National Preserve and the surrounding area in southwest Florida, including portions of Collier, Lee, and Hendry counties; Ocala National Forest and the surrounding area in central Florida, which includes portions of Marion, Alachua, Putnam, Lake, Volusia, Flagler, Orange, and Seminole counties; Osceola National Forest and the Pinhook Swamp and the surrounding area in northern Florida; Apalachicola National Forest and the surrounding area in the Big Bend region; and Eglin Air Force Base and the surrounding area in the Panhandle. According to biologist David Maehr, one of the foremost authorities on Florida black bears, a 1996 estimate placed the population of the Big Cypress area alone at more than 1,000 bears.

Each region contains large expanses of relatively undisturbed natural communities with comparatively few roads. A number of viable, but smaller, bear populations occur in a handful of locations that support less extensive tracts of suitable bear habitat, including Chassahowitzka National Wildlife Refuge and surrounding area in Citrus, Hernando, and Pasco counties; the Green Swamp and surrounding area in Polk and Lake counties; the Fisheating Creek area and adjacent portions of Glades and Highlands counties; Orange County's Tosohatchee State Preserve and surrounding area; and the Twelve-Mile Swamp and Durbin Swamp areas of Duval and St. Johns counties. Bears, usually males, are occasionally reported considerable distances from the population centers listed here.

Biology: The typical home range of a black bear in Florida encompasses several different habitat types; forested terrain is preferred. In most of Florida the primary types of forests used include pine flatwoods, temperate hardwood and mixed hardwood forests, bottomland and floodplain hardwood forests, sand pine scrub, oak scrub, scrubby flatwoods, cypress swamps, bay swamps, and other freshwater swamps. South Florida's bears are the only black bear populations inhabiting subtropical habitats. According to bear biologist David Maehr, bears in southwest Florida, unlike panthers, use mangrove forests extensively for foraging, denning, and rearing cubs. Habitats used to a lesser extent by bears include high pine communities, dry prairie, and tropical hammocks. Several different habitats are typically used throughout the year, depending on the seasonal availability of food.

Radiotelemetry studies in central and northern Florida have revealed home ranges for adult male black bears averaging 66 square miles (170 square km); home ranges of adult female bears average 11 square miles (28 square km). Adult male home ranges as large as 176 square miles (457 square km) have been recorded. Dens are typically found in areas having dense undergrowth, often palmetto thickets or secluded swamps. The dens or nests used for birthing and winter dormancy are dug into the earth and measure 18–30 inches (45–75 cm) across and 2–12 inches (5–30 cm) deep and may be lined with leaves. Large hollow logs are also used for denning.

In Florida, bears mate in midsummer and in midwinter bear two to four young (usually twins), which have a 50:50 sex ratio. In southern Florida, cubs are usually born in late February and early March. Cubs weigh 10.3–16 ounces (290–454 g) at birth and remain with the mother in the den until late April or May. Cubs quickly gain weight feeding on the mother's rich milk. Cubs emerge from the den after several months weighing 4–7 pounds (1.8–3.2 kg). They often stay with the mother for 16–18 months. Females tend to remain close to the area where they were reared. Sexual maturity is typically reached after two years, and first litters are usually produced after three years. Females produce young every other year. Unlike females, males typically leave their natal home range, when they are two to four years old, in search of mates and vacant territories. Male cubs frequently disperse 20–40 miles, but occasionally one will travel much farther. In the summer of 1996 state biologists tracked a 350-pound (159 kg) male bear wearing a radio collar; the bear set a record by roaming all the way to Baton Rouge, Louisiana, approximately 350 miles from its Apalachicola National Forest home

near Tallahassee. Many bears are killed during this dispersal period, when they are more vulnerable to automobile collisions and deadly encounters with beekeepers or other bears.

Bears may be active nocturnally and crepuscularly. While bears from more northern, colder locales remain dormant for as long as nine months of the year, bears in Florida, especially southern Florida, remain active most or all of the year. Bears are least active in January and February. Black bears are not averse to water, and biologists believe that during warm weather bears will enter water to cool off. Black bears are excellent climbers. They will ascend trees to locate food and to elude perceived threats. The Florida black bear is a particularly shy subspecies that avoids contact with humans at all costs. There are no reports of bears in Florida killing or attacking humans.

Though bears have a poor sense of sight, their senses of hearing and smell are exceptional. Their keen sense of smell is used to locate fruits and berries, nuts, insects, and one of their favorite meals, honey. The diet of Florida black bears varies considerably with different seasons and with geographic area. In the spring, bears take advantage of the abundance of herbaceous matter, shifting to soft mast in the summer and to hard mast, such as acorns, in the autumn. The hearts and fruits of saw palmetto and sabal palm are important foods statewide. Other important plant foods include swamp tupelo (*Nyssa sylvatica* var. *biflora*), acorns from oaks, blueberry (*Vaccinium* sp.), and gallberry (*Ilex glabra*). The fruits of exotic Brazilian pepper have become an important winter food for South Florida bears, which also consume the fruits of native plants such as royal palm, marlberry (*Ardisia escallonoides*), and parts of bromeliads. Research has revealed that black bears are important seed dispersers for many native plants as well as for exotics, particularly the Brazilian pepper.

Animals are a greater component of the bear's diet in the spring than at any other time. A wide array of animals are eaten, but none is as significant as insects. The most commonly eaten insect is the honeybee (*Apis mellifera*), a nonnative species introduced to Florida by European settlers long ago. Many other insects are eaten, however, including other bees and wasps, bessie bugs (*Odontotaenius disjunctus*), ants, beetles, flies, and cicadas. An assortment of vertebrates are eaten as well, including feral hogs, armadillos, reptiles and their eggs, birds and their eggs, and deer. Black bears are capable of running 30 mph for short distances. A number of early naturalists noted the black bear's fondness for sea turtle eggs, which probably was an important source of protein for coastal populations. The development of Florida's coastline has now eliminated access to beach areas for most bear populations. The bear's appreciation for the taste of honey is well known. In many areas, particularly Collier County in southwest Florida, Lake County in central Florida, and the Big Bend region, bears regularly raid apiaries in search of honey and honeybees. Many beekeepers have learned to protect their apiaries by surrounding them with electric fences, leaving dogs near the hives, moving hives, and by having the FWC trap problem bears. It is known that some beekeepers illegally kill bears by shooting or poisoning them.

In areas where Florida's ever-increasing human population encroaches into natural communities occupied by bears, interaction between bears and humans increases as well. Bears are opportunistic animals who will, on occasion, take advantage of an easy meal by raiding a pet's feeding bowl (and sometimes the pet itself), chicken coops, garbage bags, and bird feeders. While I was a park ranger at Chiricahua National Monument in Arizona a number of years ago, I became acquainted with a large black bear that would make a well-timed appearance at the campground for 8–10 consecutive days, just as campers were sitting down for lunch. After announcing its presence with a thunderous roar, which would generally clear the dozen or so picnic tables, the bear would go from table to table, emptying the buckets of fried chicken and other morsels, leaving no crumbs.

Other than man, bears have very few enemies. Remains of a juvenile bear were found in panther scat in Collier County, indicating that young bears may be preyed on by Florida panthers. Alligators and American crocodiles are large enough to pose a threat to young cubs. So, too, may the Florida red wolf (*Canis rufus floridanus*), an extirpated species now reintroduced in the Big Bend area. The longevity of black bears has been known to exceed 30 years; the average life expectancy in the wild, however, probably averages 6–8 years. The mortality rate is particularly high during the first two years and is considerably higher in males than females.

CAUSE OF DECLINE, THREATS

Habitat Destruction and Fragmentation:
The black bear formerly inhabited nearly
all of Florida except for the Keys. Today,
urbanization, forestry practices, and
agricultural practices have eliminated
bears from all but a few large, relatively
undeveloped areas. A number of smaller
populations are now isolated; natural
corridors that would connect populations and allow recolonization and
genetic diversity have been cut off by
highways, residential development, or
agricultural uses. Without the preservation of corridors that link population
centers, biologists believe that many isolated bear populations will be extirpated
and there will be no way to repopulate
their habitats. It is expected that several
smaller isolated colonies, such as the
population inhabiting Tosohatchee State
Reserve in Orange County, will become
extinct within the next few decades.
If black bears are to survive outside
protected public lands, the acquisition
of land is imperative in certain strategic
locations, including both suitable bear
habitat and corridors that link populations. Furthermore, certain types of
forestry practices, such as the conversion
of mast-producing hardwood forests to
slash pine plantations, eliminate an
important source of food for bears.

**Persecution by Beekeepers and
Ranchers:** Florida is the largest honey-
producing state; combined with the
state's sizable bear population, that
spells trouble for both beekeepers and
bears. Bears cause a reported $100,000
worth of property damage to Florida
apiaries each year. Beekeepers kill a
number of bears, usually with firearms
or poison, each year. Beekeepers who
erect electric fences around their apiaries
virtually eliminate bear depredation.

Automobile Collisions: Each year,
automobiles take their toll on Florida
bears; many are killed and many more
are seriously injured. In 1990 alone, 33
black bears were killed by automobiles
in Florida.

Hunting and Poaching: Before 1950,
Florida's black bears received no protection. Overhunting is believed to be the
cause of their extirpation in several
regions of Florida. Hunting black bears
is currently permitted during limited
hunting seasons in Apalachicola
National Forest and in Baker and
Columbia counties (the area of Osceola
National Forest), where the bear has
been designated a game animal.
Elsewhere in Florida, the black bear
is classified as a threatened species
and hunting is prohibited. A significant,
rangewide increase in bear poaching has
been documented in recent years. Local
poachers illegally take bears in many
areas, and bears are also poached for
high-priced parts such as gall bladders,
which are used in traditional Oriental
medicine. Of the eight bears that died
during a two-year radiotelemetry study
by state biologists, five were killed illegally by humans; two others were killed
by automobiles, and one, the only bear
to die of natural causes, was killed by
another bear.

CURRENT TREND: *Declining* overall;
however, some populations appear to
be *stable.*

Everglades Mink

Mustela vison evergladensis
FAMILY MUSTELIDAE; Order Carnivora

LISTED STATUS
FWC: Threatened, listed 1973 (endangered 1971–1972)

Description: The Everglades mink has a slender, elongated body with a small, flattened head only slightly larger in diameter than its body. Like other members of the weasel family, mink have short legs, short rounded ears, and anal sex glands. Their partially webbed feet assist them while swimming. Mink are larger than weasels and much smaller than otters. Adult male mink of the subspecies *Mustela vison mink* attain an approximate head and body length of 28 inches (711 mm), with a tail about 8 inches (203 mm) long, and males tend to be bigger and heavier than females. The Everglades race appears to be smaller on average and noticeably darker than the two north Florida subspecies. Pelage is typically a luxurious dark brown overall; many specimens bear a white chin patch, and sometimes a white chest patch is also present. The tail is well furred and darker on the terminal third. Mink walk with a hump-backed gait.

Distribution: The current known range of the Everglades mink is largely restricted to suitable habitat within southern Collier County, portions of northern and eastern Monroe County, and portions of Dade County west of the Florida Turnpike, in the Big Cypress and Everglades region. Though generally considered rare, this subspecies is not uncommon in portions of both the Big Cypress Swamp and Everglades. The author has observed mink crossing Loop Road in Big Cypress National Preserve on several occasions. Historically, it occupied a larger range covering much of the northern Everglades and Lake Okeechobee region.

During the 1930's, mink were reportedly trapped in and around Lake Okeechobee on a regular basis. There are no reliable recent records indicating the presence of Everglades mink in the northern portions of its historic range. Drainage of wetlands, conversion of suitable habitat for agricultural purposes, water pollution, and extensive trapping may have resulted in its extirpation from many areas. For reasons not evident, mink are apparently absent from most of inland peninsular Florida north of Dade and Collier counties.

Biology: The Everglades mink is a semi-aquatic mammal that occupies a variety of shallow-water wetlands ranging from long-hydroperiod swamp forests to wet saw grass prairies to short-hydroperiod spike rush marshes. Mink inhabiting short-hydroperiod environments typically move to longer-hydroperiod environments during the dry season. Some artificial canals crisscrossing portions of the Everglades are apparently also inhabited by mink, as concentrations of mink tracks, scat, and well-defined trails have been found on adjacent levees. Brackish marshes and salt marshes are also used seasonally, but to a much lesser degree than its north Florida relatives. This subspecies typically avoids deep-water areas, possibly because of the vulnerability to predation by alligators. Mink are believed to be locally common in portions of the Big Cypress Swamp and Everglades; however, they are seldom seen.

This subspecies is thought to breed earlier than northern populations. Everglades mink typically mate from September through November, with females usually bearing young during March and April. Female mink from northern populations produce one litter of three or four young annually, and this race probably does the same. Young may remain with the mother for several months. Males sometimes assist with rearing duties. Young open their eyes in about five weeks and soon accompany their parents on foraging trips.

Everglades mink are truly amphibious mammals, well adept in water. Generally mink are nocturnal or crepuscular, but the Everglades mink are occasionally observed during the day. Their diet includes many small animals, including fishes, crayfish, mollusks, frogs, snakes, turtles, small mammals, birds, insects, and bird and reptile eggs. Mink forage both in the water and on land. Known or suspected predators of the Everglades mink include American alligators, Florida snapping turtles, Florida softshell turtles, bobcats, hawks, owls, and eastern indigo snakes, eastern diamondback rattlesnakes, and Florida cottonmouths.

CAUSE OF DECLINE, THREATS

Habitat Destruction and Alteration: Changes to wetland habitats associated with numerous drainage and flood control projects and the conversion of wetlands to agricultural lands during the late 1800's and early to mid 1900's are believed to be the primary reasons mink no longer occur in northern portions of their historic range.

Water Pollution, Agricultural Runoff: Toxic pollutant discharges and nutrient-rich runoff from large agricultural areas contaminate wetlands used by the Everglades mink and their food supply.

Automobile Collisions: Automobile collisions may be the leading cause of death in wetland areas bisected by highways and roads.

Trapping: The trapping of Everglades mink is now illegal in Florida, but trapping of mink and other fur-bearing mammals was once a popular way of life for many residents near Lake Okeechobee, the Everglades, and Big Cypress to earn a living. Trapping of mink is probably no longer a common practice in South Florida.

CURRENT TREND: *Unknown.*

Key Deer

Odocoileus virginianus clavium
FAMILY CERVIDAE; Order Artiodactyla

LISTED STATUS
FWC: Endangered, listed 1974
USF&WS: Endangered, listed 1967

Description: The Key deer is generally considered a subspecies of the Virginia white-tailed deer (*O. virginianus*), and aside from its obvious difference in stature, it closely resembles its northern relative. Some authorities, however, believe this race should be afforded a full species classification. Distinctions that set this race apart include a wider skull, disproportionately long tail, and shorter legs. The most apparent distinction is the relatively dwarfed size of this race. Key deer tend to measure 24–28 inches (61–71 cm) at the shoulder. Does weigh 45–65 pounds (20.4–29.5 kg), bucks 55–75 pounds (24.9–34 kg). Their pelage varies from reddish brown to sooty gray. A dark facial mask is apparent on most animals.

Distribution: The Key deer is a Lower Keys endemic with a geographical range much like that of the silver rice rat, another mammal not found above Spanish Harbor. Like the rice rat, this deer is most abundant on keys with consistent sources of fresh water. Key deer consistently occur on Big Johnson, Little Pine, Big Pine, No Name, Little Torch, Middle Torch, Big Torch, Cudjoe, Howe, Sugarloaf, Knockemdown, and Summerland keys. Over two thirds of the population, currently estimated at between 250 and 300 animals, is found within the National Key Deer Refuge on Big Pine and No Name keys. The historic range, however, was larger and is believed to extend from Duck Key to Key West.

Biology: Key deer are habitat generalists that utilize a wide variety of habitats, including rockland pine forests, tropical hardwood hammocks, buttonwood-mangrove areas, as well as suburban yards and rights-of-way. The pine-palm community throughout much of Big Pine and No Name keys is probably the most important natural habitat. The availability of fresh water, however, has more to do with determining where deer congregate than does the type of flora present. Key deer have been known to drink brackish water in times of drought. These deer swim well and sometimes swim from key to key in search of fresh water. Key deer have become regular visitors to the yards of many residents of No Name and Big Pine keys. Some residents consider the deer a nuisance and have fenced their property. Key deer travel alone and in small groups, usually an adult female accompanied by several offspring of different ages. Does generally become sexually mature at two years of age. Breeding activity begins in September, peaks in October, and occasionally extends to February. The average gestation period is 204 days, and the single fawn (very

rarely a pair) is born between late March and the end of June; births peak in April. The sex ratio of fawns approaches or exceeds two males to one female. Fawns weigh 2–4 pounds (0.9–1.8 kg). Bucks drop their antlers in the early spring, new growth takes place by August, and they are usually in velvet until September. Males have not been recorded living beyond 8 years, but females have on occasion exceeded 20 years. The diet of the Key deer varies seasonally and includes more than 160 species of plants; woody plants, forbs, palm fruits, and flowers constitute the bulk. Favored plants include black mangrove, red mangrove, blackbead (*Pithecellobium keyense*), Key thatch palm, silver palm, dilly fruit (*Manilkara bahamensis*), acacia (*Acacia pinetorum*), pencil flower (*Stylosanthes hamata*), Indian mulberry, and grasses.

CAUSE OF DECLINE, THREATS

Habitat Destruction, Human Encroachment: Most experts agree that both Big Pine and No Name keys have now met or exceeded the permanent, seasonal, and transient human population numbers at which people and wildlife can coexist cohesively. Roads transect these keys every few hundred yards, and there are few places one can stand on either island without viewing some sort of residential or commercial development. Nearly all the land outside the National Key Deer Refuge is now developed or slated for development. Miles of mosquito ditches cut into the oolitic limestone become traps for fawns, drowning a number of them each year. Free-roaming dogs are a constant source of harassment to deer and also are responsible for fatalities. Every year, several deer die from intestinal blockage after ingesting plastic bags. The feeding of deer by residents and tourists alike, although outlawed, is a continuing problem. Feeding of deer not only provides the animal with an unnatural, often unhealthy diet but it also reduces their natural fear of humans and encourages them to congregate near roadways where they may be killed.

According to Tom Wilmer, a biologist with the National Key Deer Wildlife Refuge, "although automobile collisions are harmful to Key deer populations, protecting this species boils down to land use issues." It is difficult to manage land not owned by the refuge, and Key deer don't recognize the refuge's boundaries. The future of the population depends, in part, on how much of the remaining third of Big Pine Key habitat (now in private ownership) is acquired. Biologists fear that Key deer may be doomed to extinction if urbanization of the Lower Keys is not controlled soon.

Low Reproductive Rate, High Mortality Rate: Key deer naturally have a low reproductive rate, which probably is largely attributable to the absence of large mammalian predators in the Lower Keys. Their low reproductive frequency, coupled with the high rate of mortality, makes population increase difficult. Sadly, the chances are better than one in four that an individual Key deer observed on a visit to the Keys today will de dead a year from now.

Poaching: Uncontrolled hunting pushed the Key deer to the brink of extinction in the early 1900's. Though probably no longer a significant factor, a few deer are killed by poachers each year. In 1991 two men were convicted of clubbing a Key

deer to death. The Key deer population will never be large enough to support hunting.

Automobile Collisions: Traffic fatalities consistently account for more Key deer deaths (nearly 80 percent) than any other single cause. With more traffic inundating the Lower Keys, more deer-vehicle collisions occur. The toll was particularly high in 1995, with 94 deer killed, 66 by automobiles, surpassing the worst year on record, 1971 with 86 fatalities. The Monroe County Sheriff's Office and Florida Highway Patrol strictly enforce the 45 mph speed limit (35 after dark) on U.S. Highway 1 and 30 mph limit on smaller roads on keys that support Key deer. The speed limits were lowered to protect the deer, and they are also stringently enforced by federal officers within the Key Deer Refuge.

CURRENT TREND: *Stable.* The current population is estimated at 250–300 animals. Though considerably more than the 25–80 deer that remained in the 1950's, that number is lower than the population of 350–400 animals estimated in the 1970's.

Lower Keys Marsh Rabbit
Sylvilagus palustris hefneri
FAMILY LEPORIDAE; Order Lagomorpha
LISTED STATUS
FWC: Endangered, listed 1989
USF&WS: Endangered, listed 1990
Description: Lower Keys marsh rabbits are small to medium sized, dark brown rabbits, with a grayish white belly, small feet, and a rather inconspicuous dark brown tail. The Lower Keys marsh rabbit was first formally described by James "Skip" Lazell in 1984. He noted several

prominent differences between this rabbit and the Upper Keys marsh rabbit (*S. palustris paludicola*) and the mainland form (*S. p. palustris*), which warranted its recognition as a distinct subspecies. In a rather inventive approach to raising research funds to study the newly described subspecies, Lazell auctioned off the subspecific naming of the rabbit. The *Playboy* magazine organization demonstrated a considerable interest, presumably because of its Playboy Bunny trademark, and won the auction. Thus the subspecific portion of the Latin name is *hefneri*, after Hugh M. Hefner, the owner and editor-in-chief of Playboy Enterprises, Inc.

The Lower Keys marsh rabbit has different cranial characteristics from the Upper Keys and mainland marsh rabbits, as well as differences in overall size and coloration. When describing the subspecies, Lazell noted a shorter molariform tooth row (less than 80 percent of the dental symphysis), a higher and more convex frontonasal profile, and a broader cranium and longer dentary symphysis than other marsh rabbits.

The dorsal pelage is brownish with no red tints, and overall, it is darker and smaller than other Florida marsh rabbits. It should be noted, however, that some Big Pine Key specimens have some reddish dorsal coloration. The venter and tail underside of the race are gray. The sides of the face tend to be grayer than the dorsal pelage. Measurements for adults are: total length 12.6–15 inches (320–380 mm), tail length 0.8–1.7 inches (20–43 mm), hind foot 2.6–3.2 inches (65–80 mm), ear from notch 1.8–2.4 inches (45–62 mm), condylobasal length 2.43–2.95 inches (61.8–75 mm),

zygomatic breadth 1.25–1.42 inches (31.7–36 mm), molariform tooth row 0.50–0.54 inches (12.8–13.8 mm), frontonasal height at posterior tips of frontals 0.63–0.73 inches (15.9–18.5 mm), dental symphisis 0.64–0.69 inches (16.3–17.4 mm), cranium at posterior tips of zygomata 1.02–1.12 inches (25.9–28.5 mm), diastema 0.73–0.80 inches (18.6–20.3 mm), and width of foramen magnum 0.35–0.39 inches (8.9–10 mm). The dorsal surfaces of the parietal, frontal, and nasal bones are ornate. Adult Lower Keys marsh rabbits weigh between 35 and 50 ounces (1,000–1,400 g), and there appears to be little or no difference in weight or color between males and females.

Distribution: An endemic of extremely limited distribution, this race occurs only on a number of the oolitic Lower Keys. As of 1999, the Lower Keys marsh rabbit is known to inhabit portions of Boca Chica, Saddlebunch, Sugarloaf, and Big Pine keys, which are connected by U.S. Highway 1. They are also known to occur on the backcountry keys of Annette, Mayo, Big Munson, and Saddlehill. Approximately one third of the estimated 100–300 surviving Lower Keys marsh rabbits are found on the grounds of Key West Naval Air Station (which is actually on Boca Chica Key, adjacent to Key West). Records from the 1980's indicate this rabbit was also present on Hopkins, Welles, and Geiger keys.

In 1995 an extensive survey was conducted throughout the known historic range of this subspecies. The survey identified a total of 81 areas, comprising 783 acres (317 ha), that provided suitable habitat. Lower Keys marsh rabbits have been observed on 50 of the 81 sites. The areas occupied now total only about 625 acres (253 ha), and the majority of the sites are quite small, less than 7.4 acres (3 ha).

Marsh rabbits (of which there are three subspecies) occur throughout much of the Atlantic Coastal Plain of the southeastern United States, from the area of the Dismal Swamp in Virginia south through the Florida Keys.

Biology: Like other marsh rabbits, this subspecies occupies marsh habitats and adjacent thick sedge and grassy areas. The Lower Keys marsh rabbit is a habitat specialist, at home in the transition zone between the lower mangroves and the upland hardwood hammock communities. They depend on the grasses and sedges of the transition zone for food, shelter, and nesting sites. The areas inhabited are wetland communities in the middle of the salinity gradient in the Lower Keys. Their vegetative components often include grasses and shrubs such as saltwort, woody glasswort, and Key grass (*Monanthochloe littoralis*); succulent herbs such as sea daisy (*Borrichia frutescens*); sedges including *Cyperus* spp.; and scattered small trees such as buttonwood and blackbead. Some Lower Keys marsh rabbits utilize freshwater marsh areas dominated by sedges such as saw grass, succulent herbs like beach dropseed, and grasses including cordgrass. Coastal beach berm habitat is also used by marsh rabbits where present; these berms may be vegetated by more than 80 plant species, including gumbo-limbo, blolly (*Guapira discolor*), sea grape, poisonwood, and Spanish stopper. Mangrove communities are often utilized as corridors and occasionally as foraging areas. When nesting

in brackish habitats, they typically use growths of cordgrass or salt marsh fimbristylis (*Fimbristylis castanea*) for nesting materials. When nesting in freshwater wetlands, they typically use growths of saw grass for nesting sites.

As with other marsh rabbits, this race is primarily nocturnal but may be active in dense cover on overcast days. They are solitary in behavior. Rabbits spend most of their time in mid-marsh and high-marsh areas where food and shelter is plentiful. The home range varies considerably with individuals but averages about 0.8 acre (0.32 ha). Home ranges of adult marsh rabbits of the same sex do not overlap. Adult marsh rabbits tend to have permanent home ranges, but subadult males often disperse. These rabbits may display territorial behavior. Marsh rabbits commonly vocalize. They swim quite well, often taking to the water when pursued. They may use burrows on occasion, but that is not ordinary behavior.

The species forages on various grasses, herbs, sedges, and some tree leaves, requiring little fresh water to survive. Compared with other Lower Keys mammals, this rabbit has one of the highest capacities to concentrate urine. The three most common dietary items are cordgrass, seashore dropseed, and sea daisy. When foraging they tend to walk rather than hop.

The Lower Keys marsh rabbit exhibits classic metapopulation dynamics with its small body size, short life span, high reproductive output, and specific habitat requirements. Forty separate subpopulations of marsh rabbits occur in small disjunct portions of habitat on four keys. Individual rabbits from different disjunct portions of habitat are socially isolated from other subpopulations but interact through dispersal. Small isolated populations of marsh rabbits are vulnerable to extinction. The species depends on the recolonization of vacant habitat for survival. For it to persist in the wild, the immigration rates of the marsh rabbit have to be equal to or greater than the death rates.

Marsh rabbits of both sexes become sexually mature after approximately nine months of age. By nine months the majority of males have dispersed from their natal range, the majority of females have not. Lower Keys marsh rabbits, like other marsh rabbits, are polygamous and breed year round; unlike other subspecies, there is no apparent seasonal breeding pattern. A recent study of 24 marsh rabbits from five different populations indicates that all females breed, but only a portion of the males breed. Biologists believe that the Lower Keys marsh rabbit may be less fecund than other marsh rabbits. Marsh rabbits from mainland Florida can produce 14–18 young per female per litter; initial observations of Lower Keys marsh rabbits, however, indicate an average of only 1–3 young per nest. The average number of litters per year is also lower for the Lower Keys marsh rabbit (3.7) compared with marsh rabbits from mainland Florida (5.7 litters per year).

CAUSE OF DECLINE, THREATS

Habitat Destruction and Fragmentation: Habitat loss is the primary cause behind the decline of the Lower Keys marsh rabbit. As of the year 2000, there are few contiguous patches of marsh rabbit habitat greater than 5 hectares, and as time goes by, fewer and fewer subpopulations

are connected by corridors, which lowers the potential for genetic interchange and decreases the probability of persistence. Approximately 39 percent of the remaining suitable habitat (783 acres) is privately owned and is vulnerable to destruction or degradation.

Predation by Cats: Free-roaming cats are abundant throughout the Lower Keys and pose a major threat to juvenile and adult Lower Keys marsh rabbits. Although the loss of suitable habitat caused the initial declines of this subspecies, the high mortality attributed to domestic and feral cats is currently considered the greatest threat. Recent studies have revealed the presence of domestic and feral cats at 14 out of 19 sites occupied by Lower Keys marsh rabbits.

Automobile Collisions: The increase of both roads and traffic in the Lower Keys has resulted in an increased level of road mortality for the Lower Keys marsh rabbit and a number of other listed species. Dispersing males appear to be especially at risk. The majority of roadkills occur at night, when the rabbits are most active and visibility is poor.

Poaching: Intentional shooting or killing of Lower Keys marsh rabbits by humans does occur; however, it is thought to be infrequent.

Invasive Exotic Flora: Australian pine and Brazilian pepper are abundant in the transition zone throughout the Lower Keys, including the naval air station on Boca Chica. Both of these exotic species adversely alter the Lower Keys marsh rabbit's habitat. The needles of the Australian pine halt undergrowth, thus eliminating food, shelter, and nesting sites for the marsh rabbit. The Brazilian pepper competes with native vegetation, often displacing large areas of native trees and grasses.

Invasive Exotic Fauna: Feral hogs destroy or seriously degrade marsh rabbit habitat while foraging, and baby rabbits may fall victim to the painful biocidic bites of exotic fire ants.

Mowing: Grass mowing may kill young marsh rabbits in the nest, and it temporarily destroys shelter used by marsh rabbits, nesting sites, and food.

Contaminants: Biologists believe that marsh rabbits may be exposed to harmful pesticides or other chemicals used in marsh habitats. Chemicals such as Prival, a rodenticide used to kill black rats, are lethal if ingested.

CURRENT TREND: *Declining.* According to the federal recovery plan, "the Lower Keys marsh rabbit's recovery potential is quite low due to the lack of available habitat and increased mortality due to cats and vehicular traffic." Unchecked development of the Lower Keys will ultimately result in the extinction of the Lower Keys marsh rabbit. Although once an abundant species in the Lower Keys, including Key West, in 1991 the entire population of Lower Keys marsh rabbits was estimated to be approximately 300 individuals; by 1993 the population had dwindled to only about 100 individuals. The 2000 population estimates are between 100 and 300 individuals rangewide.

Big Cypress Fox Squirrel
Sciurus niger avicennia
FAMILY SCIURIDAE; Order Rodentia
LISTED STATUS
FWC: Threatened, listed 1973

USF&WS: Species of management concern

Description: Although noticeably larger than gray squirrels, this race is somewhat smaller than other fox squirrel subspecies in Florida. External average measurements are: total length 23.6 inches (600 mm) or less, head and body 11 inches (278 mm), hind foot 2.95 inches (75 mm), skull length 2.5 inches (62 mm) or less, skull width 1.1 inches (27 mm) or less. Adult weight averages nearly 2 pounds (900 g). As with other subspecies of fox squirrels, pelage color of Big Cypress fox squirrels is quite variable. The morph most frequently encountered is a brownish or buff color phase, followed by a black or very dark color phase; occasionally light tan squirrels are observed. The lips, nose, and ear tips are generally white regardless of the color phase. The top of the head and upper back are often black, and some squirrels appear to be masked. Fox squirrels have large, bushy tails.

Distribution: This Southwest Florida endemic is restricted in distribution to portions of Monroe, Dade, Collier, Lee, and Hendry counties. Its range is not contiguous, and it is now scarce or extirpated from several former haunts. For reasons not clearly understood, Big Cypress fox squirrel populations have recently disappeared from Corkscrew Swamp Sanctuary and Everglades City, while relatively dense populations thrive on several urban golf courses in Naples. The range of this subspecies is separated from the range of the closest subspecies, Sherman's fox squirrel (*Sciurus niger shermani*), by at least 30 miles. Historically, the range of this subspecies is believed to have extended farther east than its current range. Fox squirrels that occurred in eastern Dade County until the early 1950's were identified as intergrades between the *avicennia* and *shermani* subspecies (that population is now extirpated).

Biology: The Big Cypress fox squirrel has been observed in most habitats within its range, including oak woodland, pine flatwoods, tropical hardwood hammock, cypress swamp, and mangrove communities. This race, also referred to as the mangrove fox squirrel, does occasionally forage in mangrove forests; its use of this habitat is seasonal, however. The squirrel probably occurs most frequently in pine woodlands with minimal understory, where fire has not been routinely suppressed. Fire suppression has altered natural communities throughout its range and may have rendered many areas unsuitable. The author has observed these squirrels in a cypress strand swamp within Big Cypress National Preserve and on golf courses in Naples surrounded by urbanization. Flourishing populations have been well documented on several Naples golf courses. Fox squirrels exploit the plentiful native and exotic vegetation on golf courses and benefit from the lack of natural predators. These suburban fox squirrels consume cabbage palm fruits (which they cache), cypress cone seeds, and fruits from fig trees (*Ficus* spp.) and queen palms (*Cocos pamosa*).

South Florida slash pine cones are believed to be the chief dietary item of rural populations, but acorns, black mangrove seeds, bromeliad buds, and fungi are also consumed. An individual was observed eating a nonnative Cuban treefrog. Fox squirrels forage both on the ground and in trees.

Though typically solitary and nongregarious, these squirrels sometimes forage in small, loose groups. Activity often diminishes during the hottest, most humid weeks of summer. During the rainy season, fox squirrels inhabiting mesic habitats are more apt to travel distances through the canopy of trees than on the ground. Nests are constructed in the tops of slash pines, hardwoods, or cabbage palms of sticks, twigs, bromeliads, and Spanish moss. Mating takes place from June through August; the gestation period is approximately 42 days. Likely predators of adults or young include birds of prey, bobcats, and several snake species.

CAUSE OF DECLINE, THREATS

Habitat Destruction, Fire Suppression: Though the specific cause of decline of this animal is puzzling, biologists believe that the destruction, alteration, and fragmentation of suitable habitat are largely to blame. Rampant residential and commercial development combined with land conversion for agriculture has claimed much of the historic range of this species. Many populations are now completely isolated by urban sprawl, preventing genetic exchange and recolonization. Decades of fire suppression rangewide have resulted in widespread plant succession and ultimately eliminated much of the suitable fox squirrel habitat.

Poaching: The hunting of Big Cypress fox squirrels was permitted until 1972, and overhunting before then was no doubt a factor in the squirrel's decline. Surveys conducted by the state indicate that poaching of Big Cypress fox squirrels is still prevalent in some areas.

Other Threats: Road mortality in both suburban and rural areas and free-roaming dogs are responsible for a number of squirrel deaths each year.

CURRENT TREND: *Declining* generally, but *stable* in some areas.

Key Largo Wood Rat
Neotoma floridana smalli
Key Largo Cotton Mouse
Peromyscus gossypinus allapaticola
FAMILY CRICETIDAE; Order Rodentia

The Key Largo wood rat and the Key Largo cotton mouse are treated in the same account because their ranges are identical or nearly so, as are their habitat needs and threats to their survival.

LISTED STATUS

Key Largo Wood Rat

FWC: Endangered, listed 1972
USF&WS: Endangered, listed 1984 (threatened 1969–1983)

Key Largo Cotton Mouse

FWC: Endangered, listed 1975
USF&WS: Endangered, listed 1984

Description

Key Largo Wood Rat: The pelage of the Key Largo wood rat is grayish brown or sepia dorsally with cinnamon flanks and white or cream ventral coloration. It has large, conspicuous ears (they may exceed 1 inch), large protuberant eyes, and a hairy tail. This species differs from European rats in that its tail is not ringed with scales; the wood rat tail is covered with fine fur to its end. The forefeet are white to the wrist, and the hind feet are usually white to the ankle. Physical dimensions are head and body length 4.7–9.1 inches (120–230 mm), tail length 5.1–7.5 inches (130–190 mm), and hind foot length 1.3–1.5 inches (32–39 mm). The average weight of adult males (9.1 ounces, 258 g) is greater than the average weight of females (7.4 ounces, 210 g).

Key Largo Cotton Mouse: The Key Largo cotton mouse is a medium-sized mouse with large ears and protruding eyes. Its dorsal pelage is reddish brown, its flanks are more of a dusky brown, and the ventral pelage is white. The bicolored tail is dark brown above and whitish below. The overall dimensions are larger on average than other cotton mouse subspecies: head and body length 6.7–7.4 inches (170–189 mm), tail length 2.8–3.4 inches (72–87 mm), and hind foot length 0.8–0.9 inches (21–23 mm).

Distribution: The ranges of the Key Largo wood rat and the Key Largo cotton mouse are sympatric, and both are currently restricted to suitable habitat on the northern half of Key Largo in Monroe County, precisely, tropical hardwood hammocks north of the intersection of U.S. Highway 1 and SR905. The range has been reduced in recent decades by habitat destruction and fragmentation. The historic distribution of both species is believed to have included forested uplands once present throughout Key Largo.

The Key Largo wood rat represents the southernmost subspecies of the eastern wood rat (*Neotoma floridana*), a widespread species of the southeastern United States. The subspecific name, *smalli*, honors John Small, a botanist who located wood rat houses on Key Largo in 1932. Wood rats of several species occur throughout much of the United States and include the Allegheny wood rat (*N. magister*) and the white-throated wood rat (*N. albigula*).

The Key Largo cotton mouse is an insular race of cotton mouse (*Peromyscus gossypinus*), a widespread species of the southeastern United States. The genus includes deer mice (*P. maniculatus*) and white-footed mice (*P. leocopus*).

In 1970, 19 Key Largo wood rats and 14 Key Largo cotton mice were released on Lignum Vitae Key. It was reported that both rodent species may have been briefly established there, but they are now believed to be extirpated.

Biology: The Key Largo wood rat and the Key Largo cotton mouse are both habitat specialists that depend on the tropical hardwood hammock communities of Key Largo. Appropriately, the subspecific name for the Key Largo cotton mouse, *allapaticola*, is derived from the Seminole Indian word, *allapattah*, which describes the dry, tropical deciduous hammocks of southern Florida. The remaining tracts of tropical hardwood hammocks on Key Largo, though relatively small, represent the largest areas of tropical forest remaining in the continental United States.

Tropical hardwood hammocks represent the climax vegetative stage of the Keys upland rockland communities. Mature hammocks are junglelike in appearance and typically have a shaded, humid, and somewhat protected microclimate, with little wind and less temperature variation than adjacent, more exposed environments. The substrate is composed of porous Key Largo limestone, which sporadically juts from the surface. Hammock soils are rather thin but quite fertile and support a wide array of flora, including many tropical tree and shrub species that reach their northernmost

geographical limits in extreme southern Florida. More than 100 species of native trees have been recorded from the hammocks of the Florida Keys. The height of trees in the mature tropical hammocks of North Key Largo ranges between 30 and 40 feet (9–12 m), and the understory is generally open. Trees characteristic of the North Key Largo hammock's canopy include gumbo-limbo, pigeon plum, black ironwood, strangler fig, poison-wood, mahogany, Jamaican dogwood (*Piscidia piscipula*), and wild tamarind. Understory shrubs and trees include torchwood, soldierwood, wild coffee (*Psychotria undata*), marlberry, crab-wood (*Gymnanthes lucida*), milkbark (*Drypetes diversifolia*), white stopper (*Eugenia axillaris*), and Spanish stopper. Groundcover species, where present, may include snowberry (*Chiococca parviflora*) and yellowroot (*Morinda royoc*). Undisturbed lower elevations of Key Largo (often adjacent to tropical hammocks) support mangrove communities where three mangrove species and buttonwood comprise the dominant vegetation. Upland areas of Key Largo formerly supported areas of pineland (*Pinus elliottii* var. *densa*); however, the only islands of the Florida Keys that now support this pyrogenic habitat are Big Pine Key and some of the other Lower Keys west of the Seven Mile Bridge.

Both species achieve their highest population densities in undisturbed, mature tropical hammocks. Population density estimates for wood rats in North Key Largo hammocks vary dramatically. In 1978 Larry N. Brown estimated the density to be approximately 0.5 animals per acre (1.2 per ha), in 1981 S. L. Hersh estimated 1.0 per acre (2.5 per ha), in 1982 D. B. Barbour and Stephen R. Humphrey estimated 0.9 per acre (2.2 per ha), and in 1988 Humphrey estimated 3.1 per acre (7.6 per ha). It should be noted that methods of estimation have become more reliable; the initial estimate counted stick nests, and the most recent estimate is based on grid live trapping. In 1988 Humphrey estimated that there was approximately 2,100 acres (851 ha) of suitable habitat remaining on Key Largo. Based on the 1988 density estimates (3.1 wood rats and 15.5 cotton mice per acre), the total populations are 6,500 Key Largo wood rats and 18,000 Key Largo cotton mice. Based on Brown's 1978 estimate that only 297–395 acres (120–160 ha) of suitable habitat remained, the estimated total population for each species would be 920–1,225 Key Largo wood rats and 4,604–6,123 Key Largo cotton mice.

For reasons unknown, populations of Key Largo wood rats and Key Largo cotton mice have declined drastically in recent years (from 1995 to 2002). Recent population estimates, based on trapping surveys, indicate that the total population of Key Largo wood rats may be as low as 170 individuals. The population of Key Largo cotton mice is unknown. The significant decline of Key Largo wood rats in the wild has prompted the USF&WS to remove several specimens from the wild to develop a captive breeding population (typically a last ditch effort to save a species). Two theories to explain the extreme decline of these species are predation by feral house cats and diseases associated with a roundworm found in raccoon feces in northern Key Largo.

Key Largo wood rat populations depend on their habitat to provide adequate cover and nest-building materials. Wood rats construct large stick houses (up to 4 feet in height and 7 feet in diameter), assembled from branches, sticks, twigs, and various other objects. The sticks typically measure 1–3 inches (25–76 mm) in diameter. The stick house characteristic of this species is used for bedding, breeding, and feeding activities. Nests are frequently constructed at the base of a fallen tree, stump, or exposed limestone, or on occasion in abandoned cars or farm machinery. The typical nest will have one central nest chamber with several entrances and is generally used by only one adult wood rat. Nests may be used by several generations of wood rats, and studies of other subspecies of *Neotoma floridana* reveal that nests may be repaired, enhanced, or enlarged with repeated uses. Wood rats may use more than one nest. Other wood rat subspecies may be somewhat more inclined to build elaborate stick nests than this race; some nests encountered on Key Largo are very crude, with just a few sticks placed at the entrance of a limestone fissure. The wood rat's trait of elaborate nest-building is shared by Australia's endangered stick-nest rats (*Leporillus*). Biologists studying the Key Largo wood rat have noted tendencies for these rodents to decorate their domiciles with brightly colored objects, including seashells and the shells of tree snails, a habit well known among western *Neotoma* species (pack rats).

The habitat requirements for the Key Largo cotton mouse are similar to those of the wood rat; however, the required habitat parameters seem to be less narrow than the wood rat's. Though it prefers undisturbed mature hammock, the Key Largo cotton mouse is more likely than the wood rat to occur in early-successional and recently burned forest. The leaf-lined nests of the cotton mouse are, like the wood rat's, often placed at the base of a fallen tree or stump and are sometimes made within the larger wood rat nests. Nests may also be made within hollow logs or stumps and in rock crevices. The entrance hole of a cotton mouse nest measures approximately 1.2–3.5 inches (30.5–89 mm) in diameter. Cotton mice and wood rats travel through hammocks using networks of subterranean runways and tunnels.

The wood rats and cotton mice of Key Largo both spend a substantial amount of time in trees. Both species are predominantly nocturnal, and both are omnivorous. Their diet is composed largely of buds, leaves, seeds, and fruits. Key Largo wood rats are also known to consume cicadas, slugs, and possibly tree snails, on occasion. Freshly gnawed shells of Florida tree snails (*Liguus fasciatus*) have been found in the nests of Key Largo wood rats, indicating the snails themselves were consumed; it is possible, however, that wood rats may have simply collected and chewed shell pieces for their mineral content.

Female Key Largo wood rats are capable of reproducing year round and may produce two litters annually. Reproduction activity reportedly peaks during the winter and the summer. The average litter size is two, with one to four young reported. They are probably sexually mature after about five months, and the average life span is probably less than 1 year. The Key Largo cotton mouse also may reproduce throughout the year. Females may produce two or three litters, averaging four young per litter. Their average life span is only 2–5 months.

Known or suspected predators of both rodents include raccoons (the most significant natural predator), bobcats, great-horned owls, barn owls, broad-winged hawks (*Buteo platypterus*), rat snakes (*Elaphe obsoleta* and *E. guttata*), indigo snakes, black racers, eastern diamond-back rattlesnakes, fire ants, and feral and domestic cats. Key Largo cotton mice reportedly have been parasitized by bot flies (*Cuterebridae*).

CAUSE OF DECLINE, THREATS

Habitat Destruction and Fragmentation: The loss and fragmentation of suitable habitat is by far the greatest threat to both the wood rat and the cotton mouse. Approximately half of the tropical hardwood hammocks that historically covered the uplands of Key Largo have been eliminated as a result of residential and commercial development. In the year 2000 only a few tracts of tropical hammocks remained in the southern half of Key Largo that exceeded 10 acres (4 ha) in size. The remaining small parcels are disturbed and contain relatively immature vegetation; they no longer support wood rat or cotton mouse populations. Fortunately, a large percentage of remaining habitat occurs on protected lands within the confines of Crocodile Lakes National Wildlife Refuge and Key Largo Hammocks State Botanical Site.

Invasive Exotic Fauna: The predatory inclination of free-ranging cats and dogs poses a direct threat to wood rats and cotton mice, especially near human habitation. It is suspected that fire ants are a threat to cotton mice and young wood rats in some areas. In 1995 three Key Largo cotton mice captured in traps as part of a research program were apparently killed by fire ants (personal communication, Britt Keith, 1995). Ongoing research indicates that the black rat, a large aggressive exotic, may be a significant competitor to wood rats and, to a lesser degree, cotton mice. Biologists have noted low densities of black rats at some study sites, but at other sites the black rats trapped equaled or exceeded the number of wood rats trapped. In 1995 the author assisted state biologist Britt Keith with her research involving wood rats and cotton mice by checking traplines at her study site at Key Largo Hammocks. On 16 October, of the 100 traps located in pristine, mature hammock, 10 contained cotton mice (1 animal per trap), 5 contained black rats, and, oddly, 1 trap contained a female northern cardinal (*Cardinalis cardinalis*). No wood rats were trapped. Keith believes black rats may be displacing the wood rats in some areas. Her research indicates that in these areas, wood rat populations may be decreasing while black rat populations are increasing. The author also encountered an indigo snake and a merlin, both potential predators, at this site.

Invasive Exotic Flora: Suitable wood rat and cotton mouse habitat, once disturbed, is quickly invaded by exotic plants that may, if left unchecked, alter hammocks so much that they eventually become unable to support the native rodents. Events that precipitate the invasion of exotic flora include land clearing; dumping of trash, building materials, and plant debris; and severe weather events.

A survey recorded more than 20 exotic plant species in or near the tropical hardwood hammocks of Key Largo. **Severe Weather:** Effects of hurricanes and severe tropical storms (storm surge, wind shear, uprooting of trees, soil disturbances) can be devastating to the tropical hammock habitat of these rodents. Disturbed hammocks and immature hammocks appear to be more vulnerable to the effects of severe storms than undisturbed mature hammocks. Hurricane Andrew came ashore at Elliott Key, just north of Key Largo, in August 1992. Approximately 200 acres (80 ha) of North Key Largo hammocks lost 70 percent of their canopy as a result of this ferocious storm. Hurricanes and tropical storms are regular events in the Upper Keys, and both the wood rat and cotton mouse have survived dozens of them; however, the current limited and isolated distribution of the rodents coupled with reduced overall populations renders the species more vulnerable to extinction as a result of severe weather events. The after-effects of severe storms, such as loss of canopy or changes in vegetative structure, may make hammocks more susceptible to the invasion of exotic plants.

Automobile Collisions: Because SR905 cuts directly through the last stronghold of optimum habitat for both species, road mortality remains a constant threat.

Other Threats: Wildfire, though rare in tropical hardwood hammocks, represents a threat to wood rats, cotton mice, and their habitat. Key Largo wood rats may be susceptible to raccoon roundworms, a parasite that has plagued wood rats in other regions. Chemicals used to kill black rats at homesites near hardwood hammocks will also kill wood rats and cotton mice.

CURRENT TREND: Both rodents are *declining.*

Florida's Beach Mice (5 subspecies)

Peromyscus polionotus
Perdido Key beach mouse
Peromyscus p. trissyllepsis
Choctawhatchee beach mouse
Peromyscus p. allophrys
St. Andrew beach mouse
Peromyscus p. peninsularis
Anastasia Island beach mouse
Peromyscus p. phasma
Southeastern beach mouse
Peromyscus p. niveiventris
FAMILY CRICETIDAE; Order Rodentia

LISTED STATUS

FWC: Endangered, Perdido Key beach mouse listed 1986 (threatened 1975–1985), Choctawhatchee beach mouse listed 1985 (threatened 1975–1984), St. Andrew beach mouse listed 1989, Anastasia Island beach mouse listed 1989; threatened, southeastern beach mouse listed 1989

USF&WS: Endangered, Perdido Key beach mouse listed 1985, Choctawhatchee beach mouse listed 1984, Anastasia Island beach mouse listed 1989; candidate, St. Andrew beach mouse; threatened, southeastern beach mouse listed 1989

Description: The beach mice described here are all subspecies of the oldfield mouse (*Peromyscus polionotus*), one of approximately 55 species of the genus *Peromyscus.* Of the 16 recognized subspecies of *Peromyscus polionotus,* 8 are distinctly paler races that inhabit beach and dune areas of the Atlantic and Gulf coasts, collectively known as beach mice. This species is one of the smallest mice inhabiting Florida; its largest races rarely exceed 6 inches (152 mm) in total length. Adults weigh 0.25–0.50 ounce (8–15 g). The ears and feet of beach mice tend to be proportionally larger than the inland *Peromyscus polionotus* subspecies. The assorted beach mice races are quite variable in coloration; inland subspecies, however, tend to be considerably darker than coastal races, some of which are almost uniformly white. The differences in coloration between the inland races and the beach races are cryptic, evolutionary adaptations to the specific coastal environments. The soils where darker races dwell are dark; conversely, the very pale beach mice inhabit the bleached white sands of coastal dunes and beaches. The abdomen, sides, and cheeks of beach mice are usually pure white, and various amounts of white are present on the face and head. The eyes of all races are large and black. The feet are flesh-colored. The adjective "cute" is appropriate for these little rodents, especially when comparing them with their smelly, ugly, introduced relatives such as black rats (*Rattus rattus*), which often come to mind when one utters the word "rodent."

Perdido Key beach mouse: Though somewhat variable in color, the dorsal pelage of this subspecies is generally paler than that of the Choctawhatchee beach mouse (which occurs to the east) and the Alabama beach mouse (which occurs to the west). As with other races, the pelage of the abdomen, sides, and cheeks is white. The face has various amounts of white, often merging with the darker pelage on the forehead. The tail of this race lacks the dark stripe often present on other subspecies. The total length ranges from 4.5 to 5.4 inches (115–139 mm). The head and body measure 2.7–3.3 inches (70–85 mm); the tail is 1.8–2.1 inches (45–54 mm). The hind foot of adults measures 0.6–0.7 inches (16–18 mm) in length.

Choctawhatchee beach mouse: This beach mouse is also variable in coloration, with several different color morphs recorded. Though decidedly paler than inland races, it is generally darker than other beach subspecies. The dorsal pelage color, though variable, is typically some shade of light brown ranging from yellowish brown to an orange brown. The abdomen and lower sides are white. Various amounts of white are present on the face and nose. Total length of adults ranges from 4.4 to 6 inches (112–152 mm). The head and body length ranges from 2.7 to 3.5 inches (70–89 mm). The tail, which is the longest among the Panhandle's beach mice, measures 1.7–2.5 inches (43–64 mm). In this race, the tail may have a stripe. The hind foot is 0.6–0.7 inches (16–19 mm) long, and the ear is 0.5–0.68 inches (14–17.2 mm) long.

St. Andrew beach mouse: One of the palest beach mice subspecies, this race is typically buffy above with white fur covering much of the underparts and sides. Average measurements of adults are total length 5 inches (127 mm), head and body length 3 inches (76 mm), tail 2 inches (51 mm), hind foot 0.7 inches (18.5 mm), ear (males) 0.65 inches (16.5 mm) and (females) 0.6 inches (15 mm).

Anastasia Island beach mouse: This subspecies is typically lighter in color than the southeastern beach mouse, which occurs on the Atlantic Coast south of this race. The dorsal region is buffy with a grayish or pinkish wash. The underparts, nose, area around the eyes, legs, and feet are usually very white. The unicolor tail is also white. This subspecies and the southeastern beach mouse are among the larger beach mice. Average measurements of adult Anastasia Island beach mice are as total length 5.4 inches (139 mm), tail 2.07 inches (53 mm), hind foot 0.7 inches (18.7 mm), ear 0.55 inches (13.9 mm).

Southeastern beach mouse: The buffy-colored pelage of this race, though paler than inland races, tends to be slightly darker than the coat of the Anastasia Island beach mouse. Hairs in the dorsal region are much darker at the base. The underparts are bright white with white extending upward on the sides, throat, and face. The bicolored tail is buff above and white below. Average measurements of adult southeastern beach mice are total length 5.42 inches (139 mm), tail 2.03 inches (52 mm).

The average weight of adults is 0.4–0.63 ounces (12–18 g), with gravid females weighing as much as 0.70–1.05 ounces (20–30 g).

Distribution: Eight races of beach mice occupy certain coastal areas from northern South Carolina south and west through much of coastal Florida, coastal Alabama, and a small portion of Mississippi. One of the subspecies, the pallid beach mouse, is now believed to be extinct. Seven of the subspecies have occurred in Florida, and six are endemics. The Santa Rosa beach mouse (*Peromyscus polionotus leucocephalus*), a federal species of management concern not discussed at length here, occurs in the

Panhandle. The eighth subspecies is the Alabama beach mouse (*Peromyscus p. ammobates*), a federally endangered species that occurs just a few miles from the Florida border in Alabama. The Perdido Key beach mouse is nearly a Florida endemic, being restricted to coastal dunes on the Florida-Alabama border.

Perdido Key beach mouse: The Perdido Key beach mouse ranges farther west than any other Florida beach mouse subspecies. Historically, this subspecies occurred, probably continuously, in coastal dune habitats from Pensacola Bay, Florida, in the east, to Perdido Bay, Alabama, in the west, including portions of Gulf Islands National Seashore. Currently, the sole naturally occurring population is restricted to the western tip of Perdido Key at Gulf State Park, Baldwin County, Alabama. Hurricane Frederick, which struck the Gulf Coast near the Florida-Alabama border in September 1979, is suspected of causing the extirpation of Perdido Key beach mice from Gulf Islands National Seashore. Perdido Key beach mice have been reintroduced in several areas within the historic range, and the USF&WS plans to continue the reintroduction in an effort to establish self-sustaining populations. In recent years, Florida populations have not been faring as well as Alabama populations. According to federal biologist Jim Moyers, this race was recovering and fairing relatively well until a category 3 hurricane, Opal, blasted the Gulf Coast on 4 October 1995. Many beach mice were drowned and much of the dune habitat destroyed.

Choctawhatchee beach mouse: Historically this endemic subspecies occupied coastal dune habitats from Choctawhatchee Bay, in Okaloosa County, east to Shell Island in St. Andrew Bay, in Bay County. That range was more or less contiguous, but it is currently restricted to three disjunct populations, each only a few miles long, on Shell Island in Bay County, Topsail Hill near Destin in Okaloosa County (recently acquired by the Florida Park Service), and Grayton Beach State Recreational Area in Walton County. The population at Grayton Beach is a result of reintroduction programs during the late 1980's. A fourth population may inhabit a small stretch of dunes near Deer Lake. The area is currently owned by the St. Joe Paper Company, which has denied requests from the state to place traps in an attempt to determine whether the beach mouse is present. Much of the remaining habitat was destroyed or severely degraded by Hurricane Opal in 1995.

St. Andrew beach mouse: As of 1999, this species is restricted to a single, isolated population in St. Joseph State Park in Gulf County. This population is limited to a strip of lofty dunes no more than 5 miles (8 km) long. Historically, this race occupied a small but wider range in Gulf and Bay counties, including Crooked Island on Tyndall Air Force Base, Bay County's Mexico Beach, and the area of Port Saint Joe in Gulf County. The race occurs farther east than the other four beach mice that inhabit coastal ecosystems along the northern Gulf of Mexico.

Anastasia Island beach mouse: Development has now consumed most, if not all, of the northern two thirds of this endemic beach mouse's historic range. The race is now restricted to portions of Anastasia Island, an Atlantic barrier island off St. Johns County in northeastern Florida. Even on Anastasia Island, the distribution of this beach mouse is not contiguous, and viable populations are known from only two locations, at Fort Matanzas National Monument on the southern end of the island and Anastasia Island State Recreational Area on the northern end. Elsewhere on Anastasia Island, the rodent occurs very locally, and these smaller, disjunct populations are not likely to survive far into the future. According to the federal recovery plan, only about 3 miles of beach now supports viable populations, and the entire range is limited to approximately 14 linear miles (23 km) of coastline. The narrow strip of dune habitat occupied by the Anastasia Island beach mouse is rarely wider than 500 feet (152 m) and often as narrow as 25 feet (7.6 m) as suitable habitat is converted to residential development. In 1986 biologists tried to locate Anastasia Island beach mice at several other locations within the historic range in St. Johns County that appeared to support suitable habitat, including sites between Mickler Landing and South Ponte Vedra Beach; they were unsuccessful. The historic distribution encompassed approximately 50 linear miles (80 km) of coastline, ranging from about the boundary between St. Johns and Duval counties in the north to the area of Matanzas Inlet, St. Johns County, in the south. The USF&WS recently reintroduced the subspecies to the beach dune system of Guana River State Park in St. Johns County.

Southeastern beach mouse: Historically, this subspecies occupied a strip of Atlantic coastline approximately 175 miles long from the area of Ponce Inlet in Volusia County southward to the area of Broward County's Hollywood Beach and possibly as far south as Miami. Now extirpated from south of Fort Pierce Inlet, its current range is limited to 40–50 miles of coastline at the northern end of its historic distribution. Populations are now largely restricted to protected public lands that safeguard most of what remains of suitable beach mouse habitat. Scattered populations inhabit dune systems within Merritt Island National Wildlife Refuge, Canaveral National Seashore and Brevard County's Cape Canaveral Air Force Base, Sebastian Inlet State Recreational Area (south of the inlet), Turtle Trail Public Beach and Treasure Shores Park in Brevard County, and possibly Pepper Park and Fort Pearce state recreational areas in St. Lucie County. This subspecies has also been reported from the beach area of the Seaview residential subdivision in Indian River County.

Biology: The life history, habits, threats, and recovery objectives of each of Florida's morphologically similar beach mice are nearly the same, although certain races are more imperiled than others. The most important habitat used by beach mice is primary frontal dunes, with the densest populations in the sea oat zone of undisturbed dune systems that are devoid of exotic house mice, domestic cats, or red foxes. In rare instances, beach mice have been encountered more than 0.6 mile (1 km) inland, but the width of suitable habitat is generally much narrower. Characteristic plants of these dune environments include sea oats, beach grass (*Panicum* amarum and *P. repens*), railroad vine, camphor weed (*Heterotheca subaxillaris*), little bluestem (*Schizachyrium maritimum*), sea rocket (*Cakile constricta*), and beach morning glory (*Ipomoea stolonifera*). Older secondary dunes and scrub dunes just inland from the frontal dunes may also be inhabited. Plants in these areas may include sand live oak and scrub oak, seaside rosemary, dwarfed magnolia, saw palmetto, prickly pear cactus, sand pine, slash pine, sea grape, wax myrtle, and beach tea (*Croton punctatus*).

The home ranges of male and female beach mice are about the same size; their ranges, however, expand significantly during the spring. Young beach mice may roam extensively in their search for a vacant home range, but adults generally use an established home range area for life. Beach mice are nocturnal and are reportedly most active on still, moonlit nights. Much of the beach mouse's life centers on its burrows and network of subterranean tunnels. A mouse may excavate a burrow itself or use the abandoned burrows of other animals, such as ghost crabs (*Ocypode* spp.). A typical burrow contains a primary entrance, frequently located on a dune slope or at the foot of a tuft of grass or a shrub, and three main physical features: an entrance tunnel, which generally descends straight from the entrance; a nesting chamber, 2–3 feet (61–91 cm) into the dune; and an escape tunnel, which leads from the nesting chamber to within approximately 1 inch (2.5 cm) of the surface. A home range may contain as many as 20 burrows that serve as retreats from predators and locations to store food.

Some adult beach mice do not pair, but most form a monogamous pair that remains together until one of the mice dies. Beach mice typically breed in the winter between November and January. Large numbers of immature mice are present during the breeding season, which is when populations attain their greatest numbers. The mortality rate among beach mice is quite high, and the populations typically drop to their lowest numbers in the summer. Research involving Alabama beach mice revealed that 63 percent of captured mice lived less than four months following their capture. The mortality rate is probably similar in other subspecies. The reproductive potential of Florida's beach mice is relatively high. Litter size varies between 2 and 7 young, with an average of 4. It is believed that young become sexually mature after only six or seven weeks. Captive beach mice have been capable of producing litters as often as every 26 days and are believed to be capable of producing more than 80 young in a lifetime. Average longevity in the wild is probably less than five months.

The diet of beach mice comprises both vegetable and animal matter, but the former typically makes up the bulk of it. Beach mice feed on the seeds or fruits of sea oats, railroad vine, beach grass, prickly pear cactus, and sea rocket. Known or suspected natural predators include red and gray foxes, bobcats, skunks, raccoons, owls, coachwhip snakes, racers, and rat snakes. The great blue heron, which roosts in the dunes where beach mice forage after dark, no doubt is an occasional predator. In many areas, free-roaming domestic cats take a serious toll on beach mice.

CAUSE OF DECLINE, THREATS

Habitat Destruction: The ever-increasing coastal real estate boom in Florida continues the loss of formerly suitable beach mouse habitat within the range of all subspecies. According to the federal recovery plan, the Perdido Key, Choctawhatchee, and Alabama beach mice were reported to be "abundant and widespread throughout their respective ranges" as late as the 1940's, when the coastline of the Florida Panhandle and Alabama was largely intact. At least 80 percent of the range of those three races has been lost to development. Loss or degradation of habitat from development and intensive recreational use remains the most serious threat to beach mice populations, and the effects of other threats such as hurricanes are amplified as a result. The Florida Coastal Setback Law (enacted to protect Florida's coastline by prohibiting construction within set limits above mean high tide) has been of some help in protecting beach mice, but beach mice do occur well beyond the setback lines. Development on the coastline of Volusia and Flagler counties, coupled with predation by domestic cats, replacement by house mice, and other threats brought by humans, is responsible for the extinction of the pallid beach mouse, a formerly abundant subspecies last recorded in 1946.

Most areas currently supporting beach mice populations are state or federal lands subject to intensive human use. Such use of the fragile dune systems increases beach mouse vulnerability to extirpation. Erosion of dunes and loss of dune-stabilizing plants (sea oats) caused by vehicular and pedestrian traffic have rendered dune areas incapable of sustaining beach mouse populations.

Biologists are also concerned that routine channel maintenance conducted by the U.S. Army Corps of Engineers will damage fragile dune systems used by beach mice. The programs often remove accumulations of sand from channels and deposit it on beach areas inhabited by beach mice. Hovercraft used in military exercises conducted in nearshore areas of Tyndall Air Force Base have reportedly damaged dunes harboring St. Andrew beach mice.

Competition and Predation from Nonnative Animals: Introduced house mice often outcompete native beach mice. Evidence indicates beach mice have been displaced and possibly totally excluded from several locations invaded by house mice. In February and March 1986, biologists were able to trap several St. Andrew beach mice on Crooked Island East, within Tyndall Air Force Base in Bay County, and estimated the population there to be approximately 150 individuals. Extensive trapping in the same locality in the spring of 1987 produced many house mice but just a single beach mouse. This population is now believed to be extirpated. The presence of house mice in otherwise suitable habitat may eliminate the ability of beach mice to repopulate an area. Populations of black rats are now established within Palm Beach County's Manalapan Beach, within the range of the southeastern beach mouse. Predation of beach mice by free-running house cats, and to a lesser extent domestic dogs, is one of the more serious threats in many areas. In some Gulf Coast areas, including Perdido Key, red fox (a chief predator of beach mice) populations have become unnaturally abundant. Red foxes have been present in these areas only 50–60 years and are generally regarded as a nonnative species. **Severe Storms:** Hurricanes and tropical storms threaten beach mice and their habitats. The 1995 hurricane season delivered two devastating hurricanes to Florida, Erin and Opal, and both wreaked havoc on beach mice and their dune habitats. Opal consumed more than 100 feet of beach and foredune throughout the range of most, if not all, of the Panhandle's five beach mouse races. After Opal's wrath, biologists became concerned that one or more species may have been swept to extinction. Fortunately, field investigations soon verified that each Gulf coastal race survived. Hurricane Erin came ashore on the Atlantic Coast near Indian River County's Vero Beach and damaged frontal dune systems inhabited by southeastern beach mice. The loss of beach mice and their habitat was not as severe as Opal's destruction on the Gulf Coast. In 1985 Kate and Elana destroyed large portions of the St. Andrew beach mouse dune habitat. Frederick struck the Panhandle in 1979, destroying much of the Perdido Key beach mouse population. Severe storms often destroy beach mouse food supplies and refuges and increases their vulnerability to predation and subsequent storms.

An estimated 75–80 percent of the Choctawhatchee beach mouse population perished as a result of Hurricane Opal, a category 3 storm that delivered sustained winds of 130 mph and storm surges over 18 feet (6.6 m). All but 10 percent of Bay County's Shell Island,

which contained the largest Choctawhatchee beach mouse population, was flooded by this hurricane. About 80 traps set out on storm-ravaged Shell Island revealed good news. Three surviving Choctawhatchee beach mice were found, two of which were pregnant.

In fact, the populations and habitat of all four listed subspecies of Panhandle beach mice (including the Santa Rosa beach mouse, a federal species of management concern) were adversely affected by the storm, some worse than others. Approximately 75 percent of St. Andrew beach mouse habitat on St. Joseph Peninsula and Tyndall Air Force Base was devastated. According to state biologist Jeff Gore, Opal also claimed about 50 percent of the Perdido Key beach mouse habitat. The Santa Rosa beach mouse may qualify for federal listing after Opal's unwelcome visit. Other recent hurricanes (1995–2002) have also decimated beach mice populations. Given time, these subspecies may rebound, but the strike of another major hurricane would likely result in the extinction of one or more of them. Such an extinction would clearly not be due to natural causes. These tenacious mice and their ever-changing beach habitats have endured hundreds of hurricanes. Those hurricanes may have annihilated total populations locally, but the beaches were naturally repopulated over time from nearby, surviving colonies. Large-scale beachfront development has now isolated populations to as few as one or two small areas, significantly increasing their vulnerability to a single catastrophic event.

Other Threats: The establishment of invasive nonnative plants could potentially be detrimental to populations of beach mice. It is quite possible that the effects of global warming, primarily the anticipated rise in sea level will consume what is left of suitable beach mice habitat within the next 100 years.

CURRENT TREND: *Declining.* The Perdido Key beach mouse is generally considered to be Florida's most endangered beach mouse. The Southeastern beach mouse is *declining* generally, particularly in southern Florida, but it is *stable* in some areas.

Silver Rice Rat

Oryzomys argentatus
FAMILY CRICETIDAE; Order Rodentia

LISTED STATUS
FWC: Endangered, listed 1975
USF&WS: Endangered, listed 1991

Description: Except for color, this species superficially resembles the marsh rice rat (*Oryzomys palustris*) of peninsular Florida. It is a medium-sized rat, approximately 5.5 inches (140 mm) in head and body length and 2.1–4.2 ounces (60–120 g). The weight of males may exceed that of females. The tail is brown above, lighter below, and lightly haired. Although most rice rats are brown, often dark brown, silver rice rats are generally silver-gray laterally and are typically much lighter than mainland races. Other distinctions include the lack of digital bristles on the hind foot and a thin, delicate skull with elongated nasal bones.

Distribution: The silver rice rat is a Lower Keys endemic. It has been recorded on 12 of the Lower Keys: Little Pine, Howe, Water, Middle Torch, Big Torch, Summerland, Raccoon (which supports the largest population), Johnston, Cudjoe (type locality), Upper Sugarloaf, Lower Sugarloaf, and Saddlebunch. Suitable habitat exists on several other keys, including Annette, Big Pine, Little Torch, Boca Chica, and Crab, but to date trapping for this species has been negative.

Biology: Although the silver rice rat was first discovered in a freshwater marsh on Cudjoe Key, further fieldwork revealed that this rare rodent reaches its highest densities in salt marshes and adjacent habitats, such as low intertidal areas, low salt marsh, scrub mangrove swamp, and buttonwood transitional salt marsh. Characteristic plant species of those habitats include saltwort, saltgrass, sea oxeye, and coastal dropseed. Freshwater habitats contain cattails and saw grass. These semiaquatic rats are exceptional swimmers and also display arboreal tendencies. The species is strictly nocturnal, spending the daylight hours sleeping. An individual rat may utilize well over a dozen different nests in a period of a month. Nests, usually constructed of grass, stems, and leaves, are assembled in slightly elevated tufts of grass. In disturbed areas, piles of debris are sometimes used. Breeding activity peaks in September and October but may occur at any time. The gestation period is 21–28 days, with typical litters of 3–6 young. Longevity is unknown, but individuals have been known to live longer than one year. Home ranges are exceptionally large (occasionally more than 20 acres), probably because fresh water is limited. They feed on the seeds of saltwort, buttonwood, nonnative coconut palms (*Cocos nucifera*), and other plants and on fiddler crabs, snails, and other invertebrates. Predators include raccoons, owls, hawks, snakes, and house cats.

Although silver rice rats are fairly widely distributed in the Lower Keys, they occur at extremely low densities and were probably never abundant. Densities may be lower than one animal per hectare (2.471 acres) in suitable habitat and may naturally fluctuate greatly.

CAUSE OF DECLINE, THREATS

Habitat Destruction and Degradation: Habitat destruction and the adverse effects of human encroachment are the most serious threats. Activities associated with commercial and residential development (filling of wetlands, alteration of natural hydrologic cycles, invasion of exotic vegetation, use of off-road vehicles) have destroyed or severely degraded this endangered rodent's habitat throughout its historic range.

Invasive Exotics: Nonnative black rats have successfully invaded many occupied sites. Young rice rats may be preyed on by black rats. Interspecific competition between larger, more aggressive black rats and silver rice rats is believed to be a factor in rice rat population declines. Rice rats are also preyed on by domestic cats and by raccoons, which are unnaturally abundant near human habitations. Exotic fire ants are suspected of killing young rice rats. Raccoon Key's introduced rhesus monkeys have degraded much rice rat habitat. Australian pine and Brazilian pepper have invaded and adversely altered formerly suitable habitat in several areas.

Sea Level Rise: A grave though not immediate threat is the expected rise in sea level attributed to global warming. Experts predict that most of the Lower Keys will be submerged by the year 2100.

CURRENT TREND: *Unknown,* probably declining, but little long-term data are available. Entire population estimated at 200–500.

Florida Salt Marsh Vole

Microtus pennsylvanicus dukecampbelli

FAMILY SIGMODONTIDAE; Order Rodentia

LISTED STATUS

FWC: Endangered, listed 1993

USF&WS: Endangered, listed 1991

Description: The Florida salt marsh vole is a subspecies of the meadow vole, a species occurring throughout much of the eastern, midwestern, and northwestern United States and Canada. This small rodent has a short tail, blunt head, and diminutive ears. Compared with the meadow vole, the Florida salt marsh vole is darker in color, larger in overall size, and has relatively smaller ears, with certain distinctive skull characteristics. The pelage is dark black-brown dorsally and dark gray ventrally. This vole measures 7.0–7.8 inches (178–198 mm) in length, averaging 7.3 inches (186 mm); average tail length is 1.9 inches (48.8 mm); average hind foot length is 0.92 inch (23.36 mm). Diagnostic skull characteristics are: greatest length of skull 31.17 mm, condylozygomatic length 24.65 mm, incisive foramen length 5.68 mm, diastema length 9.22 mm, cranial breadth 11.71 mm, and zygomatic breadth 16.89 mm.

The subspecies of *Microtus pennsylvanicus* that are morphologically most similar to the Florida subspecies are *M. p. nigrans,* a race inhabiting salt marshes of Maryland's eastern shore, and two insular races from eastern Canada, *M. p. magdalenensis* from Magdalen Island, Quebec, and *M. p. copelandi*, which inhabits Grand Manan Island, New Brunswick.

Distribution: The Florida salt marsh vole was inadvertently discovered in 1979 by biologists studying Scott's seaside sparrow at Island Field Marsh, a coastal salt marsh in Waccasassa Bay near Levy County's Cedar Key. It was subsequently (1982) described as a new subspecies by Charles A. Woods, a mammalogist with the Florida Museum of Natural History. Despite extensive searches in road-accessible public lands within Levy County and neighboring counties of Citrus, Dixie, and Taylor, the Florida salt marsh vole has not been found anywhere other than its type locality.

This subspecies is believed to represent a relict population of the meadow vole (*Microtus pennsylvanicus*) that subspeciated and is now separated from the range of the nearest other subspecies (which occurs as far south as Newton County of central Georgia) by more than 300 miles. The meadow vole is now largely absent from much of the southeastern United States, but numerous fossil records indicate that it formerly occurred in northwest peninsular Florida. Fossilized specimens, believed to be 8,000–30,000 years old, have been found in late Pleistocene deposits at four locations in Alachua, Citrus, and Levy counties. Dramatic shifts in climate reduced the habitat suitable for this species in Florida and elsewhere, isolating Florida's population from the larger contiguous population for at least 5,000 years. The present range is more

northerly and covers much of the eastern and northern United States, portions of western states, and Canada. The Pleistocene relict adapted to Levy County's harsh salt marsh environments when its grassland communities receded from central and northern Florida.

Biology: Island Field salt marsh, the type locality and only known location inhabited by Florida salt marsh voles, is dominated by seashore saltgrass, with perennial glasswort and smooth cordgrass also occurring. The salt marsh vole has also been associated with the margins of black needlerush growth within the marsh. The very dense marsh vegetation is 18–24 inches (45–60 cm) tall. Island Field salt marsh is adjacent to a maritime live oak hammock. Biologists trapping within Island Field salt marsh and adjacent areas also found marsh rice rats, hispid cotton mice, and cotton mice. The marsh itself is inhabited by the Florida salt marsh vole and the marsh rice rat, but each species tends to occupy specific microhabitats. The Florida salt marsh vole typically occupies much the same vegetation zone as Scott's seaside sparrow, being most abundant in saltgrass flats. The marsh rice rat apparently prefers areas dominated by black needlerush. Hispid cotton rats and cotton mice are most abundant in forested areas adjacent to the salt marsh but generally avoid all but the edges of the black rush flats close to the maritime forest. Both are occasionally encountered deep in the marsh.

The Florida salt marsh vole population appears to fluctuate cyclically. Substantial numbers have been trapped some years, very few in some years, and none in others. Survival is not easy for salt marsh voles. Their salt marsh habitat is subject to repeated battering and flooding by violent storms. The meadow vole, of which this is a subspecies, is largely terrestrial and does not typically occur in marsh ecosystems. This race has, as an evolutionary adaptation, adjusted to life within the hostile environment of the low-lying Gulf tidal marsh. It is unknown exactly how Florida salt marsh voles survive severe flooding, but they do, or at least some do. Among the survival mechanisms they may employ are taking refuge atop the highest vegetation in the marsh, temporarily vacating the marsh, and swimming. California voles (*Microtus californicus*) have been observed diving more than a yard (1 m) beneath the water's surface, swimming below the surface for approximately 20 feet (6 m), and swimming across a 40 foot (12 m) slough. It is possible that Florida salt marsh voles may have a more widespread distribution than is currently known and may occur in other salt marshes along Levy County's Gulf Coast. If that is the case, they would be able to recolonize areas where the resident population has been lost to severe storms.

This subspecies, like other *Microtus pennsylvanicus* subspecies, has a very high reproductive potential, which may help to facilitate its recovery after catastrophic weather events. Females may produce as many as 17 litters each year. Breeding may occur year round, though it is thought to peak during February and March. Salt marsh voles construct a weather-resistant nest from grasses in vegetation above the high tide line. Voles have a gestation period of about

21 days, and the average litter size is 5. Young are weaned after about 14 days and may begin breeding after only two months. Life expectancy probably averages less than six months.

Salt marsh voles may be active day or night. Known food items include a variety of plant matter (seeds, grass, roots, and bark), but these rodents may also eat insects, spiders, snails, crabs, and possibly the eggs of seaside sparrows and marsh wrens. Known or suspected predators include barn owls, short-eared owls (*Asio flammeus*), northern harriers (*Circus cyaneus*), other hawks, raccoons, foxes, and snakes.

CAUSE OF DECLINE, THREATS

Climatic Changes: Florida salt marsh voles differ from other species discussed in this book in that their decline and range reduction may be attributed largely to natural causes. Prairielike habitats were widespread in Florida during the Pleistocene Epoch, when glaciers covered much of North America. Sea level was significantly lower, with prairie and savanna habitat extending westward from the type locality into what is now the Gulf of Mexico, as well as eastward and northward. When the glaciers receded, suitable upland and lowland habitats were eliminated, isolating northwest Florida's vole populations.

Severe Storms: Because of the Florida salt marsh vole's extremely limited distribution and its extremely low-lying salt marsh habitat, this animal may be subject to extinction by a single catastrophic storm. In the past, flooding and high winds from hurricanes and severe storms have been blamed for population declines. Between 1900 and 1975, 21 major hurricanes struck Florida.

Hurricanes passed over or close to Waccasassa Bay in 1966, 1970, 1979, 1983, and 1995. It was feared that Hurricane Elana, which remained parked just off Cedar Key's coast for more than 24 hours in August 1985, had eliminated this species. Fortunately, a few tenacious voles survived.

Rising Sea Level: Experts predict that by 2100, global warming will cause sea level to rise 3.3–6.6 feet (1–2 m) above current levels in Levy County. That will greatly reduce the extent of salt marsh locally and globally.

CURRENT TREND: *Unknown.*

Florida Manatee

Trichechus manatus latirostris

FAMILY TRICHECHIDAE; Order Sirenia

LISTED STATUS

FWC: Endangered, listed 1979 (threatened 1974–1978)

Florida Manatee Protection Act of 1978 (protected under Florida law since 1893)

USF&WS: Endangered, listed 1967

NATL MARINE FISHERIES: Protected under the Marine Mammal Preservation Act since 1972

Description: The Florida manatee, also known as sea cow, is one of North America's largest coastal mammals. Adults of both sexes average approximately 11.5 feet (3.5 m) long and weigh an average of 2,200 pounds (1,000 kg); extraordinary individuals exceed 3,500 pounds (1,588 kg). The manatee's immense seallike body is covered by thick gray to grayish brown skin that is sparsely covered with small, thick hairs. Manatees are sometimes covered with barnacles and algae. The manatee's head is indistinct from its body and has an elongated, muzzlelike snout with whiskers. Its small, wide, deeply set eyes have no visible upper or lower eyelids but are covered by a protective membrane. Its vision is believed to be quite good at distances. Manatees have no external ears, though internal ears enable them to hear exceptionally well. Manatees communicate through a series of low chirps, squeaks, squeals, groans, and grunts. Their nostrils are equipped with specialized valves that keep water out while submerged. Unlike other mammals, the lungs and diaphragm of the manatee run lengthwise, not crosswise. Manatees may remain submerged for up to 15 minutes. Powerful muscles surrounding their lungs enable them to exhale rapidly and submerge quickly. The manatee's body lacks hind limbs but has two rather dexterous paddlelike forelimbs or flippers, which are used to steer. The dorsal surface of each flipper has three or four heavy nails, which are used to dislodge vegetation from the bottom of rivers and canals. The species name *manatus* means "having hands." The manatee's large, horizontally flat, paddlelike tail is used for propulsion and serves as a rudder. The manatee's teeth resemble the teeth of its closest living terrestrial relative, the elephant. As front teeth wear down from consuming hundreds of pounds of coarse vegetative matter daily, rear replacement teeth move slowly forward to replace them, as though on a conveyer belt. Although manatees are sexually dimorphic, the differences between the sexes are often not immediately obvious. Females often appear bulkier than males and have a single prominent mamma or teat behind the axilla of each forearm and a short anal-genital distance. The male's urinary and reproductive opening is located just beyond the naval. Newborn calves average about 4 feet (1.2 m) long and weigh 60–80 pounds (27–36 kg). Newborns are darker in color than adults but lighten after several weeks.

Distribution: The Florida manatee is a resident of the southeastern United States, primarily the coastal and inland waterways of peninsular Florida and, to a lesser degree, southeastern Georgia. During the warmer months of summer, manatees may disperse along the Atlantic Coast as far north as Rhode Island (on rare occasions) and along the Gulf Coast as far as the mouth of the Rio Grande in Texas. Florida manatees have also been recorded on occasion in the Bahamas. Water temperatures below 68 degrees F (20 degrees C) generally create distributional limits to the range of the Florida manatee.

When waters are warmer (April to November), manatees occur throughout much of Florida. During the cooler months (December to March), manatees usually seek the warmer waters of natural sources such as springs or man-made sources such as power plants. Population centers for manatees within Florida include, on the east coast, the St. Johns, Banana, and Indian rivers and Biscayne Bay. On the Gulf Coast, there are population centers in the Suwannee, Crystal, and Homosassa rivers; the region of Charlotte Harbor, Matlacha Pass, and San Carlos Bay; the Caloosahatchee River and Estero Bay area; and the Ten Thousand Islands. Inland they are found throughout many of the inland waterways of the Everglades and Lake Okeechobee. Manatees occur only rarely in the warm waters of the Florida Keys, probably because of the relative scarcity of fresh water. A number of sites in central and southern Florida are well known for their large winter aggregations of manatees (more than 50 individuals), including Volusia County's Blue Springs, the headwaters of the Crystal River, the headwaters of the Homosassa River and Homosassa Springs, Manatee Springs, Welaka Spring, Silver Glen Spring Run, the Biscayne Bay area, several areas within the Everglades and the Ten Thousand Islands, and at the warm outflows from power plants near the Indian River Lagoon, Canaveral, Vero Beach, Fort Pierce, Riviera Beach, Port Everglades, and Fort Lauderdale. Before the establishment of power plants throughout Florida in the 1950's, the manatee's winter range was largely restricted to areas south of Charlotte Harbor on the Gulf Coast and the Sebastian River on the Atlantic Coast.

Manatees are members of the mammalian order Sirenia, which contains four recognized families, three recent genera, and five recent species. Within the order are two recent families (Dugongidae and Trichechidae), four living species, and one extinct species. The family Trichechidae includes three recognized species: the West Indian manatee (*Trichechus manatus*), the Amazonian manatee (*T. inunguis*), and the West African manatee (*T. senegalensis*). The current range of the West Indian manatee includes two subspecies: our Florida manatee on the coasts and rivers of Florida and southern Georgia, and the Antillean manatee in much of the Caribbean, eastern Mexico and Central America, and portions of northern and eastern South America. The ranges of the two subspecies are generally separated by the deep waters and strong currents of the Straits of Florida. The family Dugongidae includes two genera (*Dugong* and *Hydrodamalis*) of aquatic mammals closely allied to the manatee, but the dugong (*Dugong dugong*) is the only living species of this family. It occurs in northern Australia and areas of the Indian Ocean. Steller's sea cow (*Hydrodamalis giga*), a former resident of the Bering Sea, was discovered by humans in 1741 and hunted to extinction by 1768.

Biology: Florida manatees frequent a variety of fresh, brackish and saltwater areas in coastal, estuarine, and riverine or spring habitats. Manatees were once considered primarily freshwater denizens; we now know, however, that these creatures spend about as much time in saline environments as they do in fresh water, although they do tend to prefer salinity levels below 25 ppt. Among the many factors contributing to the geographical distribution of manatees are access to warm water during cold spells, access to foraging areas with ample aquatic vegetation, access to fresh water, and access to channels of at least 6 feet deep. Specific aquatic habitats used by Florida manatees may vary considerably with the seasons. During the winter, when coastal waters drop below 68 degrees F (20 degrees C), large aggregations gather at various warm water refuges, usually at natural springs or near power plants. A total of 17 major winter aggregation sites have been identified in Florida. As spring approaches and water temperatures rise, some manatees leave their winter refuges while others remain. During the spring some manatees migrate great distances from their winter haunts, usually traveling northward along the Atlantic coastline. In recent years manatees have been sighted in a number of mid-Atlantic states and even in New England states. These well-traveled manatees usually migrate southward again with the coming of fall. For several consecutive years during the mid-1990's, a wayward male manatee fondly nicknamed Chessie made northward excursions to Maryland's Chesapeake Bay. On 1 October 1994, Chessie was rescued from the Chesapeake's cold waters by concerned biologists and was transported back to Florida to save his life.

Another factor important to manatees is the availability of suitable foraging habitat. Throughout much of central and southern Florida, manatees feed primarily on various submergent, emergent, and floating vegetation. In some of the northern portions of the range (e.g., St. Johns River), manatees feed primarily on floating vegetation. Favorite foraging areas within estuarine and saltwater environments include shallow sea grass beds adjacent to deeper channels. Preferred freshwater sites include calmer, quiet areas of canals, lagoons, and rivers. During the winter, manatees will typically leave the warm water areas in late afternoon to forage in nearby vegetated areas.

In 1976 the USF&WS designated critical habitat for the Florida manatee, identifying specific areas occupied by the manatee that have those physical or biological features essential to its conservation.

These semisocial animals sometimes travel in small groups and are well known for their large winter aggregations. Manatees are not territorial, and groups, when formed, have no leaders. Manatees have well-developed brains and are believed to be quite intelligent. Social interactions include apparent playing, nuzzling and touching, chasing, and considerable vocalizing.

Manatees must consume large amounts of aquatic vegetation daily (up to 20 percent of their body weight) to meet their metabolic requirements. On a typical day a considerable portion of the manatee's waking hours are spent foraging. Research has shown seasonal variances in the time spent foraging each day. More time is spent foraging during the late fall (6.9 hours per day) than during the early spring (3.2 hours per day). Manatees are opportunistic herbivores that consume more than 60 species of aquatic vegetation. Occasionally, they will consume small fish and invertebrates while devouring plants, and they have been observed feeding on algae attached to submerged objects. The most common submerged aquatic plants consumed by manatees in South Florida are turtle grass, manatee grass, and Cuban shoal grass. Many other plants are consumed, including the leaves of overhanging mangroves and shoreline vegetation such as cordgrass. In regions where submerged vegetation is scarce (as in northeastern Florida), manatees depend on floating vegetation such as water hyacinth, warm water fern (*Salvinia rotundifolia*), and alligator weed. Other freshwater vegetation consumed by Florida manatees includes hydrilla and various aquatic macrophytes such as *Myriophyllum* spp.

Female manatees become sexually mature after they are 3–5 years old, males after 3–4 years of age. Manatees are believed to be fecund throughout their adult life, probably peaking between the ages of 4 and 12. A 34-year-old captive female manatee was reportedly reproductive throughout her entire adult life. When a female manatee goes into heat, a breeding herd of eligible males often gather around her. The estrous female may mate with several males. Larger, presumably older males are responsible for most pregnancies. Reproduction may occur throughout the year; most calves, however, are born during the spring or early summer. Female manatees produce offspring at intervals of at least 2–3 years and typically have only one calf at a time, although there are several records of manatees bearing twins. Manatee calves nurse underwater by burying their heads in the armpits of one of the mother's front flippers, where her nipples are located. Young begin feeding on vegetation when they are about one month old. Calves remain with their mother for up to two years. Adult females have been known to adopt and nurse orphaned calves.

Humans are the only known predator of the Florida manatee, with the possible exception of sharks. Young manatees may fall prey to alligators on occasion. Biologists believe the longevity of wild Florida manatees may exceed 60–70 years. The typical cruising speed of a manatee is 2–6 mph, although they can attain speeds of about 15 mph for short distances. Their relative slowness was not a hindrance to their survival before the arrival of powerboats and barges.

CAUSE OF DECLINE, THREATS

Watercraft Collisions: For decades now, watercraft collisions (including jetskis) have been by far the most perilous threat to manatees. Florida has more registered boats than any other state, and power boats outnumber manatees more than 500 to 1. Manatees are generally killed or injured by watercraft in one of two ways, either directly by the impact with the vessel or as a result of wounds inflicted by a boat's propeller. So many of Florida's manatees have been wounded by propellers that biologists can identify more than 900 individuals from their propeller scars.

The number of pleasure and commercial vessels and other watercraft on Florida's waterways has increased dramatically since the 1960's. In 1960 there were approximately 100,000 boats registered in Florida; by 1990 there were more than 700,000, and by 2000 there were 1.2 million. Formerly remote waterways that had once been nearly devoid of high-speed boats are now high-traffic areas, increasing the risk of collisions. Manatee deaths attributed to watercraft collisions rose an average of 9.3 percent a year between 1974 and 1992 (Table 1). In January 2002, 16 manatees were killed by watercraft collisions, the record for a single month. Of those 16 deaths, 10 occurred in or near state-designated manatee zones, where boaters are supposed to slow down to avoid hitting manatees.

When a collision kills a female manatee accompanied by a newborn calf, it can generally be assumed that the calf will perish also. Biologists believe that some manatee calves die simply from being separated from their mothers while attempting to evade passing boats. Stress associated with boat traffic and noise may induce premature births in some manatees. Perinatal deaths (stillborn and newborn calves) represent nearly 25 percent of all dead manatees recorded in Florida during 1994.

Habitat Destruction: Loss and degradation of essential manatee habitat is considered the second most notable threat. Formerly suitable habitat has been lost or seriously degraded by recreational and commercial boating, coastal construction, and pollution from sewage discharge and storm runoff. Boat propellers and wake disturbances also seriously degrade sea grass beds.

Red Tide: In the spring of 1996 a large number of manatees in southwest Florida began turning up dead from what was for some time a mystery illness. Most manatee carcasses were recovered from Lee County, followed by Collier, Charlotte, and Sarasota counties. At least 158 manatees died between 5 March and 29 April, in the greatest single mortality event ever recorded for manatees. A thorough investigation revealed that red tide, or more specifically the toxins released from a bloom of *Gymnodinium brevii* dinoflagellates, was responsible. Autopsies revealed the presence of the toxins in the animals' stomach contents and in liver, kidney, and lung tissues. That year was Florida's worst for manatee deaths: the 1996 death toll was 415, mostly as a result of red tide.

Adverse Weather Conditions: Sustained exposure to low water temperatures

TABLE I. *Manatee Deaths Attributed to Watercraft Collisions in Florida*

1974: 3	1984: 34	1994: 46
1975: 6	1985: 33	1995: 42
1976: 10	1986: 33	1996: 60
1977: 13	1987: 39	1997: 54
1978: 21	1988: 43	1998: 66
1979: 24	1989: 50	1999: 82
1980: 16	1990: 47	2000: 78
1981: 24	1991: 53	2001: 81
1982: 20	1992: 38	
1983: 15	1993: 33	

(below 61 degrees F) can be fatal to manatees. The number of cold-related manatee deaths varies considerably from year to year; there were none in 1992 but at least 46 in 1990. Hurricanes and severe tropical storms are certainly another threat to Florida's manatees.

Poaching, Malicious or Criminal Mischief: Fortunately, the shooting and intentional slaughter of manatees are now rare within the United States. In times gone by, the harvest of manatees for meat, bones, oil, and hide extirpated them from much of their historic range. Overhunting of manatees in the last three centuries has resulted in their disappearance from a number of coastal areas in Mexico, Honduras, and the Virgin Islands. In 1893 the first state law was passed in Florida outlawing the killing of manatees. In 1995, while the author was a federal law enforcement officer, an investigation of illegal harvesting of protected wildlife in southwest Florida implicated some residents of a rural community in the illegal harvest of manatees for consumption.

Water Control Structures: Flood gates and canal locks have been responsible for numerous manatee deaths. In an attempt to reduce manatee mortality, the gate opening procedures were modified in the late 1970's and early 1980's. Initially the deaths attributed to these structures decreased, but in later years they rose again. In the late 1970's an average of 8–9 manatees were killed annually in Florida. During the entire 1980's the annual death rate dropped to 4. In 1994 alone, however, 16 manatees were killed. The latest federal recovery plans for the manatee include alternative measures at water control structures to reduce manatee mortality.

Net Entanglement: In Florida as many as six manatees have died in some years from entanglement in inshore shrimp boat nets or crab pot float lines. The majority died in northeastern Florida from drowning after becoming entangled in nets.

CURRENT TREND: *Stable* generally; however, manatee populations are *declining* in some regions. Aerial surveys conducted in February 1996 produced estimates of at least 2,639 manatees in Florida's waters, 1,182 of them along the west coast, including the west coast of Everglades National Park, and 1,457 along the east coast, including the Florida Keys and Florida Bay.

The manatee is Florida's official state marine mammal. It is cherished by many Floridians. The extremely popular manatee license plate, first released in 1990, has raised millions of dollars to protect these gentle giants. The Save the Manatee Club, a popular conservation organization cochaired by well-known singer-songwriter and longtime Floridian Jimmy Buffett, boasts about 40,000 members. This organization, founded in 1981 by Buffett and former governor Bob Graham, promotes public awareness and education relating to endangered manatees. To learn more about the Save the Manatee Club, write to S.M.C. at 500 N. Maitland Ave., Maitland, FL 32751; call 1-800-432-JOIN (5646); or e-mail education@savethemanatee.org or membership@savethemanatee.org.

Least Tern
Sterna antillarum antillarum
FAMILY LARIDAE; Order Charadriiformes
LISTED STATUS
FWC: Threatened, listed 1975
Two other least tern subspecies breed in North America, the interior least tern (*Sterna antillarum athalassos*) and the California least tern (*S. a. browni*); both are federally endangered.

Description: This is North America's smallest tern, 8.5–9.5 inches (21.5–24 cm) long, with a wingspan of 20 inches (50 cm). No sexual dimorphism exists. Adult birds in breeding plumage are gray above with white underparts, a black cap, and white forehead, with an orange-yellow bill and legs. The two outer primaries are dark and are quite noticeable in flight. The bill has a dark tip. Tails of adults are short and moderately to deeply forked, but the tails of immature birds are only slightly forked. The bill and legs of first-summer birds are black. Adult plumage is acquired before the birds are two years old. The least tern's flight is typical of terns: buoyant and irregular. The wingbeats of this species are quicker than other terns'. Its voice includes a sharp, high-pitched, repeated *kit*, a hoarse *chir-ee-eep*, or *zeek*.

Distribution: Formerly considered a subspecies or form of the little tern (*Sterna albifrons*), an Old World species, it is now recognized as a distinct species. The subspecies of least tern that occurs in Florida (*S. antillarum antillarum*), often called the eastern least tern, occurs as a breeding bird sporadically along the Atlantic Coast from Maine to the Florida Keys and scattered sites along the Gulf Coast from southern Florida to Texas and Mexico. It also breeds in the Greater and Lesser Antilles and on the Caribbean coast of Mexico, Central America, and northern South America.

Least terns winter in Central and South America as far south as Brazil and Peru. This species breeds along both Florida coasts but is apparently most common in the Panhandle and the Keys. Inland breeding colonies have been documented in portions of Leon, Volusia, Seminole, Orange, Polk, Highlands, Okeechobee, and Glades counties.

Biology: The least tern is a bird of seacoasts, coastal lagoons, and large rivers, but it also nests close to larger interior lakes, including Lake Monroe and Lake Placid. Natural nesting habitat consists of beaches and sandbars, where it nests colonially, often in association with black skimmers. As a rule, these birds select colonial beach nesting sites that are at least 30 feet (10 m) wide.

Least tern colonies sometimes exceed 500 pairs. Nests are usually nothing more than shallow scrapes in sand or gravel. The female lays two or three, rarely one, dark-spotted, cream-colored eggs, which are incubated by both parents. The incubation period ranges from 14 to 21 days, but 20 or 21 days is the norm. Least terns will protect their eggs from any perceived threat, regardless of size, with much bravado. Young are quick studies and may begin leaving the nest vicinity only one or two days after hatching. By 1 September, the majority of least terns have departed nesting beaches and begun their migration to their wintering grounds.

While humans have been largely responsible for the decline of the least tern, they have unwittingly helped the species by providing artificial nesting sites in many areas. Much of the tern's historic nesting beaches have been lost to residential and commercial development. In Florida, least terns nest during late April and May, a time when millions of humans blanket the beaches, encroaching on many of the remaining tern colonies. In response to the loss of natural nest sites, least terns have increasingly become dependent on man-made nesting habitats, particularly gravel roofs of large commercial buildings and dredge-material sites. Artificial sites have now become the preferred nesting sites in many areas. While writing this species account, the author repeatedly observed these least terns foraging over a freshwater canal, two miles inland from the Atlantic, in Palm Beach County. As very few if any natural nesting sites occurred in this highly developed area, the birds were most likely nesting on a nearby rooftop. Recent studies indicate that rooftops have been more productive in terms of eggs and chicks produced than ground beach sites. A study of nesting least terns in the Panhandle by biologists J. A. Gore and M. J. Kinnison in 1989 revealed that 10.4 percent of eggs from ground colonies hatched, but 29.4 percent of eggs from rooftop colonies hatched. Similar studies in the Florida

Keys found that of the 689 breeding pairs observed, all but 7 were on rooftops or dredge material; the remaining 7 were on coral boulders placed in a man-made lake. Another study of nesting least terns in eight Florida counties concluded that 81 percent of the least terns nested on rooftops. Chicks and adults use the shade provided by air conditioners and other rooftop structures to avoid exposure to midday summer temperatures. Man-made nesting sites are generally not permanent, however, and in recent years many gravel rooftops have been replaced with plastic, rendering them unsuitable for nesting.

Small fish represent the bulk of the least tern's diet, plucked from coastal waters on the wing or by plunge-diving from a considerable height. Terns also take shrimp and insects on occasion. These long-lived birds are known to live more than 21 years.

Predators of adults and juvenile terns include falcons (kestrels, merlins, and peregrines), other hawks, laughing gulls (*Larus atricilla*), fish crows, red foxes, raccoons, snakes (*Coluber, Masticophis,* and *Elaphe*), ghost crabs, and ants. Great white herons (*Ardea herodias* morph) and great horned owls have been seen raiding tern colonies. Introduced predators include black rats and free-ranging cats and dogs, which in some areas are the most prolific predators of hatchlings and young birds.

CAUSE OF DECLINE, THREATS
Habitat Destruction: Undisturbed beaches, the natural nesting habitat for least terns, are now a rare commodity anywhere in Florida, often prompting terns to use alternative sites. Unfortunately, the construction sites, landfills, and other

man-made alternatives that this species is drawn to are often destroyed, along with tern nests, after nesting has begun.

Disturbance of Nesting Colonies: The second most menacing threat in Florida, the disturbance to colonies by pedestrians, automobiles, off-road vehicles, and free-running dogs can have serious effects. Disturbance may force terns off nests (causing eggs to overheat when exposed to the sun), reduce overall reproductive success, and lead to the abandonment of nesting sites.

Other Threats: Exotic animals are serious threats to least terns in many areas. Black rats and domestic dogs and cats prey on tern eggs and hatchlings. Off-road vehicles kill terns and destroy eggs. Historic threats, once very serious, include plume hunting and egg collecting.

CURRENT TREND: *Stable* or *increasing.*

Caribbean Roseate Tern

Sterna dougallii dougallii
FAMILY LARIDAE; Order Charadriiformes

LISTED STATUS

FWC: Threatened, listed 1975
USF&WS: Threatened, listed 1987 (New England and Canadian populations endangered)

Description: This is a medium-sized tern, 14–16 inches (35–41 cm) in length with a 29-inch (74 cm) wingspan. Sexes are alike. Breeding adults have a pale gray back and whitish underparts. Underparts display a rosy tint in good light, hence the name. Breeding birds have a jet-black cap and nape and bright orange-red legs and feet. The bill is normally all black, except in the breeding season, when the basal half is reddish.

The Caribbean population, which breeds in Florida, generally has more reddish basal coloration on the bill than birds from the northeastern breeding population. The deeply forked white tail projects well beyond the wing tips in standing birds. The cap and nape are faded in winter adults and immature birds, and the entire bill and legs become black. Adult plumage is attained by the second spring. First-summer birds have a white forehead but otherwise resemble adults.

This species resembles Forster's, common, and Arctic terns. Roseates are distinguished from common and Arctic terns by paler coloration, slimmer build, lack of dark trailing on the underside of outer wings, and bill color. Forster's terns (spring birds) have gray tails, predominantly red bills, and much slower wingbeats. The distinct vocalizations of roseate terns include a loud *pink* and *pi-vik* and a louder *yaaach* alarm call.

Distribution: This is a widespread species, with five subspecies occurring on six continents. Roseate terns of the United States form two distinct and widely separated breeding populations. The northeastern population nests locally in colonies scattered along the Atlantic Coast from Nova Scotia to Virginia or North Carolina, but colonies are scarce south of Long Island. The Caribbean population, referred to as Caribbean roseate terns, includes Florida's breeding population and is separated by 700–800 miles from the nearest northeastern birds' breeding grounds.

This Caribbean population has been known to breed in the Florida Keys, Dry Tortugas, Bahamas, Puerto Rico, Virgin Islands, Jamaica, Honduras, and

Hispaniola. In Florida, this species occurs as a breeding bird in the Florida Keys only, between Marathon and the Dry Tortugas. Breeding colonies have been recorded at Key West, Stock Island, Pelican Shoal, Boca Chica, Hospital (or Sand), Bush, Long, Indian, Vaca, Crawl, and Raccoon keys; islets near Pigeon Key; islets near Matecumbe Keys; Molasses Reef Dry Rocks; and the Dry Tortugas, where they have nested consistently since at least 1917. In April 1832 John James Audubon noted the abundance of roseate terns on Indian Key.

Most birds from both the Caribbean and northeastern populations are believed to winter in South America, although there are several reports of roseates wintering along Florida's southwest coast and the Keys. Banded birds from the northeastern population have been recorded in Florida during migration. **Biology:** A pelagic species much of the year, the roseate tern comes ashore only to nest. The Caribbean and northeastern populations favor island habitats for nesting, which offer some protection from mammalian predators. For the birds' purposes, natural islands, artificial islets, and rooftops have all qualified as island habitat in Florida. Roseates, like most terns, are colonial nesters, often mingling with nesting least terns in Florida. Colonies of several hundred roseates have been recorded in the Lower Keys. Roseate terns usually arrive at their Florida nesting grounds in late April or early May and actually nest in late May or early June. The species' tendency to nest early is advantageous to the chicks, who are usually long gone when the hurricane season arrives. These birds may lay eggs directly on the ground or construct crude scrapes in the sand, usually above the storm high-tide line and sometimes lined with bits of vegetative matter, coral, or shells. Rooftop nesting has been recorded in the Lower Keys. Clutches of one or two speckled brownish eggs are the norm in Florida, with replacement clutches usually containing a single egg. The incubation period is three to four weeks long, with both parents incubating. The chicks fledge after 22–29 days.

The roseate tern's flight is buoyant with rapid wingbeats. Roseates are competent fishermen and catch their quarry (fish 3–4 inches long) by plunge-diving from a hover at 20–50 feet above the water. Predators of adult roseate terns, their chicks, or their eggs include raccoons, black rats, domestic dogs and cats, magnificent frigatebirds, kestrels, peregrine falcons, red-tailed hawks, cattle egrets, laughing gulls, night-herons, great white herons, rat snakes, and land crabs. The average longevity of this species is unknown, though a banded roseate tern was recorded as living 14 years.

CAUSE OF DECLINE, THREATS

Human Encroachment and Disturbance: Pedestrian traffic, boat traffic, recreational activities, and other forms of human interference with nesting colonies, together with other threats associated with human presence (free-running dogs and cats, black rats), constitute the most serious threat to this species. Nesting terns disturbed by human activities have abandoned their nests. Loss of suitable habitat may also be a factor limiting the abundance of this species in the Keys.

Plume Hunters (historic threat): Before the Migratory Bird Treaty of 1918, roseate terns were commonly shot for their feathers. Egg collecting remains a significant threat to many Caribbean colonies outside Florida.

Pollution: This species is vulnerable to pollutants in the waters in the vicinity of nesting colonies. In 1988 a mass of sewage from Key West was suspected of causing nest failures in a colony of roseate terns on Tank Island.

Other Threats: Severe weather events (storm tides and high winds) are a serious hazard to nesting colonies. Free-running dogs and cats threaten colonies by harassing and killing birds. Black rats, an exotic species abundant in the Keys, may raid colonies at night in search of eggs and chicks. Predation and displacement by gulls are serious factors in the decline of northeastern populations.

CURRENT TREND: *Stable.* South Florida population in 1998 estimated at approximately 300 breeding pairs; combined U.S. and Canadian populations estimated at fewer than 7,000 birds.

Southeastern Snowy Plover
Charadrius alexandrinus tenuirostris
FAMILY CHARADRIIDAE; Order Charadriiformes

LISTED STATUS
FWC: Threatened, listed 1985 (endangered 1975–1984)
USF&WS: Species of management concern

Description: Averaging 6.5 inches (16 cm) in length, with a 12-inch (30 cm) wingspan, this small plover is about the same size as the piping plover. Like most plovers, it has a stockier build and thicker neck than most sandpipers. This is a pale bird, and Florida birds are noticeably more pallid than the western snowy plover (*Charadrius alexandrinus nivosus*). Specimens of *C. a. nivosus* were reportedly collected in Bay County during the 1890's but have not been reported since then. Both sexes are patterned similarly, but males tend to have darker markings than females. Adults and juveniles have a light tannish back and a white abdomen, throat, and forehead, with a slender, dark bill and dark legs. Snowys have a dark (often black) ear patch and a dark patch on the top of the head. Immature birds are similarly patterned, but the dark areas are more subdued. The snowy plover's calls include a whistling *pe-wee-ah* or *ku-wheet.*

Distribution: The snowy plover is a widespread species, nearly cosmopolitan, and it occurs in both North and South America, Eurasia, Africa, and Australia. Almost 90 percent of the estimated 21,000 snowy plovers inhabiting the United States are believed to nest west of the Rocky Mountains. The southeastern snowy plover inhabits areas along the Gulf Coast of the southeastern United States, portions of the southern Great Plains, and several locations in the Caribbean, including the coast of the Yucatan Peninsula, Greater and Lesser Antilles, and islands off northern Venezuela. The species is now reported to be extirpated as a breeding bird on St. Croix in the Virgin Islands. In Florida it occurs as both a nesting and winter resident, along the Gulf Coast sparingly from the Alabama border to Collier County's Marco Island.

Biology: In Florida, snowy plovers inhabit expanses of sandy beaches away from human activity and disturbance. They forage on sand flats, in the surf, and occasionally on mudflats. Nests are generally placed well above high tide and usually close to vegetation, including sea oats, railroad vine, and other fore-dune plants. Nests are shallow (less than 2 cm) scrapes in the sand, usually on slightly elevated, windblown micro-dunes, and are often lined with tiny shells. In nearly all cases, nests are with-in view of the Gulf. Western populations, which nest on hard salt pan, often nest in footprint depressions left by coyotes, horses, and humans. Snowy plovers rarely nest near human habitations or areas with constant human traffic. They often nest close to least terns; therefore, protection offered to either species benefits the other.

Florida snowy plovers may pair as early as late winter. Nesting takes place from March through June or July, often peaking in late April and early May. A territory is established by males but defended by both sexes. Females lay on average three smooth oval eggs, which hatch after 24–27 days. Eggs are covered with small black or brown spots that blend in well with beach substrates. Chicks fledge after about a month but remain with one or both parents for several weeks. Parents often renest if the brood is lost and sometimes produce second broods after nesting successfully.

Snowy plovers feed on small crus-taceans, mollusks, worms, and insects, which are plucked from sand or mud. Predators are known to include ghost crabs (*Ocypode quadrata* and *O. albicans,* which prey on eggs), raccoons, striped skunks, falcons, accipiters, great blue herons, fish crows, and domestic dogs and cats. Red foxes, black racers, and coach-whip snakes are also suspected predators.

CAUSE OF DECLINE, THREATS

Habitat Destruction and Human Encroachment: Intensive studies of Florida's snowy plovers by state biologists Jeffrey Gore and Charles Chase have produced interesting but not surprising findings. Snowy plovers cannot endure human disturbance near their nesting sites. Much of their historic Florida nesting beaches are adjacent to congested residential areas, and those areas protect-ed from development are heavily visited recreation areas. Snowy plovers are philopatric, returning each year to the same general nesting area. Areas still supporting suitable nesting habitat are now scarce, particularly along Florida's southwest coast.

Other Threats: Free-roaming cats and dogs are known to torment and kill adults and chicks and may separate chicks from their parents. Trash accumulations in beach areas often attract an abundance of predators, including raccoons and skunks. Ironically, wire fencing erected to protect nesting colonies from predation and dis-turbance have been responsible for colli-sion-related deaths. Plovers have also died after becoming entangled in discarded monofilament fishing line.

CURRENT TREND: *Declining.* Florida's population of nesting snowy plovers probably does not exceed 400 individuals (200 pairs).

Piping Plover
Charadrius melodus
FAMILY CHARADRIIDAE; Order Charadriiformes
LISTED STATUS
FWC: Threatened, listed 1985

USF&WS: Threatened, listed 1985; Great Lakes populations endangered
CANADA: Endangered

Description: These pint-sized but stocky plovers attain lengths of 6–7.5 inches (15–19 cm). Adults weigh approximately 2 ounces (56 g). Wingspan is approximately 15 inches (38 cm). This is North America's palest plover, paler even than the snowy plover. The species shows little if any sexual dimorphism. Breeding plumaged adults have a pallid, sand-colored back and white abdomen, breast, and throat. A black neck ring (which may or may not be complete) and a black forehead band are present. Legs are yellow to orange; bill is yellow with a black tip. At close range, a very fine orange eye ring can be detected. A distinctive white rump is seen in flight. Adult plumage is acquired eight months or so after fledging; therefore, juveniles wintering in Florida often resemble adults. Birds in winter plumage have a black bill and darker legs, and they lack the conspicuous neck ring of summer birds. Piping plovers emit a descending *peep lo.*

Distribution: The breeding range of the piping plover can be divided into three geographic regions, and it occurs extremely locally within each. The two primary regions are, first, the Great Plains of the United States and Canada and, second, scattered Atlantic Coast segments from maritime Canada to North Carolina. The third region, the Great Lakes district, contains only 20 or so breeding pairs. Piping plovers winter on the Atlantic and Gulf coasts of the southeastern United States, Mexico, the Bahamas, and the Greater Antilles. The species does not breed in Florida,

although the state's beaches remain an integral wintering area; the Tampa Bay area provides winter refuges to an estimated 5 percent of the total population. Piping plovers from Atlantic Coast populations (*Charadrius melodus melodus*) and Great Plains populations (*C. m. circumcinctus*) have been documented wintering in Florida, with the former greatly outnumbering the latter. It is probable that Great Lakes birds (also *C. m. circumcinctus*) winter in Florida.

Biology: Piping plovers are winter visitors to Florida's coastal regions (especially the barrier islands), where they frequent sandy beaches and dunes. The author has found that wintering piping plovers in Florida congregate more on the calmer, sandy landward side of sand spits of barrier islands than on the ocean or Gulf side.

Atlantic Coast populations arrive at their respective breeding grounds at varying times, with birds nesting in Virginia arriving by mid-March and New Brunswick birds arriving as late as late April. The male plover makes grandiose attempts to woo a prospective mate by strutting around the female with feathers puffed, stomping his feet, uttering peeps and whistles, and flying figure eights. If the female is taken with her suitor, they mate and choose a nest site. The nest, positioned well above the high-tide line, is usually no more than a well-camouflaged scrape in the sand. An average of four finely spotted, buff-colored eggs are laid and are incubated by both parents. Eggs hatch after 27–30 days. If a clutch is destroyed, the pair will renest. During the course of one season, a female piping plover in Cape

Cod nested and laid eggs a total of five times. Piping plovers may nest as young as one year old. Parent birds often feign injury by limping and acting as though they have a broken wing to lead predators away from the nest (a common plover tactic). The chicks accompany the parents on food-finding missions well away from the nest, sometimes after only one day.

Like most of the 67 plover species, pipers have the habit of running quickly in short spurts, stopping abruptly, then sprinting once again. Piping plovers feed primarily on insects and aquatic invertebrates, which are plucked from beach areas and mudflats. In Florida, known or suspected predators include striped skunks, raccoons, opossums, foxes, night-herons, crows, raptors (peregrine falcons, merlins, and accipiters), and domestic dogs and cats. Eggs and chicks from Atlantic and Great Lakes populations are subject to predation from introduced Norway rats and from gulls. Average life expectancy is probably less than 5 years, but individuals are known to live more than 14 years.

CAUSE OF DECLINE, THREATS

Overhunting: Pipers were nearly hunted to extinction before the Migratory Bird Treaty of 1918. They made a substantial comeback until other threats, such as habitat destruction, appeared later in the century.

Habitat Destruction and Disturbance: Beach recreation activities, beachfront construction, and water projects (in the Great Plains) now constitute the most serious threats to the species. Each year, piping plovers find less suitable wintering habitat in Florida. Jetty construction and inlet stabilization projects threaten remaining wintering habitat. Much of the plover's historic nesting habitat in the northern United States and Canada have been destroyed or severely degraded by human activities. Some of Florida's wintering habitat has been degraded by hurricanes and tropical storms. Hurricane Opal, which slammed Florida's Panhandle in 1995, destroyed significant areas of wintering habitat. Severe storms in 1995 washed away a Woman Key site where piping plovers had wintered for many years.

Other Threats: Free-roaming dogs and cats are known to harass and prey on adult plovers and their eggs and chicks. Their camouflaged nests have been trampled on by humans, and many have been run over by off-road vehicles and construction equipment. The diversionary tactics performed by parent birds do nothing to fend off all-terrain vehicles. The accumulation of garbage at Florida's beach areas has increased mammalian predators, including raccoons, rats, opossums, skunks, and foxes.

CURRENT TREND: *Stable:* Atlantic Coast breeding populations; *declining:* wintering populations in Florida, as estimated in recent winter censuses. *Declining:* Great Lakes and northern Great Plains breeding populations.

Wood Stork
Mycteria americana
FAMILY CICONIIDAE; Order Ciconiiformes
LISTED STATUS
FWC: Endangered, listed 1972
USF&WS: Endangered, listed 1984
Description: America's only native stork, this large white, long-legged wading bird has highly contrasting, jet-black primary

and secondary feathers and tail, with a naked black or dark colored head and neck. The bald black head of this species (which earned it the nickname "ironhead") may have been the salvation of the bird during the late 1800's when plume hunters were decimating the populations of more exquisitely plumed wading birds in Florida. The sexes are identical. This species attains a height of 40–47 inches (102–118 cm) and a wingspan of more than 61 inches (155 cm). Adults weigh 4–7 pounds (1.8–3.1 kg). Wood storks have long, down-curved bills that are dark in adults and yellowish in juvenile birds. The legs are black; the feet are peach to orange in color but turn bright pink in breeding adults. Usually silent, these birds occasionally give off a rasping croak.

Distribution: Wood storks historically nested throughout much of the southeastern coastal plain from South Carolina and Georgia throughout Florida and along the Gulf Coast through Alabama, Mississippi, Louisiana, and Texas, and south through much of Mexico, Central America, and South America. The American wood stork is the only one of four species of wood storks (*Mycteria*) found in the New World. Though the species continues to breed throughout much of its Latin American range, its breeding range in the United States is now limited almost entirely to peninsular Florida, with small numbers in Georgia and South Carolina. The birds in Florida are permanent residents, although colonies of storks are known to disperse throughout large areas in reaction to seasonal changes and changes in hydroperiods. Storks from northern Florida often move southward during the coldest

months. Wood storks are also well known for lengthy postnesting dispersal; numerous records show Florida individuals turning up as far away as Delaware and Tennessee. Wood storks apparently from Mexican breeding populations are regular visitors to the Salton Sea in California and have wandered as far north as British Columbia. Though wood storks commonly fly extended distances overland to and from feeding sites, they apparently are reluctant to fly over large expanses of water, which may explain their scarcity in the Lower Keys. Fairly large wood stork rookeries can still be found in Florida in areas such as Collier County's Corkscrew Swamp Sanctuary and Everglades National Park.

Biology: Wood storks utilize a variety of subtropical wetlands, including cypress and mangrove swamps; however, their primary nesting sites (freshwater and brackish marshes, wet prairies, roadside ditches, flooded pastures, and depressions in flood plains) are primary foraging areas. The specialized technique used by wood storks to capture prey (mostly small fish) is called tactolocation, and successful feeding by this method requires shallow water with high concentrations of fish. Unlike other wading birds that often share the same hunting grounds, the wood stork does not depend on keen eyesight to capture prey. The wood stork wades tediously through pools of muddy water, usually no more than a foot deep, stirring up the water even more with its feet in an attempt to flush fish from their cover. Simultaneously, the stork keeps its partially open bill in the water, anticipating the impact of scurrying fish. When a fish grazes the stork's 9-inch (23 cm) mandible, the stork grasps the prey with its bill, often within 25 milliseconds. This bill-snap reflex is among the fastest known reflexes of any vertebrate. The fish most commonly preyed on by storks include mosquito fish, sailfin mollies (*Poecilia latipinna*), flagfish (*Jordanella floridae*), and several species of sunfish. In addition to fish, wood storks also prey on frogs, aquatic salamanders, snakes, crayfish, insects, and an occasional baby alligator.

Wood storks are gregarious creatures, and it is rare to find a lone individual. They nest in large rookeries, sometimes containing hundreds of pairs. Wood storks may fly as far as 80 miles between roosting and foraging areas, taking advantage of thermals for soaring. They may be seen circling like hawks while exploiting thermals. Storks south of Lake Okeechobee tend to begin nesting in the winter months (November-January), but colonies north of the lake are generally spring nesters (February-May). The timing of nesting depends largely on water levels within the storks' feeding grounds. Nesting pairs of storks require as much as 450 pounds of fish during the nesting season, which amounts to 2.6 million pounds of fish for a rookery of 6,000 pairs. Prior to mating, storks participate in a courting ritual that includes head bobbing and preening of the prospective mate's plumage. Rickety nests constructed of sticks, vines, Spanish moss, and leaves are most commonly positioned in the upper branches of large cypress trees or atop mangroves. Females construct the nest with materials collected by the male. Clutches of two to five cream-colored eggs, measuring 2.7 inches (68 mm) in length, are laid often at a rate of one egg per day. Eggs hatch after approximately one month, with an average of two young fledged per each successful nest. Because the nests are often exposed to direct sunlight and high temperatures, the parents keep the young cool by shading them with their outstretched wings and dribbling water on them carried back to the nest in the bill. The young fledge and are capable of sustained flight within two months. Although mortality is high in the first year of life, some wood storks may live more than 10 years in the wild.

Predators known or suspected of preying on adult wood storks include alligators, bobcats, and (historically) Florida panthers. The young or eggs may be preyed on by yellow rat snakes (*Elaphe obsoleta quadrivittata*), fish crows, great horned owls, barred owls, and possibly raccoons.

CAUSE OF DECLINE, THREATS

Habitat Destruction: Wood storks depend on wetlands for survival, but unlike other species, they require a specific type of wetland. The birds rely on ephemeral wetlands, with isolated pools of shallow water that dry up and contain a high density of fish that have no escape. If storks cannot locate enough of these particular microhabitats within range of their nesting rookeries, nesting failures commonly occur. Storks are for the most part limited to their unique tactolocation technique to capture prey, which proves futile in typical wetland habitats. The drastic decline of South Florida's wood storks correlates with the human alteration of the Everglades' natural sheet flow, which formerly provided sufficient habitat suitable for wood storks. Additionally, runoff from sugar farms south of Lake Okeechobee contains high amounts of nutrients, altering the vegetative communities where storks traditionally feed and making them unsuitable for foraging. Biologists refer to wood storks as the barometer of the Everglades because they are an indicator of the ecosystem's health. In central and northern Florida, the cutting of large nesting trees coupled with the draining of wetlands has been detrimental as well. The wood stork is Florida's most endangered species of wading bird.

Pollution: High concentrations of DDE, a metabolite of the infamous DDT, have been found in wood stork eggs from several central and northern Florida rookeries.

CURRENT TREND: Generally considered *stable,* South Florida breeding populations *declining,* Georgia and South Carolina populations *increasing.* An estimated 75,000 wood storks bred in Florida during the 1930's; the current population is estimated at fewer than 9,000 birds. The total U.S. breeding population now numbers approximately 5,000 pairs.

Whooping Crane

Grus americana
FAMILY GRUIDAE; Order Gruiformes
LISTED STATUS
FWC: Species of special concern (experimental population)
USF&WS: Threatened (experimental population); naturally occurring U.S. population listed as endangered in 1967
CANADA: Endangered, listed in 1978

Description: Standing erect at just over 4 feet (132 cm), the whooping crane is the tallest North American bird. The wingspan may exceed 7.5 feet (229 cm). Adult males may exceed 16 pounds (7.25 kg) and females 14 pounds (6.35 kg). Adults are nearly all white with red facial skin; their black primaries can seen in flight. Adults have black legs; those of juveniles are lighter. Whoopers, like other cranes, have a characteristic tuft of feathers on the rump, long legs, and a long heavy bill. Chicks are cinnamon brown until about four months, when they gradually begin turning white. Until their first autumn, immature birds retain a rust or reddish brown wash on their feathers, especially about the head and neck. Migrating cranes often fly in a formation similar to geese, with their necks extended. The voice of the whooping crane has best been described as a piercing buglelike *ker-loo, ker-lee-loo.*

Distribution: The only wild population of whooping cranes (approximately 150 birds) nests within Wood Buffalo National Park on the border of Alberta and the Northwest Territories in Canada and migrates to wintering grounds on the Aransas National Wildlife Refuge on the Texas Gulf Coast. Its former breeding range included a large area from the Canadian provinces of Alberta, Saskatchewan, and Manitoba south through portions of North Dakota, Minnesota, Illinois, and Iowa. The birds were believed to have migrated to wintering grounds in the southeast, including South Carolina, Georgia, and Florida, and to separate locations in central Mexico. Another, nonmigratory population existed in Louisiana until the 1940's, when a hurricane killed the last remaining few.

In Florida the whooping crane occurred as a wintering bird, and most records are from central or northern Florida. Pleistocene fossils have been discovered at a number of locations. O. E. Baynard, an experienced naturalist, reported seeing a flock of 14 whooping cranes in flight near Micanopy, Alachua County, in 1911. Two more whoopers were reported near the Kissimmee River in January 1936. Currently, efforts are under way to establish a nonmigratory population in the half-million acres of the Kissimmee Prairie region of Central Florida.

Biology: The Wood Buffalo and Aransas population summers on the flat, moist muskeg country of Canada; the introduced breeding populations in more southern latitudes, as well as wintering birds, favor similar prairies and freshwater marshes. Whooping cranes mate for life and will take a new mate only after the death of the partner. Whoopers participate in a truly amorous courtship ritual known as the crane dance, in which two love-smitten cranes flap their wings and bob their heads up and down, then jump as high as 12 feet in the air, often in unison. Nesting takes place in the spring, when the cranes construct a bowl-shaped nest of grass and reeds on elevated piles of debris, usually within a marshy area. The clutch of eggs averages two, rarely three. Eggs hatch after 29–31 days of incubation. Chicks are capable of flight after approximately three months. Pairs of cranes generally return to the same nesting area year after year.

Whooping cranes are omnivorous, and their diet includes fish, crustaceans, reptiles, amphibians, and insects as well as grain and berries. Few species regularly prey on whoopers, but the number of individual predators in a given area may be high. Predators in Florida include bobcats and alligators. Whooping cranes are long-lived; they are known to exceed 22 years in the wild and may live 40 years.

By 1941 the number of whoopers reached an all-time low of 15 animals; the outlook for the species was bleak. The story of recovery efforts, past and current, involving the whooping crane is a fascinating chronicle of trial and error in a last-ditch effort to prevent this grand species from going the route of the Carolina parakeet and passenger pigeon. A number of recovery efforts conducted in western North America were not as successful as envisioned. Because migration proved to be a significant source of mortality, a decision was made to establish a nonmigratory population in the eastern United States. After considering several locations, the Kissimmee Prairie of Central Florida was selected. Plans to establish a breeding colony in Florida began in the late 1970's, but the first birds were not released until 1993. The reintroduction endeavor is a cooperative effort of the USF&WS and the FWC. The goal of Florida's introduction program is to establish a resident population of approximately 25 breeding pairs by 2020.

The first 14 whooping cranes were soft-released at the Three Lakes Wildlife Management Area, with more whoopers released in subsequent years. (Soft-release provides a gradual transition for captive-raised birds from a sizable open-topped enclosure to life in the wild.) Three Lakes contains large expanses of habitat types favored by sandhill cranes, including wet and dry prairies with numerous lakes and marshy areas. At first, mortality was extremely high among the newly released birds and was attributed almost entirely to predation by bobcats. By 1995, biologists were happy to report that they had observed pair bonding and then breeding behavior, and it appeared as though introduction efforts were successful.

On a sunny day in November 1995, the author had the good fortune of photographing a flock of five whoopers on the 14,000-acre Escape Ranch, where many of the released cranes had recently relocated.

CAUSE OF DECLINE, THREATS

Overhunting (historic threat): Shooting of these stately birds decimated their population in the late 1800's and early 1900's and was a major factor in bringing them to the brink of extinction. One of the last whoopers in Florida was reportedly shot in 1927 or 1928 near St. Augustine.

Habitat Destruction: A primary cause of the decline of this noble bird within its historic range has been the loss of suitable wetland habitat, particularly in wintering areas and along historic migration routes.

Human Encroachment and Disturbance: Whoopers have little tolerance for human disturbance. Disturbance from airboats near Florida release sites may have been a factor in the death of one crane.

Power Lines: Collisions with power lines has been a leading cause of death in fledged birds.

Pollution: Texas' wintering population is vulnerable to offshore oil spills.

Avian Tuberculosis: This is one of several communicable diseases that could be deleterious to populations. Efforts are being made to prevent this disease from being introduced to wild birds.

CURRENT TREND: *Increasing.* Status in Florida looks promising despite heavy predation, but yet undetermined.

Florida Sandhill Crane
Grus canadensis pratensis
FAMILY GRUIDAE; Order Gruiformes
LISTED STATUS
FWC: Threatened, listed 1974 (endangered in 1972)
CITES: Appendix 2

Description: The typical Florida sandhill crane is usually just slightly taller than the great blue heron, a species commonly confused with the sandhill. This stocky, long-necked bird averages nearly 4 feet (122 cm) tall and may have a wingspan of 6–7 feet (183–213 cm). Males are slightly larger than females but are otherwise indistinguishable. Males average 10 pounds 5 ounces (4.7 kg) in weight, while females average 9 pounds (4 kg). Other sandhill subspecies vary in size from the Florida race; however, it may be difficult to make a distinction in the field. Adults are uniformly gray or grayish blue with a red crown that is quite noticeable. The upper throat and cheeks are white. As with other cranes, sandhills have a bustled rump. Dark primary feathers can be seen in flight. Immature birds lack the red crown and whitish facial feathers and often have a considerable number of brownish feathers. Adults are often adorned with brown-stained plumage as a result of preening themselves with a ferrous solution found in the mud where cranes forage. Adults and juveniles have black legs. Adult plumage is attained between 1 and 2.5 years. Sandhills fly with the neck well extended (unlike great blue herons). Sandhills emit a repeated, shrill, clattering *garoo-a-a-a* that can be heard for more than a mile.

Distribution: The Florida sandhill crane is one of six sandhill subspecies; it and two other subspecies are nonmigratory. This race is a permanent resident of peninsular Florida, with a disjunct population occurring in the Okefenokee Swamp of extreme southern Georgia. It is a locally common breeding bird in suitable habitat from Levy and Flagler counties south, but it is most numerous in the Payne's Prairie region of Alachua County, Kissimmee Prairie region, and the prairie region north and west of Lake Okeechobee. This race is seldom encountered south of central Dade and Monroe counties. Sandhills are generally absent from the Keys, although there is one record from the Dry Tortugas. Records of this bird are rare in the Big Bend region of the state, and it is considered an accidental in the Panhandle.

The more common migratory greater sandhill crane (*Grus canadensis tabida*) is widespread, breeding in Siberia, Alaska, much of Canada, and throughout portions of many western and midwestern states. These birds winter in portions of the American southwest and Mexico and also in southern Georgia and Florida. Migrating sandhills are known to fly in formations, similar to geese, at extremely high altitudes. Approximately 25,000 greater sandhills, mostly from the Great Lakes area, winter in Florida each year, easily outnumbering the 5,000 or so Florida sandhills. Other subspecies, including the smaller northern race (*G. c. canadensis*) and federally endangered Cuban (*G. c. nesiotes*) and Mississippi (*G. c. pulla*) sandhill cranes, may turn up in Florida from time to time.

Biology: Typical Florida sandhill crane habitats include marshes with low vegetation, margins of shallow lakes and ponds, wet and dry prairies, pastureland, and cultivated fields. Characteristic plant species found in the marshy areas most commonly inhabited by this bird include maiden cane and pickerelweed. Sandhills may forage away from wetlands diurnally, but they typically roost standing in the water, which offers some protection from predators. Sandhills are generally wary of humans and do not congregate near populated areas. Florida sandhills typically utilize the same general territory year round.

Florida sandhills often mingle with loose flocks of greater sandhills during the autumn; however, they segregate themselves in the winter when pairs are formed. Cranes usually remain paired for life; birds will find another mate if their original mate dies. The courtship of cranes includes a dance in which birds leap 10 feet or more into the air and execute an elegant series of hops and bows. This race nests from January (southern Florida) to mid-March, but nesting is delayed if water levels are low. Pairs tend to use the same nesting site year after year. Nests are usually constructed in several inches of water; the birds use sticks and a variety of vegetative matter to form an elevated, bowl-shaped mound approximately 3 feet in diameter. Pairs have been known to build additional nests nearby, possibly to confuse predators. Two (rarely three) eggs are laid in February or March and hatch after being incubated by both parents for 29–32 days. The young are quick learners and will accompany the parents away from the nest within 2 days. Young take their first sustained flight within 65–70 days. Birds reach sexual maturity and are capable of reproduction after 3 years. Life expectancy is known to exceed 25 years.

Sandhill cranes feed on a variety of small animals and vegetative matter. Their large bills snatch roots, seeds, bulbs, frogs, sirens, insects, crayfish, and snakes from shallow waters of marshes and lake margins. Sandhills have also been known to foray into oak woodlands to feast on acorns, but only on infrequent occasions have they been seen damaging crops. Natural predators include bobcats, coyotes, alligators, and, historically perhaps, the Florida panther. Bald eagles have been known to prey on injured sandhills. Chicks and inexperienced young birds are much more vulnerable to predation than adults.

CAUSE OF DECLINE, THREATS

Overhunting and Shooting: Shooting cranes for sport and fun caused the initial decline of this species in Florida. The state now outlaws the hunting of sandhills, although a few cranes are undoubtedly shot each year.

Habitat Destruction: Many wetlands inhabited for generations by sandhill cranes have now been drained for agriculture and development. The crane's specialized habitat is shrinking within its limited range. Sandhills do forage in improved pastures; however, these areas do not usually furnish adequate nesting sites.

Fences: Entanglement in barbed wire and other fences is a leading cause of serious injury and death to Florida sandhill cranes.

Other Threats: Drought conditions (natural and man-made) can seriously threaten sandhills during the breeding season. Their relatively low reproductive rate unfortunately is not conducive to a rapid recovery. Free-ranging dogs have injured and killed sandhill cranes.

CURRENT TREND: *Stable.* Population as of 2000 estimated at 5,000 birds.

Everglades Snail Kite
Rostrhamus sociabilis plumbeus
FAMILY ACCIPITRIDAE; Order Falconiformes

LISTED STATUS
FWC: Endangered, listed 1972
USF&WS: Endangered, listed 1967

Description: The Everglades snail kite is a medium-sized raptor, 15–19 inches (38–47 cm) in length with a wingspan of 41–46 inches (104–117 cm). It weighs 12–21 ounces (340–520 g). Females are often slightly larger than males. Unlike other Florida kites (swallow-tailed, Mississippi, and white-tailed), which have the tapered wings of falcons, snail kites have paddle-shaped wings resembling those of a buteo. Wing tips of perched snail kites extend beyond the tail tip. The bill is deeply curved, enabling the bird to extract its primary prey, apple snails, from their shell. The sexes are clearly dimorphic. Adult males are slate-gray to slate-black with a slightly darker back, head, and upperwing. The tail (on both sexes) has a broad white band at the base, easily observed in flight, and a less conspicuous narrow gray band at the tip. The adult male's legs and facial skin adjoining the beak are vivid reddish orange. Adults have deep red eyes; the eyes of juveniles are brown. Adult females are brownish with a streaked chest and abdomen; legs and cere are yellowish, though more subdued than the male's. The sides of the face are whitish with a distinctive dark line running from the rear of the eye toward the rear of the head. Older females may be darker and lack the dark eye line. Juveniles closely resemble adult females but have brown eyes. Juvenile males obtain adult plumage between their second and third years. Snail kites fly with unhurried, floppy wingbeats and keep their wings slightly cocked or bowed upward when soaring. This species emits several types of shrilling calls that have been described as *kor-ee-ee-a, kor-ee-ee-a; ka-ka-ka-ka-ka-ka;* and *kak-kak-kak.*

Distribution: The snail kite reaches the northernmost limit of its range in Florida and Cuba, where the Everglades race occurs. Two other subspecies inhabit the tropical wetlands of the West Indies, Mexico, and Central and South America. Historically, snail kites occupied suitable habitat throughout much of peninsular Florida. The current range, however, has been reduced to a number of localized colonies in the freshwater marshes of the Kissimmee and St. Johns rivers and in the Lake Okeechobee-Everglades ecosystems.

Biology: Unlike bald eagles and ospreys, which are both habitat generalists utilizing various aquatic habitats, the Everglades snail kite is a habitat specialist. It is largely restricted to freshwater marshes, shallow lakes, and other wetland habitats that support apple snails, its principal prey. Though the apple snail's range extends a considerable distance north of the snail kite's range, abundant foraging habitats suitable for the kite do not. Typical marsh plants of the emergent, long-hydroperiod, palustrine wetlands inhabited by snail kites include spike rush, maiden cane, and saw grass.

Habitat specialists are often more vulnerable to population declines as a result of habitat alteration or degradation. Fluctuations in the apple snail's abundance are likely responsible for this kite's habit of relocating nesting and roosting sites. Snail kites may hunt by flying low (6–35 feet) and leisurely, over open marshland where submerged snails are easily seen, or from a perch. Upon targeting a snail, kites simply snatch them with their talons. They often transfer snails to the beak in flight. Snails are generally plucked while ascending to respirate, usually within 4 inches (10 cm) of the surface. Everglades snail kites have been observed feeding on small turtles and freshwater crabs, which superficially resemble apple snails.

Snail kites are a gregarious species, hence the Latin name *sociabilis.* They tend to nest and roost colonially; however, roosting congregations are generally larger than nesting congregations. In 1985 (a drought year), 372 snail kites were counted roosting at the Palm Beach County Solid Waste Authority's water impoundment area. Breeding activity typically occurs from February to July but may occur in any month. Courtship displays include aerial acrobatics, and males furnish their mate with food. This species often nests in association with anhingas, herons, and ibises. Nests are usually assembled over water (to impede predation) in southern willows, pond apples (*Annona glabra*), or other small trees. The male constructs the nest of sticks, twigs, and foliage. Two to four oblong, blotched, light-colored eggs are laid; they hatch after 26–28 days. Nestlings fledge after four or five weeks. During wet years, males (occasionally females) may abandon mates and nestlings to renest with another mate. This habit, known as ambisexual mate desertion, is an evolutionary adaptation enabling species to survive in environments with drought and flood cycles.

Natural predators of adult snail kites in Florida include barred owls and great horned owls. Nestlings and eggs are preyed on by rat snakes, Florida cottonmouths, raccoons, fish crows, and boat-tailed grackles. Biologists believe average life expectancy to be 5–8 years; individuals older than 17 have been recorded.

CAUSE OF DECLINE, THREATS

Habitat Destruction: Florida's snail kite populations began a sharp decline in the early 1900's with the widespread drainage of wetlands. The most significant changes involve conversion of wetlands for agriculture and diversion of water to urban areas. Snail kites rely on apple snail abundance and accessibility, which are affected by water levels. If water levels are too low, snails perish. If the water is too high, it submerges the vegetation that apple snails cling to, making them inaccessible to kites.

Critical habitat was designated for the Everglades snail kite in 1977.

Invasive Exotic Species: Introduced exotic aquatic plants such as the water hyacinth, water hydrilla, and water lettuce have created vegetative blankets over many former snail kite foraging areas, impairing the kites' ability to hunt. Melaleuca trees have rapidly taken over many freshwater marshes, displacing native vegetation, changing the landscape, and lowering water levels.

Water Pollution: Nutrient-rich runoff, particularly phosphorus from agricultural sources, has degraded water quality throughout much of the kite's range. Such runoff is believed to be injurious to apple snail populations and to encourage invasion of nonnative vegetation. High levels of arsenic (0.02–0.08 ppm) were detected in Palm Beach County's snail kite foraging sites.

CURRENT TREND: *Stable.* By 1965 the Everglades snail kite was nearing extinction, with only 10–25 birds remaining. From 1969 to 1994, annual counts rose from 96 to 996, but the increases have been interrupted by many steep declines (Table 2).

Southern Bald Eagle
Haliaeetus leucocephalus leucocephalus
FAMILY ACCIPITRIDAE; Order Falconiformes

LISTED STATUS

FWC: Threatened, listed 1972
USF&WS: Threatened (endangered 1967–1995)
CITES: Appendix 1

Description: A bald eagle soaring over a high mountain lake or perched above an Everglades prairie is an awe-inspiring sight, not soon forgotten. The bald eagle is truly a magnificent creature. That is

TABLE II. *Annual Counts of Everglades Snail Kites in Florida*

1969: 96	1976: 142	1983: 452	1990: 418
1970: 120	1977: 152	1984: 668	1991: 372
1971: 72	1978: 267	1985: 407	1992: 733
1972: 65	1979: 431	1986: 562	1993: 849
1973: 95	1980: 652	1987: 326	1994: 996
1974: 81	1981: 109	1988: 500	
1975: 110	1982: 302	1989: 464	

why our forefathers chose to adopt this noble raptor as our national symbol in 1782. The bald eagle and America's only other regularly occurring eagle, the golden, are by far our largest birds of prey. External measurements of a typical adult bald eagle are length 27–37 inches (70–94 cm), wingspan 71–90 inches (180–229 cm), and weight 4.4–13.6 pounds (2.0–6.2 kg). Southern bald eagles (*Haliaeetus leucocephalus leucocephalus*) tend to be smaller than northern bald eagles (*H. l. alascensis*), and females may be slightly larger than males. Adults are nearly unmistakable, with the vivid white head and tail and contrasting dark brown body. Legs are yellow or yellow-orange in all plumages. The species is not sexually dimorphic. Aberrant plumages, including partial albinos and cream-colored birds, have been observed in the wild. The voice is an acrimonious, cackling *kleek-kik-ik-ik-ik*, or lower pitched *kak-kak-kak*.

The full adult plumage is attained after 4–6 years. Young adults may still have brown coloration on the head, but it eventually dissipates. The beak and cere of adults are bright yellowish orange; the iris is light yellow. Juvenile and subadult birds may closely resemble golden eagles; the chance of seeing a golden eagle in Florida, however, is remote. Four fairly distinctive plumages are attained before full adult plumage is reached. *Immature plumage:* Birds under a year old are uniformly dark brown above, including head and breast. From below, some feathers, particularly axillars, may have a whitish wash. The abdomen is paler than the breast; beak and cere are black; the iris is dark brown. Tail feathers are longer in this plumage than in all others. *White-belly 1 plumage:* After approximately

one year, these birds have a lighter beak, cere, and iris, and a buffy superciliary line on the face. White feathers appear on the back, forming an upside-down triangle, which remains throughout the subsequent white-belly 2 phase. A large proportion of the abdomen feathers are now white. *White-belly 2 plumage:* After approximately two years, the iris, bill, and cere become even lighter. Head feathers also become lighter, and the superciliary line becomes more pronounced, as does the dark bib of the upper chest. *Adult transition plumage:* Between three and four years, birds exhibit characteristics of both white-belly and adult plumages. Body feathers darken; head and tail feathers lighten. A dark eyeline similar to an osprey's is often present.

Distribution: Two bald eagle subspecies occur, in localized populations, over a wide range from Alaska and northern Canada throughout much of the United States and portions of northern Mexico. Northern bald eagles inhabit Canada and Alaska, and southern bald eagles breed in the lower 48 states, including Florida, which supports the largest breeding population of bald eagles outside Alaska.

Bald eagles may nest (and winter) virtually anywhere in Florida where suitable habitat exists. Florida state studies revealed that nearly 75 percent of Florida's nesting eagle populations nest within five primary geographic regions: Everglades National Park; coastal areas of Lee, Charlotte, and Sarasota counties; lakes and prairie region of Osceola and Polk counties; Ocala National Forest region; lakes and prairie region of Alachua and northern Marion counties.

Biology: Bald eagles are usually associated with large bodies of water (seacoasts, lakes, and rivers) where their dietary staple, fish, is readily available. They are sometimes encountered far from water, especially in migration. The author has observed bald eagles perched atop mesquite trees and saguaro cactus in Arizona's Sonoran Desert in late winter, far from lakes and rivers. Winter (after nesting) is also the time for this fairly gregarious species to gather at communal roost sites, where several dozen eagles may share a single tree. Eagles are sometimes observed in mock aerial combat (actually a courtship behavior known as talon grappling), in which two birds barrel-roll through the sky with talons locked.

These piscivorous raptors are competent anglers, but they are also opportunists that will pirate prey from other birds, especially ospreys. Bald eagles in Florida also readily consume waterfowl, especially American coots (*Fulica americana*), wading birds, carrion, and occasionally mammals and herptiles.

In Florida, nesting usually begins in October and may extend into February. Eagles construct the largest nests of any North American bird, often more than 50 feet high in large trees providing unobstructed views. Pairs may use the same nest for decades, refortifying and enlarging the nest each year. One Florida nest measured nearly 10 feet wide and 12 feet deep. Clutch sizes range from one to three eggs, averaging two. The incubation period is 34–35 days, with young fledging after 10–12 weeks. Bald eagles defend nesting territories with vigor, announcing their presence to intruders with blaring grunts and loud *whee-he-he-he*s that sound almost like a horse. When eagle nests are vacated for the season, great horned owls sometimes use them to raise their own families.

CAUSE OF DECLINE, THREATS

DDT Poisoning: Dichloro-diphenyltri-chloroethane, or DDT, is the infamous insecticide that nearly exterminated bald eagles, ospreys, peregrine falcons, and brown and white pelicans from our planet. Before being outlawed in 1972, it was widely used throughout this country. Quantities of DDT ended up in wetlands and many wetland species. Over a relatively short time, DDT made its way through food chains, becoming concentrated in predators of contaminated prey (in this case, in eagles that ate contaminated fish). Among the residual effects of DDT in eagles was a severe reduction in calcium in their eggshells, resulting in very brittle shells that usually broke during incubation. Now that DDT is largely a historic threat, bald eagles have recovered throughout much of their former range, prompting the USF&WS to downlist it to threatened status in 1995. It is important to note, however, that illegal DDT use continues in this country, and it is regularly used in several Latin American countries where many susceptible birds winter. Surprisingly, DDT is still manufactured in the United States and legally exported to other countries.

Habitat Destruction: Destruction of eagle habitat, particularly nesting habitat, now constitutes the foremost threat to Florida's eagles. Many former nesting areas have been lost to residential, commercial, or agricultural development. Some Florida landowners and developers are suspected of killing eagles and felling active nest trees in an attempt to rid their property of the protected species.

In one such incident, on land slated for development, an active nest containing two eggs was chainsawed down, causing the eggs to fall 50 feet to the ground. Amazingly, one egg survived and was incubated and hatched with the help of Resee Collins of the Florida Audubon Society's Bird of Prey Center in Maitland. The lucky eaglet, dubbed Seminole Wind, was successfully reared and released into the wild on 9 February 1993.

Human encroachment and disturbance of nesting eagles is a related threat to Florida's eagles, as urban sprawl consumes wild areas statewide. Most Florida eagle nests are closer to roads or highways than they are to the nearest body of water.

Shooting: Unfortunately, illegal shooting remains a serious threat to bald eagles in many parts of their range. Reasons range from financial motives (feather and artifact trade) to an outright disregard for living things.

Electrocution: Many eagles are killed while perching on the crossbars of powerlines. Where hot wires and ground wires are closely positioned, large birds can come in contact with both wires simultaneously and be electrocuted.

Metallic Poisoning: Many eagles have died after consuming waterfowl containing toxic lead pellets from hunters' shotshells. Steel shot has replaced lead shot (now illegal), which is expected to reduce lead poisoning in the years to come. Mercury poisoning, however, may be on the rise, particularly in South Florida, where toxic levels of methylmercury have been detected in many organisms including fishes, panthers, and bald eagles.

Automobile Collisions: Automobile collisions (mostly with eagles feeding on roadkills) are responsible for 40 percent of eagle deaths in some areas.

CURRENT TREND: *Increasing.*

Audubon's Crested Caracara

Caracara cheriway audubonii
FAMILY FALCONIDAE; Order Falconiformes
LISTED STATUS
FWC: Threatened, listed 1974
USF&WS: Threatened (Florida population only), listed 1987

Description: The crested caracara is a robust member of the falcon family, about the size of a red-tailed hawk. It more closely resembles, both in appearance and behavior, the New World vultures (family Cathartidae). Though there is no disputing that the caracara belongs to the Falconidae, it often has been unofficially characterized as half falcon, half vulture.

These crested, boldly patterned, prairie-land raptors are 20–23 inches (50–58 cm) long, with a wingspan of 48–52 inches (122–133 cm), and the tail measures 8–10 inches (20–25 cm) long. Adults typically weigh 1.8–2.8 pounds (800–1,300 g). Sexes are similar in appearance, though females may be slightly larger. Compared with typically sleek, streamlined falcons with pointed wings, the caracara has a massive head and beak, broad rounded wings, and an elongated neck. Its featherless, yellowish legs are exceptionally long, with the large feet characteristic of falcons (except that the talons are flatter, making it easier to pursue prey on the ground). The caracara's naked facial skin may be various shades of orange, yellow, or pinkish; it has the remarkable ability to change color, apparently triggered by emotional stimuli, generally showing bright orange-red when the bird is at ease but quickly changing to a much paler, washed yellow when a threat is perceived. The tip of the bill is bluish, sometimes bright blue. The iris is brownish.

Adults are long-legged black and white birds recognizable at some distance. The lower back, abdomen, wings, crown, and crest are dark brown or black. The throat, cheeks, sides and rear of head, neck, upper breast, lower abdomen, and undertail coverts are white. Black barring occurs on the midbreast, merging into a solid black belly band. The tail is white, with numerous thin black bands and a prominent broad black band near the tip. Like the black vulture, the only bird it is likely to be confused with, the caracara has conspicuous whitish patches toward the tip of each dark-colored wing. Black vultures are distinguished from caracaras by their uniformly dark body, shorter tail and neck, and lack of white throat and crest. Also like both black and turkey vultures (*Cathartes aura*), with which caracaras commonly associate, the underwing coverts are several shades darker than the secondaries, producing a two-toned effect.

Adult plumage is usually attained after four years. Subadults are quite similar to adults but somewhat duller. Juveniles are also similar in color and pattern but are more brownish, their facial skin is pinkish rather than red, the breast is streaked rather than barred, and the legs are grayish.

When soaring, a caracara's wings are held straight, in contrast to the dihedral position of the turkey vulture. The caracara's flight is forceful and eaglelike. This bird is commonly called the Mexican eagle in Texas and Mexico.

When excited, caracaras emit a loud, distinctive rattling call, which inspired their common name.

Distribution: The range of Audubon's crested caracara, one of four recognized subspecies, extends from portions of the southeastern, south-central, and southwestern United States, Cuba, and the Isle of Pines south through much of mainland Mexico and Baja California to Panama. This race (until recently known as *Polyborus plancus audubonii*) is the only subspecies native to the United States. Other subspecies inhabit Mexico, Central America, and South America. Fossils found in Florida indicate that two other species of caracara (*Caracara prelutosa* and *Milvago readei*), both extinct, inhabited Florida during the Pleistocene Epoch.

Within the United States, the caracara occurs within three disjunct, nonmigratory populations, all three of them in southern states. The most western population occupies the area of the Tohono O'Odham Indian Reservation in the Sonoran Desert of southern Arizona, where it is relatively rare. The largest population within the United States inhabits the vast mesquite scrub and savanna regions of southern Texas, where caracaras are locally abundant. Stragglers from that population occasionally reach extreme southwestern Louisiana and southern New Mexico. The Texas and Arizona populations are not truly disjunct, as their range is more or less continuous south of the Mexican border.

The third and smallest population is restricted to the 10-county prairie region of central and south-central peninsular Florida. Only this population is designated as threatened under the Endangered Species Act. The nucleus of the current

Florida range is the Kissimmee Prairie and other open expanses studded with cabbage palms within five contiguous counties (DeSoto, Glades, Highlands, Okeechobee, and Osceola) north and west of Lake Okeechobee. Caracaras also occupy portions of Charlotte, Hardee, and Polk counties, and individuals (usually immature birds) are occasionally reported as far north as Orlando and as far east as Florida's St. Johns River. Stragglers have been recorded as far north as Nassau County, as far south as the Lower Keys, and as far west as the Panhandle's Bay County. The historic range of the caracara in Florida is known to be considerably more expansive; the bird's habitat has been shrinking for many years and is likely to continue to dwindle as the state's human population increases. The caracara was a former resident from St. Johns County (the type locality is near St. Augustine, where Audubon first collected this bird) south to portions of Dade County on the Atlantic Coast and from Alachua County to portions of Collier County on the Gulf. Although now considered uncommon to rare in Florida, caracaras are locally common and are not difficult to find if one knows where to look. Among several likely viewing locations, the author has found a stretch of State Highway 70, between U.S. Highway 27 in Highlands County east to the vicinity of the city of Okeechobee, to be the most reliable. **Biology:** Before the arrival of Europeans, caracaras were plentiful residents of the once widespread dry prairie ecosystems of central and south-central Florida. These vast expanses of open country included both dry and wet prairies, palm-studded native grasslands dotted with numerous shallow, marshy wetlands. The typical caracara habitat in Florida was and is these now less expansive areas of prairie, unimpeded by large tracts of dense forest but with numerous scattered cabbage palms. Caracaras are closely associated with the cabbage palm, the state tree, which serves almost without exception as their nesting sites. It also provides lofty hunting perches for these stately, scavenging predators. Sporadic hammocks of cabbage palms and live oaks dot the flatlands, and other typical plants include saw palmetto and assorted grasses and forbs. These falconids also inhabit open wooded areas with tracts of grassland, and pastures. Fortunately, caracaras have demonstrated an ability to adapt, to some degree, to habitats altered by some human activities and have flourished in certain areas converted to cattle country or agricultural lands, if sufficient nesting and foraging habitat remains. The habitat and habits of the Florida population of Audubon's crested caracara are remarkably similar to those of Africa's largely terrestrial secretary bird (*Sagittarius serpentarius*).

Florida's population of crested caracara is now isolated by hundreds of miles from the primary distribution of its species, as are several other predominantly western species like the burrowing owl and Florida scrub-jay. Central Florida populations are relics from a time when Florida's environment was more arid and the ranges of these Florida species or subspecies were contiguous with their western counterparts. While many species retreated as climatic conditions changed, the caracara and a few other species adapted, evolved, and flourished in the more xeric natural communities of peninsular Florida.

Characteristic faunal species that share the caracara's domain include eastern meadowlarks, turkey and black vultures, northern bobwhites, bald eagles, northern harriers (winter only), eastern coachwhip snakes, eastern diamondback rattlesnakes, and threatened eastern indigo snakes. The caracara trox beetle, known to science from only two specimens, is possibly restricted to life within the confines of the shabbily constructed nest of the caracara, the microhabitat where it was discovered in Florida. The continued existence of caracaras and other species of Florida's prairie habitats depend on the preservation of substantial intact tracts of dry prairie.

Though a great deal is yet to be learned about the courtship and breeding behavior of caracaras, it is believed that these birds are monogamous and mate for life. Birds are thought to be sexually mature by their fourth year. Adults become more vocal during the breeding season, when their unusual contortionist display and accompanying vocalization is most often witnessed. Birds often arch the neck and head extremely far back and utter loud rattling calls that are forever associated with the caracara. Pair bonding in these birds is very strong, with the male and female generally remaining together throughout the year. In caracara country, two of these birds huddled snugly together atop a telephone pole or other perch is a familiar sight.

Unlike true falcons, the caracara does construct a real nest, although it is somewhat crude. The nest is nearly always assembled in the crown of a cabbage palm, 12–55 feet (3.7–16.8 m) above the ground, but nests as low as 7 feet (2.1 m) have been found. Only a handful of caracara nests in trees other than cabbage palms have been recorded in Florida, the most unusual of which was reportedly in mangroves on an islet off Lee County's coast. Both sexes share the duties of nest building, which include gathering branches, twigs, roots, and vines. Egg-laying generally takes place in February and March, but eggs have been recorded between September and April. Usually two or three oval eggs are laid, measuring close to 2.4 inches by 1.9 inches (6.1 by 4.9 cm). The ground color of the eggs is typically light but is quite variable. The eggs are commonly splashed with colors, including reddish brown and chocolate. Incubated by both parents, they hatch after approximately 28 days. The offspring remain in the nest for as long as 60 days. The parents feed their young small pieces of meat carried to the nest, sometimes over considerable distances, rather than regurgitating meals. The pair will raise additional broods only if the first brood of eggs is destroyed. The same nest is often used for many years. Because caracaras tend to nest and roost atop sabal palms that tower above their prairie habitat, the eggs and nestlings are usually afforded a fair degree of protection from most predators. Those predators include crows, raccoons, owls, rat snakes, and bobcats. This species is long-lived, exceeding 30 years in captivity.

Crested caracaras are opportunistic in their feeding habits and readily take nearly any kind of prey, living or dead. They are equally capable of hunting from an elevated perch or foraging on the ground. Caracaras are swift, powerful, and agile in flight, capable of exceeding 40 miles per hour, and are equally dexterous on land, capturing lizards, snakes, and small rodents in the manner of a roadrunner. The enormous appetite of this bird is matched by the variety of prey it consumes. Live prey commonly taken includes frogs, fishes, snakes, lizards, crabs, rodents, crayfish, insects and arachnids, small birds, rabbits, juvenile alligators, the eggs of birds and reptiles, especially turtles. Larger prey such as opossums or wading birds are sometimes subdued by the combined efforts of a pair of caracaras.

These birds are primarily scavengers, and carrion is the mainstay of their diet. The face of the caracara, like the vulture and most true scavenging birds, is featherless, which helps when the bird immerses its head in a ripe roadside corpse. It often feasts on roadkills in the company of both turkey and black vultures, usually without feuding. Caracaras are clearly the more dominant species and sometimes demonstrate their assertiveness by pilfering food from the other scavengers or harassing the vultures to the point that they regurgitate their meal, which is then consumed by the aggressor. Caracaras have also been known to pirate food from other caracaras, gulls, pelicans, and even bald eagles.

CAUSE OF DECLINE, THREATS

Habitat Destruction: The distribution and the number of caracaras inhabiting Florida have been substantially reduced in recent decades, and the primary cause is habitat loss. The Florida population of Audubon's crested caracaras is now estimated to be a third of what is was in the early 1900's. The specialized nesting and foraging habitat required for its survival continues to recede as agricultural and residential land use expands. Over 95 percent of Florida's caracaras inhabit

unprotected private lands, making it difficult to restore and protect a viable population. Recently permits have been approved authorizing the development of more than one million acres of citrus groves on land that is of great significance to caracaras.

Automobile Collisions: Caracaras regularly forage on roadkills, which puts them in constant jeopardy. Automobile collisions are the second most serious threat to Florida's caracaras. Ironically, the high-speed vehicles traveling the roads bisecting the caracara's prairie domain yield a consistent and effortless source of sustenance for these and other scavengers; however, the take of an easy roadside meal too often becomes their last supper.

Other Threats: Illegal shooting, trapping, and poisoning of caracaras undoubtedly still occurs, although these threats are no longer as serious as they once were. Historically, caracaras were routinely shot by ranchers who believed they were a threat to newborn livestock. Caracaras with gunshot wounds still turn up, providing evidence of illegal shooting. Trapping and deliberate killing of many vultures by ranchers was another common practice early in the last century; now illegal, it also took its toll on caracaras. Effects of pesticides and pollutants are not well known, although a study concluded by Kiff et al. in the early 1980's revealed that eggshells of Florida caracaras taken after 1945 were 8.2 percent thinner than eggs taken before then. Caracaras may be susceptible to lead poisoning in areas where hunters illegally use lead shot to hunt waterfowl, doves, and quail, which are consumed by caracaras. Egg collecting was another historic threat. Thousands of caracara eggs were removed from Florida nests during the early 1900's, when egg collecting was in vogue.

CURRENT TREND: Florida population currently considered *stable* by federal biologists. Population and habitats, however, have experienced long-term *declines.* Biologist Joan L. Morrison (1996) states, "The problem with a long-lived species is that until you know something about recruitment of juveniles, you may not notice a population decline until the breeding adults start to die off, then there will be a huge crash and it is usually too late to do anything." Statewide population estimates for 1997 range from 400–500 individuals to 700–800 individuals.

Peregrine Falcon
Falco peregrinus
FAMILY FALCONIDAE; Order Falconiformes
LISTED STATUS
FWC: Endangered, listed 1972
CITES: Appendix 1

Description: The peregrine is a superlative, muscular, slaty blue falcon, about the same size as a red-shouldered hawk. Adult peregrines reach a total length of 15–20 inches (38–51 cm), with a wingspan of 39–45 inches (99–114 cm). Females attain a greater size and weight than males but are otherwise very similar in appearance. Adult males weigh an average of 1.3 pounds (0.60 kg); adult females average 1.9 pounds (0.85 kg). Like other falcons, the peregrine has long pointed wings that are bent at the wrist, and the tail is fairly long and narrow. The peregrine falcon is the only North American falcon whose wing tips extend to the tail tip when perched. The crown and nape

are black, and there is a prominent broad, dark streak on each side of the face, referred to by birders as a mustache.

The two North American races that may occur in Florida as migrating or wintering birds are the Arctic peregrine falcon (*Falco peregrinus tundrius*), also known as the tundra peregrine falcon, and the American peregrine falcon (*F. p. anatum*), sometimes called the continental peregrine falcon. (A third race, Peale's peregrine falcon, *F. p. pealei*, a resident of the American and Canadian northwest, is the largest, darkest, and most heavily streaked peregrine in North America.) The species designation *peregrinus* means "wandering." The Latin subspecies designation *tundrius* refers to the environment inhabited by the Arctic peregrine during the summer months; the subspecific designation of the American peregrine, *anatum*, means "of ducks." The plumage of slightly smaller Arctic peregrines is generally paler than the other two subspecies. Adults typically have a white abdomen, chest, and throat that are barred with dark brown or black, the barring being more pronounced on the abdomen. The abdomen, chest, and throat of adult American peregrine falcons are generally more tan in color, and the back is darker. The mustache of the American peregrine is thicker than in the two other North American races. The tail has five or six narrow, dark bands, with the terminal band being broader. The tip of the tail is white. The legs and feet of adults are yellow and the talons black. The cere and eye rings in adult birds are yellowish. The iris is dark brown. In immature birds, the underparts are brownish and often heavily streaked lengthwise. The cere, legs, feet, and eye rings of juvenile birds are often grayish or blue. The tail of immature birds is longer, and the wing tips may not extend quite to the tail tip. In recent years, the majority of peregrines observed in Florida have been of the *tundrius* subspecies. A hodge-podge of peregrine races have been used in relocation efforts in the eastern United States, however, to the extent that intergrades of *tundrius* and *anatum* are not uncommon and pure-form American peregrines may be observed as well.

The merlin, which is a fairly common wintering bird in Florida, resembles a miniature peregrine; at a length of 10–13 inches (25–34 cm) and wingspan of 23–26 inches (58–66 cm), it is considerably smaller than the peregrine. Also, the merlin lacks the peregrine's thick, black mustache. The American kestrel is decidedly smaller than even the smallest peregrine, at 10 inches (27 cm) in length, with a 23-inch (58 cm) wingspan, and both sexes have a conspicuous rufous-colored upper back.

Calls issued by peregrine falcons include the cacking call, a brief, raspy, high-pitched call, often repeated rapidly at the approach of a perceived threat; the wailing call, a long drawn-out call, also high-pitched, that rises toward the end, most often uttered during courtship and nesting activities; and the creaking call, described under "Biology."

Distribution: The range of this species is nearly cosmopolitan; it occurs on every continent except Antarctica. A total of 19 peregrine subspecies are currently recognized. Three subspecies occur in North America, and two, the Arctic peregrine and the American peregrine, occur in Florida. The Arctic subspecies breeds north of the tree line from Alaska eastward across northern Canada to Greenland, and winters from the southern United States, including Florida, as far south as Chile in South America. The American race formerly bred throughout much of Canada, south of the tree line, and south throughout much of the United States, excluding Florida and Ohio, to the mountains of northern Mexico. It had been extirpated from nearly all of its historic range in the eastern United States but has now been reestablished in many areas through the release of captive-bred birds. Research has revealed that the third North American peregrine, Peale's, is an essentially nonmigratory, permanent resident of the Pacific Northwest, from the Aleutian Archipelago in Alaska south to the Queen Charlotte Islands of British Columbia.

The peregrine falcon occurs in Florida only in migration and as a wintering species; it does not breed within the state. Peregrines may occur virtually anywhere in the state but are most frequently observed in coastal areas where ducks, gulls, and other seabirds congregate.

A 1995 survey of breeding pairs of peregrine falcons in the United States counted 98 nesting pairs in the eastern states, 68 pairs in the central United States and south-central Canada, and 829 pairs in the western states. Arizona made the top of the list, with more than 250 pairs, and several states had only 1 known pair, including Kansas, Nebraska, Kentucky, South Carolina, and Washington, D.C. Concentrations of migrating peregrines following southbound seabirds are often observed at Cape May in New Jersey, in the Assateague and Chincoteague areas of the Delmarva Peninsula, and on Padre Island, Texas.

Biology: The habitat utilized by migratory peregrines during the breeding season (late spring, summer) is often quite dissimilar from habitats used during migration and the winter months. The peregrine's aerie is usually situated on a cliff or other setting that is nearly inaccessible to mammalian predators, whether among land-locked mountains or on a seacoast. Peregrines hunt for prey in open places, sometimes far from their nest site but often in open terrain bordering a rocky crag. The winter haunts of the peregrine falcon in Florida include various coastal habitats, lakeshores, wet and dry prairies, freshwater and saltwater marshes, and urban areas, including Miami, Tampa, and Jacksonville. A direct correlation exists between the type of habitat utilized and the available avian prey base.

The home range of a peregrine falcon covers between 6 and 19 square miles, but on rare occasions nests have been as little as 1,500 feet (457 m) apart. During the late winter and early spring (less frequently at other times), lone peregrine falcons may try to attract a mate by flying back and forth in the vicinity of the potential nesting site, or by emitting a loud creaking call from multiple locations near a suitable nesting spot. The creaking call has been described as a repeated, variable, two-syllable call with an emphasis on the first syllable. After pairing, the birds engage in courtship rituals consisting of flight displays (high-speed loop-the-loops, figure eights, and steep dives), mate-feeding by the male, and cooperative hunting. Falcons can copulate in midair; in a slow, bouncing flight (known as slow flight), the male approaches the female from behind and presses his tail downward while the female crouches down, leaning her tail to one side.

Natural nest sites are usually on a cliff face, about halfway up, often with a southern exposure. In coastal areas, cliff caves are commonly used. Peregrines that have established breeding populations in urban areas commonly nest on the urban equivalent of cliffs: the ledges of tall buildings, bridges, and towers. Well-used aeries are often visible by the whitewash of droppings on the ledges below. The nest itself is usually no more than a shallow scrape in a ledge, about 1 foot (30 cm) in diameter and 1–2 inches (2.5–5 cm) deep. Both sexes use their feet and bill to excavate the scrape. No vegetative matter is added to the nest site. On rare occasions, peregrines have been known to nest in the hollowed top of tree trunks that have been struck by lightning or in abandoned raptor or raven nests in trees. Egg-laying peaks in late March and early April. Three or four brown-blotched pinkish or cream-colored eggs are laid at two- or three-day intervals; they are incubated for 28–33 days, primarily by the female. Hatchlings are covered with whitish down feathers and are virtually sightless and quite helpless. Nestlings quickly become more capable, and after about a month they often become so aggressive that the parents leave food for them on the ledge rather than feeding them directly. Peregrine falcons typically fledge after about six weeks, with males often fledging before females. Young-of-the-year birds sometimes remain together until migration, especially in the far north. Nesting peregrines generally do not tolerate human encroachment and often flee the nest when humans approach within

1,200–1,500 feet (366–457 m); on rare occasions they abandon the nest. It should also be noted that these formidable birds fiercely protect their nests against intruders, including humans. They have been known to attack other large birds that venture too close to the aerie, including ravens (*Corvus corax*), turkey vultures, other hawks, and even eagles. The peregrine falcon typically begins breeding at 2–3 years of age. It is believed that the average wild peregrine lives about 6–8 years, with a maximum life expectancy of less than 20 years.

The peregrine's former name, "duck hawk," is quite appropriate. Birds, often ducks, constitute the primary source of prey for the peregrine falcon year round, throughout its range. This falcon is considered by many authorities to be the fastest of all God's creatures. This streamlined, feathered bullet is believed to exceed 200 mph (possibly as fast as 270 mph) in free-falling stoop dives that trace the shape of a teardrop. The peregrine's remarkable ability to capture, on the wing, the swiftest of birds, including swifts and swallows, is well documented. At dusk, peregrines are also known to capture bats. The peregrine's list of avian prey is quite varied; in addition to swifts and swallows, it takes doves, pigeons, gulls, terns, shorebirds, passerines, and even other raptors. Rock doves (domestic pigeons) and European starlings often represent the dietary mainstay of urban peregrine falcons. Peregrines migrating to Latin America usually follow coastal routes, feeding on other neotropical migrants such as black-necked stilts (*Himantopus mexicanus*), lesser yellowlegs (*Tringa flavipes*), and blue-winged teal (*Anas discors*). Fledgling peregrines

have been known to catch insect prey such as dragonflies. Death from above, a catchphrase sometimes used by U.S. Army Airborne Rangers, would be an apt description for the manner in which peregrines take their feathered quarry. They stalk their unwitting airborne prey from above and plummet into the victim in a high-speed stoop dive, usually making the kill instantly with their talons. Peregrines also hunt from perches. The falcon may either grab its prey immediately after the strike or may release it and grasp it before it falls to the earth. In January 1995, while birding at Point Lobos State Park on California's Big Sur, I was fortunate enough to witness a peregrine hurtling down out of the heights like an F-16, delivering a fatal blow to a pelagic cormorant (*Phalacrocorax pelagicus*) as it ascended from the surface of a lagoon. Pelagic cormorants average about 26 inches (66 cm) in length, substantially larger than an 18-inch peregrine (although their wingspans are both about 40 inches). Natural enemies of the peregrine falcon are few. Known predators include the great horned owl and the golden eagle (*Aquila chrysaetos*).

CAUSE OF DECLINE, THREATS

Bioaccumulation: DDT (dichloro-diphenyl-trichloroethane), its metabolite DDE, and other organochlorine pesticides exterminated the peregrine falcon in the eastern United States in the two decades preceding the 1960's, as well as eliminating the species from much of its historic range. Organochlorine contaminants caused birds to lay thin-shelled eggs that broke under the weight of an incubating parent. Peregrine populations in Europe and other parts of the world declined severely for the same reasons. The use of

DDT within the United States was outlawed in 1972, though it and other harmful contaminants, including dioxins, are still used in many countries where wintering peregrines congregate. Though the pesticide threat is now mostly historic, it has not disappeared entirely.

The three North American peregrine subspecies did not suffer equally from the effects of DDT. The Arctic peregrine and the American peregrine, both migratory, were hit hard by the bioaccumulation of DDT, but the nonmigratory Peale's peregrine was relatively unaffected. Also, other migratory birds that have accumulated these pesticides in fat tissue are eaten by peregrine falcons in this country.

Habitat Destruction: Many authorities now place the destruction and alteration of wintering habitats among the most perilous threats to this species in Florida. More than 10,000 acres of Florida wetlands are lost each year. The loss of breeding habitat is also a serious and worsening threat to the peregrine in many parts of its range.

Illegal Take: Each year, a number of peregrines are taken alive by unscrupulous falconers for use in their sport. Falconry, which reached its peak in Europe during the Middle Ages, remains a flourishing avocation in many parts of the world. Illegal methods of procuring peregrine falcons range from removing eggs or young birds from aeries to trapping, including the trick of tying monofilament line to a duck's foot, restricting it from flying more than 10–15 feet above a beach, and netting adult peregrines as they approach to snare an easy meal. Peregrine falcons and gyrfalcons, among the most prized of all raptors for falconry, may sell for thousands of dollars each

in Iran, Iraq, Saudi Arabia, the Republic of Georgia, and other countries.

Other Threats: Peregrines are sometimes shot by pigeon breeders, duck hunters, and ranchers. Some pigeon breeders, who may pay more than $1,500 for a pair of good pigeons, shoot peregrines because they consider them a threat to their valuable pigeons. In an April 1991 *National Geographic* article, a roller pigeon breeder in Los Angeles proclaimed that he knew of 14 peregrines that had been shot and killed by pigeon breeders, adding, "I've seen their leg bands."

Nocturnal predation by great horned owls is believed to be responsible for limiting the range expansion and reestablishment of peregrine falcons in the southern Appalachian Mountains. Conversely, peregrines easily establish breeding populations in urban areas where these large owls are rare.

Collisions with automobiles, wires, fences, and other objects remain a threat to peregrines and other birds of prey.

CURRENT TREND: *Increasing.*

Southeastern American Kestrel

Falco sparverius paulus
FAMILY FALCONIDAE; Order Falconiformes
LISTED STATUS
FWC: Threatened, listed 1975
USF&WS: Species of management concern
CITES: Appendix 2

Description: Kestrels are America's smallest and most colorful hawks, built for speed with long pointed wings, bent back at the wrist, and a long tail. They are easily distinguished from other falcons by the two black mustaches and the rufous back and tail. The sexes are clearly dimorphic. Females average 11.5 percent larger than males. Males are more colorful, with a rufous breast, back, and tail and bluish gray upperwing coverts. Males also have a wide black band near the tail tip. The upperwing coverts of the female are rufous, like the back and tail, and the light-colored breast and abdomen are heavily streaked with rufous. The entire tail, the back, and upperwing coverts of the female have a series of narrow dark bands, and the overall coloration is more subdued than on the male. A pair of false eyes toward the rear of the head are believed to deter predators. Unusual plumages occasionally seen include total and partial albinos and gynandromorph females possessing male plumage. The southeastern race is slightly smaller than most of the other 16 kestrel races, including the eastern American kestrel (*Falco sparverius sparverius*), which winters in Florida in large numbers. Mean body mass of this subspecies is 22–26 percent less than the eastern American kestrel. Typical external measurements are 8.75–11 inches (22.2–28 cm) in length and 20–24 inches (51–61 cm) of wingspan. Males of this subspecies have few if any spots on the abdomen, unlike eastern American kestrels, and when spotting is present it is generally restricted to wingpits and doesn't extend as far onto the abdomen and breast as it does on *Falco s. sparverius.* The colors of male southeastern American kestrels are often slightly richer and more vibrant, and the buff coloration that covers approximately two thirds of the breast and abdomen is typically darker than on the eastern. Females of both races are virtually identical.

Distribution: Seventeen American kestrel subspecies range from central Alaska and Canada through nearly all of North America and much of Central and South America. The southeastern American kestrel is the resident subspecies from southeastern South Carolina and Georgia through most of Florida and west through portions of southern Alabama, Mississippi, and Louisiana. Florida's highest concentration of nesting southeastern American kestrels inhabit the uplands of the Central Ridge from Suwannee County south through Highlands County. Breeding populations have been extirpated from much of southeastern Florida because of habitat loss. Migratory eastern American kestrels arrive in Florida in the fall and depart by early spring.

Biology: Optimum kestrel habitat is composed of several different components, each used for a distinct purpose. Open, pasturelike expanses with a low herbaceous vegetative cover, such as grasslands, are used for foraging. Higher vegetative cover greatly reduces the kestrel's ability to observe and catch prey. Perches such as snags, living trees, poles, and wires are used by kestrels searching for prey. During the breeding season (February through May) snags and trees containing cavities, generally close to foraging areas, are needed for nesting sites. Kestrels often take advantage of man-made nesting sites, including structures (abandoned and occupied) and nest boxes. Fresh water is not necessarily an element, as kestrels obtain sufficient hydration from their prey. State studies show that the kestrel's average home range is approximately 124 acres (50 ha) in areas containing suitable habitat, expanding to nearly 800 acres (317 ha) in marginal habitat. The kestrel's diet is largely insects, reptiles, rodents, and small birds. Increases in the take of lizards during the breeding season may indicate changes in nutritional requirements during this time. Although perch hunting is the most common hunting method, kestrels are well known for their hover-hunting abilities. Kestrels often hunt by hovering 50–100 feet (15–30 m) above the ground, especially on windy days and in areas lacking perches. They can be quite vocal, often emitting the characteristic rapid *killy-killy* or *klee-klee-klee*, especially when menaced or their nest is approached. Breeding behavior begins in late January and February with acrobatic aerial displays, feeding of mate by males, and nest site selection. Abandoned woodpecker cavities are often used, and this species has been known to evict current occupants. The majority of cavities are found in standing dead trees known as snags. Three to five blotched, light-colored eggs are laid from mid-March through May. Both parents incubate the eggs over approximately 30 days. Young develop rapidly, approaching adult weight in fewer than 20 days and fledging in about one month. Pairs occasionally rear two broods in one season. Kestrels may use the same nesting site and foraging grounds for many years and often remain in the area year round.

Placement of kestrel nesting boxes has proven to be an effective alternative to natural cavities, which have become very scarce in many regions. The box shown in the diagram should be attached to a snag, live tree, or utility pole (if authorization is provided), approximately 20–25 feet high. Select a tree or structure in a relatively open area, at least 150 feet from forested areas. The nest box should

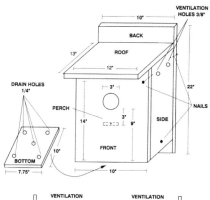

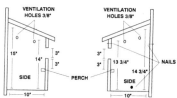

Kestrel nest box design. Wood is 1 inch thick. Half of the circle cut out for the entrance is attached to the inside of the box with a screw and used as the perch. Two nails at the top of one side panel act as hinges to swing the side open for cleaning. A single nail at the bottom is used to secure the side shut.

be placed in the vicinity of a roost or perch tree (roost sites close to the nest provide both cover from predators and initial perches for fledglings). The entrance hole of the box should face south or east, and it should provide an unimpeded flight path. Disturbance near the nest should be prohibited during the courtship, breeding, and nesting period (January–August). The nest box should be checked for routine maintenance and removal of other species twice a year, during the nonreproductive season (September–December). If the tree or pole becomes decayed or unsuitable for the nest box, the box should be relocated to a nearby suitable structure during the nonreproductive season. Removal or relocation of a nest box that has been used by kestrels requires a permit from the FWC and USF&WS.

CAUSE OF DECLINE, THREATS

Habitat Destruction: Destruction and fragmentation of suitable habitat is by far the most serious threat. Optimum habitat contains the four components described above (perch site availability, suitable foraging habitat, food supply, and suitable nesting sites), and they must be close to one another. Removal of snags and standing trees has eliminated suitable habitat throughout much of the kestrel's historic range. Habitat loss has also been attributed to conversion of upland habitats for citrus groves and transformation of formerly open foraging sites to densely overgrown areas after decades of fire suppression. North-central Florida's kestrel populations have decreased nearly 80 percent between the early 1940's and the early 1980's, and the kestrel has been extirpated as a breeding bird in South Florida's tropical pinelands.

Automobile Collisions: The kestrel's inclination to nest near roads and forage along rights-of-way makes them vulnerable to road mortality.

CURRENT TREND: *Declining.*

White-crowned Pigeon
Columba leucocephala
FAMILY COLUMBIDAE; Order Columbiformes

LISTED STATUS
FWC: Threatened, listed 1975
USF&WS: Species of management concern
Description: At first glance this stout, 13-inch (33 cm), square-tailed, fast-flying pigeon resembles its domestic cousin the rock dove. From a distance, adult birds may appear uniformly dark grayish black, with a highly contrasting pearl-white forehead and crown. The crown of adult females and juveniles of both sexes is more drab than that of adult males and frequently tinged with brown. The white crown is sometimes stained with dark resins from poisonwood trees, a favored native foraging tree. Birds examined at close range display a myriad of subtle variances in plumage. Adults (both sexes) have a greenish iridescent collar, a white or pinkish eye ring, and a bright white iris. The bill is reddish with a white tip. The legs and feet are also pinkish red. The underparts are grayish but lighter than above. This species can be distinguished in silhouette from the slightly smaller and slimmer mourning dove (*Zenaida macroura*) by its square tail, and from the increasingly common, introduced Eurasian collared dove by its darker color. Calls include a low, resonant *coo-cura-coo*, or *coo-croo*.

Distribution: The white-crowned pigeon is one of those specialties of the Keys that birders travel long distances to see and add to their life lists. It occurs as a breeding bird throughout many of the uninhabited Florida Keys and locally on the extreme southern periphery of the peninsula. It is a common summer bird in the Keys and is not uncommon on coastal areas and islands of Biscayne Bay and Florida Bay, including adjacent portions of Everglades National Park. It is suspected that this species also breeds within the Ten Thousand Islands of Monroe and Collier counties. White-crowns regularly wander north of their breeding range and have been reported from numerous (usually coastal) locations as far north as St. Petersburg and Fort Pierce. This pigeon has become an increasingly common wintering species in Florida, although most birds migrate early (mid-September to mid-October) to warmer locales, returning in April. The breeding, migration, and wintering patterns of Florida populations of white-crowns were poorly understood until recently. Using radiotelemetry, biologists discovered that many breeding birds from the Upper Keys migrate to their tropical wintering grounds via the Bahamas, but most Lower Keys birds winter in Cuba. Apparently, more of these birds winter in the Upper Keys, particularly Key Largo, than in the Lower Keys.

The historic breeding range of this species is quite expansive, stretching from the Florida Keys and Bahamas on the northern periphery through many of the West Indies as far south as Antigua, with birds occurring locally on islands of the western Caribbean and off the east coast of the Yucatan Peninsula, Belize, Nicaragua, and Panama. Populations have been extirpated from several areas. *Biology:* In Florida, the white-crowned pigeon is largely dependent on two distinct ecosystems, the tropical hardwood hammocks (which provide food) and the offshore mangrove islands (which provide nesting sites). Each morning during the breeding season, flocks of frugivorous white-crowns depart from mangrove islet nest sites and fly to tropical hammocks to forage on various fruit-bearing trees and shrubs. After feeding, the birds return to their nesting and roosting sites. The distance between nest sites and feeding grounds may be considerable. Mangrove islets, which generally lack

mammalian predators, are favored over coastal mangrove forests.

The white-crown's diet consists almost entirely of fruits, with poison-wood, strangler fig, short-leaf fig (*Ficus citrifolia*), and blolly considered the most important, but it includes fiddlewood (*Citharexylum fruticosum*), strongbark (*Bourreria ovata*), pigeon plum, gumbo-limbo, coco plum, and other fruits as well. Flowers of black mangroves are reportedly consumed on occasion. White-crowns usually forage within the canopy of tropical hammock trees and, with less frequency, in rockland pine forests. During the winter, they often feed lower in trees or on the ground. This keystone species is an important seed disperser of many plants of the Keys. The fruits of some exotic trees are also eaten, and individuals have been observed eating insects, small tree snails, and cultivated grain. Raccoons are the primary predator of white-crowns (including eggs and offspring) in the Keys; they constitute a serious threat in areas where human encroachment spawns an overabundance of raccoons and facilitates their dispersal to pigeon colonies. Other predators include black rats, birds of prey, and rat snakes.

This species nests colonially on remote mangrove islets, often using the higher mangrove branches. Nesting in Florida occurs from May through early September. Egg-laying often peaks from late May through early June, and a second, larger peak usually occurs in late July and early August, when the fruit of the poisonwood ripens. These are shy birds, especially during the nesting season, and they generally nest far from human activity. Relatively small nests are assembled from twigs and lined with grass and roots. Males typically obtain nesting materials while females construct the nest. Two eggs, rarely one, are laid and hatch in about two weeks. Males usually incubate eggs during the day, with females incubating at night. Hatchlings are fed nothing but crop milk (an excretion from the membranous lining of the parent bird's crop) for several days. Fruit is offered after three or four days, and the percentage of fruit consumed by chicks increases (and the percentage of crop milk decreases) as the young grow. Young fledge after two or three weeks.

CAUSE OF DECLINE, THREATS

Habitat Destruction: Loss of habitat, especially foraging habitat, is a serious threat to this species. Much of the tropical hardwood hammock habitat that produces virtually all of the bird's food supply has been destroyed by urban sprawl. Many remaining parcels are threatened with development. Native poisonwood trees, a primary source of nourishment, may cause an irritating rash in humans if brushed against, which is why they are often cleared from residential and commercial lots.

Shooting: Historically, nesting colonies containing thousands of white-crowned pigeons were reportedly slaughtered in the Bahamas during the late 1800's; in one incident reported during that period, several hundred nesting pigeons were killed in a single day near Indian Key. Though now protected from hunting in the United States, pigeons that breed in Florida continue to be shot on their wintering grounds and during migration. Overhunting of white-crowns has resulted in their extinction on Caribbean islands where they formerly bred.

Other Threats: Pesticides sprayed on trees where these pigeons forage, in Florida and in wintering areas, may constitute a threat. Collisions with automobiles along the Overseas Highway and other thoroughfares certainly take their toll on this species. Collisions with power lines also kill many of Florida's white-crowned pigeons each year.

CURRENT TREND: *Stable* in Florida; however, this species has suffered significant declines throughout much of its range.

Ivory-billed Woodpecker

Campephilus principalis principalis
FAMILY PICIDAE; Order Piciformes

If you are familiar with the ivorybill, you may wonder why this species is included in a book about endangered and threatened animals. For the last couple of decades, one would be hard put to find a reputable source that would suggest that a population of this large and boldly marked woodpecker remains in the wild. That is primarily because the kinds of places capable of sustaining an isolated and undiscovered population of such a conspicuous species are themselves extinct within our borders. This species account is provided, however, because the ivorybill is still officially listed by both the FWC and USF&WS as an endangered species and because on several occasions species, even birds and large mammals, that have been officially pronounced extinct have resurfaced in the wild, sometimes many years later, proving the assumption of extinction to be premature. The Bermuda petrel, or cahow (*Pterodroma cahow*), was exploited for food by early settlers and thought to be extinct for nearly 300 years, whereupon it was rediscovered nesting on small islets just a mile or so offshore from the heavily populated Bermuda of the 1950's. The once wide-spread black-footed ferret was presumed extinct by the 1970's, but to the surprise of many, a population was discovered in 1981 near Meeteetse, Wyoming. Even the large Sinai leopard (*Panthera pardus* ssp.), proclaimed extinct at the turn of the last century, escaped detection for 75 years, until it was rediscovered in 1975.

LISTED STATUS

FWC: Endangered, listed 1972
USF&WS: Endangered, listed 1967
Description: The ivorybill is or was the largest woodpecker native to the United States, reaching 20 inches (50 cm) in length, with a wingspan of 30–33 inches (76–84 cm). The pileated woodpecker, commonly mistaken for the ivorybill, ranks a close second, at a length of 16–19 inches (40–48 cm) and a wingspan of 25–28 inches (64–71 cm). Though both are large black and white woodpeckers, the ivorybill is distinguished from the pileated by its large white wing patches visible when perched as well as in flight. The large area of white on the wings of the pileated is not visible when perched. Also, the trailing-edge feathers on the ivorybill's wing are white; on the pileated they are black. Both male and female pileateds have prominent, bright red crests; in ivorybills the crest is red in the male and black in the female. Ivorybills have a massive, ivory-colored bill (hence the name), about 2.5 inches long; although the pileated's bill is also large, at 1.7–2 inches long, it is proportionately smaller and is darker. Also, the chin of

the ivorybill is black, and the pileated woodpecker's chin is white. The pileated flies in the typical undulating woodpeck-er fashion; the ivorybill usually flies fast and straight, like a duck. Finally, the calls of the two birds are quite different. The ivorybill's call has been described as a sharp, nasal *kent, pate* or *yank,* like a nuthatch. The pileated's call is a loud, rising and falling *kik-kik-kikkik, kik-kik,* like a flicker.

Distribution: Historically, the ivory-billed woodpecker is the northernmost representative of the genus *Campephilus,* which contains 11 recognized species. The ivorybill formerly ranged sporadically from southeastern Oklahoma and eastern Texas in the west northward with the Mississippi River Valley to southern Illinois and Indiana, and throughout much of the Gulf Coastal Plain from Texas to Florida and the Atlantic Coastal Plain northward to southeastern North Carolina, with a closely related sub-species, *Campephilus principalis bairdii,* inhabiting Cuba.

The ivory-billed woodpecker is cur-rently believed extirpated in the United States, but a glimmer of hope exists that there may still be a few Cuban ivorybills surviving in the montane forests of east-ern Cuba's Oriente Province. There was definite evidence of ivorybills in Cuba as late as 1988.

Museum records and detailed natural-ist accounts indicate that ivory-billed woodpeckers were fairly common in Florida before the late 1800's and occurred nearly statewide. Florida remained one of the last strongholds for the ivorybill in the United States. In 1950 a trio of ivorybills was reportedly located in a remote area along the Apalachicola

River. In Highlands County, one or two ivorybills were reported on numerous occasions from 1967 to 1969. This area was established as a sanctuary for the birds in one of several last-ditch efforts to save the ivory-billed woodpecker. Many accept the last confirmed report to be from northeastern Louisiana's Tensas River valley in the mid-1940's. That population was lost after the land was cleared for soybean production in 1948. Other areas where ivorybills continued to be reported include the Hyazoo River and Pascagoula River floodplains in Mississippi, the Santee River floodplain in South Carolina, and along Georgia's Altamaha River. The most recent unverified sightings in Florida are from the Fakahatchee Strand (Collier County) in 1990 and the lower Apalachicola and Chipola river swamp in the Big Bend in 1991.

In 1986 the USF&WS hired Jerome Jackson, a Mississippi State University ornithologist, to conduct an exhaustive search for ivory-billed woodpeckers in eight states within the bird's historic range. No ivorybills were ever seen. It now appears that the efforts to save the ivorybill from extinction, though noble, were too little, too late.

Biology: Most accounts of this species depict the ivorybill as a bird of the wilderness, inhabiting expansive tracts of old-growth floodplain forests in the Southeast and Cuba's mature montane pine forests. Approximately 2,000 acres may be required for one pair of ivorybills. In the late 1800's and early 1900's virtually every acre of old-growth forest was harvested, and when that forest was all but gone, so were the ivorybills.

Early naturalists described the ivorybill as a quiet and sedentary species, spending all or most of its life within an area of old-growth forest no larger than a few square miles. They reported that ivorybills remained paired throughout the year and that breeding activity took place from January through April. Nest cavities are excavated by both sexes 15–70 feet above the ground in large, usually live trees, often bald cypress. Oval entrance holes may be as large as 6–7 inches (15–18 cm) high by 4 inches (10 cm) wide, and the cavity may be a yard (0.9 m) deep. The two to five glossy white eggs, measuring 1.4 by 1 inch (3.3 by 2.5 cm), hatch after about three weeks.

The diet of the ivorybill is primarily insects and vegetable matter. The larvae of wood-boring beetles (family Cerambycidae) represent a major source of nourishment, but fruit and seeds of various trees, including southern magnolia, are also important elements of the ivorybill's diet. Early ornithologists witnessed these stately birds using their chisel-like bills to scale off tree bark while foraging for insects. Natural predators include peregrine falcons and rat snakes, which readily scale nest trees to prey on eggs and young.

CAUSE OF DECLINE, THREATS

Habitat Destruction: The ivorybill, like the grizzly bear, is doomed to extinction in areas where wilderness is eliminated; unfortunately for the ivorybill, that describes its entire range. Soon after the arrival of European man, the old-growth forests of the Southeast were felled tree by tree, and with them went the ivory-billed woodpecker. The pileated woodpecker was able to adapt and even prosper in the changing environment; the ivorybill was not.

Hunting and Collecting: American Indians reportedly hunted ivorybills for their skin, feathers, and bill, though the effects on the bird's population were probably negligible. After the arrival of Europeans, things changed. Collectors tromped through great river swamps, rifle in hand, searching for ivorybills and their eggs. Early Floridians reported that its flesh was better than that of ducks. The similarity to ducks in size and flight also caused the woodpecker to be shot by duck hunters.

CURRENT TREND: Almost certainly *extirpated* in the United States, very possibly *extinct.*

Red-cockaded Woodpecker
Picoides borealis
FAMILY PICIDAE; Order Piciformes

LISTED STATUS
FWC: Threatened, listed 1974
USF&WS: Endangered, listed 1970

Description: At about 8.5 inches (22 cm), with a wingspan of 14.5 inches (37 cm), the red-cockaded woodpecker is sized between the smaller downy woodpecker (*Picoides pubescens*) and the larger hairy woodpecker (*Picoides villosus*), both of which may occur in the same area as the red-cockaded. Adult birds weigh approximately 1.6 ounces (45 g). Both sexes look very much alike. This species can be identified by its large white cheek patch, black cap, and black and white zebra-barred back that lacks the broad white vertical strip present in both the downy and hairy woodpeckers. The abdomen, chest, and throat are white. The tail is black edged with white. The tiny red cockade present on the male's head is often not visible in the field and usually not displayed unless the bird becomes agitated. Immature males lack this small red field mark but may have a red crown patch, which dissipates after the first molt. Calls of the red-cockaded woodpecker include a nasal, rasping *sripp,* which sounds much like a young starling, and a higher-pitched *tsick.*

Distribution: The historic range of this woodpecker consisted of the great pine (especially longleaf pine) forests of the southeastern United States, from southeastern Oklahoma and the Big Thicket region of Texas in the west, east through most of Louisiana, Mississippi, and portions of Arkansas, Tennessee, and Kentucky, and nearly all of the Atlantic Coastal Plain pine forests from Maryland (possibly New Jersey), south to southern Florida.

Currently, the species occurs within the perimeter of the range described above; however, massive depletion of the mature pine forests required by this species now limits it to local, isolated colonies. In Florida the largest populations occur in the Apalachicola National Forest (currently, the largest population on Earth) and Eglin Air Force Base. Smaller populations exist at Blackwater River and Withlacoochee state forests, Ocala and Osceola national forests, Big Cypress National Preserve, Avon Park Bombing Range, Three Lakes and Babcock-Webb wildlife management areas, Ochlockonee River State Park, and several other sites.

Biology: Red-cockaded woodpeckers occupy a narrow ecological niche, which increases their vulnerability to extinction. Their habitat consists of open, frequently burned, mature pine forests. Flatwoods and high pine communities are both utilized, with mature longleaf pines, at least 65–90 years old, being the preferred tree species, although slash pine, loblolly pine, pond pine, Virginia pine, pitch pine, and shortleaf pine are also used. Stands of trees selected for nesting sites generally contain large trees infected with red heart disease, a nonlethal fungus (*Phellinus pini*) that softens the heartwood of the trees and makes it easier for birds to excavate nesting cavities. This is the only Florida woodpecker that habitually excavates nesting cavities in living trees; a number of other birds and animals, however, will readily use the cavities it makes. Each woodpecker has its own roosting cavity. Red-cockaded woodpeckers, unlike the majority of Florida's bird species, are cooperative breeders and have a well-defined social structure within each family or clan. Typical clans, composed of a nesting pair and several helpers, have territories of 200–300 acres.

The nest cavity usually has a southerly or westerly exposure, and the entrance hole is 20–50 feet (6–15 m) above ground; in southern Florida, however, where mature pines are generally smaller, entrance holes are excavated as low as 6 feet (2 m). The roosting cavity of the clan's breeding male is used by the breeding female for the nesting cavity. Regular fires are important, as they preclude the understory from encroaching on the nesting cavity and help to impede predation. A cluster of nesting cavities may be excavated within the territory by a family of woodpeckers, with each cavity taking as long as a year to complete. These very social birds are altruistic and have as many as six helpers assisting the breeding pairs with various duties, including excavating cavities, defending the territory, incubation, and feeding young.

Red-cockaded woodpeckers employ a rather novel means of repelling terrestrial predators. They drill a series of small holes, called resin wells, on the trunk of nest trees, above and below the entrance hole. The resin wells ooze sticky sap from the tree's resin canal system, which has proven to be a deterrent to many predators, particularly snakes. Nesting takes place from April to June. The three to five white eggs are incubated by both parents, at times by helpers during the day, and solely by the father at night; they hatch after 10–13 days. Young remain in the nest for nearly a month before fledging. Typically, clans have only one nest, but double brooding, though rare, has been recorded.

The red-cockaded woodpecker's diet is composed chiefly of insects but also includes some vegetable matter. These birds work trees within their territories in the morning hours and again in the late afternoon. Females often forage lower than males. Arboreal rat snakes (*Elaphe obsoleta* and *E. guttata*) and southern flying squirrels are among the predators of young and eggs. Birds of prey, particularly accipiters, may prey on adults.

CAUSE OF DECLINE, THREATS
Habitat Destruction: This species, much like the northern spotted owl (*Strix occidentalis caurina*), depends on large tracts of old-growth conifer forests for its survival. Rampant clear-cutting of mature pine forests continued until this species was extirpated throughout most of its

former range. Today more than 90 percent of the original longleaf pine forest in the United States has been destroyed. Short-rotation forestry management (harvesting trees after only 20–50 years) precludes the growth of habitat capable of sustaining red-cockaded woodpeckers. Because of the value of timber, protection of the red-cockaded woodpecker became a political issue similar to the efforts to save the spotted owl.

After decades of fire suppression, underbrush has grown thick and tall, rendering the habitat unsuitable for these woodpeckers and causing their dispersal. Once extirpated from a locality, they have never been known to recolonize the site. Fire exclusion also permits various hardwoods to invade the pine forest, and with the hardwoods come several animals that compete for nesting cavities, including southern flying squirrels and other woodpecker species.

Hurricanes: Larger populations of red-cockaded woodpeckers are concentrated in several isolated tracts of remnant old-growth pine forest. A direct strike from a hurricane will decimate the population and their habitat, as happened when Hurricane Hugo struck the South Carolina coast in the late 1980's, destroying 100,000 acres of woodlands in the Francis Marion National Forest, which formerly supported the largest red-cockaded population. High winds damaged or destroyed nearly every bit of the bird's habitat and killed approximately 60 percent of the population. Hurricane Andrew, which scoured South Florida in 1992, killed red-cockaded woodpeckers and toppled many of Dade County's remaining pine trees capable of supporting their colonies. Hurricane

Opal, a category 3 storm that collided with the Panhandle in October 1995, felled thousands of mature pine trees at Eglin Air Force Base and Blackwater State Forest, including trees used by this species.

Other Threats: Infestations of southern pine beetles (*Dendroctonus frontalis*) have eliminated nesting and foraging habitat in some areas.

CURRENT TREND: *Declining.* Total population estimated at 7,500 individuals.

Florida Scrub-jay

Aphelocoma coerulescens

FAMILY CORVIDAE; Order Passeriformes

LISTED STATUS

FWC: Threatened, listed 1975 (endangered 1972–1974)

USF&WS: Threatened, listed 1987

Description: This is an average-sized jay, 11–12 inches (28–30 cm) in length, about the same size as the blue jay (*Cyanocitta cristata*) but lacking the blue jay's crest and white markings on wings and tail. The tail and wings, along with the side, rear, and top of the head, are generally blue, in shades that vary considerably from dingy blue in juvenile birds to a brilliant turquoise blue. Immature birds (less than six months old) have a dusky brown head and neck. The back and abdomen are grayish; the throat is whitish gray and separated from the slightly darker abdomen by a streaked, blue-gray breast band. Florida scrub-jays can be distinguished from western scrub-jays by their whitish forehead. Both have a whitish eyeline, though it is often more pronounced in the western species. Sexes look alike. As do many other birds, breeding females acquire a brood patch during the breeding season; however, it can be found only by handling the animal. The voice of the Florida scrub-jay includes a raspy *kwesh* and a low-pitched *zhreek*. Females are known to emit a distinctive, clicking hiccup call during territorial displays.

Distribution: The Florida scrub-jay is the only species of bird whose range is completely confined to Florida. It is a nonmigrating permanent resident. A map of the remaining tracts of Florida scrub and scrublike habitats in peninsular Florida and a map of the Florida scrub-jay's range would be nearly one and the same. This Florida endemic occurs in a number of scattered populations from portions of Clay County in north-central Florida south along the Atlantic Coast to the Boca Raton area of southern Palm Beach County, upland areas of central Florida, and portions of the Gulf Coast from Levy County south to Lee and Collier counties. The elimination of suitable habitat is responsible for the recent extirpation of this bird from portions of its historic range, including Broward, Dade, Hendry, Pinellas, Gilchrist, St. Johns, and Duval counties.

Two other species of scrub-jays occur in the western United States. The western scrub-jay (*Aphelocoma californica*) is a widespread resident of the western United States and Mexico. It has several races, the closest of which is separated by nearly 1,000 miles (1,600 km) from the range of the Florida scrub-jay. The island scrub-jay (*Aphelocoma insularis*) is limited to several islands off the California coast. The range of the Florida scrub-jay once joined the range of the western scrub-jay when the physical environment of Florida and much of the

southeast was more arid and desertlike. After Florida's climatic patterns changed during the Pleistocene, only isolated patches of xeric habitat remained. Scrub-jay populations isolated in Florida during that period eventually evolved into a distinct species.

Biology: The Florida scrub-jay is a true avian habitat specialist. Optimum habitat consists of oak-dominated Florida scrub and scrubby flatwood regions with open areas of exposed sugar sand. The oaks that occur throughout this habitat are not tall, spreading shade trees but rather several species of shrub-sized oaks often not as tall as a human, including the Archbold oak, Chapman's oak, myrtle oak, sand live oak, and running oak in thin-canopied scrubby flatwoods. Other characteristic plants of this ecosystem include scattered sand pine or slash pine, scrub palmetto, saw palmetto, and rosemary. Researchers hypothesize that the exposed areas of this nutrient-poor sand are important to this scrub-jay because they provide locations to bury acorns for later use.

The most significant difference between the Florida scrub-jay and its western counterparts is its well-developed social system, which involves cooperative breeding. The well-defined family structure is dominated by a male breeder, followed in rank by male helpers, the female breeder, and finally the young nonbreeding females. In birds of the same sex, older birds are dominant over younger birds. Family members share the duties of defending nesting territories and even feeding young birds not yet fledged. The center of the Florida scrub-jay family is a pair of breeding birds that mate for life. As many as six birds from previous broods, and occasionally adoptees, remain with the pair as helpers for several years. Males generally remain as helpers longer, as females usually disperse after one or two years to start families of their own. Florida scrub-jay families vigorously defend their territories, which average 25 acres (9 ha). Studies of several species of cooperative breeders have shown that in these particular species, pairs with helpers fledged more offspring than pairs without helpers. Other North American birds that are cooperative breeders include Mexican jays (*Aphelocoma ultramarina*), barn swallows (*Hirundo rustica*), red-cockaded woodpeckers, and chimney swifts (*Chaetura pelagica*).

Nesting occurs from late February or early March through June. Each spring the breeding pair constructs a new nest, usually in a shrubby oak 3–10 feet (1–3 m) above the ground. Nests are assembled from oak twigs and lined with cabbage palm or scrub palmetto fibers. Clutch size varies from one to five (average three) mottled light blue and brown eggs. Eggs hatch after approximately 17 days, and the young fledge after another 17 days or so, eventually becoming helpers themselves. If nesting failure occurs, Florida scrub-jays may attempt to raise additional broods. Florida scrub-jays are long-lived, with a maximum life span of about 15 years.

During the spring and summer months, insects and other small animals constitute a significant part of this species' diet. A variety of arthropods, including lepidopteran larvae, beetles, spiders, centipedes, millipedes, scorpions, and even vertebrates such as treefrogs, toads, lizards, small snakes, and mice are extracted from the vegetation and leaf litter. Acorns are an important source of nourishment for the Florida scrub-jay, particularly in the fall and winter months. A typical scrub-jay may harvest and cache 6,000–8,000 acorns a year. The birds bury their acorn stockpiles in the oak scrub sugar sands, and they may help to disperse the scrub oak species. Scrub-jays are preyed on by a number of animals, including raccoons, bobcats, coachwhip snakes, eastern indigo snakes, racers, great horned owls, crows, Cooper's and sharp-shinned hawks, and merlins. Blue jays are known to raid scrub-jay nests near more wooded habitats. Domestic cats are also frequent predators in many areas.

Much of what has been learned about this fascinating bird is a result of over two decades of intensive research conducted by biologists Glen E. Woolfenden and John W. Fitzpatrick at Archbold Biological Station.

CAUSE OF DECLINE, THREATS

Habitat Destruction and Fire Suppression: The variations of Florida scrub habitat that this species depends on are among the most threatened ecosystems in the country. Many decades of fire suppression have transformed areas of suitable oak scrub habitat into habitats that can no longer support scrub-jays. The oak species require a regular cycle of fires every 10–15 years or so to produce the large quantities of acorns needed to support scrub-jays.

Many coastal areas that formerly supported scrub-jays have been lost to development, and most of the original scrub-jay habitat on Lake Wales Ridge has also been lost to development and conversion to citrus groves. More than

85 percent of the Lake Wales Ridge scrub habitat is now gone.

Pesticides: Scrub-jays are vulnerable to pesticides, which they ingest when they consume insects from areas that are heavily sprayed, such as golf courses, citrus groves, and residential areas.

Predation by Domestic Animals: As a result of human encroachment, predation by domestic cats has become a serious threat to scrub-jays in many areas.

Other Threats: Competition with and predation of young by aggressive blue jays in ecotonal areas jeopardize some populations. Between September 1979 and February 1980, an unidentified catastrophic epidemic swept through a scrub-jay population being monitored at Archbold Biological Station, rapidly taking the lives of approximately 50 percent of adult birds and 92 of the colony's 93 juveniles. Automobile collisions are a significant cause of death, especially to younger birds, in scrub habitats transected by heavily traveled roads.

CURRENT TREND: *Declining.* Florida's scrub-jay populations have declined by more than 50 percent in the last century; the population was estimated at 7,000–11,000 individuals in the year 2000.

Kirtland's Warbler

Dendroica kirtlandii
FAMILY EMBERIZIDAE; Order Passeriformes
LISTED STATUS
FWC: Endangered, listed 1975
USF&WS: Endangered, listed 1967
Description: Kirtland's warbler is the country's second rarest wood warbler. A large, tail-wagging *Dendroica,* it measures approximately 6 inches (15 cm). Both sexes are bluish gray above, yellow below, with black streaks on the back and sides and a finely pointed bill. A broken white eye ring can be seen at close range. Breeding males are brighter, have a black mask and lores, and two faint white wing bars; the duller females lack dark lores and masks. Immatures and nonbreeding adults are browner. This is the only gray-backed wood warbler that consistently bobs its tail. The male's loud, melodious song is a series of low, staccato notes followed by higher pitched whistles, ending abruptly (*chip-chip-cheway-o*); it resembles the song of the northern waterthrush (*Seiurus noveboracensis*).

Distribution: The breeding range of Kirtland's warbler is limited to an area roughly 100 miles by 60 miles in the northern portion of Michigan's southern peninsula. In recent years, the breeding range has expanded, thanks to recovery efforts. Solitary males have been sighted during the breeding season in nearby Wisconsin and Ontario.

Kirtland's warbler winters in the Bahamas. Young birds leave Michigan as early as August, but some older males may not depart until October. Though the birds are rarely observed in migration, most Florida records are from October and April. Museum records and confirmed sightings suggest that they migrate in a southeasterly direction from their breeding grounds, to the mid-Atlantic coast and then southward to the Bahamas. Fewer than 20 verified sightings exist for Florida, with the majority recorded along the Atlantic Coast north of the Keys. Sightings of this rare warbler may increase as the breeding population continues to increase.

Biology: As a breeding bird, Kirtland's warbler is a true habitat specialist. It nests only in young jack pine (*Pinus banksiana*) stands with thick ground-cover, in the well-drained grayling sands of north-central Michigan. A nesting pair requires a minimum of 85 acres (optimally more than 500 acres) of suit-able habitat, which consists of jack pines 6–20 years old that are 4–16 feet in height. Jack pine ecosystems are maintained by periodic wildfires, which induce cones to disburse seeds and avert vegetative suc-cession. In the early 1900's, when many settlers arrived in northern Michigan, an era of fire suppression began to spur widespread plant succession and significantly reduce the warbler's habitat. Migrating and wintering birds apparently favor dense scrubby areas.

Nesting typically occurs from May to July, occasionally August. Females assemble well-concealed ground nests from grass, moss, and leaves, often in fern or blueberry brambles near grassy openings. The four or five brown-spotted eggs are incubated by the female. The male feeds the female during the 13–16 days of incubation. Young fledge after 12–13 days. Parents may feign injury to distract potential predators.

Kirtland's warblers are primarily insectivorous during the breeding season, occasionally consuming blueberries; wintering birds, however, are largely frugivorous. Predators of adults, young, and eggs may include owls, hawks, blue jays, snakes, squirrels, and domestic cats. Average life span is two years.

CAUSE OF DECLINE, THREATS

Habitat Destruction: Much of the original jack pine ecosystem that represents this species' sole breeding habitat has been lost or degraded by the effects of human encroachment. Habitats are threatened by continued fire suppression and com-mercial and residential development. Efforts to restore and create viable nesting habitats have proven quite successful. Wintering habitats in the Bahamas are thought to be fairly secure.

Cowbird Parasitism: The brown-headed cowbird (*Molothrus ater*), a resourceful blackbird that lays its eggs in the nests of other birds, represents perhaps the most menacing threat to Kirtland's warbler. The cowbird's eggs are incubated by the host bird, which also raises the chick. The more aggressive and larger young cowbird soon takes over the nest, and the young warblers usually perish. The cowbird's range has greatly expanded in recent decades, wreaking havoc on many species of songbirds. By 1994 more than half of all Kirtland's warbler nests were parasitized by cowbirds.

Other Threats: Though fire is a natural and necessary element of the jack pine ecosystem, fires set during the warbler nesting season could have devastating consequences. Disturbance by overzeal-ous birders, hikers, and off-road vehicles threatens this ground-nesting warbler, which is why most nesting areas are closed during the nesting season.

CURRENT TREND: *Increasing.*

Bachman's Warbler
Vermivora bachmanii
FAMILY EMBERIZIDAE; Order Passeriformes

LISTED STATUS
FWC: Endangered, listed 1974
USF&WS: Endangered, listed 1967

Description: This small wood warbler, measuring only 4.25–4.75 inches (11–12 cm), resembles the hooded warbler (*Wilsonia citrina*) and rare Lawrence's warbler (a hybrid of *Vermivora chrysop-tera* and *V. pinus*). Adult males have a black crown and bib that are not contiguous, and a yellow shoulder, forehead, lores, eye ring, chin, and underparts. Immature males resemble females. Both sexes have an olive-green back, white undertail coverts, a slender bill slightly downcurved, and they lack wing bars. Females are more uniform in color, lacking any black markings, and have a whitish eye ring. The song of Bachman's warbler has been described as series of one-pitch buzzing notes, *bzz-bzz-bzz* or *zip-zip-zip.*

Distribution: Bachman's warblers formerly inhabited numerous localities within the southeastern United States; breeding populations, however, occurred very locally within this expansive range. Breeding records exist for southeastern Missouri, northeastern Oklahoma, northeastern Arkansas, southwestern Kentucky, Louisiana, Mississippi, and Alabama, east to Maryland, Virginia, South Carolina, and Georgia, but not for Florida. The species winters in western Cuba and the adjacent Isle of Youth, so Florida lies within the migratory flight path to and from this warbler's wintering grounds. The one winter record for Florida (Melbourne, 27 January 1898) is the sole wintering record for the United States. Some authorities have hypothesized that Atlantic Coastal Plain populations and Mississippi Valley populations represent two distinct subspecies; too few specimens are available to investigate the theory.

If not extinct, Bachman's warbler is currently on the brink of extinction. A March 1977 Brevard County sighting was the last confirmed Florida record; the last

sighting anywhere was in Louisiana in August 1988. Several reliable sightings were also reported from Cuba during the late 1980's. Among the species' last strongholds were Alabama's Moody and Bear swamps and South Carolina's Santee and I'on swamps near Charleston.

Before 1900, Bachman's warblers were a common migrant in Florida. The species was the seventh most common migrant along the lower Suwannee River in the late 1800's.

Biology: The scanty records available indicate that this species may have rather narrow nesting habitat requirements. Habitats where Bachman's warblers have nested include undisturbed southern hardwood swamps, floodplain forest, and dense bamboo (*Arundinaria gigantea*) canebrakes. They may prefer to nest at the periphery of natural openings within these communities where cane and undergrowth flourish. Wooded areas (especially canopies) and thickets are used during migration. The species reportedly frequents flowering hibiscus trees on its wintering grounds.

Bachman's warblers nest from late March to early June. Camouflaged nests, constructed of leaves, moss, and grass and lined with lichen fibers, are placed in dense vegetation, often blackberry (*Rubus allegheniensis*), within 5 feet of the ground. Clutches of three or four glossy white eggs are laid.

This bird migrates earlier than most wood warblers. Spring migrants have been seen in Florida as early as late February, and fall migrants have been recorded as early as mid-July, with migration peaking in late August. Most spring records are from the Suwannee River; most fall records are from Key West. During a four-day period in August 1888, collector J. W. Atkins observed 42 Bachman's warblers in Key West, 8 of which he shot. After the 1930's, Bachman's warblers were no longer reported from the Keys. The species passes through Florida at a time when few birders are watchful for rare birds to add to a life list. The optimist in me hopes that a birder vacationing in the Keys during the dog days of August will happen to train a spotting scope and then a camera on an odd-looking hooded warbler, providing indisputable proof of this species' existence.

The bird's foraging behavior is premeditated and intentional. It methodically gleans foliage for ants, caterpillars, and other animals, but it may also catch insects on the wing. Numerous predators inhabit its favored habitat types, including various snakes, birds, and mammals.

CAUSE OF DECLINE, THREATS

Habitat Destruction: Several theories explain the severe and rapid decline of this bird during the early 1900's, and all relate to human intrusion. Most authorities blame the decline on the loss and alteration of nesting or wintering habitat. Drainage of wetlands, logging of old-growth forests, and hurricanes are probable factors, although hurricanes have also created suitable habitat. Depletion of formerly abundant canebrake communities may be a significant factor, as early authors often noted its close association to this species.

Other Threats: The species also suffered from plume harvesting and egg collecting. Large numbers of Bachman's warblers were shot and many nests and eggs collected during the late 1800's for sale to museums. Collector J. W. Atkins alone reportedly shot hundreds of migrating Bachman's warblers annually, year after year, in Key West. A nest has not been found since 1937. Collisions with structures such as lighthouses and microwave towers pose a threat to night-migrating warblers.

CURRENT TREND: *Unknown,* possibly *extinct;* only two confirmed Florida sightings since 1909.

Cape Sable Seaside Sparrow
Ammodramus maritimus mirabilis
FAMILY EMBERIZIDAE; Order Passeriformes
LISTED STATUS
FWC: Endangered, listed 1967
USF&WS: Endangered, listed 1972
Description: The Cape Sable seaside sparrow is a medium-sized sparrow, averaging about 6 inches (14–15 cm) in length. This subspecies is the palest race of the relatively dark seaside sparrows, and it is typically greener than other subspecies. The tail is short and pointed, and the long bill is broad at the base and thin at the tip. Adults display a yellow patch between the eye and the upper mandible; the color may extend above the eye. A dark stripe runs from the base of the lower mandible down to the upper chest, separating the whitish throat from the darker cheeks. The abdomen and chest are whitish, with dark olive-gray or olive-brown streaking that is more pronounced on the flanks. A gray triangular patch is often visible on the cheek. When perched, the bird sometimes shows a small yellow patch on the wrist area of each wing. Legs are flesh-colored to gray; the bill is gray. Seaside sparrows have proportionately larger feet than other *Ammodramus* species, which assists them in walking in grass, on mud, and

wading in shallow water. The yellow lores in males tend to be brighter than in females, and they are generally more stout. Young birds often lack the whisker marks and yellow lores of adults and will have brown streaks on the back. Singing males emit a buzzing *cutcut zhe-eeeeeee,* similar to a sharp-tailed sparrow (*Ammodramus caudacutus*), or a *chack,* similar to a red-winged blackbird. Females may respond with a churble that sounds like *che-che-che-shu-shu-shu.*

Distribution: The Cape Sable seaside sparrow is limited to several nonmigratory populations in the Everglades and Big Cypress regions of extreme southern Florida. As of 2000, the known range of the Cape Sable seaside sparrow is limited to two areas on the east and west sides of Shark River Slough and to Taylor Slough. The geographic areas inhabited by this sparrow are separated from one another by physiographic barriers (unsuitable habitat). Much of the land now occupied by the Cape Sable seaside sparrow is within Everglades National Park and Big Cypress National Preserve. In recent years the race has inhabited areas of suitable habitat within Taylor Slough, Cape Sable, southern Big Cypress Swamp, and Ochopee. The population of Cape Sable (where the bird was first discovered by Howell in 1919) is now believed to be extirpated.

This is one of nine recognized subspecies of the seaside sparrow, which are distributed along the Atlantic Coast from Massachusetts south to northern Florida (formerly east-central Florida), the southern tip of mainland Florida, and along the Gulf Coast from the area of Pasco County, Florida, to eastern Texas. Seven of the nine have occurred in Florida. The

northern seaside sparrow (*Ammodramus maritimus maritimus*) appears as a wintering bird. The dusky seaside sparrow (*A. m. nigrescens*), a former resident of coastal Brevard County, is recently extinct. Florida's five other resident seaside sparrow subspecies are the Smyrna (*A. m. pelonata*) and MacGillivray's (*A. m. macgillivraii*), which both occur along the northeast coast of Florida, and the three Gulf Coast subspecies, the Wakulla (*A. m. juncicola*), Scott's (*A. m. peninsulae,* a species of special concern), and Louisiana (*A. m. fisheri,* in part). With the exception of the Cape Sable seaside sparrow, and formerly the dusky seaside sparrow, the ranges of these subspecies are fairly contiguous.

The Cape Sable seaside sparrow was formerly recognized as a distinct species, the Cape Sable sparrow (*Thryospiza maritima,* or *A. mirabilis*). When it was accepted as a new species, in 1919, it represented the last new bird species described in the continental United States. It was reclassified as a subspecies in 1973. Some contemporary authorities on the Cape Sable seaside sparrow (for instance John Curnutt and Stuart Pimm in 1993) assert that this bird should be recognized as a distinct species, mainly because the habitats it utilizes are markedly different from those of other seaside sparrows.

Biology: The Cape Sable seaside sparrow inhabits fresh and brackish marsh habitats within the Everglades, East Everglades, and Big Cypress landscapes that are virtually devoid of woody shrubs and trees. It is now known that the preferred nesting habitats of this race are the short-hydroperiod marl prairie communities dominated by muhly grass. Optimum nesting habitat consists of moderately dense clumps of muhly grass with an abundance of open spaces. The tie between the Cape Sable seaside sparrow and muhly grass prairies is apparently so strong that it has not been reported outside this habitat during the wet season. This bird avoids sites with permanent water cover, long-hydroperiod wetlands with tall dense vegetation, sites sustaining woody vegetation, taller saw grass–dominated communities, dense cattail monocultures, and coastal spike rush marshes. Areas supporting this subspecies are subject to a cycle of low-intensity fires. Fire plays an important role in maintaining suitable nesting habitat by preventing the invasion of woody plants and the accretion of dead plant material. Much less is known about the habitats used by this reticent bird during the winter months, but biologists plan to use radiotelemetry to learn more. Habitats where Cape Sable seaside sparrows have been observed during the winter months include the edges of hammocks and salt marshes.

The importance of particular food items shifts with availability, but the bird's diet is known to include spiders, caterpillars, grasshoppers, moths, beetles, dragonflies, wasps, shrimp, marine worms, and grass and sedge seeds. The chief food in terms of biomass is spiders, followed by grasshoppers and crickets and caterpillars. Known or suspected predators include raccoons, rice rats, and rat snakes. Life span is probably less than five years.

Nesting may occur from late February through early August, but it peaks in the spring when marl prairies are dry. Male seaside sparrows defend the same territory for two or three successive years. Males are far more vocal than females, usually singing from atop a fairly conspicuous perch. The typical song is a series of clicks and trills lasting approximately 1.5 seconds; it may be repeated 10–13 times in a minute. The males will bob his head up and down while uttering the initial clicks and will generally tilt his head back while completing the song with a buzzy trill. Most singing takes place in the early morning and late afternoon. Singing, as well as other breeding activity, also declines or stops when the water level rises above 4 inches (10 cm).

Pairs will typically raise two broods in a season but may produce three if weather conditions are favorable. A new nest is built for each brood. Nests are placed in clumps of grass, usually species of *Muhlenbergia* or *Spartina,* about 5 inches (14 cm) above the ground. Saw grass is often used with finer grasses for the lining. Nesting activities typically end with the beginning of the summer rains. Most but not all pairs remain together for successive nest cycles; some females changed mates after one nest cycle.

Clutches contain three or four eggs. Incubation lasts about 12–13 days. Young are fed by both parents and fledge after 9–11 days. Parents often continue feeding and rearing the young for 10–20 days after fledging. Young are apparently not able to fly until 16–17 days old. If a predator approaches when young are flightless, they freeze perfectly still until the danger comes within about 3 feet (1 m), when they attempt escape by running.

CAUSE OF DECLINE, THREATS

Habitat Destruction and Changes in Hydroperiod: The Cape Sable seaside sparrow was originally listed as an endangered species because of its limited distribution and threats to its habitat posed by large-scale conversion of land in South Florida to agricultural uses. Several areas that were formerly inhabited by this sparrow have now been altered to the point that they cannot support the bird. During the 1970's, an area of 8.5 square miles (3.4 ha) northeast of Shark River Slough that supported Cape Sable seaside sparrows was developed without obtaining permits; it is now devoid of seaside sparrows. This subspecies evolved in a changing and variable environment, and historically it has probably adapted to natural disturbances and changes in habitat suitability by varying its distribution within its limited range.

The replumbing of the Everglades by humans during the twentieth century has spelled big trouble for the Cape Sable seaside sparrow and a number of other species as well. The landscape of South Florida was historically able to support simultaneously a number of different bird species, as each depended on different niches within the natural landscape. While Cape Sable seaside sparrows require dry or very shallow marl prairies for nesting and foraging, wood storks require ephemeral wetlands with very shallow water to secure prey, and Everglades snail kites require deeper, open water that supports apple snails for survival. Human alterations to South Florida's ecosystems and water delivery systems have made it difficult to maintain that range of different habitat niches at the levels necessary to support viable populations of their habitat specialists. According to federal biologist Kim Livengood, however, the problem may be reparable (personal communication,

21 April 1996). The question is, can it be repaired in time? Much of the area west of Shark River Slough is now too wet for seaside sparrows, while much of the area east of the slough is too dry. According to the 1998 federal recovery plan, "If we manage the system to mimic the conditions that historically existed, the needs of the Cape Sable seaside sparrow should not conflict with other native Everglades species."

Invasive Exotic and Woody Plants: Succession to woody vegetation and the invasion of exotic plants and trees are commonly linked to the disappearance of this subspecies from formerly occupied sites.

Severe Storms: The existing populations of this sparrow are now so isolated and small that a series of tropical storms or possibly a single hurricane could result in its extinction. Hurricane Andrew, a devastating storm, passed directly over the bird's entire range in August 1993, eliminating 50–65 percent of the total population (personal communication, Jane Tutton, 1996). Before that storm, the Cape Sable seaside sparrow was more numerous and widespread. In fact, the 1984 *Birds of Everglades National Park* listed it as a common species within the park. Between 1871 and 1971, 138 hurricanes and tropical storms passed over or close by the range of the Cape Sable seaside sparrow. The bird's current low numbers and extremely limited range render it vulnerable to extinction from severe weather events.

Hurricanes also pose an indirect threat to sparrow populations and habitat by precipitating shifts in vegetation, succession of woody plants, or invasions of exotic plant species. In 1935 a powerful hurricane that passed through southern Florida is believed to have caused the succession of plant communities in the Cape Sable area, replacing the dominant freshwater plants with salt-tolerant plants. Before that hurricane, the Cape Sable area contained the only known breeding population of the Cape Sable seaside sparrow, hence the name. After the hurricane, the habitats of the Cape Sable area were no longer suitable for the species.

CURRENT TREND: *Declining.* In 1981 the population was estimated at 6,624; after Hurricane Andrew in 1993, the estimate dropped by half, to 3,264, and in 1994 it was down to 2,368. The estimated population increased slightly by 1997, to 3,920, but declined again in the years to follow.

Florida Grasshopper Sparrow

Ammodramus savannarum floridanus
FAMILY EMBERIZIDAE; Order Passeriformes

LISTED STATUS
FWC: Endangered, listed 1975
USF&WS: Endangered, listed 1986

Description: The Florida grasshopper sparrow is a diminutive species, approximately 5 inches (12.7 cm) in length and weighing less than 1 ounce (28 g). Like other grasshopper sparrow races, this subspecies has a brownish back, buffy breast and sides without conspicuous streaking, a flat rather than rounded head, and a short sharp tail. There is a pale white median stripe on the crown, a faint white eye ring, and a yellowish orange patch in front of each eye. The feet and legs are flesh-colored. This is the darkest of the grasshopper sparrow subspecies. The feathers of the head, back, nape, rump, wings, and tail are various shades of dark brown and gray. The abdomen, breast, and throat are usually lighter than in other races, however. The feathers at the bend of each wing are yellowish. The Florida grasshopper sparrow also differs from the eastern grasshopper sparrow (*Ammodramus savannarum pratensis*), which commonly winters in Florida, in that it lacks the reddish streaks on the nape and has a slightly larger bill. In late summer, juvenile birds with streaked breasts are observed. Immature birds are just as dark as adults, and the sexes look alike. The Florida grasshopper sparrow has two songs; both are frail and do not carry far. The primary song is initiated with two high-pitched *chip* notes, followed by a buzzing *pi-tup zeeeeeeeee,* like a grasshopper, hence the common name. The second is a thin, buzzy tumbling of notes that go up and down in pitch.

Distribution: The range of the Florida grasshopper sparrow is limited to the prairie region of south-central Florida, where it is a nonmigratory resident. The range of this race is separated from the breeding range of the eastern grasshopper sparrow by more than 300 miles. Currently, only seven localized populations are known; they occupy portions of southern Osceola County and portions of Polk, Highlands, Okeechobee, and Glades counties. Populations formerly known from northern Osceola County and from portions of Hendry and Collier counties are now believed to be extirpated. The largest population (43 breeding pairs) occurs on the public land within Avon Park Air Force Range, approximately 12 miles east of Avon Park on the border of Highlands and Polk counties. Another breeding population exists at the Audubon Prairie Preserve in Okeechobee

County. Historic records of nesting grasshopper sparrows in Florida are from Payne's Prairie in Alachua County (1913), near Titusville in Brevard County (1917, 1925), and Manatee County (about 1924).

A dozen subspecies of grasshopper sparrow are distributed from Washington and southern British Columbia in the west, east to southern Quebec and Maine, and south locally to portions of Mexico, Central and South America, and the Greater Antilles. Two other subspecies are known to winter in Florida, the more frequent eastern grasshopper sparrow and the common grasshopper sparrow (*A. s. perpallidus*).

Biology: The Florida grasshopper sparrow is a bird of frequently burned and poorly drained treeless expanses, a prairie habitat with stunted vegetation, often no more than 2 feet high, and occasional patches of bare ground. This habitat niche preferred by the Florida race differs somewhat from the habitat used by the eastern grasshopper sparrow. The most characteristic plants associated with the Florida race's habitat are saw palmetto (usually the most prolific plant species), dwarf live oak, gopher apple, St. John's wort, and papaw (*Asimina* spp.). The more common grasses and herbaceous vegetation found in these areas are wiregrass, flat-topped goldenrod (*Euthamia tenuifolia*), and bluestems (*Schizachyrium* spp.). The vegetation used by Florida grasshopper sparrows is almost always shorter than in adjacent habitats, which often support Bachman's sparrows but lack grasshopper sparrows. Much of the habitat where these sparrows occur is on large private ranches with cattle present. Although cattle will occasionally trample on and destroy sparrow nests,

moderate grazing may be somewhat beneficial in the maintenance of this niche, and biologists generally believe that cattle are not a serious threat to the survival of this species. Ranchers typically conduct prescribed burns in these areas during the winter at two- to three-year intervals, which helps maintain the habitat required by the sparrows.

Florida grasshopper sparrows are shy and not easily approached. The author can certainly testify to the extreme difficulty of photographing them in their natural habitat. This race spends a considerable amount of time on the ground or just above it. Individuals often forage by walking on the ground between clumps of palmettos, into which they may run if threatened. Analyses of the stomach contents of these birds by Arthur H. Howell in 1932 revealed a diet of 69 percent animal matter, mostly crickets, beetles, and other insects, with the remainder being vegetative matter.

Nesting territories range from 2 to 12 acres. They are defended by males. Males may sing throughout the day, but they are heard more frequently in the early morning and just before dusk. Individual territories are often separated by a considerable distance. This ground-nesting bird constructs a domed nest of fine grasses, usually concealed at the base of a clump of grass, below the shelter of a dwarf live oak or papaw or under a palmetto frond. Breeding activity has been observed from March to May, and it is known that these birds occasionally produce second broods. The three to six (usually four or five) white eggs speckled with reddish brown measure about 0.75 inch by 0.5 inch (1.8 cm by 1.4 cm). Laid between early April and June, they are incubated by the female and hatch after 11–12 days. Because they nest on the ground, these sparrows are vulnerable to a large number of predators, including several species of snakes, eastern spotted skunks, striped skunks (*Mephitis mephitis*), and feral hogs. Recent studies conducted on the Avon Park Bombing Range have revealed that these little birds are fairly long-lived, for sparrows, despite heavy predation. An adult bird banded by biologists in 1990 was recaptured in 1995, indicating that life spans may exceed five years.

CAUSE OF DECLINE, THREATS

Habitat Destruction: When people began settling in the dry prairie region of south-central Florida, they quickly and repeatedly extinguished the frequent natural fires that kept back the succession of tall woody plants. Without the regular wild-fires, habitats that had supported nesting populations of Florida grasshopper sparrows became incompatible for the continued existence of this habitat specialist. Fire suppression and other changes in land use have caused the abandonment of six breeding sites since the bird was listed as a federally endangered species in 1986. Populations are quite sedentary and do not readily relocate to suitable new habitat. Widespread pasture improvement in the form of near total removal of palmetto and other shelter vegetation is considered the primary cause of decline. Bush hogs and other mechanical land-clearing equipment destroy nests and eggs and kill birds. According to the federal recovery plan, "a continued loss of habitat is expected due to increased pasture conversion and changes in intensity of management of existing pastureland."

Cowbird Parasitism: Nest parasitism by the brown-headed cowbird is not presently a threat because the range of the Florida grasshopper sparrow is south of the current known breeding range of the cowbird. It has, however, been a factor in the decline of many passerines. Cowbirds deposit their eggs in the nests of other, usually smaller birds, where they are cared for by the host birds, often in lieu of their own. The breeding range of the temperate brown-headed cowbird is rapidly spreading south, and the range of the tropical shiny cowbird (*Molothrus bonariensis*) is apparently extending north. These range extensions cause ornithologists to fear that cowbirds may threaten grasshopper sparrow populations in the future.

Other Threats: Introduced feral hogs commonly occur in areas inhabited by this species. They root through dry prairie habitats consuming virtually anything they encounter, including eggs and young of ground-nesting birds.

CURRENT TREND: *Unknown, probably declining.* Early naturalists reported the Florida grasshopper sparrow to be relatively abundant in south-central Florida. Currently, seven population sites are known, with individual population estimates ranging from 1 bird to more than 82 birds at the largest site. Total population is presently estimated at 150–200 individuals.

American Crocodile

Crocodylus acutus

FAMILY CROCODYLIDAE; Order Crocodilia

LISTED STATUS

FWC: Endangered, listed 1972 (protected 1967–1971)

USF&WS: Endangered, listed 1975

CITES: Appendix 1

Description: Crocodiles, like alligators, are large, primitive, lizardlike reptiles. In size comparisons without regard to range, the American crocodile is a larger animal than the American alligator. American crocodile specimens taken in South America have exceeded 23 feet (7 m), whereas the largest recorded alligator, a Louisiana specimen killed in 1890, measured 19 feet 2 inches (5.8 m). Within Florida populations, however, these two distantly related crocodilians average roughly the same size. In recent times, adult crocodiles in Florida are 7–11 feet (2.1–3.4 m) in length, and adult alligators are 6–9 feet (1.8–2.7 m). The largest American crocodile recorded from Florida was a 15-foot (4.6 m) male; Florida's largest recorded American alligator, also a male, measured 17 feet 5 inches (5.18 m). Female crocodiles are smaller than males, at 6–8 feet (1.8–2.4 m). The American crocodile is not as stout or heavily bodied as the alligator. A large female measuring just short of 10 feet 5 inches (3.17 m) weighed only 289 pounds (131 kg).

Adult American crocodiles are lighter in color than alligators, typically olive-gray, gray-brown, or tannish gray. The belly is whitish or yellowish. Hatchlings and young are similar in color to adults but often have rows of spots on the back and sides or black crossbands. The spectacled caiman, a nonnative species well established in some areas of southern Florida, is similarly colored but has a discernible curved, bony ridge in front of the eyes. Unlike alligators, American crocodiles have a long, tapered snout, with the fourth tooth on the lower jaw protruding when the jaws are closed, which is quite noticeable on larger individuals. The fifth tooth of the lower jaw is actually the largest tooth, but it fits into a cavity in the crocodile's jaw and is not visible when the jaws are closed. The nostrils are at the end of the snout. The ear is shielded by a movable flap. Eyes, nostrils, and ears are situated in such a way that the animal can see, smell, and hear with all of the body submerged except the top of its head. The crocodile's back is covered with longitudinal rows of prominent, bony, keeled scales. Belly scales are much smaller than dorsal scales. The muscular tail is nearly 50 percent of this reptile's total length. The crocodile's legs are short; the front feet have five toes, and the webbed hind feet have four.

Distribution: At least 29 species and subspecies of crocodilians, comprising three families and eight genera, are found throughout the tropics and the warmer temperate regions of the world: there are

18 species and subspecies of crocodiles, 8 species and races of caimans, 2 species of alligators, and 1 species of gavial.

The American crocodile is widespread throughout much of the American tropics but is endangered throughout its range. Southern Florida represents the northernmost limit of its distribution. Its range includes much of the Greater Antilles, including Cuba, Jamaica, and Hispaniola (and formerly the Bahamas); the Caribbean coast, from southern Mexico, including portions of the Yucatan Peninsula, through Central America to South America, including Colombia and Venezuela; and the Pacific coast from Sinaloa, Mexico, south to the Rio Tumbes in Peru. With the exception of several large inland, freshwater lakes in Central America, the range of the American crocodile is generally restricted to coastal areas.

The Florida population is coastal and not contiguous with other populations; it has been isolated for more than 60,000 years. Historically, crocodiles occurred at least as far north as Fort Myers on the Gulf Coast and Lake Worth on the Atlantic Coast. The current range is largely limited to the area of Crocodile Lakes National Wildlife Refuge on northern Key Largo, the mangrove islands of Florida Bay within Everglades National Park, the area of Turkey Point Nuclear Power Plant south of Miami on Biscayne Bay, and, on the Gulf Coast, a small, apparently nonbreeding population in the area of Sanibel Island and Estero Bay in Lee County. A breeding population of crocodiles formerly inhabited the Lower Keys (nests were found on Little Pine Key as late as the 1960's), but it is now believed that crocodiles no longer breed there, and individual crocodiles are rarely seen in the Lower Keys.

Biology: The Florida population of American crocodiles is usually associated with mangrove swamps, mangrove-bordered creeks and estuaries, bays, and isolated ponds with shallow water (2–5 feet). *Crocodylus acutus* is the only New World crocodile that occurs primarily in salt water. Crocodiles are primarily active by night and often spend the day basking, often in secluded locations, at the water's edge or concealed in dens or dense vegetation. Unlike alligators, crocodiles often bask with the mouth held wide open. Crocodiles may wander into open water, even open seas, when foraging at night.

Just the word "crocodile" is enough to inspire fear in many people who grew up watching Tarzan movies featuring hordes of man-eating crocs gliding into a tropical river in pursuit of a raft of helpless tourists. It is true that several of the larger Old World species, particularly the Nile crocodile (*Crocodylus niloticus*) of Africa and Israel and the pelagic saltwater crocodile (*C. porosus*) of Australia and portions of Asia, are genuinely dangerous to humans and cause many fatalities each year, but the same cannot be said of the rather shy *Crocodylus acutus* in Florida. American crocodiles are generally more timid, to a point, toward humans than are alligators, and few conflicts have been documented. There is only one known account of a crocodile attacking a human in Florida, and this very old account, involving a wounded crocodile, is generally considered questionable. It should be noted, however, that the Cuban crocodile (*Crocodylus rhombifer*), an insular species restricted to Cuba and the Isle of Pines, not far from the Lower Keys, has perhaps the worst reputation among crocodilians.

When swimming, a crocodile uses its muscular tail to propel its streamlined body through the water at speeds over 15 mph. Crocodiles can remain submerged for 3–5 minutes. Fish make up a large part of the crocodile's diet in South Florida. Other prey items of crocodiles include such animals as birds (especially wading birds and nestlings), crabs, diamondback terrapins (*Malaclemys terrapin*) and other turtles, snakes, and small mammals. Larger mammals are occasionally taken and may be stored under a shore bank, where they may be revisited for future meals.

American crocodiles court and breed from February through April, sometimes earlier, in Florida. Their courtship and breeding rituals are quite complex. The male crocodile, in an apparent attempt to attract females, may slap his head on the water several times, and if interested, a female may respond by arching her tail upward and tilting her head up. While forming a pair, the male and female may blow bubbles, rub snouts, and ride one another before copulating repeatedly. Nesting activities, conducted solely by the female, begin about a month later. The rather crude, mound-shaped nest is often no more than an accumulation of surrounding soil (sand, peat, or marl) scraped together by the female above the high-tide line on a beach, abandoned canal levee, or creek bank. Nest mounds may measure as much as 20 feet (6 m) in diameter and as high as 2 feet (0.6 m). The female deposits 19–50 white,

leathery shelled eggs, which hatch after 85–90 days, usually in July or August. The sex of the hatchlings depends on the temperature at which the eggs are incubated. Unlike alligators, female crocodiles are not known to defend their nests, at least not from human intrusion, but they do remain close to the nest during incubation. Both crocodile and alligator mothers do, however, routinely open the nest and carry the hatchlings in their mouth to the water. Mother crocodiles do not usually remain with the young for more than a few days, and the young are left to fend for themselves. Hatchlings feed largely on small fish, including sailfin molly (*Poecilia latipinna*), as well as crabs, snails, insects, spiders, and snakes, and the hatchlings in turn are heavily preyed on by wading birds. Hatchling crocodiles may not be as tolerant of salt water as adults; it is believed that they can obtain fresh water from a temporary freshwater lens that forms on the surface of salt water following a shower or directly from rain drops. Juvenile crocodiles grow rapidly during the first few years. Females typically become sexually mature after 11–13 years of age.

CAUSE OF DECLINE, THREATS

Automobile Collisions: Road mortality currently represents one of the dominant causes of death for adult American crocodiles in Florida. The two main roadways where crocodiles are regularly killed by automobiles are U.S. Highway 1 and SR905 (Card Sound Road) on northern Key Largo, the only two vehicular links to the Florida Keys from mainland Florida. On Sunday, 22 September 1996, the author made a sorrowful discovery on Card Sound Road at power pole 67, within Key Largo's Crocodile Lakes National Wildlife Refuge. A 3-foot crocodile had been hit and killed by an automobile and left near the center of the road. This crocodile was killed within the section of road that has been fenced in an attempt to prevent collisions with automobiles. Another crocodile, approximately the same size, had been struck within the same fenced area several days earlier (personal communication, Barry Mansell). The USF&WS has considered removing the fence, which suggests that the fence has not been effective in reducing crocodile mortality. In the author's opinion, however, a properly constructed fence would provide a practical protective barrier for crocodiles. In 1998 there was a gap of 3–5 inches under much of the fence, which permitted smaller crocodiles to walk under it.

Habitat Destruction, Human Encroachment: Much of the habitat within the crocodile's historic range in Florida has been lost to urbanization. Ditching and channelization have also resulted in the loss of crocodile habitat. Fortunately, much of the current breeding range is protected by Everglades National Park, Crocodile Lakes National Wildlife Refuge, and Florida Power and Light's Turkey Point Power Plant. Additionally, other locations that are known, or suspected, to support smaller populations of crocodiles are protected, including Ding Darling National Wildlife Refuge on Sanibel Island and two national refuges in the Lower Keys, Key Deer and Great White Heron. Suitable habitat outside these protected areas is now greatly reduced and in danger of being further reduced.

Indirect disturbance is believed to have caused crocodiles to vacate otherwise suitable habitat. Crocodiles do not tolerate consistent recreational activities such as camping, boating, jet skiing, swimming, and even fishing. Crocodile nests have been vandalized or otherwise directly disturbed in some areas.

Severe Storms: Because the remaining crocodiles occupy just a few isolated populations, both the crocodiles themselves and their habitat are vulnerable to severe storms.

Hide Hunting: A significant percentage of Florida's crocodile population was killed by hide hunters during the late 1800's and early 1900's, but since the species received complete legal protection, the illegal take has become a minimal threat, especially when compared with more contemporary threats. A few crocodiles are still reportedly killed by commercial fishermen after being caught in nets.

CURRENT TREND: *Stable.* The current Florida population totals approximately 400–500 adults, with 40–50 breeding females.

American Alligator

Alligator mississippiensis

FAMILY CROCODYLIDAE; Order Crocodilia

LISTED STATUS

FWC: Species of special concern

USF&WS: Threatened (listed because of *similarity in appearance* to the endangered American crocodile)

CITES: Appendix 2

Description: This alligator has the distinction of being the largest North American reptile, and there is virtually no chance of mistaking it for anything else throughout its range, with the exception of southern Florida, where the American crocodile and spectacled caiman occur. Adults are large, blackish, lizard-shaped reptiles; the name "alligator" was derived from the Spanish *el lagarto,* which means "the lizard." In 1890 an alligator with a confirmed length of 19 feet 2 inches (5.84 m) was killed in Louisiana; the largest gator confirmed in Florida was 17 feet 5 inches (5.18 m). Animals approaching that size are almost unheard of these days. Adults are usually 6–9 feet (1.8–2.7 m) long, with males attaining a greater size than females. These primitive crocodilians are covered by a thick, scaly hide with a series of longitudinal ridges on the body and tail. The long, thick, muscular tail is very powerful. The alligator's mighty jaws contain 70–80 large conical teeth designed for grasping and subduing prey. The snout is broad and rounded, unlike the American crocodile's, which is elongated and tapered. Alligators are generally darker than crocodiles and lack the croc's telltale protruding lower tooth. The spectacled caiman, an introduced species that has established breeding populations in southeastern Florida, can be distinguished by its distinct, bony ridge in front of the eyes. Both albino and leucistic alligators have been encountered in the wild; however, with advertised prices for such animals exceeding $100,000, it is unlikely that they are left where they are discovered.

Hatchlings are 8–10 inches (20–25 cm) long and have bright yellowish crossbands that dissipate with age. Adults, especially males, may issue loud throaty roars that are as eery and impressive as a bull elk's bugle. Young gators emit repeated high-pitched yelps, *yeonk, yeonk,* and both juveniles and adults hiss.

Distribution: Alligators occupy wetland habitats throughout much of the Atlantic and Gulf coastal plains of the southeastern United States, from northeastern North Carolina (including the Outer Banks) south to the Florida Keys and west to extreme southeastern Oklahoma, including a considerable portion of eastern Texas, as far south as the Mexican border. The primary environmental and climatic elements that restrict the distribution of the American alligator are cold weather and the lack of wetland habitats. It occurs in every Florida county and may even be present in some urban lakes or ponds. Alligators are found on several of the Lower Keys, including Big Pine, Little Pine, and No Name.

Florida, with an estimated gator population of more than a million, has more gators than any other state. Louisiana is the runner-up, with about 750,000, and Georgia places a distant third with about 100,000. Alligators remain threatened in the states of Oklahoma, Arkansas, and North Carolina, where they are much less abundant. The urban legend about enormous sewer alligators, descended from pet baby alligators flushed down the toilet into the sewers of New York or Philadelphia, is pure myth. It never happened.

The American alligator is one of only two species of alligators. The smaller Chinese alligator (*Alligator sinensis*) inhabits the Yangtze River region of China and is critically endangered.

Biology: The American alligator is a wetlands generalist that inhabits a wide variety of lacustrine, palustrine, riverine, and estuarine habitats. Once at risk of extinction, gators are again a familiar denizen of Florida's lakes, ponds, rivers, streams, swamps, marshes, water-filled roadside ditches, and occasionally back-yard swimming pools. It has often been published that the alligator is strictly a dweller of freshwater habitats that rarely ventures into brackish or saltwater environments, but that is far from true. Locally, the alligator is an abundant resident of salt marshes in many areas, including Merritt Island National Wildlife Refuge in Brevard County and tidal mangrove swamps at Flamingo in Everglades National Park.

The alligator is to the Everglades what the gopher tortoise is to sandhill communities. These keystone species play a vital role by creating and main-taining microhabitats, in this case gator holes, that benefit a host of other Everglades animals. In areas where water levels regularly fluctuate, such as the Everglades, alligators will excavate a depression in the substrate that retains water during the dry season and provides refuge to various fishes, frogs, salaman-ders, turtles, and snakes that depend on water for survival. Gator holes are also an important source of drinking water and prey for many animals, including deer, panthers, otters, raccoons, and wading birds, as well as the host gator. Alligators will often use the same gator-created pond each dry season, frequently deepening and enlarging the crater over time. When alligators were eliminated from many wetlands in the early 1900's, their holes dried up after several years and a multitude of wetland species suf-fered as a result. Alligators also excavate den hollows in the banks of rivers or

lakes, sometimes many feet deep, where they take refuge during exceptionally cold weather.

Alligators have an elaborate social hierarchy with complex courting, breed-ing, and nesting behaviors. In Florida, courtship begins in the spring, often in early April. During this time, males may wander considerable distances in search of available females. The author was once startled to find an adult male alligator strolling through a dry, high pine forest near Tallahassee, at least a mile from the nearest lake. A gator-enticing scent is released from a pair of glands at the base of the female's tail that attracts potential mates. Courtship displays include snout rubbing, head slapping, and bellowing.

Approximately 50–60 days after mating, the female constructs her nest, a mound of compacted earth and vegeta-tion, up to a yard (90 cm) in height and 4–7 feet (1–2 m) in diameter. In an open-ing at the top of the nest, she will lay 25–50 white eggs that measure about 3 inches (7.6 cm) in length. The mother will remain close to the nest until the eggs hatch, in about two months, vehe-mently defending it from intruders. Aquatic turtles often take advantage of gator nests as nesting sites for their own eggs. Heat generated by rotting vegetation incubates the eggs. The sex of the hatchlings is determined by the incubation temperature: eggs incubated between 82 and 86 degrees F generally produce females, between 87 and 89 degrees produce a fairly equal ratio of males and females, and above 90 degrees typically produce males. When ready to hatch, baby alligators emit a high-pitched croak from inside the nest, and the mother responds by clearing debris from the top of the nest to provide an exit. Offspring stay close to their mother for several months, while they are most vulnerable to predation. Baby alligators are frequently observed basking on the mother's head and back. Although adult alligators have virtually no natural predators, neonates may fall prey to numerous mammals, wading birds, raptors, fish, snakes, turtles, other alligators, even bullfrogs. Alligators may grow a foot per year during their first 7 or 8 years, after which their growth rate slows substantially. Alligators are long-lived, with exceptional individuals exceeding 50 years.

Like most crocodilians, alligators regularly partake in the sedentary activity of basking on banks or partially submerged logs, which they often share with basking turtles. When it comes to their diet, adult alligators are living garbage disposals, consuming just about anything they can catch, kill, and swallow. Carrion is readily consumed as well. Most prey is taken in the water, where gators display remarkable agility. The large, muscular tail propels these enormous reptiles through the water with ease. Fish, ducks, wading birds, raccoons, and turtles are gobbled down whole, and large prey such as deer are pulled under water and drowned. Alligators are cannibalistic and will occasionally prey on other alligators. Newly hatched alligators take such quarry as insects and tadpoles and soon graduate to frogs, snakes, and fish.

Though typically not a danger to humans, alligators have on rare occasions attacked, killed, and even consumed humans. Between 1948 and 1993, 171 alligator attacks on humans were recorded in Florida, resulting in 6 fatalities.

Most attacks occurred in murky water, and experts believe in most cases the humans were mistaken for more typical prey. Regrettably, more attacks can be expected. With nearly 1,000 new Floridians daily, many of whom choose to live in the midst of alligator habitat, coupled with the all too common practice of throwing table scraps to gators as though they were dockside pets, it is almost inevitable. Females guarding nests or young, injured animals, and fed alligators are potentially dangerous. The FWC receives more than 10,000 nuisance alligators annually and removes approximately 4,000 alligators to prevent potential problems.

CAUSE OF DECLINE, THREATS
Hide Hunting: Before the 1850's, the alligator was an abundant species in much of its range. Native Indians hunted alligators for food, as did early European settlers, but the reptiles were generally not heavily exploited until alligator hide became fashionable in 1855. With a high profit margin and no regulations, the hide market really took off in the 1870's. The number of alligator hunters increased as the number of alligators decreased. Between 1870 and 1970, the year federal law banned the interstate shipment of gators, approximately 10 million of Florida's alligators were killed and converted into handbags, belts, boots, wallets, and briefcases. Poachers hunted gators at night using spotlights to illuminate the unmistakable bright red shine of their eyes. When a population was exterminated in one area, hunters simply moved to other areas supporting large populations. In 1940 Alabama became the first state to enact laws fully protecting alligators, after they were

nearly extirpated. An estimated 90 percent of Louisiana's gators were killed during the 1940's and 1950's alone. State by state, the alligator was afforded legal protection, but the state laws were often ignored by market hunters motivated by money. In 1972 officials from Everglades National Park announced that 90–95 percent of the park's alligators had been illegally hunted out. That same year experts estimated Florida's gator population to be as low as 40,000, a tiny fraction of the presettlement population of more than 2 million. When the harvesting of American alligators slowed, the expanding market shifted to other crocodilians, causing disastrous declines in some species that continue to this day.

Habitat Destruction: Destruction and fragmentation of Florida's wetland ecosystems is currently the most serious threat. After a quarter century of strict protection, this reptile has bounced back from near extinction and is once again abundant in many areas. Here lies a problem—what to do with all those alligators. The ever-expanding loss of wetland habitats remains a continuing threat to this large, primitive reptile, which may again become rare outside national parks or refuges. As we continue to convert alligator habitat to human habitat, the remaining locations where gators have courted, nested, fed, basked, and dug their gator holes for thousands of years will disappear.

Illegal Feeding: Florida statute 372.667 (1) makes it a misdemeanor for anyone to feed or entice with food an alligator in the wild. The warning "a fed alligator means a dead alligator" is all too often proven true. Feeding alligators is the precursor to deadly encounters between alligators and pets or humans. A fed gator soon loses its instinctive fear of humans and becomes a problem gator, which must be removed and is generally killed.

Automobile Collisions: Automobiles kill or seriously injure thousands of alligators in Florida each year. Gators are frequently killed on high-speed multilane highways that traverse large expanses of wetlands, such as Alligator Alley and Tamiami Trail as they cross the Everglades or I75 and U.S. Highway 441 where they bisect Payne's Prairie.

Pollution: Occupying the top of the food chain, the alligator is susceptible to the bioaccumulation of certain contaminants ingested by its prey. The majority of gators inhabiting Lake Apopka, Lake Jessup, and other polluted bodies of water are visibly deformed or internally mutated. Many hatchling male alligators from highly polluted Lake Apopka have shrunken penises, malformed cells of their testes, and low testosterone levels, and many hatchling females have abnormal ovaries; this population has had low reproductive success for many years. Tissue samples from Lake Apopka alligators have high concentrations of DDE, a DDT derivative.

CURRENT TREND: *Stable, recovered.*

Sea Turtles
Atlantic Green Turtle
Chelonia mydas mydas
Atlantic Hawksbill Turtle
Eretmochelys imbricata imbricata
Atlantic Ridley Turtle
Lepidochelys kempi

Atlantic Loggerhead Turtle
Caretta caretta caretta
FAMILY CHELONIIDAE; Order Testudines
Atlantic Leatherback Turtle
Dermochelys coriacea coriacea
FAMILY DERMOCHELYIDAE; Order Testudines
LISTED STATUS
FWC: Endangered, Atlantic green listed
1975 (threatened 1974), Atlantic hawks-
bill listed 1975, Atlantic ridley listed
1975, Atlantic leatherback listed 1979;
threatened, Atlantic loggerhead listed
1975
USF&WS & NATL MARINE FISHERIES:
Endangered, Atlantic green listed 1978
(breeding populations in Florida and
Mexico's Pacific Coast; all other populations threatened), Atlantic hawksbill
listed 1970, Atlantic ridley listed 1970,
Atlantic leatherback listed 1970; threatened, Atlantic loggerhead listed 1978
CITES: Appendix 1, all five species
Description
Atlantic Green Turtle: The "green" in
the common name refers to the turtle's
calipee (a greenish fatty substance
removed from the body for soup) and
not the color of its skin or carapace. This
is a large sea turtle; the adult carapace
is 36–48 inches (90–122 cm) long, and
full-grown adults weigh 250–450 pounds
(113–204 kg). Occasional individuals may
exceed 60 inches (152 cm) in carapace
length and weigh more than 650 pounds
(295 kg). Carapace length of hatchlings
is 1.6–2.4 inches (4.1–6 cm). The adult
carapace is brownish but may range from
tannish to dark brown or olive. The carapace often bears a radiating or mottled
pattern that may be obscured in older
individuals. Green turtles are easily
distinguished from loggerhead turtles

(at close range) by the presence of a single pair of prefrontal plates between the
green turtle's eyes. There are four costal
scutes on each side of the carapace, the
first of which does not touch the nuchal
scute (unlike the loggerhead). There are
four scutes on the bridge of the plastron.
Hatchlings are usually very dark above,
often black, with a contrasting whitish
plastron. Hatchlings and young have a
keel on the carapace, a pair of keels on
the plastron, and their flippers are fringed
with white. These characteristics dissipate with age. The green turtle has specialized electrolyte balance mechanisms
and physiological respiratory mechanisms,
evolutionary adaptations to life at sea
common to all marine turtles.

On very rare occasions, green turtles
have been known to hybridize with
hawksbill turtles, producing offspring
that may be quite confusing.

Atlantic Hawksbill Turtle: The hawksbill is the second smallest species of
sea turtle in Florida's marine habitats.
Its adult carapace length is 30–35 inches
(76–89 cm), and adult hawksbills typically weigh 95–165 pounds (43–75 kg). Large
individuals may weigh as much as 280
pounds (127 kg), with a carapace exceeding 36 inches (90 cm). The carapace of
the hawksbill turtle is shaped much like
a shield. It is yellowish in color, with a
mottled greenish, reddish brown, or black
tortoiseshell pattern. The radiating
tortoiseshell pattern is more distinct
in young adults than in older individuals.
The skin color is usually yellowish. The
plastron of the male hawksbill is slightly
concave, which makes it easier for males
to mount females when mating. This
species has a prominent, sharply pointed,

beaklike snout, hence the name. There are four costal scutes on each side of the carapace. Unlike loggerhead and ridley turtles, the nuchal scute of hawksbill turtles (and green turtles) does not touch the first costal scutes. There are two pairs of prefrontal plates between the eyes in this species. There are two claws on each paddle-shaped flipper. As in other sea turtle species, the tail of the male turtle extends well beyond the shell's edge. Hatchlings measure 1.5–1.9 inches (3.8–4.8 cm) long and are black or very dark brown above and below. Some authorities recognize the hawksbill turtles inhabiting the Pacific Ocean as a distinct subspecies, the Pacific hawksbill turtle (*Eretmochelys imbricata squamata* or *E. i. bissa*), based on differences of carapace shape and coloration.

Atlantic Ridley Turtle: The Atlantic ridley turtle is the smallest of Florida's five species of sea turtles. The adult carapace is 23–27 inches (58–70 cm) long, and adult ridleys typically weigh 80–100 pounds (36–45 kg). Unlike other sea turtles, which usually have oval carapaces, the ridley has a heart-shaped, nearly circular carapace. The Atlantic ridley, also commonly known as Kemp's ridley turtle, is one of two ridley species, the other being the olive ridley turtle (*Lepidochelys olivacea*). Both ridleys are sometimes referred to as bastard turtles, because of the fallacious belief that they are the hybrid progeny of green turtles and loggerhead turtles. The carapace of adult Atlantic ridley turtles is generally olive-green, and the plastron is yellowish. The tail of adult males extends well beyond the edge of the shell. The nuchal scute of the carapace touches the first costal scute, which is one of several

characteristics that readily distinguish this relatively small species from green and hawksbill turtles. The Atlantic ridley has five costal plates on each side of the carapace, usually four (rarely five) enlarged bridge scutes, and a small inter-anal scute on the plastron. The olive ridley differs from the Atlantic ridley in having six or seven, sometimes as many as nine, costal scutes on the carapace. Also, the olive ridley's middle marginal scutes (carapace) are typically longer than they are wide, but those of the Atlantic ridley are generally wider than they are long. Hatchlings are 1.5–1.75 inches (3.8–4.4 cm) long and are often uniformly dark gray in color.

Atlantic Loggerhead Turtle: Though historic records of loggerheads exceeding 1,000 pounds (455 kg) exist, specimens of that weight have not been encountered for many years now. Loggerhead turtles recorded by biologists in recent years measure 31–45 inches (79–114 cm) in carapace length and weigh 170–350 pounds (77–159 kg), with occasional individuals exceeding 48 inches (122 cm) and 500 pounds (227 kg). Among Florida specimens, the loggerhead is generally larger than ridley and hawksbill turtles but smaller than green turtles and leatherbacks. The loggerhead can often be distinguished from other sea turtles by its reddish or reddish brown skin and disproportionately large head (relative to carapace size), which may be as wide as 10 inches (25 cm). The species has 5 or more costal scutes (the first touches the nuchal scute), 11–12 marginal scutes that are lateral to the costal scutes, and 5 vertebral scutes on the carapace, with 3–4 pairs of bridge scutes on the plastron. Turtles with asymmetrical scute arrangements (e.g., 12 marginals on one side and 11 marginals on the other) have been reported. The carapace of adults and subadults is generally reddish brown or orange, and the plastron is typically yellowish or light brown. Albino loggerhead turtles have been reported. At hatching, the carapace is 1.6–1.9 inches (4.1–4.8 cm) long. Hatchlings are quite variable in color; the three-keeled carapace ranges from beige to nearly black, and the two-keeled plastron is somewhat lighter. The keels present on hatchlings dissipate with time and eventually disappear.

Atlantic Leatherback Turtle: The leatherback turtle cannot be confused with any other species. With a maximum carapace length of at least 74 inches (188 cm) and a maximum weight of more than 2,000 pounds (916 kg), the leatherback (also called trunk turtle, or leathery turtle) is by far the largest of all living sea turtles. The total length of a large individual, including head, body, and tail, may exceed 10 feet (305 cm). The carapace length of typical adults is 53–70 inches (135–178 cm); adults typically weigh 650–1,200 pounds (295–544 kg). Besides size, the most obvious characteristic that sets this species apart from other sea turtles is the lack of scutes on both the carapace and plastron. Instead of scutes, leatherbacks have a dark, bluish black, rubbery shell. Adult leatherbacks retain many embryonic characteristics that are present in other sea turtles only as hatchlings. The carapace of an adult leatherback is approximately 2 inches (5 cm) thick. Males have a concave plastron and a thick tail that extends well beyond the edge of the carapace. Seven prominent, narrow, longitudinal ridges extend along the length of the carapace, and five ridges extend along the plastron. Lighter patches of pink or white may be sporadically present, but they are usually more pronounced on the plastron. The crown of the head in adult females often has a pinkish wash. The flippers of the leatherback contain a countercurrent heat-exchanging circulatory system, similar to that of a beaver's tail. This specialized adaptation, together with this turtle's well-insulated skin, provides superior insulation to that of most other pelagic turtles. The unique oily substance present in the flesh and skeleton of the leatherback is believed to function much like oils in the flesh of certain whale species that routinely dive to great depths while foraging. The oil may help to lessen decompression problems as these turtles dive or surface rapidly. Young are 2.3–3 inches (6–7.5 cm) long at hatching. The light markings present in adults are usually more conspicuous in juveniles. Hatchlings are typically covered with numerous small, beady scales, which shed after several months, and have a keeled ridge on the tail.

Distribution

Atlantic Green Turtle: The green turtle occurs in tropical and subtropical waters worldwide and often strays into temperate waters. (The darker and slightly smaller Pacific green turtle, known as the black sea turtle, *Chelonia mydas agassizi,* is considered by some authorities to be a distinct species, *C. agassizi.*) There are approximately 30 major nesting sites worldwide. Only two of them—Aves Island in the Lesser Antilles and Tortuguero, Costa Rica (the largest nesting congregation)—are in the western Atlantic Ocean north of South America. Within the United States, the Atlantic green turtle has been recorded nesting from Massachusetts south to Florida, where the large majority nest, and sparingly along the Gulf Coast to Texas. This species also nests at numerous locations within the Caribbean, including the Virgin Islands and Puerto Rico, and as far south as Argentina in South America. The greatest percentage of green turtles in the continental United States nest along Florida's Atlantic Coast between Volusia County and Dade County, with the highest densities occurring on the southeastern coast between Brevard County and Martin County. Green turtles nest on Florida's Gulf Coast only rarely. Several regions within Florida appear to be important foraging areas for immature Atlantic green turtles, including Florida Bay, Indian River Lagoon on the Atlantic Coast, and a portion of the Gulf of Mexico between the Cedar Keys in Levy County and Homosassa Bay in Citrus County. Immature green turtles are also frequently observed in the Gulf Stream surrounding Bermuda, some 600 miles off the coast of North Carolina.

Atlantic Hawksbill Turtle: Of all the sea turtle species, the hawksbill is generally considered to be more restricted to the warm waters of the tropics. Although some authorities contend that hawksbill turtles are less inclined to travel long distances than other sea turtles, some do migrate considerable distances. Juvenile hawksbills tagged in the U.S. Virgin Islands have turned up in Puerto Rico, the British Virgin Islands, and St. Martin. One juvenile hawksbill tagged in Brazil was recovered six months later 2,300 miles away in Senegal, Africa. Most hawksbills encountered in Florida are

juvenile turtles. This species wanders to the north when foraging during the summer months and has been recorded from every state bordering the Atlantic Ocean and the Gulf of Mexico with the exception of Maine and Connecticut. Hawksbill turtles may be encountered in pelagic habitats anywhere in Florida, but they occur more frequently in the coral reefs and coastal waters of southeastern Florida and the Florida Keys than anywhere else in the continental United States.

Although nesting hawksbills are extremely rare in Florida, a small number have been recorded within the state nearly every year for the past decade. Nesting has been recorded in Volusia, Brevard, Martin, Palm Beach, Broward, Dade, and Monroe counties. The world's largest known population of nesting hawksbill turtles is on Milman Island, Queensland, Australia. Other important nesting areas include other portions of Queensland and Western Australia, Papua New Guinea, Indonesia, the Seychelles, and Mexico's Yucatan Peninsula. Locations believed to support moderate nesting populations of hawksbill turtles include islands in the Torres Strait, several islands in the Red Sea, islands in the Persian Gulf, Oman, northern Australia, Palau, and possibly Cuba.

Atlantic Ridley Turtle: The range of the adult Atlantic ridley is generally associated with the Gulf of Mexico. Some authorities believe that most if not all of this species' life cycle is spent in the Gulf of Mexico; other experts, however, contend that many juvenile Atlantic ridley turtles migrate to the western Atlantic Ocean, rarely the eastern Atlantic Ocean, and return to the

Gulf of Mexico as adults. Adult ridleys are seldom encountered in the Atlantic Ocean. The type locality of the Atlantic ridley turtle is Key West, where it is, today, a very rare animal. Likewise, the species nests in Florida only rarely. One adult female attempted unsuccessfully to nest on Florida's Atlantic Coast in Palm Beach County in 1989, and another nested successfully on the Gulf Coast in Pinellas County the same year. The only location within the United States where Atlantic ridleys have historically nested in substantial numbers is southern Padre Island, on the Gulf Coast of southern Texas. The largest concentrations of nesting Atlantic ridley turtles gather each year on the beaches of Tamaulipas, Mexico, near Rancho Nuevo; today they represent but a small fraction of the numbers that nested there several decades ago.

The closely related olive ridley, often called the Pacific ridley turtle, also inhabits portions of the Atlantic Ocean and may on rare occasions occur in Florida's coastal waters. A very few specimens that have apparently migrated from western Africa have been encountered quite close to Florida in the coastal waters of northern Cuba and Puerto Rico and have established nesting colonies on several beaches in northern South America (Trinidad and the Guianas).

Atlantic Loggerhead Turtle: The range of the loggerhead turtle encircles the globe, but it reaches its greatest abundance, as well as its densest nesting congregations, in subtropical and warmer temperate regions. This turtle prefers subtropical over tropical regions for nesting sites, and its favored areas are just north of

the Tropic of Capricorn and just south of the Tropic of Cancer. The loggerhead also nests in smaller numbers at other Florida locations, including the Dry Tortugas and some of the Florida Keys, as well as scattered sites along the Gulf Coast. Loggerheads regularly nest along the Atlantic Coast from New Jersey south to southern Florida (sporadically in the mid-Atlantic states), in portions of the Caribbean including Puerto Rico, and sporadically on Gulf coastal beaches from Florida to Texas. The loggerhead is the most common sea turtle in Florida, and the beaches of Florida's Atlantic Coast have a worldwide significance in the protection of loggerhead turtles. The east coast of Florida, particularly Brevard County south to Broward County, has the world's second largest population of nesting loggerheads, as many as 450 nests per kilometer of beach. Only the beaches of Masira Island, Oman, in the Arabian Sea, have more nesting loggerheads. Other significant loggerhead nesting areas include Jamaica, Brazil, Colombia, Mexico, Greece, Mozambique, Madagascar, South Africa, and Australia.

Some authorities believe that two distinct geographic nesting populations exist along the Atlantic states: one along the coast of Georgia, the Carolinas, and states farther north and the other primarily on the Atlantic Coast of Florida. Recent research indicates the populations nesting north of Florida are declining and not faring as well as those along Florida's coast. Recommendations have been made to consider listing the Atlantic nesting populations north of Florida as endangered, while retaining the threatened designation for nesting populations in Florida. There is evidence of declines of loggerhead populations in many other areas as well.

Recent in-depth research by several scientists, including Jeff Seminoff and Jay Nichols of the University of Arizona, has revealed, or more appropriately confirmed, extensive east-west migrations of logger-heads. A tagged Pacific loggerhead turtle, released near Santa Rosalia on the west coast of Baja California on 19 July 1994, was captured 478 days later and 6,400 miles away, off the coast of Kyushu, Japan, by a fisherman. Genetic affinities between loggerhead populations of the eastern Pacific and those nesting in Japan (and, to a lesser extent, Australia) had led biologists to believe that loggerheads made transoceanic journeys, and the catch of this sole turtle finally provided proof. In August 1996 biologists from the University of Arizona released a second turtle, again in Baja California, this time fitted with a satellite transmitter that allowed them to track the turtle's path; as of April 1997, the turtle was within 1,000 miles of Japan, having traveled a fairly direct route skirting Hawaii (personal communication, J. Seminoff).

Atlantic Leatherback Turtle: The leatherback ranks among the farthest-ranging of all reptiles, regularly migrating great distances in search of its dietary mainstay, jellyfish. This species has frequently been encountered (during the summer) in the cold waters of the North Atlantic; it occurs farther north and tolerates colder water than any other sea turtle. The Atlantic leatherback has been recorded as far north as Newfoundland, Canada, and as far south as the Cape of Good Hope in Africa and Argentina in South America; the Pacific leatherback

(*Dermochelys coriacea schlegeli*) has been encountered as far north as the Gulf of Alaska near Cordova and the Aleutian Archipelago. Its skin contains a whalelike blubber that helps to insulate the animal when traveling in near-frigid waters. This species is, however, much more at home in subtropical and tropical seas.

Within the western Atlantic, leather-backs nest most frequently in Mexico, Central America (especially Costa Rica and Panama), and South America (espe-cially Brazil, Venezuela, and the Guianas), with lesser numbers nesting in the West Indies and other Caribbean locales. The U.S. Virgin Islands (St. Croix) and Puerto Rico (Culebra) support the largest nesting populations of leatherbacks within the United States, though the numbers are relatively small. The world's largest nesting congregation of leatherbacks is a population of Pacific leatherbacks that gather on the beaches of Michoacan, Mexico, near Mexiquillo on the Pacific; about 50 percent of all adult female leatherbacks nest along Mexico's Pacific Coast. The number of leatherback turtles nesting near Mexiquillo and elsewhere has declined dramatically in recent years. About 4,800 nests were counted at this location during the 1986–1987 nesting season; in the 1993–1994 season, only 70 nests were counted. The same trend holds true for Yalimapo–Les Hattes in French Guiana, historically the largest nesting site for Atlantic leatherbacks. Important leatherback nesting locations in the western Atlantic include Costa Rica (Limon to Parismina), Panama (Chiriqui Gulf region), Trinidad (Matura Bay region), French Guiana (Silebache–Pointe Isere), Guyana (Shell Beach), Suriname (Bigisanti and Marowijne beaches), and Colombia (Gulf of Uraba). Major nesting locations within the eastern Atlantic include Angola, Gabon, Ghana, Ivory Coast, Liberia, Senegal, Togo, and Zaire in Africa and several smaller sites in the Mediterranean Sea (Israel, Sicily). Formerly significant Old World nesting sites where populations have been severely depleted include a portion of the Bird's Head Peninsula in Irian Jaya, where an estimated 75-percent reduction in the number of leatherbacks has been documented, and a beach at Rantau Abang, in Terengganu, Malaysia, where similar declines have occurred. Declines have also been reported in Thailand, India, and Sri Lanka. Leatherbacks are also now much less common in Florida's offshore waters than they once were. In recent years, only about 100–200 leatherbacks have been reported from Florida waters. Biologists believe that fewer than 12 individual leatherback turtles may be nesting in Florida each year. Surveys have revealed summer concentrations of leatherbacks off the coast of Brevard County, in waters 66–132 feet (20–40 m) deep. These enormous sea turtles reportedly nested on the beaches of the Florida Keys fairly frequently. Most records of leatherbacks nesting in Florida, however, are from the Atlantic Coast, from Flagler County south to Dade County, with Hutchinson Island in St. Lucie County being especially favored.

Biology: The oceans contain various pelagic environments inhabited by Florida's five sea turtle species. Only nesting adult females intentionally make their way onto land, and then only for a short distance and for a short time. Turtles that have been severely injured or are very ill occasionally become stranded ashore. Studies have revealed that all species of sea turtles are subject to long-distance movements. Species such as leatherbacks, green turtles, and loggerheads typically nest in tropical areas but commonly travel long distances to forage in temperate or even subpolar waters. Habitats utilized by different species of sea turtles may vary considerably. Also, the habitats required by hatchlings and the habitats used by subadults and adults are often quite different.

Green and loggerhead hatchlings and small juveniles are known to spend a considerable amount of time cryptically foraging amid offshore mats of floating pelagic vegetation, especially sargassum.

Adult hawksbill turtles are often associated with hard bottom communities, including coral reefs, and other benthic communities, where they feed extensively on sponges, especially two orders of Demospongiae.

Atlantic ridley hatchlings are thought to drift among currents and, if they reach the Atlantic Ocean, to take refuge in sargassum drift lines and other stable areas, where they feed at the surface until attaining a carapace length of about 8 inches (20 cm). At that size ridleys typically become benthic foragers and often migrate to sea grass beds and other inshore habitats, where they prey on crabs and other bottom-dwellers. During the warmer months, juvenile ridley turtles congregate in sounds, inlets, and bays of the mid-Atlantic and northern Gulf coasts; when the water temperatures drop in the fall, most ridleys leave these inshore areas for warmer waters farther south.

Loggerhead turtles that hatch in Florida occupy a variety of oceanic habitats during the course of their life and have been documented as far away from Florida as the Azores and Europe. Pacific loggerheads have recently been confirmed making transpacific migrations. Hatch-lings make their way to floating mats of sargassum, where they typically spend several lost years. Larger juveniles and adults often frequent estuarine habitats, bays, and other lagoonal communities and have been found buried in the mud off the coast of Palm Beach County.

Unlike the hatchlings of other sea turtles, leatherback hatchlings do not appear to congregate in sargassum or other epipelagic debris. Adult leatherback turtles inhabit open seas, bays, and estuarine habitats.

The diet of Florida's five marine turtle species is as diverse as the marine environments they inhabit.

Green turtles are unique among marine turtles in their ability to digest plant material and are the only sea turtles that feed largely on vegetation. Turtle grass ranks high on the list of aquatic vegetation consumed by green turtles. Hatchling green turtles, however, may be quite carnivorous, although adults tend to be largely herbivorous.

Invertebrates make up the bulk of the hawksbill turtle's diet; these turtles are known to prey on highly toxic sponges, which is why their flesh is sometimes poisonous to humans.

Ridley turtles are voracious carnivores. Crabs are often their chief food item, but they also feed on a variety of mollusks, shrimp, crustaceans, fishes, and sea urchins and occasionally consume plant material.

Subadult loggerhead turtles are considered omnivores and feed on a variety of invertebrates, including crustaceans, sponges, sea urchins, and mollusks, as well as marine vegetation. Adult loggerhead turtles are carnivorous and prey largely on a variety of crustaceans, mollusks, and arthropods such as horseshoe crabs. The jaws of the loggerhead turtle are capable of crushing hard-shelled crustaceans and mollusks as well as encrusting organisms that colonize on coral reefs, pilings, and shipwrecks.

Jellyfish, including *Stomolophus, Chrysaora,* and *Aurelia,* are the chief food item of the colossal leatherback turtle, but tunicates (salps and pyrosomas) and cnidarians (siphonophores and medusae) are also consumed. The leatherback's mouth and esophagus are lined with spines that assist the turtle in swallowing slimy jellyfish. The leatherback turtle is capable of diving several thousand feet deep into the abyss of open ocean, and individuals often travel thousands of miles traversing tropical, temperate, and even arctic waters in search of prey. The leatherback turtle, if injured, may issue groans or cries.

Florida ranks first among the states in the number of sea turtles annually nesting within its borders. Most sea turtles exhibit a high degree of nest-site fidelity. Marine turtles often demonstrate remarkable navigational capabilities in returning to their natal beaches and offshore waters to mate and nest. Collectively, sea turtles excavate 40,000–70,000 nests each year on Florida's beaches. In descending order, the species regularly nesting on Florida's beaches are loggerheads, green turtles, leatherbacks (a distant third), and Atlantic ridley and Atlantic hawksbill turtles in extremely small numbers. The high reproductive potential of marine turtles helps offset the high losses of eggs, hatchlings, and subadults to predation. The gender of sea turtles is determined by the temperature of the sand that surrounds the eggs. Cooler temperatures tend to favor males, and warmer temperatures tend to favor females.

Green turtles typically nest on high-energy beaches. In Florida, this species nests nocturnally from May to September (the nesting season varies in other parts of the turtle's range) and may produce as many as six or seven clutches per season. Females usually nest at intervals of 12–14 days. The average clutch size for green turtle nests in Florida is 136 eggs, but clutches may range from 100 to 200 eggs. The incubation time depends largely on the temperature, ranging from 48 to 70 days. The Atlantic green turtle rarely nests in consecutive years and usually nests every third year, with some individuals nesting in two- or four-year cycles.

Hawksbill turtles are believed to mate in shallow waters adjacent to nesting beaches. They usually nest at very low densities on isolated shores, often on small islands. Nesting usually, but not always, takes place during the night, and nests are frequently excavated in areas surrounded by woody vegetation. The primary nesting season for hawksbill turtles is mid-June to mid-November, but nesting has been recorded during every month. A long-term study (1955–1983) of nesting hawksbill turtles at Tortuguero, Costa Rica, revealed that

clutches averaging 158 eggs were deposited by gravid females at intervals averaging 16.4 days. The incubation period at this site varied from 56 to 61 days. Studies of nesting hawksbills in Antigua revealed that females deposited an average of 4.4 clutches, with a clutch range of 70 to 203 eggs (average 147), laid at a mean interval of 14.8 days. The average incubation period at this site was 68 days. It is believed that female hawksbill turtles usually nest at intervals of two to three years.

Unlike other sea turtles, both species of ridley turtles nest during the day. The annual assemblage of nesting Atlantic ridley turtles on the beaches near Rancho Nuevo in Tamaulipas, Mexico, is known as La Arribada ("the arrival"). One of nature's most spectacular events, it typically lasts four days. Turtle biologists believe the nesting emergence at Rancho Nuevo may be stimulated by strong onshore winds. Historically, tens of thousands of Atlantic ridleys emerged from the Gulf of Mexico to nest along this one-mile-long section of beach. A Mexican engineer witnessed, and filmed, an estimated 40,000 Atlantic ridley turtles nesting on this beach during a single day in 1947. Since 1978 there have been fewer than 1,000 nests per season, and in recent years no more than 500–600 females have gathered here. The nesting asssemblages of the related olive ridley turtles on the Pacific beaches of Costa Rica may reach the hundreds of thousands, rivaling the historic numbers of Atlantic ridleys that converged on the beaches of eastern Mexico. Nesting takes place from April through mid-August, but most records of nesting, or attempted nesting, in Florida are from May. Research has revealed that at least 50 percent of adult females nest annually. Average clutch size of Atlantic ridley turtles is just over 100 eggs. The incubation period ranges from 48 to 65 days. Hatchlings typically emerge from the nest at dawn and scurry without delay toward the surf.

The nesting season for loggerhead turtles in Florida begins in late April and continues through September. Gravid females nest 2–7 times per season, at intervals that average 14 days, depositing clutches of 60–180 eggs. In Florida, clutches average 110–120 eggs. Incubation in Florida lasts 50–75 days. Hatchlings usually emerge from the nest at night. They quickly scamper to the sea, where they instinctively paddle well off-shore to reach oceanic gyres that carry them to immense floating mats of sargassum. There they spend several lost years before returning to coastal waters as subadults. The Atlantic loggerhead turtle is not usually an annual nester; typical remigration intervals for this species are 2–4 years.

Recent studies of Atlantic leatherbacks indicate that this species mates prior to or during migration to nesting beaches. Leatherbacks appear to prefer low-energy beaches with an unobstructed offshore approach. Leatherbacks nest nocturnally, typically between March and mid-July. They will nest 1–11 times in a season, averaging 5–7 nests, and renest at intervals of 9–10 days. Leatherbacks typically deposit 80–85 normal yolked eggs at a time and often lay an additional 12–24 smaller yolkless eggs. The eggs hatch after 55–75 days of incubation (averaging 60 days), and hatchlings tend to emerge from the nest in the early

evening. Female leatherback turtles appear to nest most frequently at three-year intervals.

Green turtles grow slowly and are slow to mature. It is believed that Atlantic green turtles reach sexual maturity at 20–50 years of age. The age at which hawksbill turtles become sexually mature is not known, but they may also be slow to mature. Like the hawksbill turtle, the precise age at which wild Atlantic ridleys become sexually mature is unknown; however, they probably reach their mature size after about 11–12 years. Well-fed captive ridleys have reproduced after only 5 years. Loggerhead turtles are relatively late-maturing animals. Studies of loggerheads nesting in Florida and Georgia indicate that turtles from these populations reach maturity as early as 10 years but more often at 20–30 years of age. The maximum life span of the females studied was estimated at 62 years. Unlike loggerheads, leatherback turtles mature relatively quickly. Many turtle biologists believe that leatherbacks may become sexually mature after only 2–3 years.

The mortality rate of hatchlings is extremely high for all sea turtles, but those individuals that do become adults are often long-lived, having few enemies other than humans. Sea turtle eggs and hatchlings are vulnerable to predation from myriad mammalian, bird, reptile, fish, and invertebrate organisms. In Florida and elsewhere in the United States, raccoons represent the single most important natural predator of hatchling sea turtles and eggs. Fish crows are the chief avian predator in Florida. Other animals known to prey on the eggs, hatchlings, or juveniles of one or more species of sea turtles rangewide include gray fox, coyote, coati (*Nasua nasua*), genet cat (*Genetta* spp.), water mongoose (*Ictonyx* spp.), various ameiva lizards (*Ameiva* spp.), mangrove monitor lizard (*Varanus indicus*), ghost crab, land crab (*Cardiosoma guanhumi*), black vulture, turkey vulture, crested caracara, yellow-crowned night-heron, barn owl, frigatebird, jaegers (*Stercorarius* spp.), and a variety of carnivorous fishes including black-tipped reef shark (*Carcharhinus spallanzani*), other shark species, jack fish (*Caranx* spp.), and groupers (*Epinephelus* spp.). On 27 July 1996, Larry Woods, the director of the Marinelife Center of Juno Beach, observed an adult eastern coachwhip snake eating several hatchling loggerhead turtles as they emerged from their nest (personal communication). Eggs and hatchlings still in the nest are also preyed on by ants, fly larvae (*Megaselia scalaris*), locust larvae (family Acrididae), and a variety of fungi and bacteria. Nonnative, introduced species occurring in Florida that are known or suspected predators of hatchling sea turtles include black rats, feral hogs, domestic dogs and cats, and fire ants. On St. John in the U.S. Virgin Islands and in other locations, introduced mongooses (*Herpestes auropunctatus*) have established breeding populations and have become especially problematic predators of sea turtle eggs and hatchlings. Saltwater crocodiles (*Crocodylus porosus*), which can grow to more than 20 feet (6 m), are one of the few predators large enough to take adult sea turtles, and they have been known to kill full-grown leatherback turtles. Other known predators of subadult and adult sea turtles include the killer whale (*Orcinus orca*), jewfish

(*Epinephelus itajara*), tiger shark (*Galeocerdo cuvieri*), jaguar (*Panthera onca*), and tiger (*Panthera tigris*).

CAUSE OF DECLINE, THREATS

Habitat Destruction, Human Encroachment: Widespread high-density development along Florida's coasts (as well as other coasts), accompanied by the placement of beach armoring structures, augmentation or beach nourishment programs, use of heavy construction equipment on beaches to collect discarded refuse, uncontrolled recreational use of beaches, and artificial lighting, comprises the single most significant threat to sea turtles nesting in Florida. Gravid female sea turtles, heavily laden with eggs as they make their nocturnal crawl onto the beaches of Florida to lay those eggs, are commonly blocked from suitable nesting sites by a variety of coastal armoring such as revetments, groins, erosion barriers, and seawalls. Also, formerly suitable nesting habitat is often lost when stabilizing native dune vegetation is removed, precipitating wind erosion. Sand mining has rendered formerly suitable nesting beaches unsuitable in a number of areas.

Dredging and filling activities in channels have contributed to the loss of foraging habitats in nearshore habitats frequented by juvenile sea turtles, including the critically imperiled Atlantic ridley turtle. Additionally, dredges have been known to be directly responsible for sea turtle deaths. It is estimated that dredges kill 50–500 loggerhead turtles in the United States each year.

In Juno Beach (Palm Beach County), despite numerous protests from environmentalists concerned with possible adverse effects to the 1,400 sea turtles that nest there, the construction of a

900-foot (274 m) fishing pier has been approved. Certain measures will be taken to minimize the hazard to sea turtles, including closing the pier at night and reducing the lighting during turtle nesting season.

The destruction or serious degradation of living coral reefs from indiscriminate anchoring or vessel groundings has resulted in the loss of habitat used by sea turtles, particularly hawksbill turtles. In 1988 the illegal anchoring of the 440-foot cruise ship *Windspirit* within the Virgin Islands National Park and Biosphere Reserve destroyed 338 square yards (283 square meters) of pristine coral reef. In October 1990 the anchor chain dropped from the 438-foot cruise ship *Seabourne Pride* on a nearby reef within the same reserve overturned more than 40 large living coral boulders. In February 1985 the 350-foot MV/A *Regina* ran aground within an area designated as critical habitat for hawksbill turtles off the east coast of Mona Island, spilling diesel oil and other harmful contaminants that caused extensive damage to the reef and nearby nesting beaches.

Photopollution: It has been well documented that artificial lighting disorients hatchling sea turtles as they emerge from their nest, often causing them to scamper landward toward the artificial light source instead of seaward. When hatchlings are lured landward, they become easy targets for predators, including raccoons and house cats, and may be struck by automobiles as they attempt to cross roadways. In 1988 alone, the Florida Department of Natural Resources (now a division of the FWC) received reports of more than 10,000 hatchling sea turtles

that had been disoriented by artificial lights. Artificial lighting may also deter nesting females from coming ashore to lay their eggs. Several Florida counties, including Brevard County, have now adopted ordinances restricting beachfront lighting in an attempt to further the reproductive success of sea turtles.

Oil Spills and Water Pollution: Discharges of petroleum products, domestic sewage, and industrial and agricultural runoff containing heavy metals, nutrients, pesticides, herbicides, PCBs, and other harmful substances may adversely affect sea turtles by degrading habitat or reducing their prey base. Research has revealed that sea turtles do not routinely avoid oil spills; therefore large oil spills could prove fatal to sea turtles that attempt to travel through an oil slick and ingest oil or become coated with the sticky substance. Also, small amounts of oil released as tankers and freighters empty their bilges often create tarballs, which are sometimes mistaken as food by sea turtles, including ridley turtles. Sea turtles that ingest tarballs often die from poisoning or from the obstruction of the esophagus.

Driftnets and Other Fishing Devices: Large juvenile and adult sea turtles had few enemies before the arrival of modern humans. Incidental capture and drowning due to entanglement in nets and fishing apparatus are now a serious risk to sea turtles throughout the world, and they are believed to be among the primary sources of sea turtle mortality in many areas. The National Academy of Sciences estimates that in the United States alone, 55,000 sea turtles are drowned each year in shrimp trawls.

Turtle exclusion devices, or TEDs, are designed to protect sea turtles from incidental capture by the U.S. shrimp trawl industry and are now required by federal law. TEDs save marine turtles; however, many shrimpers admittedly do not use the devices because they believe that TEDs reduce the amount of shrimp harvested, thus lessening their paycheck. Before the advent of the TED, many more sea turtles, as well as numerous other sea creatures deemed unmerchantable, were drowned or pulverized by shrimp trawlers. The dead bodies of these animals, referred to as bycatch, often greatly outnumbered the shrimp in volume and were simply shoveled overboard. Law enforcement officials suspect turtles are intentionally killed by some defiant shrimpers who oppose the mandatory use of turtle exclusion devices. Atlantic ridley turtles (juveniles) have been recovered from nets set by fisheries in Chesapeake Bay (Maryland and Virginia) and Long Island Sound (New York). In 1996 the crew of a U.S. Navy Seahawk helicopter flying over a portion of the Indian Ocean about 375 miles west of Bombay, India, spotted 11 leatherback turtles entangled in an abandoned fishing net. A Navy ship was able to save 10 of the 11 turtles from a slow, agonizing death.

Human Consumption and Egg Collecting:
Sea turtles and their eggs have been exploited by humans for centuries, and despite the enactment of laws to protect them, they continue to be harvested for their meat, shells, and eggs in many parts of the world, including Florida. The green sea turtle is generally considered the most palatable of the marine turtles and has long been exploited by humans as a source of food throughout its range. While visiting Nogales, Sonora, a border town just 60 miles south of Tucson, Arizona, in June 1997, the author was astonished to find green turtle soup and green turtle calipee advertised on the menu of a popular tourist restaurant. By 1620 green and other marine turtles had become so scarce in the waters surrounding Bermuda that the country outlawed the taking of sea turtles. Severe declines of green turtles were reported in Florida in the late 1800's. Tortoiseshell ornaments and jewelry crafted from sea turtle shell (primarily hawksbill turtle) are the most frequent contraband brought into the United States and elsewhere from Caribbean countries. Hawksbill turtle shells, which may weigh 100 pounds (45 kg) or more, have reportedly commanded $100 or more per pound. Before 1992, when the United States pressured Japan to curtail the import of hawksbill turtle shells, Japan imported more than 30,000 hawksbill shells annually; about 3,500 were purchased from Cuba alone. It has been reported that the curio trade in stuffed juvenile hawksbill turtles is increasing. Nesting populations of leatherbacks have been extirpated in locations such as the British Virgin Islands and Malaysia by commercial and subsistence turtle meat and egg markets. The illegal take of hawksbill sea turtles and their eggs continues to be commonplace in Puerto Rico, the U.S. Virgin Islands, and in the U.S. Pacific, and enforcement has been minimal. Although commercial interest in leatherback turtle products is negligible, subsistence poaching is heavy by the indigenous people of several tropical countries where leatherbacks

regularly nest. A large percentage (perhaps most) of the leatherback turtles attempting to nest on the beaches of the Dominican Republic and Guyana in recent years have reportedly been slaughtered by locals for food. Subsistence poaching of leatherbacks also takes place in Trinidad, Grenada, and St. Lucia.

Severe Storms: Unfortunately, the beginning of Florida's hurricane season coincides with the tail end of the hatching period for tens of thousands of sea turtles along Florida's coasts. Hurricanes and severe storms destroy marine turtle nests and kill sea turtles, especially hatchlings, each year in many nesting areas, including Florida. Most nesting beaches are located in tropical or subtropical regions where high-energy storms occur regularly. In 1979 Hurricane David destroyed an important green turtle nesting beach on Aves Island, in the eastern Caribbean, sweeping away the beach's deposits of sand. Gradually, the sand was redeposited, and this beach is once again being used by nesting green turtles at prestorm levels.

Other Threats: *Ingestion of plastic bags.* Thousands of sea turtles, especially leatherbacks, are killed each year when they ingest plastics and other trash that they have mistaken for jellyfish or other food items. Two thirds of the leatherback turtles that washed ashore on Long Island, New York, in the summer of 1982 died as a result of ingestion of plastic bags. In France, where eight leatherback turtles washed ashore near Rochelle, seven of the eight had swallowed plastic.

Collisions with boats and ships. Sea turtles of all species are commonly killed by pleasure boats and larger ships. Biologists estimate that 50–500 loggerhead turtles alone die as a result of vessel collisions each year in the United States. Proposals are under way to ban speedboats from the waters of Laganas Bay in Greece, where in 1993 alone, high-speed boats killed nine of the area's estimated 350 nesting loggerhead turtles.

Predation by exotic animals. Free-running cats and dogs pose a threat to hatchling sea turtles and may disturb nesting females. Introduced mongooses have become a serious threat to the eggs and hatchling young of sea turtles in some areas, including St. Croix. On Mona Island, feral hogs have destroyed nearly half of the hawksbill turtle nests in some years. Biologists also believe that many of Florida's hatchling sea turtles die each year from the stings of nonnative fire ants.

Powerplants. Powerplant intake pipes are believed to be responsible for entrapping and sometimes drowning Atlantic ridley, hawksbill, and other sea turtles each year. Turtle biologists estimate that each year 5–50 loggerhead turtles are killed by power plant entrainment in the United States.

Natural Factors. A recent lava flow at Harry K. Brown Beach Park, on the island of Hawaii, destroyed an entire nesting beach used by Pacific hawksbill turtles.

Removal of Offshore Oil Rigs. Offshore oil platforms become artificial reefs that are often frequented by sea turtles, and removal of these platforms has proven deadly for turtles. The use of high explosives to remove platforms has been documented as the cause of many loggerhead and ridley turtle deaths.

Tumors. Grotesque tumors, some as large as a foot in diameter, plague green sea turtles in many parts of the world, including the Florida Keys. Called fibropapilloma, the tumors are caused by a herpes-type virus. It is suspected that this malady is related to pollution. **CURRENT TREND:** *Declining,* all five species. It should be noted that most population estimates involving sea turtles are based on counts of adult nesting females. Less information is available pertaining to the abundance and trend of juvenile turtles and adult males.

The Atlantic ridley turtle is the most endangered sea turtle and one of the world's most endangered animals. The hawksbill turtle is considered the second most endangered sea turtle. Populations of loggerhead turtles appear to be on the decline globally; Florida's population of nesting loggerheads, however, may be stable. In 1982 the world's population of nesting leatherback turtles was 115,000; in 1995 it had dwindled to an estimated 20,000–30,000 individuals.

Bluetail Mole Skink

Eumeces egregius lividus
FAMILY SCINCIDAE; Order Squamata, Suborder Sauria

LISTED STATUS
FWC: Threatened, listed 1976
USF&WS: Threatened, listed 1987

Description: Mole skinks are smooth, slender, and shiny lizards with well-developed but diminutive legs, which are not used when burrowing (more like swimming) in the sugar sands of the Florida scrub ecosystems they inhabit. Adults are 3.5–6.5 inches (9–16.5 cm) in length, with a maximum head and body length of 2.4 inches (6.2 cm). Hatchlings are 1.9–2.3 inches (4.8–6 cm) long. The ground color of *Eumeces egregius lividus* is brown and is often darker than other subspecies. There are two dorsal stripes that widen posteriorly and sometimes separate toward the tail. The tail of juveniles and young adults is often a vivid blue. Some older individuals retain the blue tail, but in others the tail becomes duller and pinkish and may show no trace of blue at all. Skinks with rejuvenated tails, even younger skinks like the specimen pictured in this book, display little or no blue coloration. Before the discovery of this subspecies, mole skinks were often referred to as red-tailed skinks, as the tail in all other races is usually some shade of red, orange, or pink. Fortunately, these skinks were renamed mole skinks, or this subspecies would be called the bluetail red-tailed skink. The tail, which may constitute more than half the total length, is easily broken off. Males, during the winter breeding season, often show a glistening orange on their sides. There are seven upper labials on each side of the head.

Distribution: Mole skinks, of which there are five subspecies, are restricted to the southeastern United States. All but one subspecies are endemic to Florida. Their range includes much of the southern two thirds of Georgia, portions of central and southern Alabama, and most of Florida, including the Panhandle, the Keys, and the Dry Tortugas. The range of the bluetail mole skink is limited to the Lake Wales Ridge of Polk, Highlands, and the extreme northwest corner of Osceola counties in Central Florida. This race was first discovered by Robert H. Mount in 1960.

Biology: The bluetail mole skink is a true habitat specialist. Although this race is occasionally encountered in sandhill habitats, it is usually analogous with various Florida scrub associations, where it swims through the well-drained sugar-like sands. Other mole skink subspecies regularly inhabit sandhill communities, however. This species and the sand skink are among the most fossorial species of lizards and have developed their own adaptations comparable to those of reptiles found in dune areas of desert regions. Their optimum scrub habitat has an open canopy, areas of exposed loose sand free of root structures, and abundant surface litter. This species often remains 1–2 inches (2.5–5 cm) beneath the surface of the sandy substrate, under the cover of logs, pine needles, saw palmetto fronds, and man-made cover such as plywood, tin, and discarded debris. It sometimes occurs in the sand mounds of gopher tortoises, pocket gophers, and scarab beetles. Virtually all of the known bluetail mole skink habitat occurs at elevations above 100 feet (30 m).

This species, like other skinks, is a diurnal, alert lizard, quick to flee from the slightest perceived threat. Bluetails elude predation by quickly disappearing into the surrounding loose sand of their scrub ecosystem. Though much of their life is spent just beneath the surface, bluetails become somewhat more active on the surface in the autumn. The bluetail is generally considered rare throughout its range, with herpetologists finding an average of 1 bluetail for every 20 sand skinks encountered.

Within its habitat, this subspecies is believed to be somewhat gregarious. Mating takes place in the late winter. Males apparently recognize females chiefly by scent. A pair may copulate for nearly an hour and are generally oblivious to their surroundings and very tolerant of disturbance during this time. The 3–7 whitish eggs, which measure approximately 1.1 cm by 0.7 cm, are laid at a depth of several inches in the sand. The female guards the eggs during incubation and may turn the eggs as they develop.

A brooding female has been observed fiercely biting the head of an encroaching crowned snake. The eggs hatch after 31–51 days. It is typical for the hatchlings to remain very still for several hours, breathing deeply. It is believed that this race sexually matures within its first year and regularly breeds during the first autumn or winter. Mole skinks prey on a number of arthropods, including spiders, crickets, and cockroaches. They typically forage during the morning or late afternoon and often feed on surface-dwelling prey (unlike sand skinks). Known predators of mole skinks include scarlet kingsnakes, racers, coachwhip snakes, and pygmy rattlesnakes; they are also probably consumed by other animals including scrub-jays, loggerhead shrikes, glass lizards, scarlet snakes, short-tailed snakes, crowned snakes, southern ring-necked snakes, coral snakes, and several other fossorial snakes.

CAUSE OF DECLINE, THREATS

Habitat Destruction: More than 80 percent of the Florida scrub within the bluetail mole skink's range has been lost to citrus cultivation and development. The remaining tracts of suitable habitat are a series of disjunct, often small remnants of scrub surrounded by human encroachment. This subspecies is often scarce even in optimum, pristine habitat. The continued destruction and fragmentation of this endemic ecosystem may unfortunately result in the extinction of the bluetail mole skink, sand skink, Florida scrub lizard, Florida scrub-jay, Florida mouse, and a multitude of endemic invertebrates and plants. The area of sand pine scrub near Sebring (Highlands County) where the author found the bluetail mole skink pictured in this book is surrounded by a residential community and is itself slated for development.

CURRENT TREND: *Declining.*

Sand Skink

Neoseps reynoldsi

FAMILY SCINCIDAE; Order Squamata, Suborder Sauria

LISTED STATUS

FWC: Threatened, listed 1975

USF&WS: Threatened, listed 1987

Description: The sand skink is a small, slender, serpentine, smooth-scaled lizard, with adults averaging 4–5 inches (10–13 cm) in total length. The tail may be more than half the length of the lizard, measuring as long as 2.5 inches (6.5 cm). Hatchlings are approximately 1 inch (2.5 cm) long. Many of the sand skink's specialized physical characteristics are directly related to survival in the fine sands of Florida scrub habitats. The legs are greatly reduced in size, particularly the front legs, and may not be visible when the skink is burrowing (referred to as swimming) through the fine sand where it abounds. There are two toes on the rear legs; the front legs have only one toe. Lateral grooves on each side of this lizard accommodate the folded forelegs when it swims through the sand. The eyes are tiny, and there are no external ear openings. The lower eyelid contains a transparent window that allows the lizard to see when its eyelids are closed.

The snout is chisel-shaped, and the lower jaw is countersunk into the upper jaw. The belly is somewhat concave. The color may vary from a shiny white to gray to tan. There is usually a series of small, dark brown or black spots forming faint longitudinal stripes on the skink's back. Also usually present is a dark stripe on each side of the head.

Distribution: The range of the sand skink is almost entirely limited to segments of the high, dry inland peninsula scrub of Central Florida from Marion County south through portions of Lake, Orange, Osceola, Polk, and Highlands counties. Nearly all of the localities where *Neoseps* occurs are above 100 feet (30 m) in elevation. The species apparently reaches its greatest densities within suitable habitat of the Lake Wales Ridge and the Winter Haven Ridge in Polk and Highlands counties. It is relatively rare in the northern portion of its range, Lake and Marion counties. The type locality is Fruitland Park in Lake County. Efforts have been made to locate sand skinks on the Bombing Range, a ridge east of Avon Park, but have so far been unsuccessful. It is also apparently absent from the Brooksville, Lakeland, Lake Henry, and Orlando ridges.

Biology: The sand skink occurs in several xeric scrub and high pine communities along the elevated Central Florida Ridge, including oak scrub, sand pine scrub, scrubby flatwoods, and scrub–high pine ecotones. It tends to be most abundant in the rosemary balds of the southern Lake Wales Ridge in Highlands County.

Characteristic plants of sand skink habitat include rosemary (*Ceratiola ericoides*), Archbold oak (*Quercus inopina*), sand live oak (*Q. geminata*), Chapman's oak (*Q. chapmanii*), scrub palmetto (*Sabal etonia*), saw palmetto, and prickly pear cactus (*Opuntia humifusa*). It is usually absent from sandhill communities, except in some oak barrens where wiregrass has been eliminated. Important features of optimum sand skink habitat are the presence of loose sugar sand patches that are devoid of dense root systems, and a relatively open canopy.

This Florida endemic has no known close relatives, although there are several unrelated Old World lizards that have evolved similar adaptations to an environment of loose sand. It has evolved to be the most fossorial lizard in North America, even more so than lizards from the true deserts of the western United States. It is the lizard equivalent of the banded sand snake (*Chilomeniscus cinctus*) of the Sonoran Desert. The sand skink usually remains 1–3 inches (2.5–7.5 cm) below the surface in patches of loose sand, often under the cover of logs, palmetto fronds, or even man-made cover. The author has found this lizard more frequently under cover where colonies of small ants were present. When a sand skink perceives a threat, it quickly vanishes into the sand using a snakelike movement to propel itself, referred to as sand swimming. It is not uncommon to find sand skinks in proximity to mole skinks.

The sand skink is believed to mate in March and April. The species is oviparous; the female lays two grayish white eggs measuring approximately 1.2 cm by 0.5 cm, in sand under the cover of logs in May or June. The eggs generally hatch in July. Sand skinks are probably sexually mature after one year. These diurnal

lizards feed mainly on termites, beetle and lepidopteran larvae, ant lions, roaches, and small spiders. They have been known to feign death when handled, but if turned upside down, the lizard will immediately right itself. Predators are known to include larger southeastern five-lined skinks and the eastern coachwhip snake. Crowned snakes, other small snakes, and scrub-jays may also prey on sand skinks.

CAUSE OF DECLINE, THREATS

Habitat Destruction and Fragmentation: Sand skinks may be locally common, even abundant in suitable habitat. The problem is that so little suitable habitat remains. Inland peninsular scrub is the most endangered of Florida's ecosystems. Today, no more than 10–20 percent of the original Lake Wales Ridge scrub survives. The ridges of fine, well-drained sand that this species depends on also happen to be ideal for growing oranges and building homes. Sand skinks perish where scrub is converted to citrus groves or where development alters the loose, sandy substrate.

CURRENT TREND: *Declining.*

Atlantic Salt Marsh Snake

Nerodia clarki taeniata
FAMILY COLUBRIDAE; Order Squamata, Suborder Serpentes

LISTED STATUS

FWC: Threatened, listed 1975 (endangered 1975–1985)

USF&WS: Threatened, listed 1977

Description: The Atlantic salt marsh snake was first described by E. D. Cope in 1895. Salt marsh snakes (*Nerodia clarki*), are members of the genus *Nerodia*, collectively known as water snakes. Like other water snakes, the salt marsh snakes have keeled scales, a divided anal plate, a fairly stout body (though slimmer than other *Nerodia*), and a head that is distinct from the body.

Atlantic salt marsh snake are relatively small water snakes, attaining a maximum length of about 32 inches (82 cm), with most adult specimens measuring less than 24 inches (61 cm). The dorsal ground color is typically pale olive; the belly is black and has a median row of broad yellow or cream-colored spots. This race is partially striped, with dark longitudinal stripes present on the anterior portion of the body. In pure form, the striping usually accounts for more than 30 percent of the body length, with the stripes merging into a series of dark blotches posteriorly.

The taxonomic status of this race has been and remains controversial. When first listed, the Atlantic salt marsh snake was considered a subspecies of *Nerodia fasciata,* a freshwater inhabitant represented in Florida by *N. f. pictiventris* (the Florida banded water snake), and was known as *N. f. taeniata.* Extensive electrophoretic analysis of the *N. fasciata– N. clarki* complex by R. Lawson et al. in 1991 found no genetic introgression between salt marsh snakes and banded water snakes; the researchers concluded that salt marsh snakes are a distinct species. Furthermore, the studies revealed that the three recognized subspecies of salt marsh snakes are electrophoretically indistinguishable from one another.

The Atlantic salt marsh snake is one of three recognized subspecies of salt marsh snake, all of which occur in Florida. The closely related mangrove salt marsh snake (*N. clarki compressicauda*) usually has red pigmentation and is sometimes almost uniformly reddish or orange. Atlantic salt marsh snakes typically lack red pigmentation, although nearly 30 percent of specimens from near the Volusia-Brevard county line (and farther south into Indian River County) exhibit reddish pigmentation. The region where these aberrant morphs occur represents the southernmost periphery of the *N. c. taeniata* range and northernmost periphery of the *N. c. compressicauda* range. These animals are believed to occur within a zone of intergradation and are intermediates between the two subspecies. Salt marsh snakes can be distinguished from Florida banded water snakes by counting the dorsal scale rows at midbody; salt marsh snakes have 21 rows, and banded water snakes typically have 23. Also, banded water snakes are completely banded, and salt marsh snakes are at least partially striped.

Distribution: In pure form, the Atlantic salt marsh snake is apparently restricted to a narrow coastal strip of Volusia County from the area of the Halifax River in the north to the area of Indian River Lagoon in southern Volusia County. The precise southernmost boundary is difficult to determine because of the zone of intergradation with the mangrove salt marsh snake in Brevard County and perhaps northern Indian River County.

The mangrove salt marsh snake occurs in saline habitats along the Atlantic and Gulf coasts of central and southern Florida and on the north coast of Cuba. On Florida's Atlantic Coast, the range of the mangrove salt marsh snake extends northward to the southernmost boundaries of the range of the Atlantic salt marsh snake near the Brevard-Volusia county line, where the two subspecies intergrade. The Gulf salt marsh snake (*Nerodia c. clarki*) occurs in pure form in suitable habitat along the Gulf Coast from the Cedar Keys area to the vicinity of Corpus Christi, Texas.

Biology: True to its name, the Atlantic salt marsh snake is a denizen of salt marshes and mangrove swamps that vary in salinity from brackish to full-strength seawater. They are usually found in and along tidal creeks, ditches, and pools associated with glassworts and salt grass. Black mangroves are often present but rarely dominant. Farther south, where mangroves are more dominant, the mangrove salt marsh snake replaces the Atlantic salt marsh snake.

This subspecies feeds primarily on small fish that are trapped in pools by outgoing tides. It generally forages along tidal areas just above the tide line. Unlike most snakes adapted to life in salt water, salt marsh snakes do not possess salt glands that allow them to excrete excess salts. Salt marsh snakes do, however, exhibit low dehydration rates in seawater, especially compared with related fresh-water species. Salt marsh snakes refuse to drink seawater but readily exploit freshwater sources such as rain or dew. This race is chiefly nocturnal and utilizes fiddler crab burrows and dense vegetation as cover by day. Environmental factors such as tidal cycles may trigger occasional diurnal activity.

Little is known about the breeding habits and reproductive patterns of this ovoviviparous species. Unlike related freshwater inhabitants occurring nearby

(*N. fasciata, N. taxispilota,* and *N. flori-dana*), which bear 50 or more young, salt marsh snakes have relatively low fecundity. Captive females produced litters of 9 young in August and 3 young in October.

CAUSE OF DECLINE, THREATS

Habitat Destruction: Intense development of Volusia County's coastline, coupled with the limited range and the narrow habitat requirements of this snake, has resulted in population declines. Habitat has been degraded by dredge-and-fill projects, draining of wetlands, mosquito ditching, diking, placement of water control structures, and construction of piers and marinas.

Hybridization: The alteration of the natural saline habitat historically occupied by the Atlantic salt marsh snake may result in the disruption of reproductive isolating mechanisms, which can lead to hybridization with the larger Florida banded water snake, potentially swamping the gene pool of this threatened subspecies.

Rising Sea Level: Though not an immediate threat, expected sea level rises may eventually change coastal vegetative patterns and render habitat that currently supports this subspecies unsuitable.

CURRENT TREND: *Declining.*

Key Ring-necked Snake

Diadophis punctatus acricus
FAMILY COLUBRIDAE; Order Squamata, Suborder Serpentes

LISTED STATUS

FWC: Threatened, listed 1975
USF&WS: Species of management concern

Description: This diminutive subspecies of the ring-necked snake is the smallest of all the ringnecks, with a record length of only 11.7 inches (29.8 cm). The average adult length is between 8.6 and 10.3 inches (22–26 cm). Hatchlings are 3–4.5 inches (7.7–11.5 cm) long. The most distinctive characteristic of this form is that it usually lacks the neck ring found on the typical mainland ringneck. The scientific name *acricus* means "without a collar." Some specimens do bear a neck ring, although it is usually subdued and not complete. The only other American ringneck subspecies that commonly lacks a neck ring is the much larger regal ring-necked snake (*Diadophis punctatus regalis*) of the western United States. The dorsal color is slate gray, usually darkening toward the head. The ventral color is similar to the typical peninsular Florida morph in being yellow anteriorly and becoming bright orange posteriorly, with a center row of prominent black half-moons. The chin and labials are less strongly spotted than in the mainland subspecies. The scales are smooth; the anal plate is divided.

Distribution: This form is restricted to Big Pine Key and several adjacent Lower Keys. Until recently, it had not been found on any key other than Big Pine. In the late 1980's and early 1990's specimens were encountered on Little Torch and Middle Torch Key. On 19 September 1995, the author found an 8-inch (20.5 cm) Key ring-necked snake on No Name Key within Key Deer National Wildlife Refuge, which was accepted as a valid range extension for the subspecies. As a child in 1966 or 1967, the author accompanied his father on a reptile collecting trip to the Lower Keys for the Baltimore Zoo, where he found another Key ringneck under some debris on Big Pine. The subspecies was first described in 1966 by Dennis Paulson. The southern ring-necked snake (*D. punctatus punctatus*) does not occur in the Lower Keys, although it is quite common on portions of Key Largo.

Biology: This subspecies is most commonly encountered in rockland pinelands with exposed limestone, which is characteristic of much of Big Pine Key. It also occurs with some regularity at the ecotones of tropical hardwood hammocks. Like other ringnecks, this form spends much of its time under cover, ranging from pine needles to wood piles in suburban back yards. They are generally crepuscular and somewhat nocturnal and have been observed on the surface and active at dusk and after dark. They have been known to feed on Florida reef geckos (*Sphaerodactylus notatus*) and their tails, and on greenhouse frogs (*Eleutherodactylus planirostris*). Ground skinks and mole skinks (*Eumeces egregius egregius*) are probably also preyed on. Ring-necked snakes have enlarged (but not grooved) rear teeth, which assist in delivering a mild venom into prey. They are, however, harmless to humans and never attempt to bite. Natural predators of this form include black racers and raccoons (*Procyon lotor auspicatus*). When threatened, they have a tendency to twist their tail, displaying the bright red undersurface to a potential predator, which should interpret red as a danger color. Like other ringnecks, this subspecies is oviparous.

CAUSE OF DECLINE, THREATS

Habitat Destruction: Destruction and fragmentation of habitat is by far the most serious threat to this rare animal.

Within a very short time, Big Pine Key and most of the Lower Keys have been transformed from remote, nearly inaccessible islands to populated tourist hot spots with only fragmented parcels of suitable habitat. It is estimated that fewer than 5,000 Key ring-necked snakes exist in the wild. The loss of just several acres of suitable habitat could destroy a hundred or so of these fossorial animals without one ever being seen.

Other Threats: Automobiles and domestic dogs and cats certainly take their toll on this animal as well. Poaching and collection are probably not critical factors because ringnecks have little commercial value in the pet trade.

CURRENT TREND: *Decreasing.*

Eastern Indigo Snake

Drymarchon corais couperi
FAMILY COLUBRIDAE; Order Squamata, Suborder Serpentes

LISTED STATUS
FWC: Threatened, listed 1971
USF&WS: Threatened, listed 1978

Description: The majestic eastern indigo is the largest snake found in the United States; the longest recorded specimen measured 103.5 inches (262.9 cm). In recent years, snakes exceeding 7.5 feet are increasingly rare. Occasional giants are still encountered in the wild, however. Adults are typically 5–6.5 feet (152–198 cm) in length and 2–3 inches (5.1–7.6 cm) in girth. Males often attain a greater length and mass than females. Noticeably large, glossy, iridescent black or bluish black scales cover nearly all of the snake's body with the exception of the throat, chin, and side of head, which is often bright red or orange-red. Florida Keys populations often lack the red throat coloration, and animals from the Gulf Hammock area (rarely elsewhere) may have a white throat. The scales are generally smooth, although large males sometimes have several rows of weakly keeled middorsal scales. The anal plate is undivided. Hatchlings are 17–24 inches (43.2–61 cm) and resemble adults.

Distribution: The indigo snakes, or cribos, comprise a total of eight subspecies of the species *Drymarchon corais.* They range sporadically from the southeastern United States to northern Argentina. The ranges of the two subspecies that occur in the United States, this race and the Texas indigo (*D. c. erebennus*), are separated by more than 500 land miles. The eastern indigo is now largely restricted to Florida and southeastern Georgia, although isolated populations may occur in Alabama and Mississippi. This species formerly occurred in extreme southeastern South Carolina but is now believed to be extirpated there. Indigo snakes reach their greatest abundance in peninsular Florida and are fairly common on some of the Upper and Lower Florida Keys.

Biology: The eastern indigo snake is for the most part a habitat generalist, although it frequents some habitats more than others. In southern Florida it is most common in tropical hardwood hammock communities but also occurs in or near mangrove swamps, pinelands, and even agricultural lands where not harassed. In the northern peninsula and portions of the Panhandle it is most often associated with sandhill communities but also occurs regularly in pine flatwoods, scrub, coastal strand ecosystems, and also larger orange groves. Indigo snakes require large tracts of unsettled lands, with individuals often roaming well over 100 acres (40 ha) during spring and summer and utilizing several habitat types. They regularly forage at the periphery of marshes and other riparian areas where water snakes and rodents are plentiful. Eastern indigo snakes are well known for using gopher tortoise burrows as refuges from the scorching heat of Florida summers, fire, and for hibernacula. Recent studies in southern Georgia revealed that tortoise burrows constituted 94 percent of hibernacula used by indigo snakes. Gopher tortoise populations have been severely reduced in some areas, which may adversely affect indigo snake populations over time. In coastal areas of southern Florida, indigos have been documented using land crab burrows in place of tortoise burrows.

Indigo snakes are strictly diurnal and are most active in the morning. For their size, these alert, racerlike snakes are surprisingly fast. Their speed and agility enable them to capture prey, which includes nearly any animal they are able to catch, subdue, and swallow. Indigos consume rats, rabbits, snakes, amphibians, eggs, birds, turtles, and even baby alligators. Venomous snakes are sometimes eaten, and indigos are believed to be at least partially immune to the venom of native pit vipers. Indigo snakes are not constrictors; they feed like garter snakes and racers, by overpowering prey and swallowing it alive. When threatened, eastern indigos often flatten the neck vertically (unlike a cobra) and occasionally hiss.

Breeding in the wild has been observed between November and April. Between 5 and 10 large leathery eggs 2.5–3.5 inches (6.4–8.9 cm) long are laid in May or June.

After 70–85 days, the young hatch. Female indigo snakes may have the ability to retain fertile spermatozoa in the genital tract for long periods of time. In 1941 a snake collector purchased a female indigo snake that was then isolated for over four years, after which the snake laid five eggs, one of which was fertile. Recently, serious consideration has been given to the possibility of unisexual reproduction in this species and others (including the timber rattlesnake, *Crotalus horridus*).

CAUSE OF DECLINE, THREATS

Habitat Destruction: Destruction of suitable habitat rangewide and loss of winter refuges in central and northern Florida are significant threats. Large parcels of suitable habitat are required to sustain viable populations. This tropical species depends on subterranean refuges (primarily gopher tortoise burrows and stump holes) to escape extreme temperatures in many areas. Indigos have now disappeared from many areas that only a decade ago supported fair numbers, and Florida's continued, phenomenal growth will no doubt continue that trend.

Automobile Collisions: Road mortality probably ranks as the second most prominent threat to this species in Florida. Every year, more roads are constructed, causing further incursions into wilder areas and taking a significant toll on indigos. Being a large serpent, the indigo is probably hit and killed intentionally on occasion. The largest specimen encountered by the author was a roadkill 7 feet 7 inches long that could be seen from half a mile away.

Gassing of Burrows: Unscrupulous individuals sometimes gas gopher tortoise burrows in quest of eastern diamondback rattlesnakes, which also take shelter in the burrows. Such gassing often kills resident indigos and gopher tortoises. This practice, formerly a common technique employed by rattlesnake collectors seeking snakes for the skin trade, is now a criminal offense in Florida (39-25.002 in the Florida Administrative Code) but is still perpetrated by some individuals.

Illegal Collection: Although the commercial trade in this species has diminished considerably since the indigo became a federally threatened species in 1978, it remains a prized species in the growing illicit reptile market. The downside of listing a collectible species as threatened or endangered is that it often causes the black market prices of the animal to increase, thus increasing the incentive to collect the species illegally. Many of Florida's indigo snakes are taken each year and sold in the illicit pet trade. Illegally collected indigo snakes have been seized in nearly every state, and many are shipped to foreign collectors.

Some have advocated the captive breeding of eastern indigo snakes to reduce their black market value and potentially reduce the collection of wild indigos. Proponents of this concept suggest that a few carefully selected individuals be allowed to participate in a tightly controlled captive propagation program, similar to the program for American alligators. Although the theory behind the concept is sound, a proposal of this type would have to be developed with utmost care to avoid being exploited by unethical profit-motivated individuals. Loopholes in captive breeding exemptions have become legal headaches for several states.

Other Threats: Predation by domestic dogs and outright killing by humans take a toll on this species.
CURRENT TREND: *Declining.*

Short-tailed Snake
Stilosoma extenuatum
FAMILY COLUBRIDAE; Order Squamata, Suborder Serpentes
LISTED STATUS
FWC: Threatened, listed 1979 (endangered 1975–1978)
USF&WS: Species of management concern
Description: These small, seldom-seen snakes are usually 14–20 inches (36–51 cm) long; the longest recorded specimen is 25.75 inches (65.4 cm). The cylindrical body is extremely slender. The scales are smooth and in 19 rows. The snake is named for its exceptionally short tail, which accounts for only 7–10 percent of the total length. The anal plate is undivided. The short, blunt head is not distinct from the body, and it is somewhat similar to that of a kingsnake (*Lampropeltis*). The ground color is usually some shade of gray. A series of 50–80 small, irregular, dark brown or black dorsal blotches adorn the back and tail; 10–14 are on the tail. These blotches are often separated with lighter yellow, orange, or brick-red interspaces, which tend to be more pronounced in the mid-dorsal area than toward the head. A less frequently encountered gray phase lacks the colored interspaces and has a more subdued overall coloration. The belly is white with bold dark brown or black blotches, which often extend onto the snake's sides. Lateral, chin, and head scales are finely speckled with black. The

head is marked dorsally with a dark triangular blotch. Juveniles resemble adults. Formerly, two or three subspecies were recognized based largely on minor differences in scalation; however, this species is now generally considered monotypic (with only a single species in its genus). That in itself makes the species scientifically noteworthy and unique within Florida's diverse herpetofauna.

Distribution: The short-tailed snake is unique among Florida snakes in that the entire genus, with but a single known species, is endemic to the state. Populations appear to be limited to an area of north-central, central, and south-central peninsular Florida roughly 20–80 miles by about 160 miles. Short-tailed snakes have been encountered from Suwannee and Columbia counties in northern Florida south to Hillsborough and Pinellas counties on the Gulf Coast and southern Highlands County on the Lake Wales Ridge, and as far east as Seminole County. Its occurrence within the range outlined is very localized. The type locality is Lake Kerr in Marion County.

Biology: The short-tailed snake is a species of upland habitats, particularly sandhill ecosystems and, to a lesser degree, Florida scrub biotas. Optimum habitat appears to be xeric, well-drained, sandy, longleaf pine–turkey oak woodlands. It is occasionally encountered in adjacent habitats. In 1940 renowned herpetologist Archie Carr reported specimens dug out of sphagnum beds close to typical high pine-oak habitat.

This species is an accomplished burrower that only rarely ventures out on the surface. A person could search in ideal habitat for decades, perhaps a lifetime, before finding a short-tailed snake. You are more likely to stumble upon one in the middle of the path while walking your dog. Biologists spent thousands of hours in the field during the construction of the Cross Florida Barge Canal, which bisects a considerable portion of short-tailed snake habitat, yet only five of the snakes were discovered. They are seldom found under logs, boards, or other cover. Records indicate surface activity peaks in April and October. The only short-tailed snake ever encountered by the author was in mid-October 1982 at Wekiwa Springs State Park on the border between Seminole and Orange counties in characteristic sandhill habitat.

This ophiophagus snake effectively swims through loose sand, where it searches for its favorite prey, the crowned snake (*Tantilla relicta*). Though *Tantilla* is apparently the chief prey item, studies of captive short-tailed snakes by John Rossi reveal that other small snakes are readily taken. Rossi's captives consumed ring-necked snakes, brown snakes and red-bellied snakes (*Storeria*), pine woods snakes (*Rhadinaea flavilata*), rough earth snakes (*Virginia striatula*), and black swamp snakes (*Seminatrix*). Snakes of less than 7 inches (18 cm) are readily taken by adult short-tailed snakes. Ground skinks and other lizards are reportedly taken only rarely. This snake's constricting maneuvers are apparently used more to secure prey than to kill it. Predators are likely to include eastern coral snakes, kingsnakes, feral hogs, and armadillos. Little is known of the breeding habits and reproduction of this oviparous species. A wild-caught neonate bearing an umbilical scar measured 7.5 inches (19 cm). Most individuals are high-strung, vibrating the tail, emitting sneezelike hisses, and striking repeatedly if threatened.

DNA comparisons indicate that this species is related to the kingsnakes, apparently most closely to the mole king-snake (*Lampropeltis calligaster rhombo-maculata*), which it keenly resembles. The short-tailed snake also resembles the much stouter dusky pygmy rattlesnake, as does the southern hog-nosed snake. The resemblance can be astonishing; the pygmy rattlesnake, like the short-tailed and southern hog-nosed snakes, also has two distinct color phases, one with red-dish interspaces between the dorsal blotches and one without. It has been suggested that this similarity is a form of mimicry, possibly affording the two species some degree of protection from predators. The mottled pattern and colors of this cryptic species certainly hinder its detection in the leaf litter and sandy areas it inhabits.

CAUSE OF DECLINE, THREATS

Habitat Destruction: Competition for habitat with humans is the principal threat to this species. The preferred habi-tat of the short-tailed snake (high, dry, well-drained woodlands) is also favored by humans for development and citrus production. Certain forestry practices, including clear-cutting, may be detri-mental to the species as well. Longleaf pines have been totally eradicated from many of Florida's sandhill ecosystems, substantially altering the habitats as a result. Many tracts of remaining suitable habitat will be lost to development by the time this book hits the shelves.

CURRENT TREND: *Declining.*

Rimrock Crowned Snake
Tantilla oolitica
FAMILY COLUBRIDAE; Order Squamata, Suborder Serpentes

LISTED STATUS

FWC: Threatened, listed 1975

USF&WS: Species of management concern

Description: The rimrock crowned snake is one of three species of tiny burrowing snakes of the genus *Tantilla* occurring in Florida. This species is so small and secretive that most Floridians who live within its range, even life-long residents, are not acquainted with it. Adults tend to be 6–9 inches (15–23 cm) in length; the record is a mere 11.5 inches (29.2 cm). This thin, smooth-scaled serpent is tan, light brown, or pinkish above, with a white belly. The top of the head is crowned with black from the tip of the snout to the neck. Upper Keys animals may have a broken crown separated by a pale neck ring, creating a collar resem-bling that of the southeastern crowned snake (*Tantilla coronata*). The chin is black. There are 15 scale rows, and the anal plate is divided. This species pos-sesses two enlarged basal hooks on the hemipenes; all other peninsular Florida species have one. It also generally has a higher ventral scale count and fewer sub-caudal scales than other peninsula races. Hatchlings are approximately 3 inches (7.5 cm) long.

Distribution: One of approximately 50 species of petite rear-fanged snakes of the genus *Tantilla* ranging from Virginia and California to northern Argentina. These snakes are called crowned snakes, black-headed snakes, flat-headed snakes, and black-hooded snakes. The rimrock crowned snake, or Miami black-headed snake, has the most restricted range of any *Tantilla* species. This rarely encountered snake was not described or named until 1966. Its known range is restricted to a narrow coastal strip (about 80 by 20 miles) of oolitic limestone in extreme southeastern Florida from northern Dade County south to Monroe County's upper Matecumbe and Grassy keys.

The range of the coastal dunes crowned snake (*Tantilla relicta pamlica*) extends south along Florida's Atlantic Coast to within 30 miles of the range of the rimrock crowned snake; however, the rimrock appears to be morphologically more akin to the southeastern crowned snake, whose range is separated by nearly 400 miles.

Areas containing suitable habitat for this species within its historic range include the 2,000-acre Key Largo Hammocks State Botanical Site, portions of John Pennekamp Coral Reef State Park, 6,800-acre Crocodile Lakes National Wildlife Refuge, 958-acre Oleta River State Recreation Area, 5-acre Barnacle State Historic Site, and 410-acre Cape Florida State Recreation Area. Elliott Key in Biscayne National Park and Homestead Air Force Base also contain suitable habitat. Dade County manages several small tracts of protected land where *Tantilla oolitica* has been documented, or probably does occur, including the Charles Deering Estate (400 acres that include the Addison Hammock), Snapper Creek Preserve (640 acres), Matheson Hammock (630 acres), Navy Wells (353 acres), Larry and Penny Thompson Park (200 acres), Camp Owaissa Bower (110 acres), Tamiami Pineland Preserve (92 acres), Seminole Wayside Park (20 acres), Bill Sadowski Park (29 acres that include

Old Cutler Hammock), Fuchs (29 acres), Castellow (62 acres).

Biology: The rimrock crowned snake has been encountered in both south Florida rockland communities: tropical pinelands dominated by south Florida slash pine and tropical hardwood hammocks. The two habitats are characteristic (historically) of eastern Dade County's rimrock ridge. The Upper Keys locations where this species has been found consist mainly of tropical hammock. Both rockland habitats have sandy soil and exposed oolitic limestone protruding from the earth. Specimens have also been found in disturbed areas (pastures, vacant lots). Only about 35 specimens have been found to date.

This species is very reticent in nature and rarely observed. Nocturnal or crepuscular, crowned snakes remain concealed beneath palm fronds, rotting logs, pieces of limestone, or discarded rubbish during the day, venturing forth at night in search of centipedes, insect larvae, and other arachnids and insects.

Like other *Tantilla* species, this snake is mildly venomous (harmless to humans) and rear-fanged. It grasps its prey firmly and delivers its paralyzing venom with the aid of grooved fangs at the rear of its upper jaw. Predators presumably include coral snakes, scarlet king snakes, scarlet snakes, owls, large spiders, various rodents, and raccoons. It should be noted that one species of centipede (*Scolopendra atlternans*) commonly encountered on Key Largo attains a length of nearly 8 inches (20 cm) and could easily overpower and eat even the largest crowned snake.

These oviparous snakes are believed to reach sexual maturity after approximately three years. Mating takes place in early spring; one to three lilliputian oval eggs are laid in early summer under several inches of moist substrate.

CAUSE OF DECLINE, THREATS

Habitat Destruction: Although records of this diminutive snake are exceptionally scarce, it is not necessarily rare in suitable habitat. It is, however, quite vulnerable to extinction because its extremely limited range lies in the heart of the greater Miami megalopolis, one of Florida's most populated regions. Areas of remaining habitat are highly prized by real estate developers. Nearly all of the original rockland pine forest and tropical hardwood hammock within its range were destroyed long ago. The type locality for this species is now the site of a supermarket. Fortunately, unlike larger reptiles (such as indigo snakes and American crocodiles) that require sizable tracts of undisturbed habitat, this species has a small home range and can probably tolerate a moderate amount of habitat alteration.

Other Threats: Predation from introduced animals, particularly black rats and domestic cats, may threaten populations locally.

CURRENT TREND: *Declining.*

Lower Keys Reptiles
Peninsula Ribbon Snake
Thamnophis sauritus sackeni
Florida Brown Snake
Storeria dekayi victa
FAMILY COLUBRIDAE; Order Squamata, Suborder Serpentes
Striped Mud Turtle
Kinosternon bauri
FAMILY KINOSTERNIDAE; Order Testudines

On the approximately 1,700 islands of the Florida Keys are numerous species of fauna that differ from their mainland counterparts. With some animals, the differences are great enough to warrant recognition as a distinct species (for example, the silver rice rat, *Oryzomys argentatus*) or as a distinct subspecies (the Key ring-necked snake, *Diadophis punctatus acricus,* or Key deer, *Odocoileus virginianus clavium*). The three reptiles included in this section have been recognized as distinct subspecies in the past by various authorities and are still considered separate races by some, although they are officially distinguished only as populations or morphs. The same holds true for the Lower Keys population of corn snake (*Elaphe guttata guttata*), formerly known as the rosy rat snake (*E. g. rosacea*), and the Upper Keys population of yellow rat snake (*Elaphe obsoleta quadrivittata*), for many years known as Deckert's rat snake (*E. o. deckerti*). The fauna of this archipelago, particularly in the Lower Keys, have a high percentage of subspeciation, and colonies of animals disjunct from the main population usually having discernible differences in color, pattern, or other characteristics from their mainland equivalents. Oddly, many of the races occurring in the Keys resemble individuals from northern Florida more than their geographically closer counterparts from the southern tip of Florida's peninsula. For instance, the Everglades racer (*Coluber constrictor paludicola*), the subspecies occupying extreme southern Florida and the Upper Keys, is replaced in the Lower Keys by the southern black racer (*Coluber constrictor priapus*), whose contiguous range lies north of the Everglades. Another example is the ribbon snakes of the Lower Keys, which often look more like eastern ribbon snakes (*Thamnophis sauritus sauritus*) than the peninsula ribbon snakes of southern Florida.

LISTED STATUS

FWC: Peninsula ribbon snake, threatened, listed 1975

FWC: Florida brown snake, threatened, listed 1975

FWC: Striped mud turtle, endangered, listed 1979 (threatened 1975–1978)

Description

Peninsula Ribbon Snake: Ribbon snakes are the most slender races of the many garter snake species (genus *Thamnophis*), and the peninsula ribbon snake is the most slender of the ribbons. Adults are 18–25 inches (45.7–63.5 cm) in length, with the longest recorded specimen measuring 40 inches (101.6 cm). Typically, these snakes have a light brown or tan ground color, with a light-colored longitudinal stripe on the third and fourth scale rows on each side. Individuals from the Lower Keys usually have a well-developed yellow or orange middorsal stripe bordered on each side by thin black stripes; they resemble animals from northern populations more than the typical peninsula morph. Mainland snakes may have a middorsal stripe, but it is usually faint or nearly absent. Peninsula ribbon snakes have very long tails; individuals from the Lower Keys tend to have even longer tails than mainland animals. The belly is yellowish white and unmarked. Scales are keeled, and the anal plate is undivided. The Lower Keys population also differs from mainland snakes in the number of upper labial scales: mainland animals have eight,

and Lower Keys animals usually have only seven. Newborn snakes measure approximately 8 inches (20.3 cm).

Florida Brown Snake: The Florida brown snake, like other races of *Storeria dekayi*, are small brownish or tan snakes with pairs of small, dark dorsal spots running the length of the body. Florida brown snakes are slightly thinner than other subspecies and have only 15 dorsal scale rows; all others have 17. Mainland snakes are typically 9–13 inches (23–33 cm) and have been recorded as long as 19 inches (48.3 cm); Lower Keys specimens, however, are smaller on average, rarely exceeding 11.8 inches (30 cm). Insular snakes tend to have a much reduced head pattern compared with mainland snakes, which have a wide, light-colored band across the back of the head and darkly colored labials below the eye. The Lower Keys population also differs from the mainland population in having two preocular scales (usually) instead of one, and by having less ventral pigmentation. The belly is pale, usually whitish, and may have small black spots on the sides of the scales. Dorsal scales are keeled, and the anal plate is divided. Newborn snakes are 3.3–4.25 inches (8.4–10.7 cm) long and are much darker than adults.

Striped Mud Turtle: Adults of this subspecies are small, averaging 3–4 inches (7.5–10 cm), with the shells of large adults reaching nearly 5 inches (12.2 cm). Females attain a larger size than males. Lower Keys specimens typically have a darker carapace than most mainland turtles, as do specimens from Florida's Gulf Hammock region. The carapace is smooth in adult turtles. Lower Keys animals generally have three light carapace stripes characteristic of this subspecies (one middorsal stripe with a similar stripe on each side); however, their stripes are typically much less distinct than those of mainland specimens. Where mainland turtles usually have bright yellow facial stripes or blotches, Lower Keys turtles have faint markings or may lack facial markings. The plastrons of Lower Keys specimens are narrower than plastrons of mainland turtles. Mud turtles differ from closely related musk turtles (*Sternotherus*) in having much larger plastrons and triangular pectoral scutes, as opposed to the musk turtle's more squared scutes. The striped mud turtle's plastron has 11 total scutes, with 2 well-developed hinged scutes. The male's tail has a spiny tip and is larger than the female's. Mud and musk turtles possess two pairs of musk glands, located in the skin between the plastron and the carapace, which emit foul-smelling secretions when the turtle is frightened. Hatchlings are 0.6–1 inch (1.4–2.5 cm) long and have a narrow carapacial keel that fades with age.

Distribution

Peninsula Ribbon Snake: The Lower Keys population is known only from No Name, Big Pine, Cudjoe, Middle Torch, and Upper Sugarloaf keys. This population is disjunct from the principal population, which ranges from extreme southeastern South Carolina south through Georgia's coastal plain and nearly all of Florida east of the Apalachicola River, except portions of the Gulf Hammock and eastern Big Bend areas where bluestripe ribbon snakes (*Thamnophis sauritus nitae*) occur. Typical peninsula morphs occur in the Upper Keys (Key Largo and Plantation Key). The eastern ribbon snake (*T. s.*

sauritus) occurs in Florida's Panhandle west of the Apalachicola River.

Florida Brown Snake: This is a subspecies of the widespread northern brown snake, or Dekay's snake (*Storeria dekayi dekayi*), named after James Ellsworth Dekay, a nineteenth-century naturalist. The known distribution of the threatened Lower Keys population is limited to No Name, Big Pine, Little Torch, Middle Torch, and Sugarloaf keys. The principal contiguous population ranges from extreme southeastern Georgia throughout peninsular Florida and Key Largo. Two other brown snake subspecies inhabit Florida's Big Bend and Panhandle regions, the midland brown snake (*S. d. wrightorum*) and the marsh brown snake (*S. d. limnetes*).

Striped Mud Turtle: Striped mud turtles have been recorded from many keys between Big Pine and Key West. The type locality for *Kinosternon bauri* is Key West, where it is now believed to be extirpated. It has been recorded from Big Pine, Little Pine, No Name, Cudjoe, Johnston, Little Torch, Middle Torch, Big Torch, Summerland, Saddlebunch, Stock Island, and Key West. It is the Lower Keys' only native freshwater turtle. The main population ranges from southeastern Virginia south throughout peninsular Florida.

Biology

Peninsula Ribbon Snake: These snakes are semiaquatic and are usually associated with freshwater wetland habitats; in the Lower Keys, however, the ribbon snake inhabits both freshwater and brackish water environments, which include freshwater ponds and marshes, mangrove and spartina communities, and mosquito ditches. This subspecies is somewhat arboreal and often basks on vegetation overhanging water, much like water snakes (*Nerodia*). Ribbon snakes swim on the surface of water, unlike water snakes, which usually swim beneath the surface. Although diurnal throughout much of the year, this subspecies often becomes quite nocturnal during the warmest months. The typical diet of the peninsula ribbon snake includes frogs, toads, tadpoles, small fish, and insects, with individuals from the Lower Keys recorded feeding on lizards as well. Mating takes place in the spring. Ribbon snakes are viviparous; 5–8 young (a smaller clutch size than mainland snakes) are born during the early to mid summer months. Chief predators are likely to include wading birds, raccoons, and black racers.

Florida Brown Snake: Throughout its range, excluding the Keys, this snake is closely associated with aquatic environments. It is often found in mats of floating water hyacinth. Brown snakes from the Lower Keys tend to be much less aquatic than their mainland counterparts, apparently favoring tropical hardwood hammocks, but they do occur in moist areas and tropical pineland. This no doubt is an evolutionary response to the lack of freshwater habitats in the Lower Keys. These small snakes are sometimes encountered under objects or piles of debris. They may become crepuscular or nocturnal in warmer months. They feed on insects, earthworms, snails, small frogs, and lizards. They are subject to predation from various mammals, birds, and reptiles. When threatened, a brown snake may flatten its body in an effort to appear larger and may emit a

musky substance from the vent. Mating may take place in the spring or fall, with gravid females producing a dozen or more young about 3.5 months after mating. Some authorities believe that females impregnated in the fall may sometimes hold a litter over the winter for a spring birth.

Striped Mud Turtle: Striped mud turtles are closely tied to aquatic habitats; however, they are somewhat less aquatic than other mud turtle species. They are frequently encountered prowling on land. The Lower Keys population is able to tolerate and even prosper in brackish water environments in addition to freshwater ponds and marshes, which are scarce. James D. Lazell Jr., however, reports that this subspecies cannot tolerate salinities above 15 parts per thousand, which is less than half the strength of seawater. In the Keys, mud turtles often become an eternal resident of a particular pond or marshy area, but those turtles occupying seasonal hammock ponds will become transient during the winter when the ponds dry up or become too salty. Hammock ponds on higher ground where the freshwater lens is better developed support the best naturally occurring habitat for the striped mud turtle in the Lower Keys. Only a dozen or so Lower Keys ponds are known to support mud turtles. Many of them are on private property and are at risk of being developed. Man-made mosquito control ditches, which tap the subterranean freshwater lens, also support sizable populations of these turtles. The turtles are most active in the morning and afternoon hours, when they forage on land and in the water. Striped mud turtles are opportunistic omnivores that readily consume insects and their larvae, small fish, snails, crustaceans, frogs, toads, tadpoles, and carrion, as well as plant material including cabbage palm fruits. Females may lay as many as three clutches of up to four eggs each, between April and June, in shallow nests excavated on land or in decaying vegetation. The elliptical eggs, which measure approximately 1.1 inches (2.8 cm), are quite resistant to dehydration and hatch after 13–19 weeks. Young turtles and eggs are vulnerable to predators such as raccoons and wading birds, and alligators are known to prey on adults.

CAUSE OF DECLINE, THREATS

These factors apply to all three species.

Habitat Destruction: The loss of freshwater habitats is the principal threat to all three reptiles. Ironically, some mosquito control ditches supplying a lasting freshwater source important to mud turtle

and ribbon snake populations are scheduled to be filled as part of the federal Key Deer recovery plan. Commercial and residential development have already destroyed much of the Lower Keys' riparian habitat and tropical hardwood hammocks inhabited by these species. Brackish mangrove habitats, used by these species to a lesser extent than freshwater habitats, have received more protection than freshwater habitats.

Automobile Collisions: Automobile traffic poses a constant and increasing threat to each of these small, easily overlooked reptiles.

Illegal Collection: A few of these animals, particularly mud turtles, are undoubtedly collected annually as pets. Fortunately, these species are not sought-after in the reptile pet trade, as is the Lower Keys corn snake.

CURRENT TREND: *Declining.*

Shortnose Sturgeon
Acipenser brevirostrum
FAMILY ACIPENSERIDAE; Order
Acipenseriformes

LISTED STATUS
FWC: Endangered, listed 1975
USF&WS & NATL MARINE FISHERIES:
Endangered, listed 1967
CITES: Appendix 1

Description: The shortnose sturgeon is one of two native sturgeon species occurring in Florida. The other and perhaps better-known species, the Atlantic sturgeon (*Acipenser oxyrinchus*), has two recognized subspecies whose ranges are allopatric: the Atlantic sturgeon (*A. o. oxyrinchus*) and the threatened Gulf sturgeon (*A. o. desotoi*). Sturgeons are members of the class Osteichthyes (bony fish). Like other sturgeon species, the shortnose is primitive in appearance, with four odd-looking, threadlike, fleshy appendages (barbels) protruding from the ventral portions of the mouth. The ground color of the shortnose sturgeon, in fresh water, is typically a dull yellowish brown that assumes a purple or greenish cast in brackish or salt water. The head is often much darker; the sides are lighter, and the abdomen region is often yellowish or even white. Locality is sufficient to distinguish the shortnose from the Gulf sturgeon, as their ranges do not overlap. Smaller adult size and a shorter and rounder snout distinguish the shortnose from the Atlantic sturgeon. Other than the larger size of females, there is little sexual dimorphism in this species. The maximum length recorded for the shortnose sturgeon (a female collected from Canada's St. John estuary) was just over 56 inches (143 cm); the maximum weight recorded (a gravid female) was 52 pounds (23.6 kg). The largest male recorded (also from Canada's St. John River) measured just over 45 inches (108 cm) in total length and weighed 20.7 pounds (9.4 kg). Those records, however, far exceed the average adult size and weight. Shortnose sturgeons, especially those from southern populations, seldom exceed 30 inches (76 cm). By comparison, adult Atlantic sturgeon females are enormous, often exceeding 5 feet (1.5 m) in length and 150 pounds (68 kg), with historic records of 14 feet (4.3 m) and 811 pounds (368 kg). Shortnose sturgeons lack the pupil-sized bony plates between the anal base and the lateral row of scutes present in Atlantic sturgeons, which typically have 2–6 of these plates. Shortnose sturgeons have 19–22 anal fin rays and 22–29 gill rakers, averaging 25; Atlantic sturgeons typically have 25–30 anal fin rays and 22–40 gill rakers. Shortnose sturgeon at any stage, other than prolarvae, have a conspicuously wider mouth than their closely related cousin *Acipenser oxyrinchus*; also, the fontanelle is absent and postdorsal shields are almost completely lacking in the shortnose. The lateral plates number 22–33, averaging 28. Lateral and dorsal scales are relatively pallid and contrast with the dark background, unlike the Atlantic sturgeon, which has a similarly pigmented background. Additionally, the intestines of the shortnose sturgeon are quite dark, but the Atlantic sturgeon's are pale.

Young shortnose sturgeons reportedly are much lighter than mature adults but typically have melanistic blotches, which dissipate over time. Although Atlantic sturgeons attain a significantly greater adult size, hatchling shortnose sturgeons are typically larger (0.8–1.1 cm standard length) than Atlantic hatchlings (0.7–0.9 cm SL).

Distribution: The shortnose is one of seven sturgeon species in North America and one of two species in Florida. There are no recognized subspecies of the shortnose sturgeon. Though authorities continue to debate whether the shortnose sturgeon has ever occurred as a breeding fish within Florida, there is no disputing its repeated occurrences within the state. Each year, a handful of shortnose sturgeons are reported from the St. Johns River by commercial fishermen. Museum records from Florida include one fish from lower Brevard County in 1896; one from the St. Johns River, Volusia County, in each of the years 1949, 1977, and 1978 and two in 1979. Single specimens have also been documented from Big Lake George (St. Johns River) in 1949, Lake Crescent in 1949, Murphy Creek (St. Johns River) in 1977, Welaka in 1978, Cedar Creek in 1979, and the Clay-Putnam county line in 1979.

Seventeen distinct shortnose sturgeon populations inhabit 24 Atlantic Coast rivers, from Canada's St. John River in New Brunswick to northeastern Florida's St. Johns River. Biologists from the National Marine Fisheries Service have divided shortnose sturgeon populations into two distributional groups; the northeast group includes populations north of and including Chesapeake Bay, and the southeast group includes those populations south of Chesapeake Bay.

The 10 largest southeast populations inhabit these river and lake systems, listed here from north to south.

1. Cape Fear River, North Carolina. Population unknown; despite extensive sampling, only 9 sturgeon (all adults) have been documented in this river since their discovery there in 1987.

2. Winyah Bay drainages, Waccamaw, Pee Dee, and Black rivers, South Carolina. Current population unknown; however, a viable population of shortnose sturgeon occurred in this system during the late 1970's and early 1980's.

3. Santee and Cooper rivers, South Carolina. Current population unknown, but believed to be very low and decreasing. Included in this system is Lake Moultrie, which contains the second of two known landlocked populations.

4. A.C.E. Basin of Ashepoo, Combahee, and Edisto rivers, South Carolina. Current population unknown. Unlike most southern rivers inhabited by shortnose sturgeons, this system is considered relatively healthy and pristine.

5. Savannah River, South Carolina and Georgia. An accurate population estimate is difficult because this system has been heavily stocked with artificially propagated sturgeons.

6. Ogeechee River, Georgia. Population estimated at 223.

7. Altamaha River, Georgia. Estimates range from 316 to 4,226 individuals. This system drains the largest watershed east of the Mississippi River and is believed to support the Southeast's largest and most viable shortnose sturgeon population.

8. Satilla River, Georgia. Shortnose sturgeons are known from this small and relatively pristine system, but population estimates are not yet available.

9. St. Marys River, Georgia and Florida. This small system is undammed but somewhat less pristine than Georgia's Satilla River. It has only recently been surveyed and population estimates are not yet available. Shortnose sturgeons have been documented in both systems as late as the early 1990's.

10. St. Johns River, Florida. Only 6 documented from this river since 1949. This is the species' southernmost population. Unlike Canada's St. John River, which contains one of the largest shortnose sturgeon populations, Florida's heavily industrialized and degraded St. Johns River now supports at best a depauperate remnant population. Shortnose sturgeons were last positively recorded from this river during the 1970's, from upstream portions heavily influenced by artesian springs.

Biology: The seven North American sturgeon species include anadromous and freshwater species. Shortnose sturgeons are generally categorized as anadromous, with some northern populations considered freshwater amphidromous. This species spawns in the upper reaches of freshwater riverine habitats but intermittently occurs in brackish or saltwater habitats throughout much of its adult life. The shallow, inshore, saltwater habitats used most often are estuarine regions associated with the sturgeon's natal river. Shortnose sturgeons are less tolerant of full-strength sea water than Atlantic sturgeons, thus they are less likely to disperse great distances from natal rivers. Adults forage in freshwater, brackish, and saltwater habitats. The species is also quite intolerant of warm water (especially in northern portions of its range). Rises in water temperature tend to spur sturgeons to move into deeper, cooler portions of rivers.

Shortnose sturgeons migrate upstream to spawn earlier than Atlantic sturgeons in the same area. Feeding activity is greatly reduced or halted by both sexes during upstream migrations, with females fasting for months prior to spawning. Migration may take place from the fall to late winter or early spring, with fish arriving at the spawning grounds (often channels of rivers) in the fall sometimes waiting several months before beginning reproductive activities. It is believed that fall migration may avoid the risks of migration during the high water discharge periods of spring. Spawning has been documented as early as January in southern populations and as late as mid-May (rarely mid-June) in northern populations. Spawning may last two days to two weeks or more, with female sturgeons emitting a chemical attractant to lure males. Females broadcast 30,000–200,000 (average 94,000) adhesive eggs, 2–3 millimeters in diameter. Eggs adhere to submerged substrates including stones, rocks, and aquatic vegetation and are fertilized by males as they are dispatched. Adults usually vacate spawning grounds a short time after spawning and don't care for or defend eggs. The eggs hatch after one or two weeks, with longer incubation periods in northern rivers. The hatchlings are black, 0.8–1.1 cm long, and look like tadpoles, with poorly developed eyes, fins, mouth, and a large yolk sac that is absorbed during the first 9–12 days as they develop into 1.5 cm larvae. During this period, they become free-swimming larvae with well-developed eyes, fins, and mouth. Young of the year apparently remain in deeper portions of rivers. Juveniles may migrate downstream in the spring and summer and upstream in fall and winter, but they usually remain upstream of the freshwater-saltwater interface for several years. Male shortnose sturgeons are believed to spawn at two-year intervals, sometimes annually. Females are believed to spawn at intervals of three to five years.

There are fairly significant differences in growth rates, sexual maturity, and longevity between southern warm-water populations and northern cold-water populations. Shortnose sturgeons are long-lived, with one Canadian female calculated to be 67 years old. The oldest known female from Georgia's Altamaha River was calculated to be 10 years of age.

Shortnose sturgeons are generally benthivores (bottom feeders) but have been observed feeding from plant surfaces. They are known to feed nocturnally and diurnally. Sturgeons forage by vacuuming up small crustaceans, insect larvae, mollusks, and occasionally benthic fish from the substrate. This method of foraging also results in the ingestion of mud and detritus. Research indicates

that southern shortnose populations tend to fast during the summer months, contrary to the feeding pattern of most northern populations. Known or suspected predators of adults and young range-wide include yellow perch (*Perca flavescens*), gar (*Lepisosteus* spp.), striped bass (*Morone saxatilis*), alligators, harbor seals (*Phoca vitulina*), various sharks, aquatic turtles, and other fishes. A number of external and internal parasites infest shortnose sturgeons, but none are thought to be harmful.

CAUSE OF DECLINE, THREATS

Habitat Destruction: Heavy industrial development coupled with diminished water quality are believed to be the main causes of the sturgeon's disappearance from several areas. Damming of rivers has greatly affected shortnose sturgeon populations, and dams now serve as unnatural distributional limits. Dams obstruct migration routes to areas formerly utilized for spawning and alters the flow of rivers, destroying or severely degrading formerly suitable habitat, and kill sturgeons trapped in turbines. Sturgeons do not use fishways used by other fishes, including certain salmon species. Reproductive success of sturgeon populations can be directly influenced by water discharges and by releases of silt or other fine river sediments into spawning areas. Among the southeastern rivers containing dams are North Carolina's Cape Fear River and Georgia's Savannah River. Some authorities suspect that construction of the Rodman Dam on Florida's Oklawaha River, a tributary of the St. Johns, may have eliminated the shortnose sturgeon's access to possibly historic spawning habitat. Construction activities associated with dams, bridges, and power plants may adversely affect sturgeons by destroying microhabitats and their prey, producing excessive levels of turbidity, and killing sturgeons directly. Biologists suspect that activities associated with dredging may seriously threaten shortnose sturgeon populations. Hopper dredges can kill sturgeons by sucking them up through the drag arm and impeller pumps. Federal navigation channels are routinely dredged as part of channel maintenance programs. Certain human activities have destroyed or reduced thermal refuges, the deeper, cooler portions of rivers, sometimes associated with artesian spring-fed habitats, that sturgeons retreat to when water temperatures are high. This is especially true in warmer southern rivers.

Commercial Harvests and Illegal Takes: All taking of shortnose sturgeons within the United States has been unlawful since 1967. The term "take" includes killing, hunting, capturing, or harassing the fish. Caviar from this species is a delicacy that reportedly commands a higher price than that of the Atlantic sturgeon. Though most fisheries biologists interviewed do not consider illegal taking a significant threat to shortnose sturgeons, most agree that it does indeed occur. The organized, intensive harvest of both sturgeon species for more than 100 years is believed to be the primary historic cause of the decline of both species.

Before receiving protection, the shortnose sturgeon was legally harvested in several Atlantic drainages, including the Hudson and Delaware rivers. The commercial take of shortnose sturgeons was outlawed within the United States by federal law in 1967. A number of sturgeons are incidentally harvested each year by commercial fisheries, however. Commercial shad (*Alosa sapidissima*) fisheries, using gill nets, account for most accidental catches; striped bass, Atlantic salmon (*Salmo salar*), and alewife (*Alosa pseudoharengus*) fisheries have also been noted. In most cases when sturgeons are accidentally caught, it is reported that they are repatriated unharmed. Some authorities do not consider incidental take to be a significant threat, but others consider it the leading cause of unnatural mortality for long-lived sturgeons. USF&WS biologist Mary Moser reported in 1993 that the capture of shortnose sturgeons (in commercial shad nets) in the Cape Fear River resulted in the disruption and possibly the abandonment of sturgeon spawning migrations. Biologists suspect that incidental fishing mortality is a significant factor in the disappearance of shortnose sturgeons from estuarine areas of Chesapeake Bay and a major mortality factor in South Carolina. The commercial shad fishing season coincides with the shortnose's spring spawning migration.

Canada, unlike the United States, permits the commercial harvest of shortnose sturgeons. Fish over 4 feet (122 cm) in total length may be taken from the St. John River in New Brunswick in every month but June, although the majority are taken during July and August. Sturgeons are generally caught with gill nets. On the St. John River, only 3 or 4 legal-sized shortnose sturgeons are harvested annually; it is estimated, however, that more than 200 sublegal sturgeons are harvested annually. Reportedly shortnose sturgeons account for about 5 percent of the total annual sturgeon harvest from the St. John, where the shortnose population has been estimated at 18,000 adults.

Pollution: Bioaccumulation of toxic contaminants (including polychlorinated aromatic hydrocarbons, polychlorinated biphenyls, tetrachlorodibenzo-p-dioxin, and various pesticides and toxic metals that are known to accumulate in the fat tissues of certain organisms) may be especially injurious to sturgeon and other bottom-feeding species. Reduced reproductive capabilities, acute lesions, and stunted growth are examples of the adverse effects of toxic contamination. Physiological stress associated with low oxygen levels (less than 5 ppm) in riverine areas is a known threat to this and other species. Recent studies by T. I. J. Smith et al. (1993) revealed that dissolved oxygen concentrations below 3.5 mg/l caused significant mortality of juvenile sturgeons, and older fish typically died at levels below 2.5 mg/l, indicating an increased tolerance in older sturgeons. Research has shown that when water temperatures exceed 82 degrees F (28 C), dissolved oxygen levels will often become harmful to sturgeons. Thus, sources that elevate water temperature, including pollutant and sewer discharges, contribute to excessively low dissolved oxygen levels. Power plant shutdowns caused by mats of decaying aquatic vegetation that clog intake gates have greatly decreased or stopped the flow of water and have caused low oxygen concentrations downstream, killing many sturgeons.

Other Threats: Large construction and public works projects are a continuing threat to sturgeons. For instance, powerful shock waves produced by high explosives used in bridge and pier demolition

and other projects are believed to have damaging, often deadly, effects on sturgeons. The construction or removal of bridges can disrupt shortnose sturgeon concentration areas and can interfere with sturgeons' migratory movements. Researchers have documented numerous incidents, at multiple sites nearly rangewide, where shortnose sturgeons have died from impingement in the water intake screens of nuclear and electric power generating plants, particularly in Maine, Connecticut, New York, and Pennsylvania. Probably the deadliest incident took place between October 1982 and September 1983 at the Albany Steam Generating Station, where 86 young-of-the-year shortnose sturgeons were killed by impingement. Even the operation of flood-control reservoirs by the U.S. Army Corps of Engineers may impair the sturgeon's natural movement patterns by altering the flow and volume of water in rivers used by this species since prehistoric times. The success ratio of spawning sturgeons can be quickly altered by the discharge, through flood gates, of large volumes of water, which affects water depths and temperature and extends high flow periods.

Studies of some shortnose populations have revealed a high percentage of adults afflicted with fin rot, although it is unknown if this condition represents a serious mortality factor. One study of the Hudson River (New York) population, conducted in 1981, revealed that nearly 80 percent of adult fish were affected. This condition may well be associated with certain contaminants, particularly PCBs. It is well known that PCBs are heavily distributed throughout the upper portions of the Hudson River.

It is believed that PCBs may lower the sturgeon's resistance to this and other abnormalities.

CURRENT TREND: *Declining* overall; Florida's population possibly *extirpated*.

Gulf Sturgeon
Acipenser oxyrinchus desotoi
Atlantic Sturgeon
Acipenser oxyrinchus oxyrinchus
FAMILY ACIPENSERIDAE; Order Acipenseriformes

LISTED STATUS

FWC: Species of special concern, both listed 1977

USF&WS & NATL MARINE FISHERIES: Threatened, Gulf sturgeon listed 1992

CITES: Appendix 2, both subspecies

Description: Sturgeons are large, sometimes tremendous, primitive-looking fish. Old World beluga sturgeons (*Acipenser huso*) have been recorded as heavy as 2,866 pounds (1,300 kg). Adults of this species attain lengths of 35–79 inches (88–200 cm), with females growing larger than males. Adult female Gulf sturgeons taken in recent years typically weigh 120–130 pounds (54–59 kg), with males weighing 50–60 pounds (23–27 kg). An exceptional individual weighing 503 pounds (228 kg) was taken in 1936 near the mouth of the Mississippi River. According to USF&WS biologist Frank Parauka, Atlantic sturgeons are slightly larger and heavier than Gulf sturgeons. Specimens 14 feet (4.3 m) in length and more than 800 pounds (363 kg) have been recorded, though not for many years. The species has a brown or greenish ground color and is lined with five rows of bony plates, one on the back, two on the underside, and two on the sides. Four sensitive barbels protrude from the underside of the elongated snout, creating a whiskered appearance. The species is considerably larger than Florida's other sturgeon, the shortnose (*Acipenser brevirostrum*).

Of the several characteristics distinguishing the two *Acipenser oxyrinchus* subspecies, the most notable is the spleen length. In the Gulf sturgeon, the spleen comprises 12.7–17.5 percent of the fork length; in the Atlantic sturgeon it is less than 6 percent. The ratio of pectoral fin length to fork length is nearly 30 percent in the Gulf sturgeon and only 13.6 percent in the Atlantic subspecies. Differences in the ratio of head length to fork length and the length-width ratio of dorsal scutes have also been documented.

Distribution: The Atlantic sturgeon ranges sporadically along the Atlantic Coast from Labrador in maritime Canada to the St. Johns River region of Florida. It is now most likely just a rare visitor to the coastal waters of northeastern Florida and probably does not breed within the state, though authorities believe it once may have. Confirmed Florida records are few, and most are from the winter. Many are from the St. Johns River (Putnam County); some recent records, however, are as far south as Hutchinson Island in St. Lucie County. An old record exists from the northeast coast of South America, possibly indicating a former relict population.

The Gulf sturgeon's range is disjunct from the range of the Atlantic race. The Gulf race is generally confined to the northeastern Gulf of Mexico from the lower Mississippi River and Delta region of Louisiana to Florida's Suwannee River, where the largest, healthiest population occurs. Other Florida populations occur in the Apalachicola, Blackwater, Choctawhatchee, Escambia, Ochlockonee, Yellow, and Shoal rivers. The subspecies formerly occurred commonly as far south as Tampa Bay, where it was commercially harvested during the late 1800's. During cold spells, sturgeons often disperse southward. Gulf sturgeons have been reported in winter as far south as Everglades National Park.

Biology: Like most sturgeon species, this species (both subspecies) is considered anadromous; that is, most of the sturgeon's adult life is spent in brackish or salt water, but it ascends rivers to spawn in freshwater environments. The sturgeons' saltwater habitats often have little current, and the substrates vary from rock to mud, typically lacking submerged aquatic vegetation. Estuarine habitats, including tidal bays, are often exploited. Though occasionally encountered at depths of 150 feet (46 m), the species is typically a fish of shallow water that tends to remain fairly close to shore. During the winter, both subspecies may migrate southward, but occasionally Atlantic sturgeons are known to migrate more than 900 miles. Gulf sturgeons also disperse to warmer waters, but the distances traveled are usually shorter.

This species spawns in freshwater rivers, usually with a moderate to fast-moving current, often many miles inland. In Florida, Gulf sturgeons spawn from February to June, usually in deeper portions of rivers. Atlantic sturgeons typically begin spawning in April in southern portions of their range and as late as July in the Gulf of Maine. A female will broadcast 1 million to 2.5 million adhesive eggs into currents,

where they readily adhere to rocks and submerged vegetation. Females typically return to salt water soon after spawning, but males may remain until autumn. This species tends to spawn at intervals of 2–3 years. The incubation period varies from 4 to 7 days, depending on temperature and latitude, and is shorter in warmer rivers. The young measure 0.7–0.9 cm (standard length) at hatching. They remain in fresh water 3–5 years before descending to estuarine or marine environments. Both subspecies are slow growing and long-lived. Longevity records are 60 years for Atlantic sturgeons and 42 years for Gulf sturgeons. Research has shown that individuals from southern latitudes become sexually mature earlier (7–10 years) than individuals from northern, colder climes (more than 20 years). Adults loyally return to their natal rivers to spawn, which results in minimal genetic interchange between different populations.

A notable, unusual, and yet unexplained habit of the Gulf sturgeon is its inclination in fresh water to porpoise, or leap vigorously straight out of the water, often completely out. Because of the sturgeon's size, this peculiar habit has startled many, including a boating party on the Yellow River when a sizable sturgeon crashed through the window of their pontoon boat. The ill-fated fish was reportedly shot by the boat owner.

Sturgeons are bottom feeders and use their protractile mouths and barbels to vacuum their prey from the floor of rivers or marine habitats. Adults consume a variety of animal prey, including mollusks, crustaceans, worms, small fishes, and insect larvae. The diet of subadults and juveniles is believed to be primarily zooplankton, insect larvae, and benthic crustaceans. Neonate and juvenile sturgeons are preyed on by myriad piscivorous fauna. By the time adulthood is reached, the number of natural predators is substantially reduced. Humans constitute the most serious threat to adults.

CAUSE OF DECLINE, THREATS

Overfishing: This species has been commercially exploited along much of the Atlantic Coast for more than 200 years. It is prized for both its caviar and its tasty meat. Originally, sturgeons were harvested with massive gill nets, hundreds of feet long, but when few large sturgeons remained, fishermen switched to nets with smaller mesh and other devices to catch smaller sturgeons. The Atlantic sturgeon fishing season coincides with spawning migrations. Overfishing has greatly depleted populations of both subspecies throughout most of their historic range, and some populations have been extirpated.

After sturgeon fishing was outlawed in Florida, some individuals continued to harvest Gulf sturgeons illegally. In the early 1990's, a federal biologist who was diving in the Suwannee River, searching for lost sturgeon tags, was surprised to discover a submerged waterproof pipe bomb. It is believed that the unexploded device was placed in the river to harvest Gulf sturgeons illegally.

Damming of Rivers: When rivers are dammed (e.g., Jim Woodruff Dam on the Apalachicola River), sturgeons can no longer reach the spawning grounds they have used instinctively for hundreds of generations.

Habitat Degradation: Dredging and other river maintenance activities alter a river's substrate and eliminate deep holes that may be utilized by sturgeons. Pumping can cause a reduction of groundwater near streams, reducing or eliminating important cool water habitats that sturgeons rely on in warmer months.

Pollution: Gulf sturgeons from several areas in northwestern Florida have been found to contain concentrations of toxic pesticides and heavy metals, including arsenic, DDT metabolites, mercury, toxaphene, aliphatic hydrocarbons, and polycyclic aromatic hydrocarbons. Mercury, which is highly toxic to humans as well as fish, has been detected in 87 percent of the Gulf sturgeons tested. Water pollution remains a constant threat rangewide and may be a factor in population declines in some areas.

Other Threats: These fish require a long time to mature sexually, and they do not spawn annually, which will likely retard any recovery efforts. The introduction of nonnative fishes (e.g., white sturgeon) into occupied habitat is another potential threat.

CURRENT TREND

Gulf Sturgeon: *Stable,* generally. According to USF&WS biologist Lorna Patrick, the Gulf sturgeon is now in "fairly good shape" (personal communication). The Suwannee River population, estimated at 2,250–3,300 individuals (some estimates as high as 10,000), is the largest population rangewide. The Apalachicola River population, estimated at fewer than 200 individuals, was much larger before the river was dammed.

Atlantic Sturgeon: *Unknown.*

Crystal Darter
Crystallaria asprella
FAMILY PERCIDAE; Order Perciformes

LISTED STATUS

FWC: Threatened, listed 1977

USF&WS: Species of management concern

Description: The crystal darter is a relatively large darter with a slender body and a distinctly forked tail. It attains a maximum standard length of 5.1 inches (13 cm). The translucent body is yellowish green (belly is whitish), and there are 3–5 (usually 4) broad, dark dorsal saddles that extend anteroventrally to the lateral line. The saddles are less pronounced in juveniles. On the sides are 10–12 dark, oblong, midlateral blotches. Most of the body is covered with small, coarse scales. The bluntly pointed head is dark above, light below. This species has large eyes and a small mouth.

Most authorities now place the crystal darter in the monotypic subgenus *Crystallaria,* because of a number of differences that separate it from members of the subgenus *Ammocrypta,* in which it was formerly grouped. *Crystallaria* is differentiated by its larger size, greater number of scales on the lateral line, more complete scalation (only the breast and belly are unscaled), the presence of a narrow premaxillary frenum, the presence of palatine and prevomerine teeth, and a bold dorsal pattern. Identifying characteristics include 45–48 vertebrae, 83–100 lateral line scales, high and elongated dorsal and anal fins, and a single anal spine. Morphologically, this subgenus is intermediate between *Percina* and *Etheostoma.*

Distribution: This species is now largely restricted to scattered, localized populations in rivers and streams within the Mississippi Valley and other Gulf Coast drainages. Its historic distribution ranged from Wisconsin and Minnesota in the north, east to Ohio and West Virginia, and south throughout much of the Mississippi Valley to, or nearly to, the Gulf Coast and several Gulf drainages east of the Mississippi River. It has been recorded in Alabama, Arkansas, Florida, Illinois, Indiana, Iowa, Kentucky, Louisiana, Minnesota, Mississippi, Missouri, Ohio, Oklahoma, Tennessee, West Virginia, and Wisconsin. It has now been eliminated throughout much of its historic range by damming, channelization, and other types of habitat alteration. It is now believed to be extirpated in Indiana, Illinois, Ohio, and West Virginia and is rare in most regions where it still occurs. Crystal darters are locally common in several lowland streams of eastern Arkansas and southeastern Missouri and in portions of Alabama's Tombigbee River.

In Florida, the species is restricted to the upper Escambia River subbasin (Big Escambia Creek) in Escambia and Santa Rosa counties of the Panhandle. The Florida Panhandle represents the southernmost and easternmost extremes of the range.

Biology: The crystal darter (subgenus *Crystallaria*) and the six closely related darters of the subgenus *Ammocrypta* are all members of a group of fish collectively known as sand darters. *Ammocrypta* means "sand hidden." True to their name, these fishes bury themselves in sand substrates of streams and rivers, with only the top of the head and eyes protruding while they wait for passing prey. This cryptic behavior conserves energy when strong currents are present, makes them difficult to detect, and offers some protection from predators.

The crystal darter is one of only a handful of indigenous North American fishes that are largely restricted to sand and gravel benthic substrates of larger streams and rivers. It generally avoids areas composed entirely of shifting sand, which are exploited by the related Florida sand darter (*Ammocrypta bifascia*), and favors instead large sand and gravel bars and riffles within large creeks and rivers. Waters inhabited by crystal darters are usually fairly deep (more than 1.8 feet), clear to moderately turbid, with moderate to strong currents.

Its breeding behavior and life history are largely unknown. Breeding males develop large tubercles on the anal spine, on all but the last 1–3 anal rays, and on the first 3–5 pelvic fin rays (late fall to early winter in Mississippi). In Florida, it is suspected that spawning takes place from early March to late April. Eggs are probably deposited in sand and gravel substrates. Darters play an important role in aquatic food chains. They are preyed on by larger fishes, large aquatic salamanders, semiaquatic snakes and turtles, belted kingfishers, and other piscivorous birds. They in turn consume tiny crustaceans, midgeflies, mayflies, caddisflies, nematodes, and water scavenger beetles. Prey are often seized after straying too close to a well-concealed darter. The species typically inhabits deeper waters (6–16 feet) during daylight and moves into shallow waters to forage when dark or overcast.

CAUSE OF DECLINE, THREATS

Water Pollution, Habitat Alteration:
The presence of darters is usually a good indicator of a healthy aquatic ecosystem. They are intolerant of water pollution and siltation. Siltation is currently considered the primary cause of local extirpations and population and range decreases. Large stretches of formerly suitable habitat (extensive areas of clean sand and gravel) have been rendered unsuitable by heavy siltation, nutrient-rich runoff, and other forms of pollution. Dams have had a detrimental effect on this species by isolating populations and greatly reducing suitable habitat in many areas.

CURRENT TREND: *Decreasing.*

Okaloosa Darter

Etheostoma okaloosae
FAMILY PERCIDAE; Order Perciformes
LISTED STATUS
FWC: Endangered, listed 1972
USF&WS: Endangered, listed 1973

Description: The Okaloosa darter is a small to medium-sized darter, with a maximum standard length of about 1.9 inches (4.9 cm). Prolarvae, at hatching, measure approximately 0.19 inch (0.5 cm) in total length. This darter is yellowish brown to reddish brown dorsally and lighter ventrally, often with a thin, orange-red submarginal stripe on the dorsal fin. Identifying characteristics include 9–10 blotches (often dark) along each side of the body, 5–8 longitudinal rows of dark specks, a thin suborbital bar that is usually not distinct, a lateral line that is complete or nearly so and virtually straight, and 3–4 scale rows above the lateral line. Also, the cheeks, opercular area, abdomen, and nape are fully scaled, but the breast may be only partially scaled; the total scale count is usually 34–36 but may range from 32 to 37, with 4 or fewer unpored scales; the premaxillary frenum is well developed; there are usually 11–12 (occasionally 10) dorsal-fin rays, 6–8 anal-fin rays, and 12–14 pectoral-fin rays.

Distribution: The Okaloosa darter was first described in 1941 by Henry W. Fowler from a specimen collected by Francis Harper in Little Rocky Creek, approximately 7 miles northeast of Niceville, Okaloosa County, in 1939. Much of what is now known about this formerly little-known fish species is due to the extensive field research of B. B. Collette, M. F. Mettee, Ralph W. Yerger, Edward Crittenden, and R. C. Crews.

This Florida endemic is restricted in range to Rocky Bayou and Boggy Bayou of the Panhandle's Okaloosa and Walton counties. Both bayou systems drain into Choctawhatchee Bay and have three tributary streams inhabited by Okaloosa darters. Rocky Bayou comprises Swift, Turkey, and Rocky creeks, for approximately 152 total stream miles, and Boggy Bayou comprises Toms, Turkey, and Mill creeks, approximately 91 total stream miles. The total range encompasses 127,000 acres (51,396 ha), most of which is within Eglin Air Force Base.

Biology: The majority of the watershed containing the six occupied streams is largely undeveloped, well-drained, upland sandhill communities. The Okaloosa darter inhabits clear, small to moderate-sized sand-bottomed streams, 4–40 feet (1.2–12.2 m) wide, generally with moderate to fast-moving currents. Concentrations of varying amounts of detritus are often present in eddy and pool areas and along stream margins. The streams are usually less than 5 feet (1.5 m) deep. Water temperatures range from 45–49 degrees F (7–10 C) in winter to 72–75 degrees F (21–23 C) during the summer. The pH range recorded in these streams is 5.5–7.0. Many of the smaller streams inhabited by Okaloosa darters are covered by tree canopies. The darter frequents sunlit areas with submerged macrophytic vegetation, especially bulrush (genus *Scirpus*), or other cover. Some studies have indicated that in streams containing sympatric populations of both Okaloosa darters and brown darters (*Etheostoma edwini*), the two species tend to occupy slightly different microhabitats. Okaloosa darters were most commonly observed in stream areas with a stronger current where aquatic vegetation produces a barrier to the current. Brown darters were most frequently observed in the proximity of detritus in areas of reduced current, often along stream margins. A reversal of habitat roles has been observed, however.

The diet of this small fish is composed primarily of chironomid midges, ephemeropteran larvae, and tricopteran larvae, which stomach analyses have revealed account collectively for over 95 percent of the prey base. Predators include larger fishes, aquatic turtles and snakes, wading birds, and possibly large aquatic salamanders of the genera *Siren* and *Amphiuma*.

These darters may spawn from March to October, often peaking in April, with most spawning activity taking place in the morning hours. Females produce an average of 79 ova; fecundity or the rate of fertilization, however, is relatively low. Mature ova measure about 0.2 cm in diameter. This species may live as long as two or three years in the wild.

CAUSE OF DECLINE, THREATS

Introduced Species: The brown darter, a closely related species, is believed to have been introduced into Okaloosa darter streams sometime before 1964.

Brown darters are not believed to occur naturally in these streams and may have been introduced by local fishermen using them as bait. The brown darter's range virtually surrounds the Okaloosa darter's range and extends westward to southern and south-central Alabama, north to southwestern Georgia, and east to north-central Florida. Brown darters have become established in several Okaloosa darter streams, and their range and numbers have expanded. It is believed that Okaloosa darters have been displaced by the brown darter in some areas, and competition with this species is considered the most significant threat to the Okaloosa darter.

Habitat Destruction and Pollution: Okaloosa darters appear to be intolerant of siltation resulting from erosion caused by road and railroad crossings, sand and clay pits, and land clearing practices. Some stream sections, heavily silted from intense sediment runoff, are now devoid of Okaloosa darters or have suffered significant population declines. Water quality could also be degraded by the introduction of pesticides or herbicides. **CURRENT TREND:** *Declining.* Estimates of total population range from 1,500 to 10,000 individuals.

Blackmouth Shiner
Notropis melanostomus
FAMILY CYPRINIDAE; Order Cypriniformes
LISTED STATUS
FWC: Endangered, listed 1979
USF&WS: Species of management concern
Description: Shiners are small fish, and this one is a very small shiner. Adults rarely exceed 1.2 inches (3 cm)

and average only 0.8 inch (2.1 cm). The largest individual measured just under 1.5 inches (3.7 cm); the smallest individual was just shy of 0.5 inches (1.2 cm). Blackmouths are slim cyprinid minnows with large eyes and a fairly prominent black lateral stripe extending the length of the animal from the snout to the base of the tail. The snout is upturned. The scales are thin and nearly embedded, the peritoneum is black, and there are numerous elongated gill rakers. There are 36 or 37 vertebrae. The species is differentiated from other species by the anal ray count (10–12) and the pharyngeal tooth formula (4-4). Sexual dimorphism is apparent during the spawning season, when males exhibit small tubercles on the pectoral fins. Morphologically the blackmouth is apparently most closely related to the slightly larger Kiamichi shiner (*Notropis ortenburgeri*), a species inhabiting upland streams of Oklahoma and Arkansas.

Distribution: This species is but one of 110 species of *Notropis* shiners, the largest genus of North American fishes. One of Florida's 26 native minnow species, the blackmouth shiner is also known as the Pond Creek shiner. Its known distribution is limited to the lower portions of Pond Creek, the Blackwater River drainage, and, at least formerly, the Shoal River in Santa Rosa, Okaloosa, and Walton counties of Florida's Panhandle. Another, apparently disjunct population occurs in the Pascagoula River drainage in Perry County, Mississippi (Chickasawhay River and Black Creek). Biologists suspect that this shiner may be more widely distributed; however, the populations are probably localized and not continuous. The species is known from a total of 21 localities within Florida.

Biology: Until fairly recently, little was known about the species, and it was considered very rare. First discovered in 1939 by Reeve M. Bailey, it was not seen again until 1975, when additional specimens were collected by biologist Stephen A. Bortone. Much of what is now known about the habitat requirements, ecology, and life history of the blackmouth shiner is based on the extensive research and fieldwork of Bortone, under a FWC grant. Apparently, many of the searches before 1975 were not conducted in what was later determined to be the specific habitat niche occupied by this fish. The blackmouth shiner is a true habitat specialist, rarely straying from the quiet, shallow oxbows and other backwaters with no measurable flow. The rivers and streams inhabited by this species have a substrate composed mainly of quartz sand, although the bottom is often muddy. The relatively cool waters are usually fairly clear and moderately acidic with a high dissolved oxygen content. The areas where these shiners occur are often quite pristine and unspoiled. The stream and river banks are often steep. Typical tree species in the adjacent terrestrial habitats include pond cypress, sweet gum, and Atlantic white cedar (*Chamaecyparis thyoides*). The aquatic vegetation often includes pondweed, bladderwort, and bog moss (*Mayaca fluviatilis*). Blackmouths are locally abundant in large schools in the lower Blackwater River drainage.

They form tightly packed schools, ranging from 50 to several thousand individuals, which swim about 1 foot (30 cm) below the water's surface.

When pursued or startled, the school quickly becomes even more dense but may disperse only to reform seconds later. These fish typically school in approximately 3 feet (1 m) of water, at least several feet from shore. Schools of brook silversides (*Labidesthes sicculus vanhyningi*), which closely resemble and behave like the shiners, often occur just above schools of blackmouth shiners. Two spawning periods have been noted, in spring and late summer. Approximately 60–70 eggs measuring only 0.7 millimeter in diameter are produced and probably deposited on vegetation. The blackmouth shiner, a slow grower, is believed to live at least 1.5 years in the wild. This diurnal, sight-feeding species readily consumes a variety of tiny phytoplankton (plants), including diatoms and other algae, and zooplankton (animals), including small crustaceans and rotifers. Predators include larger fish, amphibians and reptiles, and piscivorus bird species.

CAUSE OF DECLINE, THREATS

Habitat Destruction: Research has revealed that blackmouth shiners are restricted to a specific riverine microhabitat that makes them more vulnerable to habitat alteration than species that readily adapt to a variety of microhabitats. Continued development in the lower Blackwater River region may alter the water table and render areas now occupied by this species unsuitable. Because populations are not contiguous, loss of habitat may result in local extirpation. Other threats include severe droughts and water pollution.

Invasive Exotics: Though currently not a problem, the introduction of certain nonnative fishes into occupied rivers and streams could rapidly become a serious concern.

CURRENT TREND: *Stable,* generally. *Declining* in some areas.

Key Silverside

Menidia conchorum

FAMILY ATHERINIDAE; Order Atheriniformes

LISTED STATUS

FWC: Threatened, listed 1985 (endangered 1977–1984)

Description: The Key silverside, like other silversides, is a small, quick fish with large eyes. It is, in fact, the smallest silverside, with a maximum length of about 2.3 inches (5.8 cm). Females are slightly larger than males. As with other silversides, this species has a silvery lateral stripe between the pectoral and caudal fins.

Compared with other *Menidia* silversides, the Key silverside has fewer anal rays (usually 12–15 versus 16–18), fewer total vertebrae, and fewer branchial lateral-line scales. It can be distinguished from other silversides in South Florida by the presence of an anal fin sheath. Research has revealed that the Key silverside appears to be more closely related to the peninsula silverside (*Menidia peninsulae*), whose range is separated by a considerable distance, than to the tidewater silverside (*Menidia beryllina*), whose range nearly meets the range of this species.

Distribution: The Key silverside is limited in distribution to the Middle and Lower Keys, from Long Key south to the Key West area. It is one of three silversides in southeastern Florida. The tidewater silverside occurs as far south as Key Largo but does not occur within the range of the Key silverside. The peninsula silverside occurs as far south as Indian River County on Florida's Atlantic Coast and Collier County on the Gulf Coast.

Biology: The Key silverside is a fish of the unique lagoonal and ponded water ecosystems of the Florida Keys. Its habitat is typified by shallow, somewhat clear, coralline pools, often surrounded by mangroves. The lagoons and pools often have a layer of floating detritus. Characteristic aquatic plants of this habitat include turtle grass and algal species, including Venus's wine goblet (*Acetabularia* spp.). This fish is highly tolerant of the extreme variations in salinity in these habitats (ranging from 0 to 115 parts per thousand). It is generally a fish of brackish water, capable of surviving in both salt and fresh water. Other fishes commonly encountered in the Key silverside's habitat include marsh killifish (*Fundulus confluentus*), longnose killifish (*F. similis*), Gulf killifish (*F. grandis*), diamond killifish (*Adinia xenica*), oyster toadfish (*Opsanus beta*), needlefish (*Strongylura notata*), sailfin molly, and mosquito fish. The Key silverside is the only species endemic to this particular habitat niche.

The species is diurnal. Schools often remain within the black mangrove's submerged cable root system at night, which offers some protection from predators. During the day, schools forage near the water's surface. Their diet consists largely of planktonic crustaceans, copepods, ants, and other floating terrestrial insects, but juvenile fish (killifish) and algae are also consumed occasionally.

Predators of this species are numerous, including various larger fishes, wading birds, belted kingfishers, and possibly terns.

The longevity of the Key silverside is believed to be one year or less. Sexual maturity is reached when the fish is about 1.6 inches (4 cm) in length. The species reproduces throughout the year, with peaks in fertility noted in the spring and fall. The female deposits a series of tiny eggs about one millimeter in diameter, connected by a single stalk. These sticky eggs adhere to almost anything, including floating plant debris, turtle shells, and the legs of wading birds. Biologist Charles Getter, an expert on the Key silverside, believes that these adhering properties may aid in the dispersal of the fish. Abundance varies seasonally, with apparent population decreases in late summer and fall and increases in winter and spring.

CAUSE OF DECLINE, THREATS

Habitat Destruction and Human Encroachment: This Florida Keys endemic is vulnerable to extinction because of its extremely limited distribution, relatively low population densities, and specific habitat requirements. The environmental conditions of this silverside's lagoonal habitats are quite variable. Certain human activities have rendered formerly suitable habitats unsuitable. Impoundment of lagoons and ponds inhabited by Key silversides has adversely affected the species, apparently causing its extirpation in some areas. Other ponds formerly containing the species have been filled. Nearly all sites where Key silversides have been found have been altered by humans.

Other Threats: Biologists suspect that pesticide use, particularly during the summer and fall when reproductive activity peaks, may harm this species. Hurricanes, which routinely occur during that same season, remain a constant threat. The introduction of invasive exotic fishes may seriously threaten this species.

CURRENT TREND: *Unknown.* Fewer than 20 Key silverside populations are known.

Squirrel Chimney Cave Shrimp
Palaemonetes cummingi
FAMILY PALAEMONIDAE; Order Decapoda
LISTED STATUS
USF&WS: Threatened, listed 1990
Description: The Squirrel Chimney cave shrimp, also known as the Florida cave shrimp, is Florida's only known species of cave shrimp. Only a dozen or so specimens have been found, and to date, there are no known photographs of this species. Like many of the other cave-adapted, decapod crustacean fauna of northern Florida's myriad aquatic cave ecosystems, this shrimp is unpigmented and its vestigial eyes are greatly reduced, an evolutionary adaptation to its highly specialized, lightless, cavernicolus environment. The adult's translucent body is about 1.3 inches (3 cm) long. Cave shrimp, like other members of the order Decapoda (which includes shrimp, crayfish, and crabs), are among the most highly organized crustaceans. The thorax and head are joined together and form the cephalothorax, which is encased by the carapace. This species, like all shrimp, has 10 pairs of jointed limbs (used for gripping, walking, and swimming) and a pair of elongated, branched antennae. The head limbs are utilized primarily for feeding, and the trunk limbs are used for propulsion, as is the telson, or hind segment of the tail. The Squirrel Chimney cave shrimp is closely related to a species of freshwater grass shrimp (*Palaemonetes paludosus*) that occurs in the same geographical area but is not cave-adapted.

Distribution: The range of this cave shrimp, Florida's only crustacean designated as threatened or endangered, is almost certainly limited to one small locality, the Squirrel Chimney Sinkhole in western Alachua County. Numerous other sinks are nearby, some within several hundred yards; however, *Palaemonetes cummingi* has not been found at any other site.

Biology: Squirrel Chimney is a subterranean, sinkhole cave system accessible to divers and spelunkers through an opening in the earth that measures approximately 12 feet (3.7 m) across. Horton Hobbs and William MacLane, who explored these mysterious caverns during the late 1930's and 1940's, are responsible for much of what is now known about the biodiversity of Squirrel Chimney and many other water-filled caves in the porous, soluble limestone strata of northern Florida. According to Richard Franz of the University of Florida, who has entered Squirrel Chimney many times, the opening leads to two vertical shafts or tubes. A side tube dead-ends within 12 feet or so, but the smooth-sided main tube, used as a crawlway, leads to an enlarged cavern above the variable water table, some 50 feet or so below the opening. Water depth varies from about 18 feet to about 48 feet and is shallowest above a cone of debris that reaches a height of approximately 20 feet. The greatest breadth of the main cavern (below the water's surface) is approximately 100 feet. The terrestrial habitat surrounding the entrance to this sinkhole is mesic, mixed pine-hardwood forest.

Only about a dozen specimens of this cave shrimp have ever been found, and most have been discovered at or near the surface of the main sink or a connected fissure.

The ecology of the cave shrimp is similar in many respects to that of its close relative, the surface-dwelling grass shrimp. Like the grass shrimp, the cave shrimp has three larval stages. A gravid female collected in July contained 35 eggs that hatched 29 days later. The eggs, when deposited, are attached to the ventral area of the mother's body. The cave shrimp lays fewer but larger eggs than its freshwater cousin, *P. paludosus*. Hatchlings resemble the surface species but are slightly larger and more developed.

Other cavernicolous crustaceans of Squirrel Chimney often associated with *Palaemonetes* include the tiny North Florida spider crayfish (*Troglocambarus* sp.), which was first discovered in Squirrel Chimney, and the larger Alachua light-fleeing cave crayfish (*Procambarus* sp.) and pallid cave crayfish. Like the cave shrimp, these three species, particularly the first two, are highly habitat-specialized; they are albinistic with vestigial eyes; they share the cave shrimp's extremely restricted geographical distribution, specific habitat niche, and vulnerability to complete extermination at a site when the hydrology or water quality changes. Each species occupies a different microhabitat within

the groundwater system. The larger, heavily built *Procambarus* typically inhabit bottoms of pools, but the slight, spidery *Troglocambarus* typically cling to protruding rocks, ledges, floating branches, and even water-surface film. Fishes inhabiting flooded portions of Squirrel Chimney include redeye chub and larger yellow bullhead catfish. Barry Mansell reports observing 5-inch "brim" (possibly *Lepomis*) in this sinkhole on at least one occasion.

These and other odd-looking, rarely observed, translucent species of crustaceans are among the most fascinating of Florida's wildlife. Many are endemic, some limited to just one or two isolated sites. These peculiar crustaceans are largely unstudied barometers of one of Florida's unique natural communities.

CAUSE OF DECLINE, THREATS

Habitat Destruction: The sole site where this species is known to occur, Squirrel Chimney, is on private land. Therefore, the sinkhole itself, the unique organisms it harbors, and the surrounding natural communities remain vulnerable to anthropogenic damage. In the not-too-distant past, Squirrel Chimney sink was used as a dumping ground for discarded washing machines, construction materials, and trash, and access to the cave was not restricted. Fortunately, the sinkhole has now been cleaned up and access is regulated. As long as this aquatic sinkhole cave remains in private ownership, however, development will continue to pose a serious threat.

Water Quality and Quantity: Groundwater pollution and depletion of the water table also represent significant threats to the Squirrel Chimney sink and its aquatic organisms. Any human activities that alter detritus input could jeopardize the cave-adapted invertebrates that depend on accumulations of organic matter, including *Palaemonetes*.

CURRENT TREND: *Unknown,* possibly *extinct.* Approximately two decades since last seen. If this species still occurs at Squirrel Chimney, the prognosis is not considered good.

Schaus' Swallowtail Butterfly
Papilio aristodemus ponceanus
FAMILY PAPILIONIDAE; Order Lepidoptera
LISTED STATUS
FWC: Endangered, listed 1983
USF&WS: Endangered, listed 1984
(threatened 1976–1983)

Description: Schaus' swallowtail butterfly was first described by William Schaus of the Smithsonian Institution in 1911, from specimens taken in Miami. Schaus' swallowtail is a large blackish brown and yellow butterfly with a pair of tails on the hindwings. The ground color is dark brown, with a dorsal oblique dull yellow band on the wings. The tails are edged with dull yellow and lack the central yellow spot found in the giant and Bahama swallowtails, which occur in the same area. The yellow-bordered tail of this species is straight-edged, not teardrop-shaped. There is a hollow red spot along the anal margin just above the anal angle, scalloped yellow on the outer edges of the wings, and chestnut patches and a row of blue spots on the underside of the hindwings. The antennae of both sexes are black; however, the tip of each of the male's antennae bears a yellow knob. The wingspan is about 3.7 inches (9.5 cm), and the forewing is 1.8–2.9 inches (4.0–5.8 cm) long. When the butterfly is perched, an area of russet brown to magenta bordered by iridescent blue scales is visible on the ventral hindwing. The giant swallowtail (*Papilio cresphontes*), the easiest species to confuse with Schaus', is larger and typically blacker with brighter yellow coloration. The giant swallowtail also has solid black antennae, teardrop-shaped tails, and distinctly different flight behavior.

Eggs of Schaus' swallowtail are green. The caterpillars are maroon with blue spots and have cream-colored patches along the sides. The head is often brownish maroon. The tubular chrysalis is tapered and horned and ranges in color from rusty brown to gray etched with green.

Distribution: The family Papilionidae, of which Schaus' swallowtail is a member, contains more than 500 species (most occur in the tropics) and includes some of the world's largest and most beautiful butterflies. This family contains the swallowtail butterflies, of which 27 species inhabit North America, including 8 in Florida. Schaus' swalllowtail is a South Florida endemic with a small geographical distribution, confined to portions of Dade and Monroe counties. Historically, Schaus' swallowtail occurred in the Upper Keys and quite possibly the Lower Keys, and on the South Florida mainland as far north as Miami, which is the type locality. Today, however, it is restricted to a few locales within the natural range, including the north end of Key Largo, on Elliott Key, and on larger islands within the boundaries of Biscayne National Park.

Reintroduction efforts conducted in 1995 and 1997 have expanded the range from Dade County's Charles Deering Estate County Park in the north to Lower Matecumbe Key in the Middle Keys of Monroe County to the south.

Though Schaus' swallowtail has been documented in the Middle Keys and Lower Keys, its presence there is not believed to be regular. Two fairly recent but unverified sightings include an individual sighted on Big Pine Key in 1966 and an individual sighted on Lignum Vitae Key in 1973.

Once considered a distinct species (*Papilio ponceana*), Schaus' swallowtail is now classified as one of five *Papilio aristodemus* subspecies, all of which inhabit the Antillean region. The other currently assigned subspecies are the nominate race *P. aristodemus aristodemus*, which occurs in Hispaniola; *P. a. temenes*, which occurs in Cuba; and two races in the Bahamas, *P. a. driophilus* and *P. a. bjorndalae*. Thomas Emmel, an entomologist with the University of Florida who is one of the foremost authorities on this butterfly, believes that Schaus' swallowtail may warrant recognition as a distinct species, however.

Biology: Schaus' swallowtail is a habitat specialist. It inhabits relict tracts of mature tropical hardwood hammocks, which at one time covered much of the uplands of extreme southern Florida and the Upper Keys. These hardwood hammocks occupy relatively high elevations, typically 10–15 feet (3–4.6 m) above sea level and generally away from tidal waters. Plant diversity is high in these unique forest communities, which occur on a substrate of Key Largo limestone,

with more than 35 species of large trees and 60 species of small trees and shrubs. Dominant overstory trees include pigeon plum, gumbo-limbo, black ironwood, wild tamarind, poisonwood, and West Indian mahogany. Plants used most frequently for nectar include guava (*Psidium guajava*), wild coffee, and cheese shrub (*Morinda royoc*), but as many as 30 plant species may be utilized. Foraging often takes place in dappled sunlight, and direct sunlight is generally avoided. Adults tend to stay within the hammock, but males occasionally wander into clearings. These butterflies are capable of dispersal over considerable distances and have been encountered over the open ocean short distances from land.

The population of these butterflies often fluctuates greatly from year to year. Populations may vary from several hundred to several thousand individuals. The determining factors in these fluctuations are not known, but rearings have demonstrated that individuals can survive a diapause for two seasons in the pupal stage. Such a delay could be in response to environmental conditions that would hinder new growth on the host plants (probably low rainfall). Maximum life span is less than three weeks, with three days being closer to the norm. Adults emerge from the chrysalis at the beginning of the rainy season and begin breeding activity immediately. Schaus' swallowtail is strictly diurnal, being most active between 9 AM and 5 PM. Courtship has been observed in open areas within hammocks such as trails and natural clearings. The earliest sightings of adults are usually in late April or very early May, and individuals have been observed as late as August and September. If ideal conditions persist, it is believed that there may be a second flight of adults in late summer. Most sightings take place during May and June, however. Females tend to remain within the hammock searching for suitable food plants on which to lay their eggs. Eggs are typically laid singly on the tops of new-growth leaves of the torchwood, the primary food plant, and occasionally the wild lime. Often there are several eggs, not necessarily from the same female, on the same plant.

Eggs take 3–5 days to hatch. Larvae are first seen in early May. They feed on the tender new growth. Eggs and pupae are heavily preyed on by birds (especially northbound migrating warblers), parasitoid wasps, ants, and flies. Adults are preyed on by various flycatchers, golden orb weaver spiders, praying mantises, and anole lizards (personal communication, Thomas Emmel, April 1996). Perhaps only 3–4 percent of the eggs become adults.

CAUSE OF DECLINE, THREATS

Habitat Destruction: Extensive habitat loss is the primary reason for the decline of Schaus' swallowtail, particularly on Florida's mainland. Destruction of mature hardwood hammocks associated with the incessant urban sprawl of Miami, Homestead, and the Keys was instrumental in the near elimination of this species. Even where the hammocks survive, however, this butterfly has declined dramatically. Clearly, other factors are responsible as well, at least in part.

Pesticides: Several reports indicate that aerial spraying for mosquito control is one of the most critical of the culprits.

Each year in Monroe County, a toxic cocktail containing 4,000–5,000 gallons of Dibrom 14 mixed with 50,000–60,000 gallons of diesel fuel is deposited by air directly on the forest canopy by the county's mosquito control district. Observations made immediately following a spraying found drastically reduced populations of Schaus' swallowtail butterflies.

Illegal Collection: Collecting, long touted by many as a harmless hobby, is now considered a major factor in the decline of Schaus' swallowtail and a number of other butterfly species. Before 1972, hundreds of Schaus' swallowtails could be seen daily in Key Largo, and collectors came from all over the United States to harvest them (personal communication, Thomas Emmel, April 1996). A large international market for butterflies has developed, with rare specimens going for top dollar. Unfortunately, the rarer or more limited in distribution a species is, the more it is worth. Wildlife protection agencies in the federal government and in some states have initiated undercover operations to infiltrate the illegal chain of collectors and dealers and to suppress this trade. One such federal operation recently resulted in several arrests and the seizure of 2,375 protected butterflies appraised at more than $307,000.

Severe Storms: Hurricanes and violent tropical storms can suddenly devastate populations of the fragile Schaus' swallowtail. Hurricane Andrew, which traversed southern Florida in 1992, nearly blew the species into extinction. Elliott Key's population dropped to fewer than 60 individuals from a prehurricane population of 600–1,000 adults. The violent 1935 Labor Day hurricane that ravaged the Florida Keys resulted in such a dramatic decline that the butterfly was temporarily considered extinct.

Other Threats: Other threats include prolonged drought, rare freezes, fire, and automobile collisions. Road-killed Schaus' swallowtails have been encountered on CR905 within Key Largo's Crocodile Lakes National Wildlife Refuge.

CURRENT TREND: *Stable.* Captive breeding programs and reintroduction efforts have been so successful that some authorities predict the butterfly's eventual delisting.

Pillar Coral

Dendrogyra cylindrus

FAMILY MEANDRINIDAE; Order Scleractinia

LISTED STATUS

FWC: Endangered, listed 1985

Description: Pillar coral is the only coral found in the Florida Reef Tract that develops tall, vertical columns or pillars, hence the name. Numerous cylindrical columns extend upward from a base mass. These vertical columns are quite thick, 3–5 inches (8–13 cm). The color of the coral ranges from pale tan to dark brown; many are golden brown. When the tentacles are extended, the coral appears somewhat hairy. Florida's pillar coral clusters average less than 3 feet (1 m) in height, only occasionally exceeding 6 feet (2 m). Pillar coral clusters in warmer Caribbean waters may exceed 10 feet (3 m) in height.

Distribution: In Florida waters, pillar coral is restricted to the Florida Reef Tract on the Atlantic side of the Keys, from the area of Key Largo south and southwest to the area of the Dry Tortugas. It is uncommon to rare in Florida waters and occurs very locally within its limited range in southern Dade and Monroe counties. Larger colonies of this tropical coral occur off North Key Largo (Upper Keys) and Key Vaca (Middle Keys). According to Bill Goodwin, a biologist with the Florida Keys National Marine Sanctuary, Florida's largest pillar coral colony, known as the pillar coral forest, is no more than a couple of hundred square feet in size. Its distribution and abundance in Florida waters are apparently restricted, in part, by water temperature and quality. Pillar coral grows larger and is more abundant in the warmer, clearer waters of the Caribbean Sea and the Bahamas.

Biology: Pillar coral inhabits reefs on flat to gently sloping substrates in shallow to fairly shallow waters, 6–70 feet (2–20 m) deep. The optimum depth for this species is 10–25 feet (3–8 m). Pillar corals are both frame builders and sediment producers. The species often occurs in isolated, single clusters on patch reefs and outer reefs. Though not common anywhere in the Florida Reef Tract, a few pillar corals occur on most major reefs. Unlike other Caribbean Scleractinia corals, pillar coral polyps extend diurnally. Pillars toppled by storms and those that simply fall over sometimes generate new pillar colonies along the length of the now horizontal fallen pillar. This continuing process helps to disburse this species.

Biologists Harold Hudson and Bill Goodwin of the Florida Keys National Marine Sanctuary have discovered surprising facts about this species. Measurements taken of pillar coral on Florida reefs revealed a rate of growth two or three times faster than previously thought. Pillar coral is long-lived, with some clusters probably centuries old.

Unlike many other corals, which are hermaphroditic, the sexes are separate in pillar coral: there are male and female corals. Pillar corals may reproduce less successfully and be less common than other species as a result.

State and federal agencies have both been involved in efforts to preserve Florida's pillar coral colonies. Florida Keys biologists have been using rather innovative techniques to restore pillar coral damaged by Hurricane Andrew. In areas where pillar coral had been knocked down, they drilled holes 3–4 inches (7–10 cm) into dead coral rock and then removed the cylindrical core. Pieces of toppled coral were then planted into the cavities and permanently fused to the coral rock using a special underwater epoxy. Within several months of being glued, the broken living coral tissue had formed a seal with the substrate. The same adhesive has also been effectively used to reattach detached pieces of pillar coral to the cylinder where the break occurred.

CAUSE OF DECLINE, THREATS

Severe Storms: Hurricanes and violent tropical storms have proven perilous to the pillar coral. After Hurricane Andrew slammed into southeastern Florida in 1992, biologists discovered extensive damage to Key Largo's pillar coral colonies. Damage sustained included toppled and dismembered cylinders. A direct strike of a class 4 or 5 hurricane on reefs containing larger pillar coral concentrations could potentially destroy a large percentage of Florida's remaining pillar coral.

Boat Anchoring and Groundings: Though sturdy in appearance, pillar corals are actually quite brittle and frail. Dropping an anchor onto or pulling it over this coral can severely damage the polyps, destroying in a moment what took many years to create. Groundings of vessels on pillar colonies can also have devastating effects.

Pollution: Corals require sunlight to live; therefore clear nutrient-free waters are required for sufficient light to reach the coral's zooxanthellae (beneficial algae). When nutrient-rich waters are introduced into reef waters, plankton growth and benthic algal growth are stimulated and water clarity is diminished. The coral reefs of the Florida Keys, especially those off Key Largo, are vulnerable to high nutrient loading from erosion, leaky septic tanks, and stormwater runoff from residential areas. Oil spills in waters harboring pillar coral could be catastrophic for this species.

Collecting: Florida statute 370.110 prohibits the collection, damage, and sale of stony corals. Before that legal protection, Florida's pillar coral was heavily collected. Between the 1950's and 1970's, collectors totally eliminated several pillar coral colonies. This attractive coral is still harvested illegally on occasion. The coral reefs of the Keys receive ten times as many divers annually as Australia's Great Barrier Reef, which is ten times larger. Florida's living coral reef is the most popular diving destination on the planet.

Other Threats: Corals are susceptible to several diseases, including white line disease, caused by a virus, and black band disease, caused by a bacterium and algae. Another condition, known as bleaching, occurs when the water becomes especially warm and stagnant, causing the zooxanthellae to vacate the coral, which in turn causes the coral to appear quite anemic. The pillar coral is apparently very intolerant of cold water; if the water stays unusually cold for an extended period of time, it could present a serious threat.

CURRENT TREND: *Stable.*

Stock Island Tree Snail
Orthalicus reses reses
FAMILY BULIMULIDAE

LISTED STATUS

FWC: Endangered, listed 1979

USF&WS: Threatened, listed 1978

Description: This fairly large, attractive tree snail, with a relatively thin cone-shaped shell is typically 1.8–2.2 inches (4.5–5.5 cm) in length, with some individuals approaching 3 inches (7.6 cm). The ground color is generally whitish or buff; there are three faint spiral bands and a series of purplish brown, vertical, undulating, axial stripes. The stripes are generally not as wide or dark as they are in the Florida Keys tree snail (*Orthalicus reses nesodryas*), a closely related form also native to the Lower Keys. The shell of the Stock Island tree snail is generally thinner and more translucent than that of other *Orthalicus* species. There are two or three white apical whorls present. The snail itself is gray to buff in color and is unmarked.

Distribution: The historic range of this subspecies was apparently limited to the tropical hardwood hammocks of Stock Island and Key West, although it may have occurred on other nearby keys. The colonies on Key West were thought to be extirpated by the 1940's, and by 1996 the race was thought to be extinct in the wild (within its historic range). Surveys conducted in 1996, however, revealed the presence of Stock Island tree snail populations on Key West.

The distribution of the Stock Island tree snail has now been artificially increased by collectors, who have intentionally released them into six different areas outside their natural range on Key Largo and on the extreme South Florida mainland.

Members of the genus *Orthalicus* are widespread in Central and South America. Only two species occur in North America, and both (*Orthalicus reses* and *O. floridensis*) are restricted in range to southern Florida. *Orthalicus reses* has two recognized subspecies, both of which are restricted to the Florida Keys. The Florida Keys tree snail (*O. r. nesodryas*) occurs throughout many of the keys, excluding Stock Island. It has been suggested that Florida's *Orthalicus* species (as well as *Liguus* species) arrived from the tropics during the late Pleistocene by floating on uprooted tropical trees.

Biology: The natural habitat of the Stock Island tree snail consists of the dense, humid, tropical hardwood hammocks that formerly covered much of the Florida Keys. Hammocks inhabited by these snails generally occur at elevations of 5–11 feet (1.5–3.6 m) above sea level. They have been found on a variety of native trees including gumbo-limbo, strangler fig, lignum vitae, poisonwood, Jamaica caper (*Capparis flexuosa*), and coco plum. Smooth-barked native trees that support an abundance of lichens and algae are preferred, especially larger, mature trees. This snail has also been found on several nonnative trees including Indian tamarind (*Tamarindus indica*).

This tree snail feeds on epiphytic cryptogams, such as fungi, lichens, and algae, found on tree limbs and leaves. A nocturnal species, it is most active during the rainy season (May–November), when it breeds and forages. Estivation generally takes place during the dry months (usually December–April), when these snails may conceal themselves in the crotches or cavities of trees and fasten the opening of the shell to the tree with a mucous seal. They may come out of estivation during dry-season rains and likewise may go into estivation during periods of wet-season drought. This snail is quite intolerant of cold weather.

The Stock Island tree snail is androgynous, having characteristics of both sexes; however, it is not capable of self-fertilization. This is beneficial in reproduction, as it allows the fertilization of each snail, not just females. Egg-bearing snails descend their host tree and lay the eggs in cavities at the base of the tree. Sexual maturity is reached after two or three years.

Predators include black rats, several species of birds, raccoons, and domestic cats. Eggs and recently hatched snails are readily attacked and preyed on by introduced fire ants.

CAUSE OF DECLINE, THREATS

Habitat Destruction: Real estate development has eliminated nearly all the snail's habitat on Key West and Stock Island, two of the most populated islands of the Keys. Continued urbanization represents a serious threat to the survival of this species.

Overcollection: Despite receiving legal protection in 1978, this species continued to be harvested from the few tropical hardwood hammocks where it remained. Overcollection of attractive arboreal snails from the wild is a principal factor worldwide in the extinction of many species. Collectors are mostly to blame for the eradication of several local color phases or races of the Florida tree snail that formerly inhabited the tropical hardwood hammocks of South Florida.

Introduced Species: Fire ants, now abundant and widespread in the Keys, including Stock Island and Key West, attack defenseless adult snails as they descend trees to lay eggs and also devour eggs laid in soil or leaf litter at the base of trees. Black rats have become increasingly common in tropical hammocks and are also known to prey on tree snails.

Severe Weather: Because the remaining wild populations of this species are so meager and isolated, they are particularly vulnerable to extinction as a result of hurricanes and other severe weather events.

Pesticides: Pesticides, including mosquito sprays, may kill snails directly and may adversely alter feeding or reproductive behavior.

Other Threats: Excessive watering of lawns and ornamental plants may induce snails out of estivation during winter and may fatally expose them to desiccation and cold temperatures.

CURRENT TREND: *Declining.* As of 2002, extirpated throughout most of its historic range.

State Species of Special Concern, Federal Candidate Species, and Federal Species of Management Concern

S, listed by the state of Florida

F, listed by the federal government

SSC, Species of Special Concern, a state classification

SMC, Species of Management Concern, a federal classification

CAND, Candidate, a federal classification

E, Endangered

T, Threatened

Within categories, species are listed alphabetically by the Latin name.

Mammals

Sherman's short-tailed shrew (*Blarina carolinensis shermani*), S-SSC, F-SMC

Florida mastiff bat (*Eumops glaucinus floridanus*), F-CAND (S-E)

Southeastern brown bat (*Myotis austroriparius*), F-SMC

Round-tailed muskrat (*Neofiber alleni*), F-SMC

Sanibel Island rice rat (*Oryzomys palustris sanibeli*), S-SSC

Santa Rosa beach mouse (*Peromyscus polionotus leucocephalus*), F-SMC

St. Andrew beach mouse (*Peromyscus polionotus peninsularis*), F-CAND (S-E)

Southeastern big-eared bat (*Plecotus rafinesquii*), F-SMC

Florida mouse (*Podomys floridanus*), S-SSC, F-SMC

Key Vaca raccoon (*Procyon lotor auspicatus*), F-SMC

Key West raccoon (*Procyon lotor incautus*), F-SMC

Englewood mole (*Scalopus aquaticus bassi*), F-SMC

Big Cypress fox squirrel (*Sciurus niger avicennia*), F-SMC (S-T)

Sherman's fox squirrel (*Sciurus niger shermani*), S-SSC, F-SMC

Insular hispid cotton rat (*Sigmodon hispidus insulicola*), F-SMC

Homosassa shrew (*Sorex longirostris eionis*), S-SSC

Eastern chipmunk (*Tamias striatus*), S-SSC

Florida black bear (*Ursus americanus floridanus*), F-SMC (S-T)

Birds

Northern goshawk (*Accipiter gentilis*), F-SMC

Bachman's sparrow (*Aimophila aestivalis*), F-SMC

Roseate spoonbill (*Ajaia ajaja*), S-SSC

Henslow's sparrow (*Ammodramus henslowii*), F-SMC

Wakulla seaside sparrow (*Ammodramus maritimus juncicolus*), S-SSC, F-SMC

Scott's seaside sparrow (*Ammodramus maritimus peninsulae*), S-SSC

Limpkin (*Aramus guarauna*), S-SSC

Southeastern snowy plover (*Charadrius alexandrinus tenuirostris*), F-SMC (S-T)

Worthington's marsh wren (*Cistothorus palustris griseus*), S-SSC

Marian's marsh wren (*Cistothorus palustris marianae*), S-SSC

White-crowned pigeon (*Columba leucocephala*), F-SMC (S-T)

Stoddard's yellow-throated warbler (*Dendroica dominica stoddardi*), F-SMC

Little blue heron (*Egretta caerulea*), S-SSC

Reddish egret (*Egretta rufescens*), S-SSC, F-SMC

Snowy egret (*Egretta thula*), S-SSC

Tricolored heron (*Egretta tricolor*), S-SSC

White ibis (*Eudocimus albus*), S-SSC

Southeastern American kestrel (*Falco sparverius paulus*), F-SMC (S-T)

Whooping crane (*Grus americana*), S-SSC (F-T experimental population)

American oystercatcher (*Haematopus palliatus*), S-SSC

Loggerhead shrike (*Lanius ludovicianus*), F-SMC

Black rail (*Laterallus jamaicensis*), F-SMC

Osprey (*Pandion haliaetus*), S-SSC in Monroe County only

Brown pelican (*Pelecanus occidentalis*), S-SSC

Mangrove clapper rail (*Rallus longirostris insularum*), F-SMC

Black skimmer (*Rynchops niger*), S-SSC

Burrowing owl (*Speotyto cunicularia*), S-SSC

Amphibians

Flatwoods salamander (*Ambystoma cingulatum*), F-SMC

Georgia blind salamander (*Haideotriton wallacei*), S-SSC, F-SMC

Pine barrens treefrog (*Hyla andersoni*), S-SSC

Gulf hammock dwarf siren (*Pseudobranchus striatus lustricolus*), F-SMC

Florida gopher frog (*Rana capito aesopus*), S-SSC, F-SMC

Dusky gopher frog (*Rana capito sevosa*), S-SSC, F-CAND

Florida bog frog (*Rana okaloosae*), S-SSC, F-SMC

Reptiles

American alligator (*Alligator mississippiensis*), S-SSC (federally listed as threatened because of its similarity in appearance to the endangered American crocodile)

LIZARDS

Florida Keys mole skink (*Eumeces egregius egregius*), S-SSC, F-SMC

Cedar Key mole skink (*Eumeces egregius insularis*), F-SMC

Island glass lizard (*Ophisaurus compressus*), F-SMC

Florida scrub lizard (*Sceloporus woodi*), F-SMC

SNAKES

Key ring-necked snake (*Diadophis punctatus acricus*), F-SMC (S-T)

Rosy rat snake, or Lower Keys corn snake (*Elaphe guttata guttata*), S-SSC

Southern hog-nosed snake (*Heterodon simus*), F-SMC

Gulf salt marsh snake (*Nerodia clarki clarki*), F-SMC

Florida pine snake (*Pituophis melanoleucus mugitus*), S-SSC, F-SMC

Short-tailed snake (*Stilosoma extenuatum*), F-SMC (S-T)

Rimrock crowned snake (*Tantilla oolitica*), F-SMC (S-T)

TURTLES

Gopher tortoise (*Gopherus polyphemus*), S-SSC, F-SMC

Barbour's map turtle (*Graptemys barbouri*), S-SSC, F-SMC

Alligator snapping turtle (*Macroclemys temmincki*), S-SSC, F-SMC

Suwannee cooter (*Pseudemys concinna suwanniensis*), S-SSC

Fishes

Atlantic sturgeon (*Acipenser oxyrinchus oxyrinchus*), S-SSC
Common snook (*Centropomus undecimalis*), S-SSC
Crystal darter (*Crystallaria asprella*), F-SMC (S-T)
Bluestripe shiner (*Cyprinella callitaenia*), F-SMC
Lake Eustis pupfish (*Cyprinodon variegatus hubbsi*), S-SSC
Harlequin darter (*Etheostoma histrio*), S-SSC
Southern tessellated darter (*Etheostoma olmstedi maculaticeps*), S-SSC
Salt marsh topminnow (*Fundulus jenkinsi*), S-SSC
Chipola bass (*Micropterus notius coosae*), S-SSC
Suwannee bass (*Micropterus notius notius*), S-SSC
Bluenose shiner (*Pteronotropis welaka*), S-SSC
Mangrove rivulus (*Rivulus marmoratus*), S-SSC
Key blenny (*Starksia starcki*), S-SSC

Crustaceans

Florida cave amphipod (*Crangonyx grandimanus*), F-SMC
Hobbs cave amphipod (*Crangonyx hobbsi*), F-SMC
Orange-Seminole cave crayfish (*Procambarus acherontis*), F-SMC
Panama City crayfish (*Procambarus econfinae*), S-SSC
Santa Fe cave crayfish (*Procambarus erythrops*), S-SSC
Black Creek crayfish (*Procambarus pictus*), S-SSC, F-SMC

Arachnids

Key gnaphosid spider (*Cesonia irvingi*), F-SMC
Torreya trap-door spider (*Cyclocosmia torreya*), F-SMC
Lake Placid funnel wolf spider (*Sosippus placidus*), F-SMC

Insects

BEETLES
Pygmy anomala scarab beetle (*Anomala exigua*), F-SMC (possibly extinct)
Archbold anomala scarab beetle (*Anomala eximia*), F-SMC
Aphodius tortoise commensal scarab beetle (*Aphodius troglodytes*), F-SMC
Big Pine Key ataenius dung beetle (*Ataenius superficialis*), F-SMC
Woodruff's ataenius dung beetle (*Ataenius woodruffi*), F-SMC
Highlands tiger beetle (*Cicindela highlandensis*), F-SMC
Copris tortoise commensal scarab beetle (*Copris gopheri*), F-SMC
Miami roundhead scarab beetle (*Cyclocephala miamiensis*), F-SMC
Fig-seed diving beetle (*Desmopachria cenchramis*), F-SMC
Spiny Florida sandhill scarab beetle (*Gronocarus multispinosus*), F-SMC
Florida intertidal firefly (*Micronaspis floridana*), F-SMC
Scrub Island burrowing scarab beetle (*Mycotrupes pedester*), F-SMC
Tortoise commensal scarab beetle (*Onthophagus polyphemus*), F-SMC
Ocala burrowing scarab beetle (*Peltotrupes youngi*), F-SMC
Everglades brownwing firefly (*Photuris brunnipennis floridana*), F-SMC
Turtle Mound firefly (*Photuris* sp.), yet to be described, F-SMC

Panhandle beach scarab beetle
(*Polylamina pubescens*), F-SMC
Frost's spring serican scarab beetle
(*Serica frosti*), F-SMC
Tantula serican scarab beetle (*Serica tantula*), F-SMC
Scrub palmetto flower scarab beetle
(*Trigonopelastes floridana*), F-SMC
Caracara commensal scarab beetle
(*Trox howelli*), F-SMC

BUTTERFLIES AND MOTHS
Florida leafwing butterfly (*Anaea troglodyta floridalis*), F-SMC
Eastern beard grass skipper (*Atrytone arogos*), F-SMC
Florida atala butterfly (*Eumaeus atala florida*), F-SMC
Tortoise commensal noctuid moth
(*Idia gopheri*), F-SMC
Sweadner's olive hairstreak butterfly
(*Mitoura gryneus sweadneri*), F-SMC
Ceromatic noctuid moth (*Pyreferra ceromatica*), F-SMC
Tortoise commensal noctuid moth
(*Schinia rufipinna*), F-SMC
Bartram's hairstreak butterfly (*Strymon acis bartrami*), F-SMC
Okefenokee zale moth (*Zale perculta*),
F-SMC

CADDISFLIES
Zigzag blackwater caddisfly (*Agarodes ziczac*), F-SMC
Florida ceraclean longhorn caddisfly
(*Ceraclea floridana*), F-SMC (possibly extinct)
Provost's ochrotrichian microcaddisfly
(*Ochrotrichia provosti*), F-SMC
Little oecetis longhorn caddisfly
(*Oecetis parva*), F-SMC
Florida oxyethiran microcaddisfly
(*Oxyethira florida*), F-SMC

Three-tooth long-horned triaenodes caddisfly (*Triaenodes tridonta*), F-SMC

DRAGONFLIES AND MAYFLIES
Say's spiketail dragonfly (*Cordulegaster sayi*), F-SMC
American sand-burrowing mayfly
(*Dolania americana*), F-SMC
Bronze clubtail dragonfly (*Gomphus townesi*), F-SMC
Westfall's clubtail dragonfly (*Gomphus westfalli*), F-SMC
Blackwater sand-filtering mayfly
(*Homoeoneuria dolani*), F-SMC
Apalachicola twilight skimmer dragonfly (*Neurocordulia clara*),
F-SMC

FLIES
Florida asaphomyian tabanid fly
(*Asaphomyia floridensis*), F-SMC
Brown merycomyian tabanid fly
(*Merycomyia brunnea*), F-SMC
Delong's mixogaster flower fly
(*Mixogaster delongi*), F-SMC
Sugarfoot moth fly (*Nemopalpus nearcticus*), F-SMC

GRASSHOPPERS
Big Pine Key conehead katydid
(*Belocephalus micanopy*), F-SMC
Keys short-winged conehead katydid
(*Belocephalus sleighti*), F-SMC
Florida Keys scaly cricket (*Cycloptilum irregularis*), F-SMC
Torreya pygmy grasshopper (*Tettigidea empedonepia*), F-SMC

Sponges
Oklawaha sponge (*Dorsilia palmeri*),
F-SMC
Kissimmee sponge (*Ephydatia subtilis*),
F-SMC

Mollusks

Florida arc mussel (*Alasmidonta wrightiana*), F-SMC

Fat three-ridge mussel (*Amblema neislerii*), F-SMC

Blue Spring hydrobe snail (*Aphaostracon asthenes*), F-SMC

Wekiwa Springs hydrobe snail (*Aphaostracon monas*), F-SMC

Dense hydrobe snail (*Aphaostracon pycnus*), F-SMC

Fenney Spring hydrobe snail (*Aphaostracon xynoelictus*), F-SMC

Helicoid spring snail (*Cincinnatia helicogyra*), F-SMC

Ichetucknee silt snail (*Cincinnatia mica*), F-SMC

Enterprise silt snail (*Cincinnatia monroensis*), F-SMC

Pygmy silt snail (*Cincinnatia parva*), F-SMC

Ponderous silt snail (*Cincinnatia ponderosa*), F-SMC

Seminole silt snail (*Cincinnatia vanhyningi*), F-SMC

Wekiwa silt snail (*Cincinnatia wekiwae*), F-SMC

Purple bankclimber mussel (*Elliptoideus sloatianus*), F-SMC

Hood ancydid (*Ferissia mcneili*), F-SMC

Narrow pigtoe mussel (*Fusconaia escambia*), F-SMC

Albany snail (*Goniobasis albanyensis*), F-SMC

Southern sandshell mussel (*Lampsilus australis*), F-SMC

Shiny-rayed pocketbook mussel (*Lampsilus subangulata*), F-SMC

Florida tree snail (*Liguus fasciatus*), S-SSC

Round ebonyshell mussel (*Obvaria rotulata*), F-SMC

Oval pigtoe mussel (*Pleuroblema pyriforme*), F-SMC

Southern kidneyshell mussel (*Ptychobranchus jonesi*), F-SMC

Keys vertigo (*Vertigo hebardi*), F-SMC

Choctaw pearly mussel (*Villosa choctawensis*), F-SMC

Glossary

Albinism   Lack of pigment in the skin and hair.

Alga   (plural, algae). Unicellular or simple multicellular photosynthetic organism lacking multicellular sex organs.

Allopatric   Occupying mutually exclusive, but usually adjacent, geographical areas.

Amphibian   A vertebrate intermediate in many characteristics between reptiles and fish, living part or most of its life on land but returning to water to reproduce because fertilization is external.

Anadromous   Of marine fish that ascend freshwater rivers to spawn.

Anal fin   The median fin behind the anus.

Antennae   Long, paired sensory appendages on the head of many arthropods.

Anterior   Front end of an organism.

Anthropogenic   Caused by humans.

Aquatic   Frequenting water, or living or growing in water. Technically, only animals that have gills for extracting oxygen from water are aquatic; others, such as turtles and water snakes, are considered semi-aquatic.

Arboreal   Frequenting trees; adapted for climbing.

Arthropod   An invertebrate with a segmented body and jointed appendages; a member of the phylum Arthropoda.

Avifauna   Birdlife of a given region.

Barbel   Small, fleshy, usually downward projection of skin near the mouth, chin, or throat in some fishes, turtles, and tadpoles.

Benthic   Occurring on or frequenting the bottom zones of bodies of water.

Bicolor   Having two colors.

Biodiversity   The total variety of life and its processes; total variety represented by all plant and animal species; variety of different habitats and ecosystems in which these species exist.

Biological accumulation   The concentration of a toxic substance (e.g., heavy metals) in living tissue as it is consumed by organisms in successive levels of the food chain.

Biota   The plants and animals of an area.

Biotic community   The assemblage of organisms living in a prescribed area or physical habitat.

Bivalve   Mollusk with a shell of two valves.

Buffer   Multiuse transition areas designed and managed to protect core reserves and critical corridors from the destructive effects of human activities.

Buteo   Any broad-winged hawk of the genus *Buteo*.

Canine   Concerning dogs; the eyetooth of mammals.

Carapace   Upper shell of a turtle; protective shell covering the head and thorax of many arthropods.

Carnivorous   Meat-eating.

Caudal fin   Fin on the hindmost part of the body.

Cavernicolous   Living in caves.

Caviar   A salty relish prepared from the eggs of sturgeon, salmon, or certain other fish.

Characteristic species   A species that is almost always present in a particular type of community, usually at higher frequency than other species.

Clastic upland lake   A lake with clay and organic substrates. The water may be clear or colored, neutral in pH or slightly acidic, and soft (with a low mineral content, particularly sodium chloride and sulfates). Nutrient levels may be relatively low to very high (eutrophic), depending on the geologic age of the lake.

Climax community   The final, relatively stable plant community in a successional series.

Community   All the organisms inhabiting a common environment and interacting with one another.

Competition   Interaction between members of the same species or population or between different species or populations in order to obtain a mutually required resource.

Conifer   A tree that bears cones (e.g., pines).

Corridor   A landscape linkage that permits large-scale and long-term ecological processes to continue operating within fragmented ecosystems.

Costal scute   An enlarged plate on the side of the carapace of a turtle or tortoise ("costal" means near or associated with the ribs).

Crepuscular   Active primarily at dawn or dusk.

Critical habitat   Specific areas determined by the Secretary of the Interior to be essential for the conservation of a species and listed in accordance with the provisions of section 4 of the Endangered Species Act.

Crop   The part of a bird's alimentary canal where food is stored prior to completion of digestion.

Cryptic   Coloring, patterning, or behavior that renders an animal less visible against its natural background.

Decapods   Crustaceans having five pairs of appendages; includes crabs, crayfish, and lobsters.

Deciduous   Shedding leaves within certain cycles or seasons.

Delist   To remove a species from a state or federal list of protected species. Species may be delisted either because they are classified as extinct or because their populations have recovered and their ecosystems are restored to a level that can support self-sustaining and self-regulating populations of the species as persistent members of native biotic communities. The federal process measures the improvement of the status of the species against the criteria set out in section 4(a)(1) of the Endangered Species Act.

Dimorphism   Difference in form, color, or structure between members of the same species (e.g., plumage differences between male and female birds).

Disjunct   Not joined; separated.

Dispersal   Movement of organisms away from a location, such as their point of origin.

Diurnal Active by day.

DNA Abbreviation for deoxyribonucleic acid, the carrier of genetic information in cells, composed of two complementary chains of nucleotides wound in a double helix.

Dominant species The principal species in a community.

Dormant In a resting state (e.g., hibernation).

Dorsal Pertaining to the upper surface.

Down feathers Small, soft feathers that lack a vein.

Downlist To move a protected species from the endangered list to the less critical classification of threatened. A species may be downlisted if it is known to be increasing in numbers in the wild or if threats to its existence are lessening in the wild.

Ecological niche The elements (e.g., food sources) of a habitat necessary to support a species; the role of a species within its ecological community.

Ecology A branch of science relating to the distribution and abundance of organisms and the relationship between organisms and their environment.

Ecosystem A dynamic and interrelating complex of plant and animal communities and their associated environment.

Ecotone An area where two or more habitats meet.

Endemic Confined to a particular geographical region.

Estivation A state of inactivity during prolonged periods of drought or high temperatures, usually while the animal is in seclusion. Animals in many drier parts of the world hide away in the summer or driest season and sleep, avoiding the danger of drying up (e.g., Stock Island tree snail).

Estuarine Pertaining to coastal wetland habitats, including salt marshes and mangrove swamps, that occur in a transition zone where the tide ebbs and flows.

Evolution The process whereby living things are believed to arise from earlier forms by gradual change; any change in the gene pool from one generation to the next.

Exoskeleton A supporting structure that is outside an animal's body, as in crabs, insects, and other arthropods.

Exotic species Any introduced species that is not native to the area, especially species that may be considered a nuisance.

Extinct No longer in existence as a population or species.

Extirpation The elimination or disappearance of a species from a part of its range; a local extinction.

Family A grouping of related, similar genera; the taxonomic category below order and above genus.

Fauna The animal life of a region.

Fecundity Fertility; the quality of producing offspring in large numbers.

Feral Relating to domestic animal species surviving in the wild.

First-magnitude spring A spring with a flow that averages over 6 billion gallons per day.

Flora The plant life of a region.

Foredune, or frontal dune The first large dune to form on the seaward side of a beach.

Fossorial Adapted for digging.

Frugivorous Fruit-eating.

Gene pool   All the alleles of all the genes of all the individuals in a population.

Genetic exchange   The exchange of genes or genetic traits between different populations or subspecies.

Genetic introgression   Occurs when gene dispersal mechanisms no longer function to maintain genetic diversity within a small, isolated population. (See *Inbreeding*.)

Genus (plural, genera)   A group of species agreeing in certain characteristics and differing from other genera within the same family.

Geomorph   A type of landscape or landform, classified according to a systematic analysis of the processes that formed it.

Gestation   Period from fertilization to birth in mammals.

Gill net   A fishing net suspended vertically in the water to entangle fish by their gills.

Gill raker   A bony or cartilaginous filament on the inside of the gill arches of fishes, which help prevent solid substances from being carried out through the gill slits.

Gravid   Bearing eggs or young, ordinarily in the oviducts; pregnant.

Groundwater   Water below ground. Its upper level forms the water table.

Habitat   A particular type of environment (e.g., marsh or dry prairie).

Habitat generalist   A highly adaptive organism that can survive within a wide range of environmental conditions; a species that is not restricted to a narrow ecological niche.

Habitat specialist   A species having special adaptations to a narrow ecological niche; an organism that is not highly adaptive.

Hammock   A slightly elevated tract of forested land, often surrounded by marsh or prairie habitats.

Hemipenes   The paired copulatory organs of male reptiles.

Herbivore   An animal that eats plants or other photosynthetic organisms to obtain its food and energy.

Hermaphrodite   An organism possessing both male and female reproductive organs.

Herpetofauna   The reptile and amphibian life of a particular region.

Herpetology   The branch of zoology that treats the study of reptiles and amphibians.

Hibernacula   The shelter or area where an animal hibernates.

Hibernation   A state of inactivity or deep sleep. Some animals (including reptiles, amphibians, and certain mammals) bury themselves away to escape freezing temperatures during the coldest months of the year.

Home range   An area within which a mammal, bird, reptile, or other animal hunts or nests.

Hybrid   The offspring of two different species or genera.

Hydric   Wet.

Hydroperiod   The time during the year when a wetland contains abundant water.

Ichthyofauna   The fish life of a particular region.

Inbreeding   The mating of individuals closely related genetically. Inbreeding depression occurs when physical isolation causes a small population of animals to inbreed.

The population becomes genetically isolated, often resulting in the loss of genetic variability, decreased semen quality, lowered fertility and neonatal survival, and other abnormalities, increasing the chance of extinction.

Indicator species A species that seems, in the context of the surrounding landscape or in comparison with related communities, to be most indicative of a particular community.

Indigenous Native to a particular area.

Instinct Inflexible, unlearned behavior or response triggered by specific stimuli, believed to be genetically determined.

Intergrade The offspring of two different subspecies; an intermediate form exhibiting a combination of characteristics of two or more subspecies.

Interspace A patch of color between two markings (such as bands or blotches on a snake).

Introduced species See **Exotic species.**

Juvenile A young or immature individual, often displaying proportions and coloration differing from that of an adult.

Keel In bats or birds, a large ridge or process on the breast bone. In turtles, a ridge down the back or along the plastron. In snakes, a longitudinal ridge on a dorsal scale.

Keystone species An animal or plant that typifies a particular type of habitat and plays a vital role in the habitat, benefiting other species in the community (e.g., the gopher tortoise in sandhill communities).

Labial Pertaining to the lip.

Lacustrine Pertaining to wetlands of natural depressions without flowing water and lacking persistent emergent vegetation except around the perimeter; applies to a lake or ponded body of water of more than 20 acres.

Landscape An area that is a composite of all the characteristics that distinguish a certain area on the earth's surface from other areas.

Larva (plural, larvae) The young form of an animal that is very different from the adult stage.

Lateral Pertaining to the side.

Lateral line System of sense organs found only in fishes and in the young stages of amphibians. It is better developed in bony fishes than in sharklike fishes. Lateral lines can clearly be seen running along the sides of sharks and bony fishes from the back of the head to the tail. Movements or vibrations in the water around the fish move the hairs and stimulate the sense cells, passing signals along the nerve fibers to the brain.

Lepidoptera An order of insects including butterflies and moths.

Lore In a bird, the space between the eye and the bill.

Marginal scute One of the plates that form the outer edge of the carapace of a turtle or tortoise.

Marine Living in salt water.

Maritime Living or found near the sea; bordering on the sea.

Marl A mixture of clay, sand, and limestone, in varying proportions, that is soft and crumbly, usually containing shell fragments.

Melanistic Having an abundance of black pigmentation, sometimes resulting in an all-black or nearly all-black animal.

Mesic Moderately moist; intermediate between xeric and hydric.

Mesophytic Moderately moist; growing in or adapted to a moderately moist environment.

Middorsal Pertaining to the center of the back.

Migration A fairly regular, instinctive movement of animals from one place to another. Migrations are normally seasonal, with populations traveling one direction in winter and the opposite direction in summer (e.g., fish going to spawning grounds, swallows flying north in the spring).

Mimicry A resemblance between species that confers some benefit on one of the species (e.g., the nonvenomous scarlet king snake is avoided by many potential predators because it resembles the venomous coral snake).

Monotypic Pertaining to the only representative of a group, such as a genus with only one species.

Morph A distinct, identifiable color phase of a species.

Morphological Pertaining to form or structure, at any level of organization.

Mustache In birds, a conspicuous stripe of color beneath the eye.

Mutation A change in a gene or chromosome that can lead to the appearance of new features in the organism.

Native A plant or animal present before the arrival of European settlers.

Neonate A very recently born or hatched individual.

Neotropical Related to the biogeographic region of the New World that stretches southward from the Tropic of Cancer and includes southern Mexico, Central and South America, and the West Indies.

Nocturnal Active by night.

Nuchal scute The single small, thin plate on the front edge of a turtle's carapace. Its different shape distinguishes it from marginal scutes.

Obligate commensal An organism that relies on a relationship with another organism for its survival; e.g., the gopher tortoise copris beetle is an obligate commensal to the gopher tortoise, the organism that creates the burrow that the beetle inhabits.

Omnivorous Eating both vegetable and animal food.

Oolitic Pertaining to rock, usually limestone, composed principally of granules of calcium carbonate.

Ophiophagous Feeding on snakes.

Order A grouping of related, similar families; the taxonomic category below class and above family.

Ornithology The study of birds.

Oviparous Egg-laying; laying fully developed eggs in which embryos are at a very early stage.

Ovoviviparous Producing eggs that undergo all or at least most of their development within the female parent.

Palustrine Pertaining to wetlands dominated by plants adapted to anaerobic conditions imposed by substrate saturation during more than 10 percent of the growing season; includes nontidal wetlands and tidal wetlands with ocean-derived salinities below 0.5 ppt and dominated by salt-intolerant species, small (less than 8 ha) and shallow (less than 2 m deep at low water) water bodies without wave-formed or bedrock shoreline, and inland brackish or saline wetlands.

Parasitic   Living in close association with another organism, often inside it, and taking food from it without giving anything in return. The host organism is not normally killed by the parasite, at least not until the parasite has completed the part of its life cycle that depends on the host.

Parotoid gland   One of a pair of external wartlike glands on the shoulder, neck, or back of the eye in toads.

Parthenogenesis   Reproduction by the development of an unfertilized egg.

Passerine   A member of the order Passeriformes, the perching birds, whose first toe (hallux) is directed backward and adapted for gripping perches.

Pectoral   Pertaining to the chest.

Pelage   The fur of a mammal.

Pelagic   Oceanic; inhabiting the waters of the open sea or large lakes but not fixed to the bottom.

Peritoneum   The membrane lining the abdominal cavity.

Pharyngeal   On the bones of the pharynx.

Phase   A distinct, identifiable individual or population that differs in color, pattern, or structure from the typical member of its group.

Physiology   The study of function in cells, organs, or entire organisms; the processes of life.

Phytoplankton   Plants of the plankton.

Piscivorous   Fish-eating.

Plankton   Free-floating organisms near the surface of the sea or lake.

Plastron   The lower shell of a turtle.

Pneumatophore   A root specialized for respiration in some plant species that grow in waterlogged or strongly compacted soils (e.g., mangroves).

Polyp   A fixed, tubelike organism.

Population   Any group of individuals of one species that occupy a given area at the same time.

Posterior   At or toward the rear end of the body.

Predator   An organism that eats other living organisms.

Premaxillary frenum   On a fish, a bridge of flesh connecting the upper lip and the snout.

Prey   An organism eaten by another organism.

Primaries   Outer wing feathers that are attached to the end or forearm of a bird's wing and strike the air at a right angle to the bird's body.

Pupa   The developmental stage of some insects, between the larval and adult stages, in which the organism is nonfeeding, immotile, and sometimes encapsulated or in a cocoon.

Pyrogenic   Pertaining to natural communities maintained and perpetuated by cyclic fire regimes.

Race   Subspecies.

Raptor   A bird of prey, including hawks and owls.

Relict   A surviving population of a diminishing or vanishing race, type, species, or natural community.

Rhizome   A creeping underground stem.

Riparian   Pertaining to habitats adjacent to rivers, streams, lakes, ponds, springs, seeps, swamps, or other permanent bodies of water.

Riverine   Related to or strongly influenced by a river.

Sclerophyllous   Having thickened leaves that resist water loss; characteristic of chaparral plants.

Scute   An enlarged scale on a reptile, also called a shield or plate.

Secondaries   The inside feathers of a bird's wing that attach to the arm.

Sinkhole   A hollow, hole, or depression in the earth into which surface water drains, often leading to an underground channel.

Slough   A broad, subtropical, seasonally inundated, shallow channel with peat over mineral substrate.

Spawn   To produce or deposit eggs; to release eggs and sperm into the water.

Species   The taxonomic category ranking below genus and above subspecies, consisting of organisms capable of interbreeding.

Spermatozoa   Male sex cells.

Standard length   A standard measure of the length of a fish: the straight-line distance from the tip of the snout, lip, or chin, whichever is farthest forward, to the rear end of the vertebral column.

Steephead   A steep-sided valley in karst substrate.

Stenothermal   Surviving only within a limited range of temperature.

Strand   Land bordering a body of water; beach.

Subcaudal scale   In snakes, a scale beneath the tail. These scales form a double row in most snakes but a single row in others.

Subspecies   A subdivision of a species; a variety or race; a category (usually the lowest recognized in taxonomic classification) ranking below species.

Substrate   The foundation to which an organism is attached.

Subtropical   Pertaining to areas that experience occasional frost but where freezing temperatures are not frequent enough to cause true winter dormancy.

Succession   An orderly process of change in a biotic community involving species structure and community processes over time.

Successional tier   A stage in the process of biotic community development, as organisms interact with their environment and the species structure changes.

Sympatric   Pertaining to two or more populations that occupy identical or broadly overlapping geographical areas.

Taxonomic   Pertaining to the classification of organisms into categories of species, genus, family, and so on.

Temperate   Pertaining to areas where freezes occur often enough to cause winter dormancy in vegetation.

Terrestrial   Adapted for living on land.

Territory   The site of breeding, nesting, or food gathering defended by an individual or a group.

Troglobite   An organism unable to live outside a cave environment, usually having adaptations to a lightless existence.

Troglodyte   Cave dweller.

Troglophile   A terrestrial organism that frequently completes its life cycle in caves but is not confined to cave habitat.

Tropical   Pertaining to areas that are practically frost-free.

Tropicopolitan   Occurring worldwide in the tropics.

Type locality   A specific location where the original specimen of a species or subspecies was obtained.

Vegetation type   A plant community with distinguishable characteristics.

Venter, ventral   Pertaining to the undersurface of an animal.

Vestigial   Of very reduced form when compared with the ancestral structure (e.g., the reduced legs of the sand skink, or the eyes and pigment of cave-adapted species).

Viable   Able to live or develop.

Viviparous   Live-bearing; giving birth to active young having been nourished inside the mother.

Water table   The upper limit of permanently saturated soil.

Wetlands   Lands transitional between terrestrial and aquatic systems, where the water table is usually at or near the surface or the land is covered by shallow water.

Xeric   Dry; pertaining to or having dry or desertlike conditions.

Zooplankton   Animals of the plankton.

Bibliography

Adams, Frank H. "Florida's Great Escape: Torreya State Park." *Florida Wildlife,* June 1996.

Alden, Peter, Richard B. Cech, Richard Keen, Amy Leventer, Gil Nelson, and Wendy B. Zomlefer. *National Audubon Society Field Guide to Florida.* New York: Alfred A. Knopf, 1998.

American Ornithologists Union. *Check-list of North American Birds,* 6th ed., 1983, as amended in the Thirty-fifth Supplement (*Auk,* July 1985), the Thirty-sixth Supplement (*Auk,* July 1987), the Thirty-seventh Supplement (*Auk,* July 1989), Thirty-eighth Supplement (*Auk,* July 1993), and the Fortieth Supplement (*Auk,* July 1995).

"And Some Good News." (Kemp's ridley sea turtles.) *New York Times,* 16 July 1996.

Anderson, Robert. *Guide to Florida Alligator and Crocodile.* N.p.: Ernie Lampert, 1985.

———. *Wilderness Florida.* N.p.: VP Publications, 1988.

Arnold, David. "Florida's Marine Turtles." *Florida Wildlife,* July–August 1995, pp. 12–15.

Associated Press. "Deaths of Key Deer Stay at Record Pace." *Palm Beach Sun-Sentinel,* 11 December 1995.

———. "Despite Protection Efforts, 80 Rare Key Deer Have Died This Year." *Orlando Sentinel,* 21 November 1996.

———. "How Do You Get a Falcon Out of the Nest?" *Orlando Sentinel,* 28 December 1995.

———. "Navy Rescues Trapped Sea Turtles." *Orlando Sentinel,* 30 June 1995.

———. "Panther Sightings Persist on Hutchinson Island." *Orlando Sentinel,* 22 November 1996.

———. "Rainy Year Has Helped Some Species, But Hurt Others." *Orlando Sentinel,* 23 November 1995.

Audubon Society. *Field Guide to North American Fishes, Whales, and Dolphins.* New York: Audubon Society, 1983.

Beatley, Timothy. *Habitat Conservation Planning.* Austin: University of Texas Press, 1994.

Beauchamp, Sylvia K. "Researchers Examine Declining Numbers of Wading Birds." *Florida Naturalist* (Casselberry), fall 1995.

Behler, John L., and F. Wayne King. *The Audubon Society Field Guide to North American Reptiles and Amphibians.* New York: Alfred A. Knopf, 1979.

Bennetts, Robert E., Michael W. Collopy, and James A. Rodgers Jr. "The Snail Kite in the Florida Everglades: A Food Specialist in a Changing Environment." In *Everglades: The Ecosystem and Its Restoration.* Delray Beach, Fla.: *Delray Beach Sun-Sentinel,* 1994.

Bent, Arthur Cleveland. *Life Histories of North American Wood Warblers,* parts 1 and 2. New York: Dover Publications, 1963.

———. *Life Histories of North American Woodpeckers.* New York: Dover Publications, 1964.

Billups, Andrea L. "Schaus' Swallowtail." *Florida Naturalist* (Maitland) 68, no. 3 (fall 1995).

Bonner, Nigel. *Whales of the World.* New York: Facts on File, 1989.

Bortone, Stephen A. *Life History, Habitat Assessment, and Systematics of the Blackmouth Shiner (*Notropis *sp.), Blackwater River Drainage.* Booklet. Tallahassee: FG& FWFC, 1993.

Bouma, Katherine. "Osceola Rancher, State Launch Rare Mix That Protects Wildlife." *Orlando Sentinel,* 18 February 1996.

Brett, James J. *Feathers in the Wind: The Mountain and the Migration, Hawk Mountain Sanctuary.* Kempton, Pa.: Kutztown Publishing, 1973.

Brown, Larry N. *A Checklist of Florida Mammals.* Tallahassee: FG&FWFC, 1987.

Bruemmer, Fred. "La Arribada." *Natural History,* August 1995.

Bruun, Bertel. *Birds of Europe.* New York: Golden Press, 1971.

Buckingham, Cheryl. "In Search of Quiet Waters." *Florida Wildlife* (Tallahassee), May–June 1993, pp. 38–41.

Burkhead, Noel M., Howard L. Jelks, Frank Jordan, Douglas Weaver. *The Comparative Ecology of Okaloosa (*Etheostoma okaloosae*) and Brown Darters (*E. edwini*) in Boggy and Rocky Bayou Stream Systems, Choctawhatchee Bay, Florida.* Gainesville, Fla.: National Biological Survey, 1994.

Burns, Anja. "Undersea Coral Garden." *Florida Wildlife,* July–August 1995.

Burt, William H., and Richard P. Grossenheider. *Peterson Field Guide to the Mammals.* Boston: Houghton Mifflin, 1976.

Cadieux, Charles L. *Wildlife Extinction.* Washington, D.C.: Stonewall Press, 1991.

"California Condors Once Again Can Call Arizona Home." *Sagi's Outdoor News* 4, no. 9 (November 1996).

Callahan, Phillip S. *The Magnificent Birds of Prey.* New York: Holiday House, 1974.

Campbell, Neil A. *Biology.* Menlo Park, Calif.: Benjamin/Cummings Publishing, 1987.

Carpenter, Betsy. "Biological Nightmares." *U.S. News and World Report,* 20 November 1995.

Carr, Archie. *The Sea Turtle, So Excellent a Fishe.* Austin: University of Texas Press, 1992.

Carter, David. *Butterflies and Moths.* New York: Dorling Kindersley, 1992.

"Caution! Manatees Moving In." *Orlando Sentinel,* 29 November 1995.

Cavanaugh, Peggy, and Margaret Spontak. *Protecting Paradise: 300 Ways to Protect Florida's Environment.* Fairfield, Fla.: Phoenix Publishing, 1992.

Cerulean, Susan, and Patricia Milsap. *What Have You Done for Wildlife Lately: A Citizen's Guide to Helping Florida's Wildlife.* Booklet. Tallahassee: FG&FWFC.

Cerulean, Susan, and Ann Morrow. *Florida Wildlife Viewing Guide.* Helena, Mont.: Falcon Press, 1993.

Chadwick, Douglas H. "Dead or Alive: The Endangered Species Act." *National Geographic,* March 1995, pp. 2–41.

Chang, Chris. "Mining for Bats." *Audubon,* July–August 1997, p. 16.

Chinery, Michael. *A Science Dictionary of the Animal World.* New York: Franklin Watts, 1969.

Clark, William S., and Brian K. Wheeler. *Hawks.* New York: Houghton Mifflin, 1987.

Cliffton, Kim. "Leatherback Turtle Slaughter in Mexico." In *Collected Papers of the Tucson Herpetological Society, 1988–1991.* Tucson, Ariz.: 1992.

Collazo, Michelle, and Frank J. Mazzotti. *Red-cockaded Woodpecker.* Brochure SS-WIS 73. Davie: Florida Cooperative Urban Wildlife Program, 1995.

Collins, Henry Hill Jr. *Complete Field Guide to American Wildlife: East, Central, and North.* New York: Harper & Brothers, 1959.

Conant, Roger, and Joseph T. Collins. *Peterson Field Guide to Reptiles and Amphibians of Eastern/Central North America.* New York: Houghton Mifflin, 1991.

Cox News Service. "Swamp Project May Get Bogged Down." *Orlando Sentinel,* 17 February 1997.

Curnutt, John L., and Stuart L. Pimm. *Status and Ecology of the Cape Sable Seaside Sparrow.* Knoxville: University of Tennessee, 1993.

Curson, Jon, David Quinn, and David Beadle. *Warblers of the Americas: An Identification Guide.* New York: Houghton Mifflin, 1994.

Dennis, Jerry. "Tracks in the Sand." *Wildlife Conservation,* January–February 1996, pp. 60–61.

Deyrup, Mark, and Richard Franz (eds.). *Rare and Endangered Biota of Florida.* Vol. 4, *Invertebrates.* Gainesville: University Press of Florida, 1994.

Domico, Terry. *Bears of the World.* New York: Facts on File, 1988.

Douglas, Marjory Stoneman. *The Everglades: River of Grass.* Marietta, Ga.: Mockingbird Books, 1947.

Duda, Mark D., Susan I. Cerulean, and Judith Ann Gillan. *Transactions of the Fifty-fourth North American Wildlife and Natural Resources Conference.* Washington, D.C.: Wildlife Management Institute, 1989.

Duquesnel, James. *1995 Roadkill Data for Key Largo State Botanical Site, John Pennekamp State Park, and Crocodile Lakes National Wildlife Refuge.* Key Largo: Florida Park Service, 1996.

Earthworks Group. *50 Simple Things You Can Do to Save the Earth.* Berkeley, Calif.: Earthworks Press, 1989.

Ehrhart, L. M., and B. E. Worthington. *Human and Natural Causes of Marine Turtle Nest and Hatchling Mortality and Their Relationship to Hatchling Production on an Important Florida Nesting Beach.* Nongame Wildlife Program Technical Report 1. Orlando: FG&FWFC, 1987.

Ehrlich, Paul R., David S. Dobkin, and Darryl Wheye. *Birds in Jeopardy.* Stanford: Stanford University Press, 1992.

Emmons, Louise H. *Neotropical Rainforest Mammals: A Field Guide.* Chicago: University of Chicago Press, 1990.

Endangered Species Act of 1973, as Amended through the 100th Congress. Washington, D.C.: U.S. Department of the Interior, 1994.

"Endangered Beach Mice Survived Opal." *Orlando Sentinel,* 26 January 1996.

Engstrom, R. Todd. "Red-cockaded Woodpecker Report." *Florida Wildlife,* September–October 1994.

Exotic Pest Plant Council. Brochure. Fort Lauderdale, Fla.: Exotic Pest Plant Council, 1993.

Fenton, M. Brock. *Bats.* Facts on File, 1992.

Fitzpatrick, John W., Glen E. Woolfenden, Mark T. Kapeny. *Ecology and Development-Related Habitat Requirements of the Florida Scrub Jay (*Aphelocoma coerulescans coerulescans*).* Nongame Wildlife Program Technical Report 8. Tallahassee: FG&FWFC, 1991.

Flicker, John. "Hope for the Everglades." *Audubon,* July–August 1996.

Florida Department of Environmental Protection. *Florida State Parks Guide: The Real Florida.* Tallahassee: Florida Park Service, 1996.

———. *Where Are the Manatees?* Quick reference sheet. Tallahassee: Florida Department of Environmental Protection, 1995.

Florida Department of Natural Resources. *Voice for the Silent Sirenian: Guardian of the Florida Manatee.* Pamphlet. Tallahassee: Florida Department of Natural Resources, n.d.

Florida Game and Fresh Water Fish Commission. *Florida Wildlife Code, Title 39.* Tallahassee: FG&FWFC, 1995.

———. *Living with Alligators.* Brochure. Tallahassee: FG&FWFC, 1994.

———. *The Snail Kite.* Brochure. Tallahassee: FG&FWFC, 1993.

Florida Keys News Service. "Survey Says People Value Animals." *Free Press,* 3 April 1996.

Florida Natural Areas Inventory. *A Guide to the Natural Communities of Florida.* Tallahassee: FNAI and Florida Department of Natural Resources, 1990.

———. *Tracking Lists of Special Plants and Lichens, Invertebrates, Vertebrates, and Natural Communities.* Tallahassee: FNAI, 1995.

———. *Matrix of Habitats and Distribution by County of Rare/ Endangered Species in Florida.* Tallahassee: FNAI, 1990.

Florida Power and Light Company. *The Bald Eagle in Florida.* Miami: FP&L, 1992.

———. *Florida's Alligators and Crocodiles.* Miami: FP&L, 1992.

———. *Florida's Sea Turtles.* Miami: FP&L, 1992.

———. *Florida's Wood Storks.* Miami: FP&L, 1985.

Fontenay, Blake. "Can Tourism and Turtles Both Survive?" *Orlando Sentinel,* 30 October 1995.

———. "Turtle Lawsuit Is Thrown Out." *Orlando Sentinel,* 21 December 1996.

Francalancia, Angie. "Changing Light Helps Turtles' Plight." *Palm Beach Post,* 3 September 1995.

Frank, Norman, and Erica Ramus. *A Complete Guide to Scientific and*

Common Names of Reptiles and Amphibians of the World. Pottsville, Pa.: N.G. Publishing, 1995.

"Gator suspected in boy's vanishing." *Arizona Daily Star,* 22 March 1997.

"Geoguide: Sea Turtles." *National Geographic,* February 1994.

Gerrard, Jon M., and Gary R. Bortolotti. *The Bald Eagle: Haunts and Habits of a Wilderness Monarch.* Washington, D.C.: Smithsonian Institution Press, 1988.

Getter, Charles D. *Ecology and Survival of the Key Silverside,* Menidia conchorum, *an Atherinid Fish Endemic to the Florida Keys.* Dissertation. Coral Gables: University of Miami.

Gilbert, Carter R. (ed.). *Rare and Endangered Biota of Florida.* Vol. 2, *Fishes.* Gainesville: University Press of Florida, 1992.

Gingerich, Jerry Lee. *Florida's Fabulous Mammals: Their Stories.* Tampa, Fla.: World Publications, 1994.

Glass-Godwin, Lenela. "Panhandle Jewels." *Skimmer* (Tallahassee), spring 1992, pp. 1–8.

Glick, Daniel. "Big Sugar vs. the Everglades." *Rolling Stone,* 2 May 1996.

Goodwin, Thomas M., and Wayne R. Marion. "Aspects of the Nesting Ecology of American Alligators (*Alligator mississippiensis*) in North-Central Florida." *Herpetologica* 34, no. 1 (March 1978).

Gopher Tortoise Council. *The Gopher Tortoise: A Species in Decline.* Gainesville: University of Florida, Museum of Natural History, 2001.

Gore, Al. *Earth in the Balance: Ecology and the Human Spirit.* New York: Houghton Mifflin, 1992.

Gore, Jeffrey A. "Distribution and Abundance of Nesting Least Terns in the Florida Keys." *Florida Field Naturalist,* August 1991.

Gore, Jeffrey A., and Charles A. Chase III. *Snowy Plover Breeding Distribution: Final Performance Report.* Tallahassee: FG&FWFC, 1989.

Gore, Jeffrey A., and Michael J. Kinnison. "Hatching Success in Roof and Ground Colonies of Least Terns." *Condor* 93 (March 1991): 759–762.

Gosner, Kenneth L. *A Field Guide to the Atlantic Seashore, from the Bay of Fundy to Cape Hatteras.* Boston: Houghton Mifflin, 1979.

Graham, Frank Jr. "The Return of the Peregrine." *Audubon,* September–October 1995.

Graulich, Heather. "Biologists on Dawn-to-Dusk Vigil to Crack Manatee Crisis." *Palm Beach Post,* 14 April 1996.

Gray, Tyler. "It's Not Easy Being Green." *Orlando Sentinel, Florida* magazine, 14 September 1997.

Greene, Ronnie. "Poacher's Turtle-Egg Love Potion Down the Drain." *Miami Herald,* 22 November 1995.

Harrison, Frederick W. *Environmental Status of Seven Species of Freshwater Sponges: Final Report.* Contract 14-16-0008-2005. Washington, D.C.: U.S. Department of the Interior, 1977.

———. "The Taxonomic and Ecological Status of the Environmentally Restricted Spangillid Species of North America." *Hydrobiologia* 65, no. 2 (1979), pp. 99–105.

Harvey, Michael J. *Bats of the Eastern United States.* Little Rock: Arkansas Game and Fish Commission, 1992.

Hendry, Laurel Comella, Thomas M. Goodwin, and Ronald F. Labisky. *Florida's Vanishing Wildlife.* Gainesville: Cooperative Extension Service, University of Florida, Institute of Food and Agricultural Sciences, 1982.

Holewa, Lisa. "Manatees Dying Off at Record Rate." *Palm Beach Post,* 9 April 1996.

Holt, Harold R. *Lane's: A Birder's Guide to Florida.* Colorado Springs, Colo.: ABA Sales, 1989.

Hovis, Julie, and Mark S. Robson. "Breeding Status and Distribution of the Least Tern in the Florida Keys." *Florida Field Naturalist* 17, no. 3 (1989): 61–66.

Humphrey, Stephen R. *Rare and Endangered Biota of Florida.* Vol. 1, *Mammals.* Gainesville: University Press of Florida, 1992.

Institute of Marine Science. *Mangrove Restoration Projects and Environmental Impact Studies.* Technical Report 30. St. Petersburg, Fla.: Institute of Marine Science, 1983.

Izaak Walton League. *Hardbottom: A Biological Community.* Brochure. Islamorada: Florida Keys Chapter of the Izaak Walton League, 1994.

Jewell, Susan D. *Exploring Wild South Florida.* Sarasota, Fla.: Pineapple Press, 1993.

Jodice, Patrick G. R., and Stephen R. Humphrey. "Activity and Diet of an Urban Population of Big Cypress Fox Squirrels." *Journal of Wildlife Management* 56(4):685–692.

Jones, Lennie. "Gator Glory? Even Though Alligator Populations Have Bounced Back, These Crocodilians Are Still Being Poached." *Reptiles* 5, no. 2 (February 1997): 32–38.

Jukofsky, Diane. "Food, Lodging, and Squirrel Monkeys." *Wildlife Conservation,* March–April 1996, pp. 64–66.

Kahl, M. P. Jr. "Food Ecology of the Wood Stork (*Mycteria americana*) in Florida. *Ecological Monographs* 34(2): 97–117.

Kastner, Joseph. *A Species of Eternity.* New York: Alfred A. Knopf, 1977.

Kautz, Randy S. *Trends in Florida's Wildlife Habitat, 1936–1987.* Tallahassee: FG&FWFC, 1988.

King, Robert P. "It's Turtle Time on Florida Beaches." *Palm Beach Post,* 6 April 1997.

Kirkland, Stan. "Hurricane Opal's Impact on Wildlife." *Florida Wildlife* (Tallahassee), May–June 1996.

Kohn, Howard. "Reefs on the Rocks." *Greenpeace Magazine,* July–August 1990.

Koontz, Fred W. "Wood Storks on the Web." *Wildlife Conservation,* January–February 1997.

Kruer, Curtis. "The Inside Story on the Monkey Islands of the Florida Keys." *Florida Naturalist* (Casselberry), spring 1996.

Kuehne, Robert A., and Roger W. Barbour. *The American Darters.* Lexington: University Press of Kentucky, 1983.

Lancaster, Cory. "'95 Was Stormy Year for Volusia Beaches." *Orlando Sentinel,* 31 December 1995.

Land, Darrell, *The Florida Panther.* Brochure. Tallahassee: FG&FWFC, 1995.

Lazell, James D. Jr. *Wildlife of the Florida Keys: A Natural History.* Washington, D.C.: Island Press, 1989.

Lee, David S., Carter R. Gilbert, Charles H. Hocutt, Robert E. Jenkins, Don E.

McAllister, and Jay R. Stauffer Jr. *Atlas of North American Freshwater Fish.* Raleigh: North Carolina State Museum of Natural History, 1980.

Lemonick, Michael. "Heading for Apocalypse." *Time*, 2 October 1995.

Lenihan, Daniel J. "Raptures of the Deep." *Natural History*, November 1996, pp. 44–46.

Leopold, Aldo. *A Sand County Almanac.* New York: Oxford University Press, 1949.

Levin, Ted. *Alaska to Everglades in 17 Days.* Excerpted in National Park Service brochure for Everglades National Park. 1994.

Line, Les. "Massachusetts Miracle." *Audubon*, March–April 1996.

———. "Silence of the Songbirds." *National Geographic*, June 1993, pp. 68–90.

"Lost Bear Sent Home." *Palm Beach Post*, 3 July 1996.

Luoma, John R. "What's Killing the Manatees?" *Audubon*, July–August 1996, pp. 18–22.

Maehr, David S. "Distribution of Black Bears in Eastern North America." *Black Bear Management Workshop.* Tallahassee: FG&FWFC, 1984.

———. "The Black Bear as a Seed Disperser." *Florida Field Naturalist* 12 (1984): 40–42.

———. "Southwest Florida Black Bear Research." *Florida Wildlife* (Tallahassee), September–October 1993, pp. 16–20.

Maehr, David S., and James R. Brady. "Florida Black Bear, Beekeeper Conflict: 1981 Beekeeper Survey." *American Bee Journal*, 25 March 1982.

———. "Food Habits of Florida Black Bears." *Journal of Wildlife Management* (Gainesville) 48, no. 1 (1984).

Maehr, David S., James N. Layne, E. Darrell Land, J. Walter McCown, and Jayde Roof. "Long-Distance Movements of the Florida Black Bear." *Florida Field Naturalist*, February 1988.

"Massive Tumors Afflict Green Sea Turtles." *National Geographic, Earth Almanac*, April 1991.

McClanahan, Tim. "Fish Critical to Coral Reefs." *Wildlife Conservation*, January–February 1997.

Means, D. Bruce, "Temperate Hardwood Hammocks." *Florida Wildlife*, November–December 1994.

Michael, Allex. "Snake Conservation: Information from Chris Scott." *Animalwatch* 2, no. 1 (September 1996).

Michigan Department of Natural Resources. "Creature Profile: Lake Sturgeon (*Acipenser fulvescens*)." *Spotting Scope*, winter 1997.

———. *Your Neighbor, the Kirtland's Warbler.* Brochure. Lansing: Michigan Department of Natural Resources, U.S. Forest Service, USF&WS, and Michigan Audubon Society, 1992.

Michigan United Conservation Clubs. "Bird of the Jack Pine." *Tracks* 15(9).

Middleton, Susan, and David Liitschwager. *Witness: Endangered Species of North America.* San Francisco: Chronicle Books, 1994.

Mihalik, Mary Beth. *North County Resource Recovery Facility Wildlife Conservation Management and Bird Monitoring Program, 1987–1993, Final Report.* Solid Waste Authority of Palm Beach County, 1993.

Millsap, Brian A., Jeffrey A. Gore, Douglas E. Runde, and Susan I. Cerulean. *Wildlife Monographs: Setting Priorities for the Conservation of Fish and Wildlife Species in Florida.* Blacksburg, Va.: Wildlife Society, 1990.

Mohr, Charles H., and Thomas Poulson. *The Life of the Cave.* New York: Time-Life Books, 1966.

Moler, Paul E. (ed.). *Rare and Endangered Biota of Florida.* Vol. 3, *Reptiles and Amphibians.* Gainesville: University Press of Florida, 1992.

Moore, Gary. "Flies as Big as Oranges, Gators as Thick as Flies." *Florida Wildlife* (Tallahassee), May–June 1996.

Mount, Robert H. "The Natural History of the Red-tailed Skink (*Eumeces egregius*)." *American Midland Natu-ralist* 70, no. 2 (October 1963): 356–385.

Myers, Ronald L., and John J. Ewel. *Ecosystems of Florida.* Orlando: University of Central Florida, 1990.

National Geographic Society. *Field Guide to the Birds of North America,* 2d ed. Washington, D.C.: National Geographic Society, 1987.

National Marine Fisheries Service. *Recovery Plan for the Shortnose Sturgeon (*Acipenser brevirostrum*).* Technical Draft. Silver Springs, Md.: Office of Protected Resources, NMFS, 1995.

———. *Shortnose Sturgeon Recovery Plan.* Silver Springs, Md.: NMFS, 1982.

———. *Synopsis of Biological Data on Shortnose Sturgeon,* Acipenser brevi-rostrum *LeSueur 1818.* NOAA

Technical Report, NMFS 14. Washington, D.C.: NMFS, 1984.

National Marine Fisheries Service and U.S. Fish and Wildlife Service. *Recovery Plan for the Kemp's Ridley Turtle.* St. Petersburg, Fla.: NMFS, 1992.

———. *Recovery Plan for Leatherback Turtles in the U.S., Caribbean, Atlantic, and Gulf of Mexico.* Washington, D.C.: NMFS, 1992.

———. *Recovery Plan for Marine Turtles.* St. Petersburg, Fla.: NMFS, 1984.

———. *Recovery Plan for the U.S. Population of the Atlantic Green Turtle.* Washington, D.C.: NMFS, 1991.

———. *Recovery Plan for the U.S. Population of Loggerhead Turtles.* Washington, D.C.: NMFS, 1991.

———. *Status Reviews for Sea Turtles Listed Under the Endangered Species Act of 1973.* Silver Spring, Md.: NMFS, 1995.

National Oceanic and Atmospheric Administration. *Florida Keys National Marine Sanctuary: Draft Management Plan, Environmental Impact Statement.* Vols. 1–3. Marathon, Fla.: NOAA, 1995.

National Oceanic and Atmospheric Administration and U.S. Fish and Wildlife Service. *Sea Turtles.* Brochure. Washington, D.C.: NOAA, 1996.

———. *The Five Sea Turtle Species of the Atlantic and Gulf Coast of the United States.* Brochure. Washington, D.C.: U.S. Government Printing Office: 1991.

National Oceanic and Atmospheric

Administration, National Marine Fisheries Service. *Protecting the Nation's Marine Species.* Brochure. Silver Spring, Md.: NMFS, 1995.

National Parks Service. *Endangered Species in National Parks.* Brochure. Washington, D.C.: Department of the Interior, NPS, 1990.

Nelson, Gil. *The Trees of Florida: A Reference and Field Guide.* Sarasota, Fla.: Pineapple Press, 1994.

New York Turtle and Tortoise Society. "Albino Loggerheads." *News Notes Newsletter* 6(1):3.

Nicholls, Janice. *The 1991 International Piping Plover Winter Census in Florida.* Asheville, N.C.: U.S. Fish and Wildlife Service, 1991.

Noss, Reed F., and Robert L. Peters. *Endangered Ecosystems: A Status Report on America's Vanishing Habitat and Wildlife.* Washington D.C.: Defenders of Wildlife, 1995.

Office of Environmental Services. *Conservation and Recreation Lands, 1995 Annual Report: A 10-year Acquisition Plan, Preservation 2000.* Tallahassee: Division of State Lands, Florida Department of Environmental Protection, 1995.

O'Meara, Timothy E., and Jeffrey A. Gore. *Guidelines for Conservation and Management of Least Tern Colonies in Florida.* Panama City: FG&FWFC, 1988.

Page, G. W., J. S. Warriner, J. C. Warriner, and P. W. C. Paton. "Snowy Plover." No. 154 in *The Birds of North America,* A. Poole and F. Gill, eds. Washington, D.C.: Academy of Natural Sciences and American Ornithologists Union, 1995.

Page, Lawrence M. *Handbook of Darters.* Neptune City, N.J.: T.F.H. Publications, 1983.

Palm Beach County Department of Environmental Resources Management. *Sea Turtle Protection Program.* Brochure. West Palm Beach, Fla.: Department of Environmental Resources Management, 1995.

"Particularly Dangerous Pollution." *Amicus Journal,* fall 1996.

Pearson, T. Gilbert (ed.). *Birds of America.* New York: Doubleday & Co., 1936.

Peltz, Jennifer. "Sea-Turtle Egg Trade Continues Despite Fines, Arrests." *Palm Beach Post,* 5 July 1996.

Peregrine Fund. *1995 Annual Report.* Boise, Idaho: Peregrine Fund, 1995.

———. "Victory Proposed." *Peregrine Fund Newsletter* 25 (fall 1995).

"Peregrine Researchers Soar with Data." *New York Times,* 25 August 1996.

Peterson, Roger Tory. *Peterson Field Guide to the Eastern Birds.* New York: Houghton Mifflin, 1980.

Peterson, Roger Tory, and Edward L. Chalif. *A Field Guide to Mexican Birds.* Boston: Houghton Mifflin, 1973.

Pimm, Stuart L. *Annual Report 1995: Population Ecology of the Cape Sable Seaside Sparrow (Ammodramus maritima mirabilis).* Knoxville: University of Tennessee, 1995.

Pinney, Roy. "AFH Profile: Archie F. Carr." *Vivarium,* May 1994.

"Poll Shows Floridians Overwhelmingly Favor Environmental Laws." *Florida Naturalist,* spring 1996.

Preston, Todd. "The Fall and Rise of the American Alligator." *Reptiles* 5, no. 2 (February 1997): 24–31.

Pritchard, Peter C. H. "Arawak Turtle Hunters: Moving from Confrontation to Conservation in Guyana." *Florida Naturalist,* fall 1995, pp. 6–7.

———. "Know Your Sea Turtles." *Florida Naturalist,* winter 1996.

———. *Rare and Endangered Biota of Florida.* Vol. 1, *Birds.* Gainesville: University Press of Florida, 1978.

———. "Sea Turtle Conservation: Science or Guesswork?" *Florida Naturalist,* spring 1996.

Pritchard, Peter C. H., and Herbert W. Kale. *Saving What's Left.* Orlando: Florida Audubon Society, 1994.

Quintana, Craig. "Opal Leaves Beach Mice Scurrying for Survival." *Orlando Sentinel,* 19 October 1995.

Rafayl, Yeub. "Herpetology Watcher." *Animalwatch* 2, no. 1 (September 1996).

Rattner, Robert. "Make Way for Manatees." *Wildlife Conservation,* September–October 1995, pp. 24–29.

Rauber, Paul. "An End to Evolution." *Sierra,* January–February 1996.

Ray, Janisse. "Clash of the Fire Ants." *Florida Wildlife,* January–February 1995, pp. 19–21.

———. "Bats Die in Cave Flooding." *Florida Wildlife,* November–December 1994, p. 27.

Reef Relief. *Florida's Coral Reef Ecosystem.* Key West: Reef Relief, 1990.

Reisner, Marc. *Game Wars: The Undercover Pursuit of Wildlife Poachers.* New York: Penguin Books, 1991.

Resendiz, Antonio, Beatris Resendiz, Wallace J. Nichols, Jeffrey A. Seminoff, and Naoki Kamezaki. "First Confirmed East-West Trans-Pacific Movement of a Loggerhead Sea Turtle, *Caretta caretta,* released in Baja California, Mexico." *Pacific Press* 1998.

Robbins, Elaine." Whale Watch: Pursued to the Brink of Extinction, Cetaceans Fight for Survival Against Man-Made Odds." *E, the Environmental Magazine* 8, no. 3 (May–June 1997): 29–35.

Robertson, William B. Jr., Oron L. Bass Jr., and Michael Britten. *Birds of Everglades National Park.* Homestead: Florida National Parks and Monuments Association, 1994.

Robson, Mark S. *Southeastern Beach Mouse Survey: Final Performance Report.* Tallahassee: FG&FWFC, 1989.

———. *Status Survey of the Florida Mastiff Bat: Final Performance Report.* Tallahassee: FG&FWFC, Bureau of Nongame Wildlife, 1989.

Robson, Mark S., and Susan Cerulean. "Florida Mastiff Bat (*Eumops glaucinus floridanus*), Florida and Federal Status: Candidate for Listing." *Florida Wildlife,* November–December 1992.

Robson, Mark S., Frank J. Mazzotti, and Teresa Parrott. "Recent Evidence of the Mastiff Bat in Southern Florida." *Florida Field Naturalist* 17, no. 4 (1989): 81–82.

Rodgers, James A. Jr., Herbert W. Kale II, and Henry T. Smith (eds.). *Rare and Endangered Biota of Florida.* Vol. 5, *Birds.* Gainesville: University Press of Florida, 1996.

Rossi, John, and Roxanne Rossi. "Notes on the Natural History and Husbandry of the Short-tail Snake, *Stilosoma extenuatum:* Primitive Mini-kingsnake of the Florida

Sandhills." *Bulletin of the League of Florida Herpetological Societies* (Orlando), 1995.

Rowell, Galen. "Falcon Rescue." *National Geographic*, April 1991.

Rudloe, Anne, and Jack Rudloe. "Sea Turtles: In a Race for Survival." *National Geographic*, February 1994.

Save-a-Turtle. *Saving the Sea Turtles.* Brochure. Islamorada: Florida Power and Light Corporation, 1995.

Schaefer, Joe. *Helping Cavity-nesters in Florida.* Brochure SS-WIS-901. Tallahassee: Florida Cooperative Urban Wildlife Program, 1994.

———. *Impacts of Free-ranging Pets on Wildlife.* Brochure. Tallahassee: Florida Cooperative Urban Wildlife Program, 1994.

Schaefer, Joe, Frank Mazzotti, and Craig Auegel. Brochure. Tallahassee: Florida Cooperative Urban Wildlife Program, 1994.

Scott, Chris. *Snake Lovers' Lifelist and Journal.* Austin: University of Texas Press, 1996.

Scott, James A. *The Butterflies of North America: A Natural and Field Guide.* Stanford, Calif.: Stanford University Press, 1986.

Scott, Virgil E., Keith E. Evans, David R. Patton, and Charles P. Stone. *Cavity-nesting Birds of North American Forests.* Washington D.C.: U.S. Department of Agriculture, U.S. Government Printing Office, 1977.

"Sea Turtle Protection." *Reptiles*, December 1995, p. 73.

Shinn, Eugene A., Barbara H. Lidz, Jack L. Kindinger, J. Harold Hudson, and Robert B. Halley. *Reefs of Florida and the Dry Tortugas.* St. Petersburg, Fla.: U.S. Geological Survey, 1989.

Simberloff, Daniel, and James Cox. *Consequences and Costs of Conservation Corridors.* Tallahassee: FG& FWFC, Nongame Wildlife Program, 1995.

Smith, Leslie Hay. "The Saltmarsh Vole." *Florida Naturalist* 63, no. 4 (winter 1990).

Snyder, Noel F. R., and Helen A. *Birds of Prey: Natural History and Conservation of North American Raptors.* Stillwater, Minn.: Voyageur Press, 1991.

Spear, Kevin, and Sandra Pedicini. "Death and Life of Lake Apopka." *Orlando Sentinel*, 3 September 1995.

Sprandel, Gary. "Small Plovers of Tampa Bay." *Skimmer* (Tallahassee), spring–summer 1995.

Sprunt, Alexander Jr. *Florida Bird Life.* New York: Coward-McCann, 1954.

Stap, Don. "Returning the Natives." *Audubon*, November–December 1996.

———. "Trail of an Ancient Wanderer." *Audubon*, January–February 1996.

Stevenson, Henry M., and Bruce H. Anderson. *The Birdlife of Florida.* Gainesville: University of Florida Press, University Press of Florida, 1994.

Strimple, Pete. "Egg Smugglers Sentenced." *Reptiles*, June 1996.

———. "Loggerhead Turtles Receive Help in Greece." *Reptiles*, April 1995, p. 10.

———. "Reptile News and Trivia: Lake Apopka Alligators." *Reptiles*, October 1995, pp. 34–35.

Stokes, Donald. *A Guide to Bird Behavior.* Vol. 1. Boston: Little, Brown & Co., 1979.

Stokes, Donald, and Lillian Stokes. *A Guide to Bird Behavior.* Vol. 3. Boston: Little, Brown & Co., 1989.

Stys, Beth. *Ecology and Habitat Protection Needs of the Southeastern American Kestrel (*Falco sparverius paulus*) on Large-scale Development Sites in Florida.* Nongame Wildlife Program Technical Report 13. Tallahassee: FG&FWFC, 1993.

Sykes, P. W. Jr., and R. E. Bennetts. "Snail Kite (*Rostrhamus sociabilis*)." No. 171 in *The Birds of North America,* A. Poole and F. Gill, eds. Washington, D.C.: Academy of Natural Sciences and American Ornithologists Union, 1995.

Taylor, Amy K., and Frank J. Mazzotti. *Florida's Changing Landscape: Impacts of Non-native Plants and Animals.* Brochure. Tallahassee: Florida Cooperative Urban Wildlife Program, 1996.

Tebo, Mary. "Chronicle of Coasts." *Florida Wildlife,* July–August 1995.

———. "Florida's Coastal Diversity." *Skimmer* (Tallahassee), spring–summer 1995.

Telford, Sam Roundtree Jr. "A Study of the Sand Skink, *Neoseps reynoldsi.*" *Copeia* 2 (24 July 1959).

Timmerman, Walter W. "Big Snakes in Big Trouble." *Florida Wildlife* (Tallahassee), September–October 1994, pp. 12–15.

"Tracking Sea Turtles from Outer Space." *National Geographic,* March 1990.

Trutwin, Carrie L. "Reptile Rehab: An interview with Dr. Nancy DiMarco." *New Directions for Better Living,* July 1996.

Turner, Raymond M., Janice E. Bowers, and Tony L. Burgess. *Sonoran Desert Plants: An Ecological Atlas.* Tucson: University of Arizona Press, 1995.

"Turtle Refuge." *Greenpeace Magazine,* July–August 1990.

U.S. Fish and Wildlife Service. *American Crocodile Recovery Plan.* Atlanta, Ga.: USF&WS, 1984.

———. *Atlantic Coast Piper Plover Recovery Plan.* Newton Corner, Mass.: USF&WS, 1988.

———. *Atlantic Salt Marsh Snake Recovery Plan.* Atlanta, Ga.: USF&WS, 1993.

———. *Cape Sable Seaside Sparrow Recovery Plan.* Atlanta, Ga.: USF&WS, 1983.

———. *Eastern Indigo Snake Recovery Plan.* Atlanta, Ga.: USF&WS, 1982.

———. *Endangered Species.* Brochure. USF&WS, 1990.

———. *The Facts on Key Deer.* Brochure. Washington, D.C.: USF&WS, 1993.

———. *Florida Key Deer Recovery Plan.* Atlanta, Ga.: USF&WS, 1985.

———. *The Florida Manatee Recovery Plan.* Atlanta, Ga.: USF&WS, 1989.

———. *The Florida Manatee Recovery Plan,* 2d Rev. Atlanta, Ga.: USF&WS, 1996.

———. *Florida Panther National Wildlife Refuge.* Brochure. Fort Myers, Fla.: Lee County Electric Cooperative, 1995.

———. *Florida Panther Recovery Plan.* Atlanta, Ga.: USF&WS, 1987.

———. *Florida Snail Kite, Revised Recovery Plan.* Atlanta, Ga.: USF&WS, 1986.

———. *Gray Bat Recovery Plan.* St. Louis, Mo.: USF&WS, 1982.

———. *Gulf Sturgeon Recovery Plan.* Atlanta, Ga.: USF&WS and Gulf States Marine Fisheries Commission, 1995.

———. *Hundreds of America's Birds Are Electrocuted Every Year*. Brochure. Albuquerque, N.Mex.: USF&WS, 1994.

———. *Kirtland's Warbler Recovery Plan*. Twin Cities, Mich.: USF&WS, 1985.

———. *Multispecies Recovery Plan for the Threatened and Endangered Species of South Florida*. Vol. 1, *The Species*, and Vol. 2, *The Ecosystem*. Technical Agency Draft. Vero Beach, Fla.: USF&WS, 1998.

———. *Okaloosa Darter Recovery Plan*. Atlanta, Ga.: USF&WS, 1981.

———. *Peregrine Falcon: Alaska Population Recovery Plan*. Anchorage, Alaska: USF&WS, 1982.

———. *Peregrine Falcon: Eastern Population Revised Recovery Plan*. Newton Corner, Mass.: USF&WS, 1991.

———. "Proposed Rules, Notice of Review, 50 CFR, Part 17." *Federal Register* 61, no. 40 (28 February 1996).

———. *Recovery Plan for the Anastasia Island Beach Mouse and Southeastern Beach Mouse*. Atlanta, Ga.: USF&WS, 1993.

———. *Recovery Plan for the Choctawhatchee, Perdido Key, and Alabama Beach Mouse*. Atlanta, Ga.: USF&WS, 1987.

———. *Recovery Plan for the Florida Grasshopper Sparrow*. Atlanta, Ga.: USF&WS, 1988.

———. *Recovery Plan for the Florida Population of Audubon's Crested Caracara*. Atlanta, Ga.: USF&WS, 1989.

———. *Recovery Plan for the Florida Salt Marsh Vole (*Microtus pennsyl-

vanicus dukecampbelli*). Technical Agency Draft. Jacksonville, Fla.: USF&WS, 1996.

———. *Recovery Plan for the Florida Scrub Jay*. Atlanta, Ga.: USF&WS, 1990.

———. *Recovery Plan for the Indiana Bat*. St. Louis, Mo.: USF&WS, 1983.

———. *Recovery Plan for the Sand Skink and Blue-tailed Mole Skink*. Atlanta, Ga.: USF&WS, 1993.

———. *Recovery Plan for Schaus' Swallowtail Butterfly with Recommendations for Bahaman Swallowtail Butterfly*. Atlanta, Ga.: USF&WS, 1982.

———. *Recovery Plan for the Stock Island Tree Snail*. Atlanta, Ga.: USF&WS, 1983.

———. *Recovery Plan for the U.S. Breeding Population of the Wood Stork*. Atlanta, Ga.: USF&WS, 1986.

———. *Red-cockaded Woodpecker Recovery Plan*. Atlanta, Ga.: USF&WS, 1985.

———. *Report to Congress: Endangered and Threatened Species Recovery Program*. Washington, D.C.: U.S. Department of the Interior, 1992.

———. *Roseate Tern Recovery Plan, Northeast Population*. Newton Corner, Mass.: USF&WS, 1989.

———. *Southeastern States Bald Eagle Recovery Plan*. Atlanta, Ga.: USF&WS, 1989.

———. *Whooping Crane Recovery Plan*. Albuquerque, N.Mex.: USF&WS, 1994.

———. *Why Save Endangered Species*. Brochure. USF&WS.

U.S. Forest Service. *Global Climate Change*. Brochure. Albuquerque, N.Mex.: U.S. Department of

Agriculture, Forest Service, Watershed and Air Management, 1990.

VanMeter, Victoria Brook. *The West Indian Manatee in Florida.* Pamphlet. Miami: Florida Power & Light Co., 1987.

Weinrich, Jerry. *The Kirtland's Warbler in 1994.* Wildlife Division Report 3222. Lansing: Michigan Department of Natural Resources, 1995.

Whitaker, John O. *The Audubon Society Field Guide to North American Mammals.* New York: Alfred A. Knopf, 1980.

Williams, Ted. "The Turtle Gulf War." *Audubon,* September–October 1995.

Winkler, Hans, David A. Christie, and David Nurney. *Woodpeckers: An Identification Guide to the Woodpeckers of the World.* New York: Houghton Mifflin, 1995.

Wisenbaker, Michael. "Cave of the Giant Catfish." *Florida Wildlife* (Tallahassee), July–August 1996, pp. 5–7.

Wood, Don A. *Florida's Endangered Species, Threatened Species, and Species of Special Concern: Official Lists.* Tallahassee: FG&FWFC, 1996.
———. *Official Lists of Endangered and Potentially Endangered Fauna and Flora in Florida.* Tallahassee: FG&FWFC, 1994.

Wood, Petra Bohall, Thomas C. Edwards Jr., and Michael W. Collopy. *Distribution, Ownership Status, and Habitat Characteristics of Bald Eagle Nest Sites in Florida: Final Report.* Tallahassee: FG&FWFC, 1989.

Woods, Charles A., and C. W. Kilpatrick. "*Microtus pennsylvanicus* (Rodentia: Muridae) in Florida: A Pleistocene Relict in a Coastal Saltmarsh." *Bulletin of the Florida State Museum, Biol. Sci.* 28, no. 2 (1982): 25–52.

Woolfenden, Glen E., and John W. Fitzpatrick. *The Florida Scrub Jay: Demography of a Cooperative-breeding Bird.* Princeton, N.J.: Princeton University Press, 1984.

Worth Publishers. *Invitation to Biology.* New York: Worth Publishers, 1981.

Wright, Albert Hazen, and Anna Allen Wright. *Handbook of Snakes.* Vols. 1 and 2. Ithaca, N.Y.: Comstock Publishing Associates, 1957.

Zambrano, Ricardo. "Least Tern Nesting." *Skimmer* (Tallahassee), summer 1996, p. 11.

Zapalac, Wil. "Turtles Here First." *Greenpeace Magazine,* March–April 1990.

Zeiller, Warren, *Introducing the Manatee.* Gainesville: University Press of Florida, 1992.

Index